CAMBODIA

Sebastian Strangio is a former reporter and editor of the *Phnom Penh Post*, Cambodia's oldest English-language newspaper. He is currently a Thailand-based journalist and analyst focusing on Southeast Asia, and is the author of *In the Dragon's Shadow: Southeast Asia in the Chinese Century*.

Further praise for *Cambodia*:

"Sebastian Strangio has written an exceptionally insightful biography of the world's longest serving prime minister. Strangio entwines his narrative of Hun Sen's life with a first-class analysis of contemporary Cambodian political history. This book is accessible to the general reader as well as Southeast Asia specialists." Carlyle A. Thayer, author of *War by Other Means: National Liberation and Revolution in Vietnam*

"An absorbing, clear-eyed evaluation of Cambodia today. Sebastian Strangio knows the country well, and has befriended many of its ordinary people. His book is a persuasive reading of the country's turbulent recent history, as it explores the connections between Hun Sen's enduring dictatorship and Cambodia's painful emergence, willy-nilly, into a larger, freer, very demanding world." David Chandler, author of *A History of Cambodia*

"As a detailed and perceptive account of Hun Sen's Cambodia, Strangio's book will remain of fundamental importance for many years to come." Milton Osborne, *Contemporary Southeast Asia*

CAMBODIA

From Pol Pot to Hun Sen and Beyond

SEBASTIAN STRANGIO

YALE UNIVERSITY PRESS

NEW HAVEN AND LONDON

For information about this and other Yale University Press publications, please contact:
U.S. Office: sales.press@yale.edu   yalebooks.com
Europe Office: sales@yaleup.co.uk   yalebooks.co.uk

Typeset in Minion Pro by IDSUK (DataConnection) Ltd
Printed and bound by CPI Group (UK) Ltd, Croydon, CR0 4YY

Library of Congress Control Number: 2020939577

ISBN 978-0-300-19072-4 (hbk)
ISBN 978-0-300-21173-3 (pbk)

A catalogue record for this book is available from the British Library.

10 9 8 7 6 5 4 3 2 1

To my grandfather, Peter Dembowski

Contents

These our actors,
As I foretold you, were all spirits and
Are melted into air, into thin air:
And, like the baseless fabric of this vision,
The cloud-capp'd towers, the gorgeous palaces,
The solemn temples, the great globe itself,
Ye all which it inherit, shall dissolve . . .

WILLIAM SHAKESPEARE, *The Tempest*

There are two futures, the future of desire and the future of fate, and man's
reason has never learned to separate them.

J. D. BERNAL, *World, the Flesh and the Devil*

A mountain never has two tigers.

TRADITIONAL KHMER

Preface to the Paperback Edition

This book first appeared at an important juncture in Cambodia's recent political history. I completed the initial draft shortly after the national election of July 2013, when the newly formed Cambodia National Rescue Party (CNRP) scored significant gains against the incumbent might of Prime Minister Hun Sen and the Cambodian People's Party (CPP). Claiming widespread voter fraud, the CNRP launched a campaign of rolling public demonstrations, which quickly evolved into the most significant challenge to Hun Sen's rule in 15 years.

The hardback edition, titled *Hun Sen's Cambodia* and presented here in revised and updated form, offered a portrait of Cambodian society as it stood on the eve of the 2013 election, when the public's dammed-up discontent briefly broke the levees and surged into the streets. It described the patronage and predation of the CPP's rule, and how the rising expectations of a young population, newly interconnected by digital technology, were straining against the limitations of its airless political consensus.

The book also tried to anatomize what I described as Cambodia's "mirage" of democracy: the facade of liberal institutions behind which the CPP governed through a latticework of personal connections, bound together by the invisible currencies of loyalty and obligation. This mirage dated back to the signing in October 1991 of the Paris Peace Agreements, an international treaty that sought to end Cambodia's endemic civil conflicts and, in the spirit of the age, to transform the nation into a liberal multiparty democracy. Desiring Western aid and support, the CPP government saw benefits in maintaining an overlay of liberal institutions, even as it subverted them from within. The result was a shimmering disjuncture between the norms the government professed, and the ways that it operated in practice.

In the six years since the publication of *Hun Sen's Cambodia*, this liberal mirage has evaporated, as Hun Sen's government, backed by a resurgent China, has shrugged off the expectations of the Western democracies and charted a more openly authoritarian course for the country's politics. In the run-up to national elections in July 2018, a CPP-controlled court abolished the CNRP and arrested its leader Kem Sokha for treason. At the same time, the government closed over many of the glades of freedom that were forced open by a United Nations peacekeeping mission in the early 1990s, and sustained since by the economic pressure and diplomatic cajoling of the Western democracies. As a result, the CPP would run in the 2018 election virtually unchallenged, winning all 125 seats in the National Assembly. Cambodia's elections had never been truly free or fair, but here, for the first time, they approached the hollow formalism of the old "people's democracies."

This updated and retitled edition of *Hun Sen's Cambodia* preserves most of the text in its original form, as a screen-capture of an important moment in 2013 and 2014, when the contradictions of Cambodia's political economy briefly manifested in the streets. While some elements of the story have changed in the years since, its broad outlines remain the same: despite an expanding economy, growing opportunities for the Cambodian population, and even some attempts to rein in the worst excesses of corruption and mismanagement, Cambodia remains a kingdom not of laws, but of men—in particular, of one man, now passing the midpoint of his fourth decade in power. The central contradiction of Hun Sen's Cambodia also pertains: that true reform would undermine the very power of those upon whom the system relies.

Even as it dissolves, Cambodia's democratic mirage remains an important part of the country's modern story. In many senses, it reflects a wider tendency in how Cambodian leaders have historically viewed and related to the outside world. As the anthropologist John Marston wrote in 2002, the key to understanding contemporary Cambodia lies in "the way transnational forces interface with local agendas. Its poverty and history of war, the ineffectiveness of state bureaucratic mechanisms, and the way that Vietnam and the United States played major roles in recent history in the creation of the current state apparatus, all bear on the fact that Cambodia stands particularly exposed to a variety of international pressures."[1] This complex dialectic between the local and the international is not just crucial to understanding Cambodia's trajectory under Hun Sen; in all likelihood, it will continue to condition the nation's politics long after the Cambodian leader has departed the scene.

Cambodia's political journey also has a wider significance. The international effort to transform Cambodia into a liberal polity was driven forward by the giddy sense of triumph that followed the collapse of the Soviet Union and the end of the Cold War. In 1991, an impoverished, conflict-torn country was swept into the slipstream of an all-pervasive *Weltgeist*: one that held that the breakup of the communist bloc would be succeeded by a global convergence towards some variant of Western liberal democracy and globalized free-market capitalism. If Cambodia embodied this hope, the country's trajectory since has traced the fading of this liberal consensus in the West, as it has been undermined by rising economic inequality, endless Middle Eastern wars, and a rapidly shifting balance of international power and prestige. Like a tiny satellite of global politics, Cambodia has reflected both the dawn, and the twilight, of the post-Cold War liberal moment.

This paperback edition includes the original version of *Hun Sen's Cambodia*, revised to correct a number of small errata and infelicities in the text. It also includes a new extended epilogue that brings Cambodia's story up to the present, describing the country's evolution beyond the closing parenthesis of the post-Cold War period, into the tense and undefined era yet to come.

Melbourne, April 2020

INTRODUCTION

A Mirage on the Mekong

It was several seconds before Bun Chenda knew what had happened. There was a thudding impact, like the blow of a hammer, which sent her falling to the ground. Then there was pain, flowering in her chest. She tasted the metallic tang of blood. As a crowd closed in blurrily around, she later said, "I felt dead already."

It was mid-February 2012, and the situation at the Manhattan Special Economic Zone in Svay Rieng was growing tense. Workers at three garment factories had walked off the job, demanding greater pay, and the Kaoway Sportswear Factory, where 21-year-old Chenda assembled running shoes, was on the verge of its own strike. The workers' demands were modest—an extra US $10 per month to cover transport costs and a $0.50 daily food allowance—but the Taiwanese factory managers refused to give ground. Instead, the police were deployed. They fired tear-gas at the protesters and union leaders, who responded with rocks and projectiles of their own.

Chenda wasn't the sort to hurl rocks. She was shy, with loose strands of hair that framed dark hazel eyes and pale angular features. Each morning she commuted to work from her home in Prek Pdav, a village of square homes and verdant rice fields a few kilometers from the sprawling industrial parks of Bavet, a town on the Vietnamese border. Here her mother and father owned a shack of corrugated aluminum, two cows, and a small plot of land. Chenda was 12 years when she finished school, 15 when she started working. She had been at Kaoway for six months. The tedious work brought in a small salary—just $81 plus overtime per month—but the extra money helped her parents hire laborers for their rice paddies and keep their rickety Daelim motorbike filled with gas. Most of the Kaoway workers had a similar story, traveling each day from villages across rural Svay Rieng, gluing soles for as long as it took to help keep their families' heads above water. As Chenda told me, "we're tired of working in the factory, but there's no choice. We have to do it for the money."

The morning shift usually started at 7:30 a.m., but on the morning of February 20, Chenda arrived to find the gates of the factory closed. Police posted outside told her to return home; the local authorities had ordered the closure to forestall further demonstrations. As more workers arrived they grew angry and demanded to speak with factory management. A protest erupted. The crowds pushed past police into the compound and a few workers began hurling chunks of concrete through the factory windows, showering the floor with glass.

Sometime after eight, a Toyota Camry edged through the crowd of protesters and pulled up to the factory's front gate. The figure who stepped out was middle-aged, with neatly parted jet-black hair. He moved languidly, a man grown comfortable in his power. After speaking with police for a moment he walked through the factory gates. As he approached a group of demonstrators, the man exchanged a few angry words. Then something snapped: he stopped, pulled out a handgun, and fired into the crowd.

Bavet, like many Asian border towns, has a shabby, desultory air. National Road 1, which doubles as the town's main drag, is lined with beer gardens and untidy concrete buildings that give way to garish casino complexes, their palm trees and faux Vegas facades fading forlornly in the tropical heat. Bavet sits at the northern tip of the Parrot's Beak, a shard of Cambodian territory that jags into southern Vietnam, close to the great delta where the Mekong River finishes its 4,350-kilometer journey by spilling into the South China Sea. During the Vietnam War, the area saw fierce battles between Vietnamese communists and American soldiers defending the United States-backed government in Saigon (now Ho Chi Minh City), an hour's drive away down NR1. Old ideological struggles have long since given way to trade and business. Semi-trailers and tourist buses roar through town, kicking up clouds of dust. Farther out begin the factories and industrial zones, concrete oceans announced by grandiose, gold-lettered arches on the highway.

The man who shot Bun Chenda and two other female apparel workers was well known in Bavet. His name was Chhouk Bundith. He was the district governor, the most powerful figure in town, reporting to the provincial governor in Svay Rieng, and, from there, all the way up to Prime Minister Hun Sen in the capital Phnom Penh. His actions at the Kaoway factory immediately made international headlines. The German sportswear giant PUMA, whose shoes were assembled by the Kaoway workers, announced an investigation. The three young victims filed complaints from their hospital beds; opposition politicians and labor rights activists demanded the governor's immediate arrest and punishment.

In Phnom Penh, the government came under immediate pressure to act. There was a huge amount at stake. With around 400 factories employing some 475,000 workers, the apparel sector was Cambodia's largest industry, earning $5.5 billion annually and making up the vast majority of the country's exports. Over the past 15 years, the country had established a niche as an ethical manufacturing base, enforcing higher labor standards than sweatshop centers like Vietnam or Bangladesh. If things started backsliding, however, image-conscious brands like PUMA, Gap, and H&M wouldn't hesitate to move their operations elsewhere. In early March, the Ministry of Interior dismissed Bundith from his post and ordered his arrest.

The case should have been clear-cut. Dozens of workers had witnessed the incident and could testify that Bundith had walked into the crowd and fired at least two shots. (The two other victims, Kao Near and Nuth Sakhorn, were injured by a single bullet.) But things in Cambodia were rarely so straightforward. While some powerful people wanted to see Bundith punished, the governor, like many high-ranking government officials, had powerful patrons determined to shield him from punishment. One of those was Men Sam An, who represented the province of Svay Rieng in the National Assembly and was the highest ranking woman in the ruling Cambodian People's Party.

In June 2013, after an acquittal and an appeal, the ex-governor was sentenced to 18 months' jail for "causing unintentional bodily harm"—a paltry charge for the daylight shooting of three unarmed protesters. But when the verdict was handed down, Bundith was nowhere to be found. His luxurious two-story villa in Bavet lay empty. He had vanished. The police claimed to have no clue about Bundith's whereabouts, even though he had been sighted several times since his disappearance. "He's staying at Men Sam An's house in Phnom Penh," said one police officer in Bavet. "It is not difficult to find him."[1] But the truth was that the case had reached an equilibrium that suited everybody. The Cambodian authorities could claim to have punished the Kaoway shooter. And Bundith, the nowhere man, could disappear—to a realm far beyond the reach of justice.

In the West, Cambodia is nearly synonymous with the terror and mass murder that engulfed the country in the mid-1970s, when the Khmer Rouge seized power and embarked on a radical experiment in communism. Led by "Brother Number One" Pol Pot, who dreamt of recreating the glories of Angkor, Cambodia's powerful premodern empire, the Khmer Rouge set about forging an agrarian arcadia of stark and uncompromising purity. They emptied the cities, abolished money, banned religion, and put the population to work in vast labor camps. For almost four years, Cambodia retreated from the world.

By the time "Democratic Kampuchea" collapsed in early 1979, an estimated 1.7 million Cambodians—about a quarter of the population—had perished and a green land had been sown with hundreds of mass graves.

Even now, four decades on, the name of this small country still has the power to conjure. Cambodia remains an international shorthand for suffering; a hazy land of skulls and spires; an ancient civilization slipped from glory and sunk, inexplicably, in madness. "I have a gloomy view of Cambodia," Henry Kamm once remarked, reflecting on the two decades he spent covering the country for the *New York Times*. "It is a nation at the end of its parabola of life."[2] But despite its dark history, the Cambodian arc persists. After many years, it is finally a country at peace and open to the world. Millions of foreign tourists visit each year to marvel at the temple-city of Angkor Wat, one of the wonders of the premodern world. Today's visitor encounters a friendly people and a small country rushing to catch up with the future, seemingly impatient to leave a horrific past behind.

Cambodia's journey to the present has been tumultuous. For two decades after their overthrow by the Vietnamese army in 1979, the Khmer Rouge lived on. Throughout the 1980s, China, the US, and their Southeast Asian allies cynically preserved the movement as a bulwark against the new Soviet-aligned regime that had replaced it in Phnom Penh. The ensuing civil war dragged on for more than a decade. Then, as the Cold War thawed and a new international order dawned, Cambodia was repackaged as a democracy. A peace plan was signed and the country became the subject of one of the most ambitious and expensive United Nations peacekeeping missions ever mounted. After years of isolation, Cambodia opened to the world. Nongovernmental organizations and charities mushroomed. Foreign aid typhooned in. A victim of Cold War power politics was offered the blessings of a global community newly confident in its ability to plan and engineer democratic government.

But the democratic renaissance, such as it was, was short-lived. The government that took office following the UN-organized 1993 election was an unsteady coalition between Hun Sen of the Cambodian People's Party (CPP), which had ruled the country since 1979, and Prince Norodom Ranariddh, the son of Norodom Sihanouk, who had led Cambodia to independence in 1953. Neither leader had much interest in democracy. Cambodians had lived under authoritarian leaders since the time of Angkor, and it wasn't long before the old patterns reasserted themselves. In 1997, Hun Sen ousted Ranariddh by force and seized power for himself, leaving the UN's democratic plans in tatters.

The CPP's stabilizing power brought decades of war to an end and opened Cambodia to economic development and investment from abroad. When the Khmer Rouge finally withered in the late 1990s, a new chapter in the country's history began—an era of peace and economic advancement. But beneath a surface sheen of modernity and pluralism, Hun Sen continued to rule in the old way, through guile and force, through gifts and threats, through an intricate hierarchy of status and power. He has been in control of the country ever since.

I came to this story in early 2008, arriving in Cambodia as a reporter for the *Phnom Penh Post*, one of the country's two English-language newspapers. The *Post* had an interesting history. Its long-time editor-in-chief Michael Hayes had founded the paper with his then-wife in July 1992, a few months into the UN mission. For its first five years, the paper was printed in Bangkok and the new editions flown in by air every two weeks. Hayes, a laconic American who always wore a crisp short-sleeved shirt and long pants despite the steamy tropical heat, had captained the publication through 16 tumultuous years, and the paper's front pages had captured all the landmark events of Cambodia's recent past: the historic 1993 election, the 1997 coup, and the final days of Pol Pot. For Hayes and his staff, each issue was "a labor of love and, at the same time, a pain in the you-know-what."[3]

The newsroom of the *Post*, which took up the second floor of Hayes's villa in central Phnom Penh, was a trove of Cambodian marginalia. Photos of old correspondents crowded the walls. A letter to the editor from the gregarious former king, Norodom Sihanouk, was taped to the side of a bookshelf, its corners curling inwards. Old press releases and reports lay in teetering piles on the floor. The back issues of the *Post*, bound in great annual volumes, offered a detailed chronicle of Cambodia's recent past, charting its twists and turns, its coronations and assassinations, the initial burst of democratic optimism and then the gradual fade.

Fifteen years on from the UN's departure, the detritus of the democratic project could be seen everywhere. The big international NGOs were comfortably entrenched, their emblems of brotherhood emblazoned on offices, signs, calendars, and reports, the last of which washed up in great dusty piles around the fringes of the newsroom. Charities and social enterprise projects abounded. International aid and its attendant foreign presence had transformed Phnom Penh into a sort of postmodern treaty-port city, a surreal settlement of cafés, bars, and restaurants. In the countryside, NGOs pursued "community-based development" projects and rice farmers wore cast-off NGO T-shirts proclaiming, "LET'S BUILD A BETTER SOCIETY." Some of the first ideas for this book were sketched out on a notepad from the UN Office of the High Commissioner for Human Rights, which bore its blue flame-and-laurel insignia above the slogan, "Human rights for everyone, everywhere."

The strong international presence made Cambodia an easy place to work as a journalist. Yearly business visas were available to any Western citizen with fresh passport pages and the necessary fee. Unlike most Asian countries, little was officially off-limits. Foreign reporters could wander into ministry buildings and knock on doors, or travel around the country interviewing the victims of land-grabs and other abuses. In few other countries could publications like the *Phnom Penh Post* or the *Cambodia Daily*, our rivals and comrades across town, be both foreign-owned and blisteringly critical of the government. In Singapore, such outspokenness would herald a hail of lawsuits; in Vietnam, a lengthy jail sentence.

As journalists in Cambodia, our main frame of reference was the global human rights regime, that patchwork of conventions and norms that had been reinvigorated by the fall of the Soviet Union in the early 1990s. We worked closely with the country's human rights groups and NGOs, the other beneficiaries of the UN mission. Together, we formed an informational symbiosis, generating huge quantities of data, much of it detailing Cambodia's persistent failure to live up to its international human rights "obligations."

But there was something curiously abstract about the freedoms we enjoyed and advocated. No matter what we and our Khmer colleagues wrote, little seemed to change. The rich and powerful remained a law unto themselves, as they had been for as long as Cambodians could remember. Businesspeople seized land and evicted the inhabitants. Forests and natural resources were sold to Chinese and Vietnamese firms for massive sums. A man like Chhouk Bundith could shoot three young women and then brazenly flout the authority of courts that had never been free from political control. The human rights groups had their own name for all of this. They called it "impunity." But the word was so frequently deployed, and so bleached of cultural and historical context, that it soon lost much of its force.

Most Cambodians lived in a very different world than the one we inhabited in Phnom Penh. Four-fifths of them still lived in the countryside, a sodden green land of rice paddies and sugar palms, where they fished, raised crops and animals, and got on with things as best they could. Village life was organized around the local Buddhist *wats*, brightly colored temples where people gathered on festival days to light incense and pray to their ancestors. Though Cambodia's official religion was Theravada Buddhism, it intermingled with a host of other ancestral deities and animist guardian spirits. In front of nearly every Cambodian house, even the poorest, there was a small spirit-house where people made regular offerings—fruit, raw meat, cans of soft drink— seeking to propitiate supernatural beings who were believed to have a strong say in worldly affairs.

At the same time, billions of dollars in international development aid had done little to improve the lot of ordinary people. Life in rural areas remained a struggle. Many households still lacked access to electricity, sanitation, and clean water. Two in five Cambodian children grew up stunted.[4] The country's development indicators languished in the bottom reaches of the international rankings, inviting comparison with the poorest states of sub-Saharan Africa and blown-out Stalinist relics like North Korea. The farther from major roads people lived, the poorer and more isolated they tended to be. With each bumpy mile, life reverted backwards in time. In some places things seemed like they hadn't changed in centuries.

But everywhere in Cambodia, even in the remotest areas, there was one constant presence. Prime Minister Hun Sen loomed over his country's political life. His name was attached to thousands of schools, often built with the donations of friendly tycoons. He was a frequent fixture on radio and TV, giving long and sometimes outrageous speeches in which he would insult political opponents and recount tales from his rural upbringing. In power since 1985, Hun Sen was modern Cambodia's longest-serving leader, a rugged survivor who had passed through repeated cycles of history. In the 1970s, he fought for the Khmer Rouge, rising to the rank of regimental commander before defecting and becoming a member of the Vietnamese-installed government that replaced Pol Pot in 1979. Over four decades he had played many roles: apparatchik and reformer, strongman and statesman, demagogue and freewheeling free-marketeer.

Beneath these various guises Hun Sen ruled in the traditional Cambodian way, through a system of personal patronage in which money was passed upward in exchange for protection. This he married to a fierce ambition, a serrated political instinct, and a genuine ability to channel the hopes and fears of rural Cambodians. Hun Sen could be violent and unpredictable. He had little tolerance for dissent. But he and his party could also credibly claim to have ushered Cambodia into an era of unprecedented peace and economic growth. In mid-2008, despite the abuses and corruption of its rule, the CPP won its third straight election by a landslide. Seeing the failure of democracy to take root in Cambodian soil, many foreign observers decided that Khmer culture, steeped in Buddhist fatalism, was inherently passive and deferential. "Most [people] expect nothing more than they have," the American journalist Joel Brinkley wrote in his 2011 book *Cambodia's Curse*. "They carry no ambitions. They hold no dreams. All they want is to be left alone."[5]

But at the same time Cambodia clearly *was* changing. Hun Sen's rule had unleashed economic forces that were slowly transforming society. When young women like Bun Chenda went to work in the garment factories, they often became the first members of their families to work outside rice-farming villages like Prek Pdav. In Cambodia there were now more mobile phones than people. The kingdom's population of 15 million was young, and with every passing year the number who had experienced Pol Pot's horrors diminished. And as the past receded, the CPP's proven system of patronage and controls, effective for so many years, began to break down. Ordinary people began standing up to demand higher wages and social justice from their government. Something was happening in Cambodia, though we weren't yet sure quite what.

By 2008, Cambodia had mostly faded from the international headlines. When the Khmer Rouge finally collapsed in the late 1990s, it had reverted to what it had been for centuries—a small, mostly unimportant country, wedged between two more prosperous and newsworthy neighbors: the economic dynamo of Thailand, the soaring dragon of Vietnam. Aside from the sclerotic trials of former Khmer Rouge leaders, about to get underway at a UN-backed court in Phnom Penh, Cambodia's travails attracted only glancing interest.

But the story of this beautiful country deserved to be told. It had experienced some of the greatest horrors of the twentieth century and then became the focus of one of its great saving ideas—the hope that democracy could be molded and implanted in a land ravaged by war. The country that emerged from this collision of opposites was unique. Few other governments had so fully absorbed the symbols and narratives of global humanism to so little apparent effect. To put in another way, few were so open, and yet so closed. The democratic project had produced a mirage on the Mekong, an illusion of Western democratic forms behind which the country operated much as it always had.

This mirage was everywhere. It hung over Cambodia's courts and parliament. It infused the Constitution and laws that Cambodia had enacted to placate foreign aid donors. It shimmered on the streets of Phnom Penh, with their fine restaurants and refractions of First World prosperity. It was especially blinding on that day in June 2013 when Chhouk Bundith was convicted of shooting three young women, only to disappear, like a human mirage, when it came time to enforce his sentence. In Hun Sen's Cambodia, accountability and change always seemed to lie just over the horizon. But what seemed tangible from a distance, on closer inspection very often melted into thin air.

The first half of this book describes the origins and history of Hun Sen's Cambodia, which arose from the ashes of the Khmer Rouge regime in 1979 and navigated through the hostile final years of the Cold War. It explores how, in the early 1990s, Cambodia joined the wider world, and the promise of a rights-based universalism collided with the realities of a poor postconflict society, burdened with a long history of autocratic rule. An important part of the story is the rise of Hun Sen, who has done the most to shape the country's recent destiny and push back against the norms imported during the UN years. The image that emerges is of a strong leader of a weak nation—a figure who is flexible, adaptable, highly strategic, adept at the manipulation of foreign interests. As the years went by, Hun Sen became a skilled illusionist, conjuring up mirages of democracy behind which he ruled in the traditional way, through an iron fist and a canny manipulation of his country's history and culture.

The second half of the book examines the country that has emerged under Hun Sen. While the CPP has presided over peace and stability, it has left many of the country's poorest and most vulnerable citizens behind. The gale force of Cambodian capitalism has swept thousands off their land, stripped the country of its natural resources, and left many stranded on the rim of Hun Sen's economic revolution. In this sense, Cambodia's story will always be that of the Cambodian people themselves, of people like Bun Chenda and her family, and how they have experienced and responded to their country's recent evolutions. In a rapidly changing country, they, too, find ways to persist.

Map of Cambodia.

CHAPTER ONE

Against the Ages

"That's where the killing fields begin." Mao Vei extended an arm eastward, past a low concrete fence and a wall of green bamboo, toward the groves and orchards of the dead. There, tall green mango and papaya trees stretched over three hectares. They were planted about 30 years before, and their roots still mingle with the remains of the thousands killed at Wat O Trakuon, a Buddhist pagoda and former Khmer Rouge prison in whose grounds the 67-year-old Vei now stood, his eyes narrowed against the afternoon sun, all the memories crowding back.

From 1974 to 1978, Wat O Trakuon served as a Khmer Rouge security center for the district of Kang Meas, which sprawls out along the Mekong River west of Kampong Cham. A tin-roofed school building within the temple grounds was converted into an office and interrogation center. The pale yellow pagoda hall, sweeping up from a base of sun-split concrete, was used as a prison. Inside the fragrant darkness, Vei crouched down and indicated where the thick wooden beams were fitted with iron bars, how the prisoners were shackled in rows by their ankles. He padded across a floor of cool brown tiles and opened a wooden door, pouring light onto a wall of Buddha images. "They couldn't clean the bloodstains," he explained, "so they put in a new floor."

During the Khmer Rouge years, Vei worked as a cook in a communal kitchen. One day in 1977, he climbed a sugar palm close to the prison walls to collect palm juice for the senior cadre. Peering down into the fields, he saw prisoners arranged in lines, their hands tied behind their backs. One by one, Khmer Rouge soldiers bludgeoned them in the back of the head with hoes and other farming implements and threw them into pits. The bodies were covered with a thin layer of earth; later, Vei told me, he could see the corpses swelling in the heat. In 1982, a few of the graves were exhumed and the bones enclosed in a white reliquary, where they still sit today, cobwebbed behind panes of dirty glass. According to a memorial inscription, 32,690 people were executed at Wat O Trakuon. Most of the remains were left undisturbed, lying beneath the fruit trees, planted to discourage people from scouring the graves for valuables.

Many of those killed at Wat O Trakuon were Muslim Chams, descendants of the kingdom of Champa that was once based in central Vietnam. The Chams' distinct language and religion immediately made them suspect in the eyes of the *angkar loeu*—the omniscient "High Organization" of the Khmer Rouge. One evening in 1977, militia squads rounded up every Cham family in Sambor Meas village and took them to the *wat*. Others were brought by boat along the Mekong. Pim Phy, an 80-year-old *achar*, a white-robed Buddhist layman, said killing began straight away and carried on all night, to the blare of revolutionary anthems. "There were two big holes to bury the Cham people," he told me. "I saw it myself—all the Chams were brought in ox-carts. They were loaded and very heavy. There were even young children and small babies. They came at night and they were all killed."

On April 17, 1975, the armies of the Khmer Rouge marched into Phnom Penh and deposed the US-backed Khmer Republic. A spokesman declared 2,000 years of Cambodian history at an end. The city's population was forcibly evacuated. The operating principle of Democratic Kampuchea (DK)—as the new regime termed itself—would take the form of a chilling aphorism: "To keep you is no gain; to kill you is no loss." Having returned Cambodia to a new zero-point, the DK leadership treated Cambodia's people as the expendable raw material from which they intended to mold a rural society of unsurpassed purity.

All traces of the old "feudal" order were to be cut away and discarded. Money was banned, families were disbanded; Buddhist monks were forced to disrobe and were shot if they failed to comply. The population was put to work on vast communes in the countryside, farming rice and digging irrigation dikes. Work began in the dark of morning and ended in the dark of night. Rations were grossly insufficient, and hawk-eyed cadres enforced a regime of inhuman discipline. Husbands were separated from wives, children from their parents. Death from starvation, overwork, and summary execution became commonplace.

Perhaps the most chilling thing about Wat O Trakuon is that there was nothing particularly remarkable about it. During the three years, eight months, and 20 days of Khmer Rouge rule, the regime established an archipelago of oppression that stretched to some 200 security centers and prisons, many with a similar satellite field of mass graves. Today, more than 40 years after the down-fall of Pol Pot's regime, piles of skulls still dot the Cambodian countryside like ghastly totems, lying in the open or disintegrating in old memorial stupas. Every now and then new killing fields are uncovered and the families of victims hold ceremonies for anonymous bones, hoping finally to give lost relatives a proper Buddhist funeral. In January 1979, the Khmer Rouge were overthrown by a Vietnamese invasion and the Cambodian nightmare came to an end. But today's Cambodia remains haunted by its past. History echoes in the bustle of the present. And as the Irish poet Ewart Milne wrote, history is always a cruel country.

Cambodia's history begins in the unique contours of its physical setting. Bisecting the country from north to south, the Mekong that bore the victims of Wat O Trakuon starts its journey far outside the country's borders, in the Himalayan mountain valleys that nurture Asia's great rivers: the Yangtze, the Irrawaddy, the Ganges. After a long journey through China, Burma, Thailand, and Laos, the Mekong arrives in Phnom Penh, where it mingles with the Tonlé Sap. While the Mekong is Cambodia's bridge to the world, the Tonlé Sap is unique to Cambodia—the only river in the world that completely changes direction, twice each year. In the dry season, the river flows southward from the Tonlé Sap Lake, a vast central expanse of water stretching over a thousand square miles. Then, when the monsoon rains come and the Mekong is swelled by Himalayan snowmelt, the pressure of its flow forces the Tonlé Sap to turn back northward, inundating the lake and flooding large parts of the country.

This annual flood-pulse provides Cambodians with an agricultural bounty, depositing rich alluvial silt across the floodplains and renewing the world's largest freshwater fishing ground. The importance of the seasons—the intertwining cycles of water, rice, and subsistence agriculture—is still marked each year by the Water Festival, when Cambodians gather in Phnom Penh for boat races on the Tonlé Sap and the Cambodian king stands at the confluence of the two rivers to preside over the churning of the waters.

A millennium ago, these fertile soils and teeming waterways nourished the empire now known as Angkor, which arose along the northern shores of the Great Lake. At its zenith, Angkor was the predominant power in mainland Southeast Asia, its influence stretching from modern-day Vietnam and Burma to the Malay Peninsula. The God-Kings who ruled Angkor were masters of hydraulics, building dikes and reservoirs to harness the monsoon floodwaters and amassing huge stores of rice. At its height, Angkor was the largest premodern settlement in the world, a city of more than 700,000 spread over an area larger than modern Los Angeles. Its crowning achievement was Angkor Wat, built at the kingdom's height in the early twelfth century. Topped by five towers, arranged in an "X" pattern like the dots on a die, Angkor Wat was designed as a microcosmic representation of Mount Meru, the center of the universe in Hindu and Buddhist cosmology. This vast complex, still the largest religious building in the world, remains a powerful representation of Angkor's military, artistic, and economic might, as well as the absolute rule of the God-Kings, who were said to "eat their kingdom," ruling with an iron fist.

Angkor Wat has since become Cambodia's talisman, the shining meridian toward which successive generations of leaders have turned their sails. An image of the temple has appeared on the flag of every Cambodian regime since independence, including the Khmer Rouge, who placed its golden silhouette on a background of blood red. Where a doctrinaire Maoist might have seen a symbol of feudal oppression, Pol Pot saw the shimmer of future greatness. "If our people can build Angkor," he said in 1977, "we can do anything."[1] But while Angkor was a source of great pride for Cambodians, it would also become a crushing burden—a symbol of the country's past achievements, and a reminder of its subsequent decline.

By the fifteenth century, Khmer power was on the wane. The Siamese kingdom of Ayutthaya had arisen to the west, and sometime during the 1400s, the royal court abandoned Angkor Wat and relocated its capital southward to Oudong, and then to Phnom Penh, both of which commanded better access to the Mekong and the flows of maritime trade. Post-Angkorian Cambodia appeared as a void on many early European maps—a featureless expanse hemmed in by the Vietnamese and Siamese kingdoms rising to either side.[2] Its diminished territory provided few natural barriers to invasion. During these dark years, the foundering Cambodian kingdom became a buffer state and object of rivalry between Siam and Vietnam, serving at various points as a vassal state to one or both.

In the 1790s, Siam moved in from the west, annexing Cambodia's western provinces (including Angkor Wat) and installing a Thai governor to oversee them. From the east, Vietnam's *nam tien*—its "southward march" from the heavily populated Red River Delta—brought it into contact with the diminished Cambodian kingdom. By the eighteenth century, Vietnamese settlers had occupied large parts of the Mekong Delta.

Cambodia's border with Vietnam, unlike its western frontier, lies along a deep cultural fault-line—the hyphen separating the two halves of what the French called "Indo-China." This gulf was geographical, political, religious, and linguistic. Vietnam's Confucian social and political system, inherited and adapted from China, contrasted sharply with the informal nature of Cambodia's political arrangements. On the Vietnamese side of the border, people aggressively shaped nature to serve their needs, clearing jungle and threading the landscape with a network of dikes and canals, while Khmer peasants adapted themselves to the natural rhythms of the land, living off the rice, fish, and fruit that they found everywhere around them. The situation along the two countries' border remains similar today. In the dry months the Vietnamese fields glow a deep green, while on the other side of the border much of the land remains parched and brown.

It wasn't long before Vietnam tried to extend more direct control. In the early 1800s, the Vietnamese emperor Minh Mang started building fortresses and forced Cambodian officials to adopt Vietnamese clothes and hairstyles. Confucian forms of administration were imposed and more Vietnamese migrants settled in the Khmer territories. In 1817, Vietnam began conscripting Cambodian laborers to build a canal linking the river town of Chau Doc to the Gulf of Thailand. The Vietnamese overseers treated their Khmer workers cruelly. According to legend, one punishment consisted of burying Khmer workers up to their necks in groups of three and using their heads to support their boiling teapots. As the Cambodians struggled and flinched in pain from the flames, the Vietnamese laughed and warned them: "don't spill the master's tea."[3]

Eventually this mini-Confucian "civilizing mission" prompted bloody revolts. By the early 1840s, imperial officials had decided that the cultural world of the "barbarian" Khmers was impervious to change. "The people do not know the proper way to grow food," Minh Mang complained. "They use mattocks and hoes, but no oxen. They grow enough rice to have two meals a day, but they do not know how to store rice for an emergency."[4] For Cambodians the period of Vietnamese domination was formative. The "*yuon*," as the Vietnamese are often pejoratively termed, became the bogeymen of the Cambodian political imagination. Again and again they would resurface as a cruel and rapacious enemy, inexorably bent on "swallowing" the rest of Cambodia's land, just as they did Kampuchea Krom ("lower Cambodia"), the former Khmer territories in the Mekong Delta. To many Cambodians, the *yuon* became synonymous with death and disunity, a force that threatened their country's very existence.

If it wasn't for the French empire, Cambodia might well have ceased to exist in the mid-nineteenth century. The first French explorers had arrived in Cambodia in the early 1860s, seeking to expand French commercial interests in Southeast Asia, and believing that the Mekong might provide a backdoor to China and its riches. By the time the French established a protectorate over Cambodia in 1863, the kingdom had endured a half-century of civil wars, rebellions, and Siamese invasions, as well as the depredations of the Vietnamese protectorate.

The Cambodian kingdom became a part of French Indochina. King Norodom welcomed the French offer of protection, which kept him in nominal power and prevented the loss of further territory to Siam and Vietnam. In 1907, the French negotiated the return of the Angkor region and the western provinces from the Siamese kingdom, and fixed Cambodia's national borders in roughly the place they remain today. But French protection soon evolved into a firmer form of control. The Cambodian monarchy became a ward of the colonial authorities, which kept it from performing any significant political activities and placed the next three Cambodian kings on the throne.

Many French officials saw their new colonial possession in romantic terms, viewing the Khmers as innocent savages—a pale vestige of the people who had produced the glories of Angkor. The French scholar George Groslier wrote, "the gods have disappeared, and ironic Death has left only slaves."[5] At the same time, French scholars did much to reconstruct the country's early past. Proclaiming the greatness of Angkor, they set about translating inscriptions and restoring monuments, including Angkor Wat. At the same time the French shielded Cambodians from the perils of freedom, judging them unready for the challenges of modernity. It was the Vietnamese, rather, who were the true dynamo of Indochina. As a derisive colonialist saying had it, "the Vietnamese grow the rice; the Khmers watch it grow; the Laotians listen to it grow."

The French attitude was largely self-fulfilling. Colonial rule did little to prepare Cambodia for the modern world. Life for most of the population remained much the same as it had been since Angkorian times, revolving around the cycles of subsistence agriculture. Instead of employing Khmers, the French brought in Vietnamese to staff the civil service and work the colonial rubber plantations.[6] Electricity and running water were rare outside Phnom Penh. Until the 1930s, practically nothing was spent on education. The country's first high school, the Lycée Sisowath, only opened its doors in 1936, and the number of Cambodian university graduates to that point was barely enough to fill a small seminar room.

Most education took place, as it had for centuries, in the country's Buddhist *wats*, where monks instructed boys in part through the use of religious treatises known as *chbap*—a series of moral aphorisms and tenets that provided students with a rigid code of worldly conduct. The *chbap* counseled passivity and acceptance and enforced strict social relationships between men and women, parents and children, rulers and ruled. In contrast with Confucian conceptions of social hierarchy, these issued from the moral worldview of Theravada Buddhism, by which a person's present fate depended on merit earned by good deeds in past lives. In the world of the *chbap*, deference and fatalism took precedence over the pursuit of social or economic justice.[7]

Slowly the modern nation of Cambodia came into relief. By 1927, the French had laid down 9,000 kilometers of roads, and a rail line linking Phnom Penh and Battambang was completed in 1932.[8] But these developments relied on a harsh system of taxes and forced labor that prompted a series of small-scale revolts in the early decades of the twentieth century. In 1925, villagers in Kampong Chhnang attacked and beat to death a French *résident* collecting unpaid taxes. The injustice of colonial rule raised hackles among Cambodia's tiny French-educated elite. In 1936, as resistance to French rule mounted in neighboring Vietnam, anticolonialists founded the country's first newspaper, *Nagaravatta* ("Angkor Wat"), which peddled a discreet anti-Vietnamese and anticolonial line. Cambodia was starting to awaken.

In 1941, King Sisowath Monivong died and the French chose as his successor Norodom Sihanouk, an 18-year-old prince whom they expected would be pliable and subservient. For the time being he was. At first, the inexperienced Sihanouk could do little but look on as his country was swept up in the tumult of the Second World War. After its surrender to Hitler's armies in 1940, France's hold on Cambodia grew weak. Indochina was placed under a Vichy French administration, which allowed imperial Japan to garrison thousands of troops in the country. Then, in March 1945, six months after the fall of Vichy France, Japanese imperial troops swept in and seized direct control from the French. During their short time in power, the Japanese encouraged the flowering of nationalist sentiment. On March 13, King Sihanouk declared Cambodia's independence from France. It didn't last long—six months later the French returned and retook control—but the colonial authorities would find the nationalist genie hard to put back in its bottle.

In 1947, to satisfy rising nationalist demands, the colonial authorities introduced the trappings of democracy—a constitution, a national assembly, and political parties—but held on to the reins of power. The young King Sihanouk soon began to buck against French control. By the early 1950s, he had grown into a headstrong monarch. The Cambodian peasantry revered Sihanouk, seeing him as a living God-King, and the king soon learned to use his immense popularity to bully opponents and confound French interests in Cambodia. In early 1953, he embarked on a "royal crusade for independence," in which he traveled the world campaigning for an end to colonial rule.

On the other side of the world, another group of Cambodians was considering the issue of independence from a very different angle. In August 1949, a 24-year-old named Saloth Sar sailed for France on the SS *Jamaique*. Born in 1925 in Kampong Thom, Sar, who would later adopt the *nom de guerre*

Pol Pot, was a quiet student who had been awarded a scholarship to study electrical engineering in Paris. On arrival, he joined a circle of Cambodian students with an interest in radical politics. The early 1950s saw the last blooming of Stalinism, the outbreak of the Korean War, and the founding, in February 1951, of the Kampuchean People's Revolutionary Party, a Cambodian communist party set up under Vietnamese auspices. Watching these events unfold from Paris, Cambodian leftists began to see Marxism and communism as a means not only of liberating the country from French rule, but also of overturning its regressive social system. Members of this circle, which included Sar, Ieng Sary, Khieu Samphan, Son Sen, and the sisters Khieu Thirith and Khieu Ponnary, would later go on to fill the upper echelons of the Cambodian communist movement.

On November 9, 1953, Sihanouk succeeded in winning Cambodia's independence from France. To a large extent he was pushing at an open door. French rule was tottering in Vietnam, where the Viet Minh, led by the communist leader Ho Chi Minh, were waging a bloody war for independence. In May 1954, the Viet Minh would defeat French forces at Dien Bien Phu, effectively spelling the end to French rule over Indochina. In Cambodia, bands of insurgents known as the Khmer Issaraks, or "free Khmers," had also taken up arms, and politicians in the Democrat Party, which dominated the new Cambodian parliament, were agitating for independence within a constitutional framework. But Sihanouk added a dynamic energy and ingenuity to the drive for independence, road-testing the unpredictability and public relations flair that would mark his years in power. To General Pierre de Langlade, the French military commander in Cambodia, he was "a madman, but a madman of genius."[9]

As independence dawned, Cambodia's prospects seemed bright. Unlike Vietnam, the 1954 Geneva Conference that ended French rule over Indochina had left Cambodia united, and, for the time being, at peace. King Sihanouk took charge of his country. Straitjacketed by the duties of kingship, he abdicated the throne in 1955 to take a more active role in politics. Over the next 15 years, Sihanouk built a powerful political movement, the Sangkum Reastr Niyum (People's Socialist Community), which monopolized Cambodian political life and provided an organizational vehicle for his enormous popularity. He also built up the education system, sculpted Phnom Penh into a modern capital, and expanded the country's small agrarian economy.

The country's "Golden Age," as many Cambodians would later remember it, was dominated by Sihanouk's personality—his foibles, obsessions, and eccentricities. Until 1970, when he was deposed in a coup, the prince (as he now was) cultivated a reputation as a great Renaissance man, combining bravura statesmanship with side roles as his country's most prominent film-maker, journalist, musician, and football coach. Like many of his royal fore-bears, Sihanouk had numerous concubines and fathered a total of 14 children by five women. "Such was his kingdom," wrote the Australian journalist John Pilger, "feudal, unpredictable, preposterous and, in relation to events in the region, at peace."[10]

As Vietnam edged toward civil war, Sihanouk struggled to keep Cambodia neutral, balancing carefully between East and West. Initially, he accepted US aid and maintained good relations with the communist bloc, forging close friendships with Chinese Premier Zhou Enlai and North Korea's reclusive leader Kim Il-sung. Sihanouk's constant political U-turns bewildered many outside observers, but the prince contended that he was motivated throughout by a consistent aim: the defense of his country's neutrality, independence, and territorial integrity. In truth, Sihanouk saw little distinction between his own interests and those of his country. The support and love of the "little people," as he referred to ordinary Cambodians, fostered a lifelong conviction that he alone could keep his country united and at peace.

Sihanouk's Cambodia was often depicted as a fairy-tale princedom—a peaceful island of golden-spired pagodas—but the country was riven with major inequalities of power and wealth. Cambodia had no tradition of power-sharing or democratic elections, and Sihanouk's modernized absolutism left little room for dissent. Throughout his time in power, he tightened the screws on his parliamentary opponents, convincing or forcing most to abandon their parties and join the Sangkum, which furnished nearly all the candidates for elections held in 1958 and 1962. Opposition newspapers were shut down and Sihanouk's security apparatus ruthlessly harassed opponents who held out. Chief among these dissidents were Cambodia's left-wing political party, the Pracheachon—driven underground in 1962—and the clandestine Communist Party of Kampuchea (CPK), whose members the prince famously dubbed the "Khmers Rouges" (Red Khmers). In 1963, dozens of leading communists fled Phnom Penh, where many worked as teachers and civil servants, and settled in remote jungle camps under Vietnamese communist protection. Among them was Saloth Sar, the CPK's new general secretary, who left behind a career as a teacher to become "a full-time revolutionary."[11]

In the mid-1960s, as the US became more deeply involved in Vietnam, Sihanouk's diplomatic high-wire act began to falter. Opposition mounted from left and right. In 1965, distrustful of US intentions and convinced that the North Vietnamese would eventually prevail over the US-backed government in South Vietnam, Sihanouk broke off relations with Washington, and quietly acquiesced in the transport of communist supplies along the "Ho Chi Minh trail" through eastern Cambodia and up from the port of Sihanoukville. He also embarked on an economically disastrous nationalization drive that stoked the opposition of Cambodia's conservative commercial elite. The disaffection of the right was accompanied by new threats from the left. In 1967, fierce rice requisitioning and communist agitation sparked a peasant uprising in Samlaut, a hilly area in the western province of Battambang. The rebellion was eventually put down with brutal force by Sihanouk's army and air force, but it was an ominous foreshadowing of the conflict to come.

As western Cambodia burned, Sihanouk retreated from the responsibilities of government into the embrace of his favorite hobbies, particularly filmmaking. Beginning in 1966, he dedicated hours to writing scripts and composing music for a string of feature films. These were characteristically self-centered affairs, in which Sihanouk served as director, producer, scriptwriter, and composer, and press-ganged senior officials and court hangers-on into embarrassing acting roles. The titles of the films—which included *Le Petit Prince du Peuple* (1967), *Rose de Bokor*, and *La Joie de Vivre* (both 1969)—provided surreal subtitles to the chaos that was slowly engulfing Cambodia.

Eventually the nimble prince fell. On March 18, 1970, a small circle of pro-American officials, led by General Lon Nol and a royal rival, Prince Sisowath Sirik Matak, engineered a parliamentary vote that removed Sihanouk from office while he was abroad. On October 9, Lon Nol and Sirik Matak proclaimed a pro-US republic, bringing the curtain down on Cambodia's centuries-old monarchy. From Beijing, where his old friend Zhou Enlai granted him a residence and a comfortable stipend, the prince raged against the coup plotters and, with Chinese promises of support, set up a resistance front with his former communist enemies, the Khmer Rouge. On March 23, Sihanouk took to the airwaves and called for the people to rise up against Lon Nol. For the prince and his country, it was a moment of no return. Thousands of rural Cambodians heeded Sihanouk's call, swelling the ranks of the Red Khmers.

The leaders of the new Khmer Republic were confronted with a deteriorating political situation. In April 1970, US President Richard Nixon sent US troops over the border from South Vietnam to root out communist base areas on Cambodian soil. The incursion failed, sweeping away the last pretenses of Cambodian neutrality and pushing the Vietnamese communists deeper into the country. As Lon Nol's officials devoured US economic and military aid, the Vietnamese and their restive apprentices—the Khmer Rouge—intensified their attacks on the new government. Cambodia had tumbled headlong into the Vietnam War.

For the five years of its existence the Lon Nol government was plagued by political and economic dysfunction. To maintain its grip on power, the regime silenced critics, arrested dissidents, and whipped up popular resentment against the Vietnamese. Lon Nol put on farcical elections, appointing himself president and marshal of the armed forces. The large influx of US aid fostered incandescent levels of corruption. This was especially the case in the army, which, fertilized by American aid dollars, grew from a force of 35,000 into an untrained and poorly led legion of more than 200,000. A common practice among commanders was to overreport the number of troops in their units, siphoning the salaries of these "phantom soldiers" into their own pockets.

In its early years, the regime drew on the deep well of opposition to Sihanouk and an outpouring of patriotism. The common animosity toward Vietnam, inflamed by the use of Cambodian territory by Vietnamese communist forces, prompted large numbers of young men, many no more than teenagers, to enlist in the military. An enduring image from the period was of the overladen Coca-Cola trucks filled with youths in baggy army fatigues—later dubbed "24-hour soldiers" for the perfunctory training they received—trundling off to the front.

Lon Nol saw the struggle against the communists as a holy war, a mission to defend Cambodia against the *yuon* and *thmil* (unbelievers) who threatened the country from the east. State propaganda posters showed Vietnamese communist soldiers, wearing conical hats emblazoned with red stars, stealing rice and murdering Buddhist monks. Anti-Vietnamese pogroms erupted. In April 1970, Cambodian troops rounded up some 800 Vietnamese Catholic laborers living across the river from the capital, shot them, and dumped the bodies in the Tonlé Bassac. By 1975, around 250,000 Vietnamese had fled the country.

Lon Nol's army was no match for the battle-hardened Vietnamese. By 1971, the republic had lost control of three-quarters of the country, and only a fierce US bombing campaign, designed to wipe out communist supply lines in eastern Cambodia, prevented it from collapse. The bombing had begun in earnest in 1969 with the launch of Operation Breakfast and was followed in due course by a euphemistic "Menu" comprising "Lunch," "Snack," "Dinner", "Supper," and "Dessert." Over the next four years, this horrific repast, conducted in secret and away from the scrutiny of the American public, devastated large swathes of the Cambodian countryside. From 1965 to 1973, the US dropped around 500,000 tons of bombs on Cambodia, more than three times what it dropped on Japan during World War II.[12]

On the ground, the B-52 sorties sowed terror. They killed tens of thousands of people in rural Cambodia, and drove many more into the arms of the Khmer Rouge. Lumphat, the remote provincial capital of Ratanakkiri in northeast Cambodia, was abandoned in the late 1960s after being bombed into rubble by American aircraft. Today the town remains little more than a village, its past dimly visible in the shattered infrastructure built during the Sihanouk years: a shrapnel-scarred water-tower and smashed concrete classrooms slumbering in the jungle behind a faded sign still announcing, with haunting optimism, the "Samdech Eav Junior High School." Policy-makers in Washington saw this destruction as the necessary price of victory in Vietnam. In a theater of toppling dominoes, Cambodia remained, in William Shawcross's eternal phrase, a "sideshow."[13]

"Who are the Khmer Rouge?" When the journalist Elizabeth Becker posed the question to readers of the *Washington Post* in March 1974, little was known about the communist movement that now controlled more than three-quarters of Cambodia's territory. Aside from Sihanouk, who headed the government-in-exile from Beijing, the identity of the CPK's top leadership was shadowy. Prominent leftists like Khieu Samphan had leading roles in the resistance front, but the limited extent of their activities suggested the existence of a higher authority. For the first time, Becker identified the head of the party as Saloth Sar, the leftist school teacher who had disappeared during government crackdowns in 1963. (He wouldn't take the name Pol Pot until 1976). She also wrote of the growing discord between the Khmer communists and their Vietnamese mentors, contradicting the prevailing American view that the Khmer Rouge were subservient to Hanoi.[14] Indeed, it would later turn out that Sar's rise to the CPK leadership had marked a decisive shift in power toward a faction of communists who were highly suspicious of the Vietnamese—a tension that would flare into open enmity after 1975. But for the time being, US officials simply assumed that the Khmer Rouge took their orders from Vietnam.

Even Sihanouk stressed the benign intentions of the Khmer Rouge. Leading communists like Khieu Samphan had served as ministers in his government during the 1960s, and he thought he knew them well. In early 1973, the prince and his wife Monique toured the CPK's "liberated zone," posing with pasted-on smiles in the black pajamas worn by the communist troops. He later wrote to several Democrats in the US, reassuring them (and maybe also himself) that the Khmer Rouge would not set up a communist system after coming to power, but rather "a Swedish type of kingdom."[15] In private he was more pessimistic, predicting that the Khmer Rouge would spit him out "like a cherry pit" once they gained power.[16]

By 1973, as Becker wrote, there were already signs that Sar and the Khmer Rouge leadership were striking out into more radical territory. That year a small book, titled *Regrets for the Khmer Soul*, appeared for sale in Phnom Penh. Before long, everybody was reading it, from pedicab drivers to high-ranking government officials. Its author was Ith Sarin, a former teacher and defector who had produced a rare first-hand account of the policies of the *angkar*—the mysterious Khmer Rouge "organization" which ruled the liberated zones. According to Sarin, the Khmer Rouge had won support among the rural people by building dikes, ponds, houses, and bunkers to provide shelter during US bombing raids. In the areas under its control, *Angkar* was omniscient and beyond criticism. Life was strictly regimented; communist cadres forced the population to wear black, banned idle chatter, and severely punished any violations of their orders.[17] Sarin also noted down a chilling phrase that would soon become ubiquitous: "*Angkar*," it was said, "has as many eyes as a pineapple and cannot make mistakes."[18]

At around the same time, Kenneth Quinn, a young US foreign service officer stationed in South Vietnam, sent a 45-page airgram to Washington detailing the Khmer Rouge policies in southern Cambodia. Quinn, an Ohio native working as a rural development officer in the Mekong Delta, was then based in Chau Doc, a Mekong River town close to the Cambodian border. One Saturday in June 1973, he had hiked up Nui Sam, a nearby hill dotted with Buddhist shrines, which commanded views far over the Cambodian plains. What he saw from the hilltop shocked him: "All the Cambodian villages that you could see—you could see out probably fifteen to twenty miles—every village, every one, was on fire on the same day. I had no idea what was going on, other than these strange columns of black smoke pouring up into the sky."[19] Cambodian refugees soon poured over the border into Vietnam, fleeing the conflagration. Intrigued, Quinn starting speaking to them.

Like Sarin's account, Quinn's report suggested the unique fanaticism of the Khmer Rouge and their de facto independence from Vietnam. Refugees described how the Cambodian communists marched them out of their villages, which were razed to prevent their return, and then forced them into collective labor brigades. Violence and terror were used to strip away old attitudes and impose a new "collective" consciousness. "Death sentences are relatively common," Quinn wrote. "Usually people are arrested and simply never show up again, or are given six months in jail and then die there."[20] When Quinn's prescient airgram reached Washington in February 1974, however, it was ignored. Like Becker's article, his analysis ran counter to the conventional wisdom that the Cambodian insurgency was being controlled from Hanoi. "It was a hard sell," he recalled later. "Even after the Khmer Rouge took over, people would still treat me politely when I would talk about the horror. Nobody believed me, because no one would accept it—no one."[21]

Back in Phnom Penh—one of the few parts of the country it still controlled—the Khmer Republic faced collapse on every front. The war had triggered wild inflation, currency devaluation, and food shortages. With the US seeking an "honorable" disengagement from Indochina, vital American support began to taper off. In August 1973, the US Congress ordered a halt to the aerial bombing, leaving the Phnom Penh government vulnerable to communist offensives.

Decision-making took on a vague, improvisatory quality. After suffering a stroke in 1971, Lon Nol had retreated into a small circle of advisors and court astrologers. As the Khmer Rouge tightened their noose on Phnom Penh, he sent Buddhist monks up in a helicopter to sprinkle blessed sand and holy water over the capital, hoping to "protect" it from attack. By early 1975, the Khmer Rouge had the city surrounded. Rockets rained down on Phnom Penh, terrifying the population. On April 1, Lon Nol and his entourage abandoned Cambodia, flying to Thailand, and thence to the US Pacific Command Headquarters in Oahu, Hawaii. As his country slipped into the abyss, Lon Nol moved into a four-acre property in suburban Oahu and settled into civilian life. From his living-room sofa he described his plans for forming a government-in-exile and returning to power, but his schemes never attracted much support. The marshal sank into an obscure, listless retirement, growing vegetables and raising geese and rabbits.[22] He never saw Cambodia again.

The end came quickly for the Khmer Republic. On April 12, US Ambassador John Gunther Dean ran down the embassy's flag and choppered out of Phnom Penh. The morning of the 17th, a Thursday, rippled with dry season heat. Shortly after dawn the first teenaged Khmer Rouge troops marched into Phnom Penh, casting long shadows on the tarmac. The frenzy of battle gave way to an ominous calm.

At first, Phnom Penh's inhabitants welcomed the end of the war. Crowds gathered in the street, cheering and waving white flags. "An almost physical sense of relief led to general rejoicing," wrote François Ponchaud, a French Catholic priest who witnessed the fall of the city and later wrote of his experiences in the book *Cambodia: Year Zero*. There were "no more rockets to fear; no more blind slaughter; no more compulsory military service . . . At last, the peasants could go back and cultivate their rice paddies."[23]

From his home in central Phnom Penh, Kassie Neou watched and waited. Up until that morning, he had been an English teacher, heading a government department that broadcast English-language materials over the radio, using old reel-to-reel tapes imported from Britain and the US. The past year had been particularly tough, with its food shortages and barrages of rocket-fire.

Like many others, Kassie hoped the arrival of the black-clad peasant soldiers, strange as they seemed, would at least mean a return to normality. "We were so sick and tired," he told me. "We longed for peace and we were led to believe it was the end of a bloody war."[24]

But within hours the atmosphere changed. The Khmer Rouge suddenly ordered the entire population to evacuate, claiming the Americans were about to bomb the city. Young soldiers walked the streets with bullhorns mounted on pedicabs, shouting the evacuation order. Others went door-to-door forcing inhabitants out of their homes and into a frenzied exodus along the highways. "Go, go, go!" urged the voices on the loudspeakers. "You will meet *Angkar*! *Angkar* will help you!"[25] In their haste, many left almost empty-handed, forgetting to take any rice, fish, or pots and pans to cook them in. Hospitals were emptied at gunpoint, and their patients, some still with IV lines attached, were pressed into the sinister procession.

In the fierce dry season heat, the evacuation from Phnom Penh soon became a death-march. Kassie Neou was swept into a crowd moving southward out of the city, leaving him no time to locate his wife. As the crowd moved south, dead bodies started appearing by the roadside—the victims of starvation and dehydration. Others started going missing at night. It rapidly became clear that the "new people" from the city were being singled out for harsh treatment. For the Khmer Rouge, city-dwellers bore the original sin of association with the "parasitic" urban culture spawned by US imperialism. All the accoutrements of city life, right down to glasses and knowledge of foreign languages, were suddenly marks of the spy and saboteur. Along the roadside, Kassie had his family discard their Western-style clothes and pose as a family of peasants from Battambang. "I started changing my identity, behavior, mannerisms," he said, "the way I talked, the way I walked, the way I dressed." An estimated 20,000 people died in the evacuation of Phnom Penh.[26]

Sihanouk returned to the city in September. After five years away he was disturbed to find the graceful capital, with its tree-lined boulevards and golden spires, empty and quiet. Sihanouk's communist allies were in a triumphant mood, crowing that they would soon embark on a "super great leap forward" that would outpace even the achievements of China's Great Proletarian Cultural Revolution. Khieu Samphan and Son Sen, the new army's commander-in-chief, told him that Cambodia's name would "be written in golden letters in world history as the first country that succeeded in communization without useless steps."[27]

As Sihanouk had feared, the authorities of Democratic Kampuchea soon cast him aside. In April 1976, the prince resigned in frustration and was shut up in a small house in the grounds of the Royal Palace, where he remained imprisoned for the next three years with his wife, his mother-in-law, and other relatives who had accompanied him home. More than a dozen members of Sihanouk's family would eventually perish under DK. His Chinese patrons, meanwhile, provided vital shipments of economic and military aid that kept the regime afloat. In the coming years, Beijing would send as many as 15,000 Chinese advisors to DK, along with artillery, tanks, and other materiel.[28]

DK's leadership, centered on a six-member CPK Standing Committee led by Pol Pot and "Brother Number Two" Nuon Chea, was paranoid and secretive. Cambodia's new rulers saw their revolution as under constant threat from foreign agents of every stripe. To root out internal enemies, the regime established a network of crude prisons and detention centers, a matrix of repression that converged on a three-story concrete high school in the southern suburbs of Phnom Penh. Over the next three and a half years, Tuol Sleng prison, codenamed S-21, grew into an elaborate bureaucracy of death, where at least 12,272 "enemies of the revolution" were tortured, forced to confess often imaginary crimes, and then butchered at a mass "killing field" on the city's outskirts. Just a handful of those who entered S-21 as prisoners came out alive.[29]

After his evacuation from Phnom Penh, Kassie Neou ended up at a work camp in Battambang, where he was forced up at 4 a.m. and toiled until dark, ploughing hard earth with skinny draught animals. One day his disguise slipped and he uttered a few words in English to a workmate. He was arrested and sent to Kach Roteh, a nearby prison, where he was shackled to the floor of a leaky hut along with dozens of other prisoners. For six months Kassie was beaten and interrogated, accused of being an agent of the "CAI"—as his illiterate torturers mistakenly termed the US Central Intelligence Agency.

Of the 72 men then imprisoned at Kach Roteh, Kassie was the only one who survived. After his arrival, he slowly won the trust of the young guards by telling them stories—Aesop's fables and Asian folktales he had learned by heart from the old tapes he once played over the radio. One morning, when the prisoners were assembled in the yard, one of Kassie's teenage guards walked up and pulled him out of the line and shackled another man in his place. Shortly afterward the prisoners were marched off and killed. "I was needed to tell the stories," Kassie said. "But somebody had to die in my place, which is not a good feeling."

The plight of Kassie Neou and millions of his countrymen remained nearly invisible to the outside world. After April 1975, Cambodia's only link to the outside world was a single weekly flight to Beijing. China and Vietnam, the two countries that had done the most to bring Pol Pot to power, remained silent about conditions inside the country. In the US, meanwhile, the lack of information was compounded by the lack of interest. Books like Ponchaud's *Cambodia: Year Zero*, published in France in January 1977, were mostly ignored. After the fall of Saigon in April 1975, Cambodia was no longer even a sideshow—it was, like Vietnam itself, a lost and forgotten cause.

Between 1970 and 1975, the *Washington Post* and the *New York Times* had published more than 700 stories on Cambodia each year. In 1976, after the Indochinese dominoes had toppled, they ran just 126.[30] In September 1975, when *Newsweek*'s Latin America bureau chief James Pringle filed an exclusive interview with DK's foreign minister Ieng Sary, he found it pulled from the US edition of the magazine. Pringle had encountered Sary during a non-aligned meeting in Lima. It was an unexpected scoop: for the first time a leading member of the new Cambodian government was offering a peek behind the shroud that had fallen over the country. But *Newsweek*'s American desk wasn't interested. Pringle picked up the phone and requested an explanation. "The editor said that they felt Americans wanted to put the Vietnam and Cambodian wars behind them and turn to more happy subjects," he recalled. "The emphasis was on more upbeat stories."[31]

A similar Vietnam fatigue prevailed in the US government. When Phnom Penh fell in April 1975, Charles Twining was a Foreign Service Officer stationed at the US embassy in Bangkok, monitoring the trickle of information coming from inside Cambodia. Then 33 years of age, Twining had just spent eight months diligently learning the Khmer language in preparation for a posting to Phnom Penh. His plans disrupted by the fall of the city, he put his language skills to use along the Thai border, where as many as 6,000 Cambodian refugees had gathered by the middle of the year. "It took me a while," Twining said. "It was only in August or so of 1975 that I started to piece together a few of the refugee stories. It suddenly struck me that some of the awful abuses of Nazi Germany were being relived in Cambodia." He wrote up his reports and cabled them back to Washington, where, like Quinn's 1974 report, they met with a general lack of interest. Only a handful of policy-makers maintained any interest in Cambodia. Otherwise, Twining said, "the United States was pretty much tuned out of Indochina."[32]

On August 12, 1978, the chairman of the Swedish-Kampuchean Friendship Association arrived in Phnom Penh on a flight from Beijing. Gunnar Bergström and his delegation were warmly received. Accompanying him were three Swedish leftists, including the prominent radical Jan Myrdal; also on the flight were a few Chinese advisors and a "Carpathian mountain garland art troupe," bringing fraternal greetings from the dim high-noon of Ceauşescu's Romania. In early 1978, hoping to improve its international image, DK began allowing small groups of sympathetic Westerners to visit Cambodia, along with journalists from friendly socialist countries. Since 1975, Bergström's group had written repeatedly to the DK embassy in Beijing requesting a visa to visit Cambodia. Then, one day, there was a response. "In spring of '78 we got a letter," he remembered. "They said we were allowed to send four people."[33]

As a student in Stockholm, Bergström had grown attracted to the ideology of Maoism. He was enraged by the American bombing of Cambodia and sympathized with the pro-Chinese peasant revolutionaries fighting to free themselves from the yoke of US imperialism. To Bergström, as to communist radicals across the Western world, DK seemed like a model of political zeal and self-reliance, smeared by what David Kline, a writer for the American communist magazine *The Call*, termed an "anti-Kampuchea propaganda war."[34] Later, when reports emerged of starvation and killings in DK, Bergström reasoned them away as reactionary lies. The US government had lied to the world about so much during the Vietnam War. Why would Cambodia be any different?

Less radical figures on the left had similar doubts. In June 1977, Noam Chomsky and Edward S. Herman penned an article for *The Nation* in which they questioned the accounts of Ponchaud and others, implying that reports of Cambodian atrocities were part of "a campaign to reconstruct the history of these years so as to place the role of the United States in a more favorable light."[35] Thirty years later, Bergström returned to Phnom Penh for a second time and admitted that he, like many of his fellow leftists, was wrong. After visiting S-21, now a museum to the horrors of DK's rule, he apologized to Cambodians, explaining that his youthful fanaticism had blinded him to the grim reality of Democratic Kampuchea. As he later told me, "we could not imagine that the people we supported could become oppressors."

Even during his 1978 visit, Bergström recalled, he found theory and reality hard to reconcile. In Phnom Penh, he walked through a cityscape of overgrown gardens and rusting gas stations. In Kampong Cham, the bus station was being used to dry corn. He noticed that the Angkor temples were well maintained, but silent except for the sound of birds and insects. Touring the communes and factories of the new Cambodia, the Swedish delegation was fed lies of the most transparent kind. Bergström was shown a technical high school where the blackboards were covered with advanced physics equations. Every teacher, the visitors were told, was "a peasant who had learned from the revolution." Most disturbing of all were the reactions of ordinary people, who shuffled off in fear when the Swedish visitors approached. "They gave stupid, evasive, crazy answers of why we couldn't talk to them," he said. "Deep inside I started to suspect some of the rumors were true—that these people were being killed."

Before returning home, the Swedes were granted an audience with Pol Pot. It was a stiff encounter. All questions were submitted in writing ahead of time, and only Pol Pot and Ieng Sary spoke. During an interview with Myrdal, later broadcast on Swedish television, Pol Pot claimed that 1.4 million Cambodians had been killed by the "US imperialists and their lackeys."[36] Afterwards, over a banquet of oysters and bony fish, Pol Pot was aloof; there was no hint of the charm noted by many others who knew him. He delivered a rote address denouncing Vietnam, the Soviet Union, and the Warsaw Pact. His guests then shook hands and left. Driving through the dark streets, Bergström's driver turned and asked what he thought of "Brother Number One." Bergström kept his thoughts to himself. Fourteen days in Democratic Kampuchea were enough to shake even the strongest revolutionary conviction.

In late 1978, a few months after his return to Sweden, Bergström publicly denounced the DK regime. The move alienated his radical friends, but he was relieved at the passing of his illusions. Just before leaving Cambodia, he had reluctantly given a radio interview that he would regret until his return to Phnom Penh in 2008. "Every place we visited," he told DK radio, "we saw the Kampuchean people working arduously and busily with a great sense of responsibility in order to build a new society free from misery, famine, disease, injustice, and oppression . . ."[37]

The same month that Bergström was in Cambodia, DK repression was reaching its terrifying crescendo. Pol Pot and his colleagues, holed up in their empty capital, lived in a dreamscape, haunted by real and imaginary threats. Purges begat purges, generating lists of enemies that kept the turbines of S-21 humming with terrifying efficiency. Under the control of a disciplined, ascetic cadre named Comrade Duch, Tuol Sleng ultimately cannibalized much of the regime's senior leadership. "S-21 was the end of the line," Duch later told the filmmaker and Khmer Rouge survivor Rithy Panh. "People who got sent there were already corpses."[38]

Khmer Rouge suspicions centered on the traditional enemy—Vietnam. By late 1976, DK was referring to its former mentor and ally as an "aggressor" and "enemy" of the Khmer people.[39] Pol Pot drew up delusional plans for the reconquest of Kampuchea Krom, the former Cambodian territories in the Mekong Delta. In 1977, Cambodian troops began cross-border raids in which they sacked Vietnamese villages and butchered their inhabitants. At the same time, the CPK Party Center embarked on a wholesale purge of cadres in the Eastern Zone bordering Vietnam, who were accused of being Vietnamese spies, of having "Khmer bodies and Vietnamese minds." The purges uncovered so many "enemies" that by April 1978, trucks delivering prisoners to S-21 were being turned away.[40] Many Eastern Zone personnel revolted or fled into Vietnam to avoid the purges. Among them was a 24-year-old regimental officer named Hun Sen, soon to begin his rapid climb to the apex of Cambodian politics.

China, the main supporter of the Khmer Rouge, saw little reason to discourage Pol Pot's warmongering. Relations between Beijing and Hanoi had soured since the mid-1970s as a reunified Vietnam drifted into the Soviet orbit. For China, DK was a country which could be dependably expected to resist the expansion of Soviet power in Southeast Asia. For their own part, the war-weary Vietnamese hoped that the conflicts with DK could be overcome through negotiations. It was a futile hope. On December 31, 1977, the regime broke off diplomatic relations with Hanoi. When the Cambodian troops launched their invasion, Pol Pot predicted, they would "kill the enemy at will" and leave nothing but "piles of the enemy's bones."[41]

In early 1978, Hanoi started making preparations to remove the DK regime by force. At former US army bases in southern Vietnam, officers began molding Cambodian defectors and other communist veterans into a guerrilla army. On December 2, in a clearing on a rubber plantation east of Snuol, a few kilometers from the Vietnamese border, Cambodian rebels and their Vietnamese overseers announced the formation of the Kampuchean United Front for National Salvation (KUFNS, or the Front), which denounced the "barbarous policy of the Pol Pol-Ieng Sary gang" and promised to drive it from power.[42]

The invasion was launched on Christmas Day 1978. More than 100,000 battle-hardened Vietnamese troops, accompanied by 20,000 rebels from the KUFNS, poured across the border into DK. Despite Pol Pot's prediction of a quick victory, the regime imploded with surprising speed. The Cambodian population, starved and weakened by nearly four years of revolution, gratefully welcomed its liberation. Freed from his work-site in Battambang, Kassie Neou remembered running down to the highway to kneel in supplication as the Soviet-built T54 tanks rumbled past. The Khmer Rouge "disappeared overnight. Even the village chief, his whole family. It was a liberation."

Pol Pot and the DK leadership fled west toward the Thai border, leaving homes, offices, and many government archives intact. On January 6, Sihanouk and his wife Monique were released from house arrest and flown out of the country aboard a Chinese Boeing 707, bound via Beijing for New York and the United Nations. Accompanying them were about a hundred Chinese diplomats and advisors, a troupe of Chinese acrobats, and two Khmer Rouge "minders" who kept a close eye on the prince as he prepared to denounce Vietnam's invasion to the world.[43]

Vietnamese advance units entered Phnom Penh the next morning, driving unimpeded into the empty city center. Shortly after noon, rebel radio announced the collapse of "the regime of dictatorial, militarist domination of the Pol Pot-Ieng Sary clique."[44] The nightmare of Democratic Kampuchea was over. The insurgents' flag—a gold, five-towered silhouette of Angkor Wat on a red field—flew over the capital. But the new war for Cambodia had only just begun.

CHAPTER TWO

The Second Revolution

The invading Vietnamese troops entered a ghost city. By January 7, 1979, just 20,000 Khmer Rouge soldiers and workers remained in Phnom Penh—a small fraction of the prewar population. Elizabeth Becker, who visited the capital days before the invasion, later described a cityscape in an eerie state of suspended animation:

> Government buildings were freshly painted; the railway station was a muted coral colour, the old ministry of information a soft yellow. The parks were immaculate, the lawns reseeded and mowed, the flower beds weeded and in bloom. There was no litter on the streets, no trash, no dirt. But then there were no people either, no bicycles or buses and very few automobiles.[1]

Behind this showcase facade, four years of neglect had taken their toll. Backstreets were strewn with trash and vegetation sprouted from cracked pavements. The empty Central Market, a domed Art Deco gem from the French era, was surrounded by overgrown palms. Nearby, the old National Bank lay in ruins, blown up by Khmer Rouge soldiers in April 1975. Cars, furniture, clothes, and consumer goods stood everywhere in rusting heaps, the decaying relics of a submerged era of wealth and middle-class prosperity. Parts of the city were strangely untouched by the upheavals of the past four years. Many survivors recalled finding their family possessions right where they had left them in 1975, troubled only by the patter of rodents and the encroachments of the tropical climate.

At Tuol Sleng in the city's south, two Vietnamese journalists stumbled across a three-story concrete school building ringed with barbed wire. Like many government offices, S-21 had been abandoned during the hurried evacuation of the capital. In their haste, the prison's staff, including its chief, Comrade Duch, had no time to cover up the evidence of their grisly work. In the tiled classrooms, torture victims, recently executed, remained strapped to metal bed frames. Elsewhere, the Vietnamese found thousands of prisoner confessions and eerie monochrome snapshots of the prison's victims, each bearing mute witness to the horror and paranoia that had consumed Democratic Kampuchea until its final days.

On January 11, 1979, four days after the fall of Phnom Penh, two American-made Dakota aircraft bounced down on the cratered runway at Pochentong airport, carrying the leadership of the newly proclaimed People's Republic of Kampuchea (PRK).[2] Little was known about the four men who walked across the tarmac toward the dilapidated terminal building. One of them was Pen Sovan, an austere and steely figure who had spent most of his 42 years steeped in the study of Marxist dialectics and theories of class struggle. Sovan, who would be appointed the PRK's first prime minister in 1981, had joined the struggle against the French as a teenager and was one of a large number of Cambodian revolutionaries who departed for Vietnam after the 1954 Geneva Conference. After spending much of the past 20 years undergoing political and military training in Hanoi, these "Khmer Viet Minh" (as Sihanouk derisively termed them) were deployed to Phnom Penh with the expectation that they would remain loyal to Vietnamese interests.

The other three men on the aircraft were part of a second group that had remained in Cambodia, served DK, and then fled to Vietnam to escape Pol Pot's purges in 1977 and 1978. One of these was the new head of state, Heng Samrin, a slight former military cadre who had served as a division commander in the Eastern Zone before fleeing to Vietnam in October 1978. Two months later, Samrin surfaced at the head of the Kampuchean United Front for National Salvation (KUFNS), the Vietnamese entity set up to act as a Cambodian spearhead for Hanoi's assault against the Khmer Rouge. The third was Chea Sim, a 47-year-old who had begun his revolutionary career in the 1940s as an organizer among the monkhood and rose to the post of district chief in the Eastern Zone. After defecting in mid-1978, he became the PRK's first interior minister and soon carved out a prominent niche in the new regime.

The last of the four wasn't much to look at. After years of living rough in the *maquis*, Hun Sen was as thin as a rake, his body worn down by chronic disease and malnutrition. Despite having been appointed foreign minister, at just 26 years of age, Hun Sen seemed uncomfortable in public settings, and his cheap glass eye, fitted in his left socket to replace the eye he lost during the final assault on Phnom Penh in April 1975, gave him an occasional look of confusion. Ouk Bunchhoeun, a fellow DK defector who first met Hun Sen in Vietnam in 1978, echoed what was probably a common view at the time: "I didn't think he was really that important . . . I didn't think he would ever do anything very significant like he has."[3]

Hun Sen, like many of the PRK leadership, came from humble beginnings. He was born Hun Bunnal on August 5, 1952,[4] in Peam Koh Snar, a village of brown-roofed stilt houses spread along the Mekong north of Kampong Cham. He grew up in a small house surrounded by clusters of bamboo, the youngest son of a family that farmed rice and tobacco. Even as a schoolboy, villagers in Peam Koh Snar remembered young Bunnal standing out from his peers. Ros Thorn, a former schoolmate, described him as a clever boy with the ability to convince others: "He was different from other children. Bunnal always came before class, never late. He was always an upright person . . . When he said something, he would do it."

It was an indication of the esteem with which Bunnal's parents regarded their youngest son that they chose him to send downstream to continue his schooling in Phnom Penh. They had little money, so the 13-year-old Bunnal boarded at Wat Neakavoan, a Buddhist pagoda in the city's north, while attending the Indra Devi High School. To pay his board, he served as a "pagoda boy," carrying food and running errands for the resident monks—an episode of hardship that would later become a much-mythologized part of Hun Sen's life story. It was here also that a teenaged Bunnal first became involved in politics. Hun Sen later told the historian Ben Kiernan that he worked under the tutelage of an older cousin, running small errands for the communist underground and delivering loaves of bread stuffed with secret communications.[5]

According to his official biography, Bunnal left school in 1969 and joined the communist rebellion on April 14, 1970, shortly after hearing Sihanouk's broadcast call to arms from Beijing. Hun Sen (he adopted the name in 1972) thrived in the rough conditions of the *maquis*. He went about his missions with single-minded dedication, finding purpose in the routines and discipline of military life. One of the few surviving photos of Hun Sen from the Khmer Rouge years shows a skinny 19-year-old youth clad in dark shirt and military beret, a pistol strapped to the side of his gaunt frame. He stares skeptically at the camera, his right hand poised as if ready to draw. Hun Sen climbed quickly through the ranks. By the time of the fall of Phnom Penh in April 1975, he was serving as an officer in the Special Forces regiment of Region 21, which commanded a 50-kilometer stretch of the Vietnamese border. Before his defection, he would rise to become its deputy commander.[6]

Hun Sen fled to Vietnam much earlier than most of his colleagues. In June 1977, as the purges of the Eastern Zone threatened to engulf his regiment, the young commander crossed the border on foot with four companions, leaving behind his pregnant wife, Bun Sam Hieng (later known as Bun Rany). For the first few months Hun Sen and his fellow defectors were imprisoned and grilled by Vietnamese interrogators. Hun Sen, who took the Vietnamese name Hai Phúc in a gesture of solidarity, soon won over his captors by offering information about Cambodian troop movements and planned cross-border attacks.[7] He later told his biographers Julie and Harish Mehta that he forged a close relationship with General Le Duc Anh, the Vietnamese general who would go on to lead the Vietnamese military effort in Cambodia throughout the 1980s. Anh put Hun Sen in charge of forming Cambodian exiles into a viable military force.[8] In late 1978, he was given a prominent position in the Front that invaded Cambodia with the Vietnamese military. Now, walking across the Pochentong tarmac four days after the fall of Phnom Penh, Hun Sen stepped onto a new battlefield: politics.

Returning to Phnom Penh in January 1979, the PRK leaders and their Vietnamese allies confronted a new Year Zero. Most of the country's physical infrastructure—along with much of its skilled workforce—had been severely damaged or destroyed, and the social system faced collapse. The education, health, and judicial systems had been eradicated. In the countryside, agricultural production had regressed half a century under the Khmer Rouge's crash-collectivization program, and rice fields lay fallow as disoriented Cambodians, suddenly freed from the bondage of the communal worksites, wandered the countryside in search of their original homes and lost relatives. Red Cross and UNICEF officials estimated that just 5 percent of the country's fields remained under cultivation in July 1979, and famine threatened.[9] A new economy and system of administration had to be built from scratch and the newly installed "government" immediately set out to assemble the few qualified individuals who could be found. "We enlisted anybody who could read and write," recalled one government official. "In that way, somehow we managed to get a government together."[10]

For the PRK, liberation from Khmer Rouge rule meant a second revolution, a more "authentic" form of communism constructed along Vietnamese lines. The ruling Kampuchean People's Revolutionary Party (KPRP), officially unveiled in 1981, claimed to represent the "true" lineage of Cambodian communism. It adopted both the name and history of Cambodia's first communist party, founded by the Vietnamese in 1951, and continued to extol April 17, 1975 as a shining victory: one that had been hijacked almost immediately by Pol Pot and his "genocidal clique." Launching the KUFNS on December 2, 1978, Heng Samrin promised that DK's most hated policies would be abolished. "Everywhere," Samrin said, "our people have witnessed massacres, more atrocious, more barbarous, than those committed in the Dark Ages or perpetuated by the Hitlerite fascists."[11]

PRK rule was benign next to the hecatomb of the Pol Pot years, but the regime remained staunchly communist. When the schools reopened, portraits of Heng Samrin, Stalin, and Ho Chi Minh were hung from classroom walls and government workers were subjected to tedious political education sessions. More problematic from the perspective of many Cambodians was the regime's near-total reliance on Vietnam. Until 1989, the PRK was propped up by a Vietnamese occupation force of more than 100,000, and assisted by a separate corps of Vietnamese advisors posted in every ministry and party office. To oversee this shadow administration, Hanoi appointed Le Duc Tho, the communist *éminence grise* most famous for helping negotiate the 1973 Paris Peace Accord with the United States, and then, when he was awarded the Nobel Peace Prize along with Henry Kissinger, for turning it down.

Tho had dedicated his life to the cause. In 1941, he became a founding member of the Viet Minh front, and had played a key role in the communists' struggle against the French and the Americans. In 1978, three years after Vietnam was reunified under communist rule, Tho was given the mission of assembling a group of Cambodian revolutionaries and defectors, and shaping them into a force capable of advancing Vietnamese interests in Cambodia. He would remain in Cambodia until 1982, "guiding" the Cambodian revolution and keeping a close watch over his hand-picked protégés. His appointment was an indication of the importance Hanoi placed on the survival of its new Cambodian satellite.

As the leadership of Democratic Kampuchea retreated west, their reign of terror continued. Cadres herded frightened villagers toward the Thai border at gunpoint. Emaciated refugees arriving in Thailand told of widespread massacres in areas of western Cambodia that fell back under Khmer Rouge control in the chaotic months following the invasion. "Many of us died at the last moment," said Kassie Neou, who was recaptured briefly by the Khmer Rouge after liberation, before escaping on foot into Thailand. By the end of 1979, around 100,000 former DK cadres, soldiers, and their families had arrived at the Thai border, where they settled in a series of makeshift camps. The defeated regime was in disarray, its senior leadership hemmed into an unwelcoming sliver of territory along the Thai border, a thickly forested area traditionally inhabited by outlaws and bandits.

Only intense international lobbying prevented the disappearance of the Khmer Rouge as a political entity. When Pol Pot was overthrown, China, the US, and the anticommunist Association of Southeast Asian Nations (ASEAN) all condemned the Vietnamese overthrow of DK and withheld recognition of the new government in Phnom Penh. When a barefoot Ieng Sary crossed into Thailand four days after the fall of Phnom Penh, officials from the Chinese embassy in Bangkok were there to greet him, with fresh clothes and shoes to replace the sandals he had lost in the confused retreat from Phnom Penh. DK's foreign minister was then placed aboard a Thai military helicopter to Bangkok and flown to Beijing.[12] The next morning, Sary met Chinese leader Deng Xiaoping, who criticized his government's excesses and "deviations," but pledged to back a guerrilla war to unseat the Heng Samrin regime, securing Thai support for the shipment of aid and military supplies to DK sanctuaries along the Cambodian border.

Deng followed up this show of hospitality with a more pointed "lesson" for Hanoi. On February 17, after heavy shelling, waves of People's Liberation Army troops invaded northern Vietnam. Fierce fighting dragged on for nearly three weeks and laid waste to the Vietnamese border region. As a pedagogical exercise, Beijing's invasion had mixed results—Chinese forces sustained heavy casualties and were soon forced to withdraw—but it set the geopolitical battle-lines that would determine the course of the Cambodian civil war for the next decade. Each year between 1979 and 1989, the Chinese provided $80–100 million to fund Pol Pot's fight against the Soviet-backed PRK, including cash payments which were made available directly through the Chinese embassy in Bangkok.[13]

The US, whose friendship with China was the key plank of its new policy orientation in Asia, "winked, semi-publicly" at Beijing's support for the Khmer Rouge. "I encouraged the Chinese to support Pol Pot," President Carter's National Security Advisor Zbigniew Brzezinski said in 1985. "Pol Pot was an abomination. We could never support him, but China could."[14] At a tense session in September 1979, the UN General Assembly voted 71–35 (with 34 abstentions) to continue recognizing DK as Cambodia's legitimate government—the first government-in-exile ever to be accorded the privilege. It would hold the position in various guises until 1991. Robert Rosenstock, the American delegate to the UN Credentials Committee, which drafted the resolution, recalled later how he was instructed to "engineer" the results in a manner favorable to the US and its allies. "I think I know how Pontius Pilate must have felt," he commented to a colleague after a grateful Ieng Sary came up to thank him after the vote.[15]

By the end of 1979, the tragedy of Khmer Rouge rule had given way to a full-blown moral farce. Despite occupying more than nine-tenths of Cambodia's territory, the new regime in Phnom Penh was diplomatically isolated and politically ostracized, while Pol Pot's emissaries were welcomed in the UN as the representatives of their former victims. Nursed back to health by the Chinese, and shielded by Western diplomatic cover, the DK forces quickly rebuilt themselves into a viable military force. Many in the West—including American officials like Rosenstock—professed to be disgusted with the moral contortions of Cold War realpolitik, but Washington's overriding strategic interest was the isolation of the Soviet bloc and its Vietnamese client. Cambodia and its sufferings, as always, remained of secondary importance.

The isolation of the PRK held back much needed assistance and prolonged the painful period of reconstruction. Strong US lobbying failed to prevent Western nations from mounting a massive humanitarian effort in the early 1980s—the largest ever to that point—but support dried up in 1983 when UN member states declared the period of "emergency" at an end. Since it was under diplomatic embargo, UN agencies were barred from providing development aid to the PRK, and only those with emergency mandates—like UNICEF and the UN High Commissioner for Refugees—could operate inside the country.

Humanitarian aid was used as a political tool by both sides. Western governments led by the US imposed a ban on bilateral aid to Phnom Penh, forcing the PRK to survive on handouts from Vietnam, the Soviet bloc, and Western volunteer organizations like Oxfam UK, which insisted on working inside Cambodia. The PRK likewise used aid to advance its own military and political objectives, demanding sole responsibility for its distribution and lobbying for the withdrawal of assistance to the Thai border camps. Sir Robert Jackson, the UN representative in charge of coordinating the relief effort, remarked in 1980 that "no humanitarian operation in this century has been so totally and continuously influenced by political factors."[16]

The upshot was that international relief efforts were concentrated in the refugee camps along the Thai frontier, now home to some 300,000 refugees. Scattered in a long arc along the border, the camps were hotbeds of fear, starvation, and ennui, menaced by bandits, thugs, and remnants of the DK regime. The first large-scale aid shipments reached the area in October 1979. In the lawless atmosphere of the border, the influx of aid provided easy pickings for the Khmer Rouge, who were soon running their own regimented camps and appropriating aid supplies for their own use. Conditions in the DK-controlled camps recalled the strict discipline of the Pol Pot years. Belgian journalist Jacques Bekaert recalled a "totally different atmosphere" than in the other camps. "We were constantly being watched and we never knew whether people were telling us what they thought, or what they were told to say," he said.[17]

Although many lives were undoubtedly saved by the aid effort on the border, it also helped rehabilitate the Khmer Rouge, bolstering its capacity to fight the PRK and giving it access to a population base and a ready pool of recruits.

Other resistance groups soon surfaced in the Thai border camps. Arriving in February 1979 was Son Sann, an ex-president of the Cambodian National Bank who had served briefly as prime minister under Sihanouk. Then in his seventies, Son Sann had spent the DK years in Paris, heading an organization of Cambodian exiles. On October 9, in the jungle along the Thai border, Son Sann announced the founding of the Khmer People's National Liberation Front (KPNLF), which united a raft of Lon Nol-era figures and obscure anti-communist rebel groups opposing the Vietnamese occupation.[18] Meanwhile Prince Sihanouk, who had rebuffed an earlier request to head the KPNLF, assembled a rival group of exiles under his own banner. The National United Front for an Independent, Neutral, Peaceful and Co-operative Cambodia (known almost universally by its French acronym, Funcinpec) was founded in Paris in February 1981, and took as its guiding star the legacy and principles of the Sangkum regime. All three factions—the Khmer Rouge, the KPNLF, and Funcinpec—received military aid from China. Funcinpec and the KPNLF also received direct economic and military support from the US.

As detailed reports of Pol Pot's atrocities began to circulate in the West, the Khmer Rouge gave themselves a political makeover. The architects of Cambodia's communist nightmare were now more "Khmer" than "Rouge." In December 1981, Pol Pot officially disbanded the Communist Party of Kampuchea and started referring to his faction as the Party of Democratic Kampuchea (PDK), which proclaimed its embrace of "capitalism," and exchanged its Maoist-inspired doctrine for an extreme strain of Cambodian nationalism focused on excoriation of the Vietnamese. In 1980, Khieu Samphan admitted to journalists that "mistakes" had occurred under the rule of DK, but rejected accusations of genocide or mass killings. "To talk about systematic murder is odious," he said. "If we had really killed at that rate, we would have no one to fight the Vietnamese."[19]

Few were convinced by the rebranding exercise. In June 1982, at the urging of their foreign backers, the three Cambodian resistance factions came together in Kuala Lumpur to form a unified "resistance coalition" to oppose the Vietnamese. Like Sihanouk's alliance with the Khmer communists in the early 1970s, the Coalition Government of Democratic Kampuchea (CGDK) was an offspring of expedience, absorbing the Khmer Rouge into a diplomatically palatable front that would occupy Cambodia's seat at the UN. Sihanouk, based in Beijing and Pyongyang, became the coalition's traveling spokesperson. When the UN was in session in New York, he put on grandiose soirées at the Waldorf-Astoria Hotel, where the champagne flowed freely and the prince occasionally serenaded guests to the backing of a Khmer band flown in from Paris.[20]

From the start the CGDK was an unstable fiction. As the journalist John Pilger wrote, it was "neither a coalition nor a government: nor was it democratic, nor was it in Kampuchea."[21] The only thing that rivaled the three factions' hatred of Vietnam was their hatred for each other. Sihanouk was understandably uneasy about remaining yoked to the DK leadership, but between the Vietnamese occupation and the desires of his Chinese backers, saw it as the only way of retaining a role in Cambodian affairs. "He had to walk a very fine line on this issue," said Prince Sisowath Sirirath, Sihanouk's representative at the UN. "We needed the Khmer Rouge as a bargaining chip."[22]

Behind the coalition's facade of parity, the PDK was by far the most significant military force, fielding as many as 35,000 troops compared with 11,000 for the KPNLF and 5,000 for the Armée Nationale Sihanoukienne (ANS), Funcinpec's military wing.[23] Its soldiers were more motivated and more disciplined than those of the other factions, and conducted most of the fighting against the Vietnamese. The PDK faction also controlled the all-important foreign affairs portfolio, meaning that it continued to occupy Cambodia's seat at the UN. For the US and other Western powers, the CGDK was the perfect diplomatic fig-leaf, deflecting criticisms of Western and Chinese support for the Khmer Rouge while allowing Pol Pot's forces to keep the Vietnamese army bogged down in its own unwinnable "Vietnam."

At first, the Vietnamese were unimpressed with the men they had selected to lead their satellite government in Phnom Penh. Chea Sim was "conciliatory, craven, and undecided," read one biographical sketch compiled and translated for East German intelligence in 1979. Heng Samrin had "a low education, does not talk a lot, and sometimes he has an inferiority complex." His political understanding was "limited."[24] Cambodia's young foreign minister, however, was a different story. To be sure, Hun Sen was an awkward transplant into the world of international diplomacy. In his 27 years, he had known nothing but war and political struggle. He had never been outside Cambodia or Vietnam, and spoke no other foreign languages. On the whole, his outlook was heavily conditioned by his poor rural upbringing in Kampong Cham. But Hun Sen was intelligent, and he had the practical bent of a soldier who had endured years of service in a civil war marked by relentless B-52 bombings and cruel violence on both sides. He now embarked on his political career with all the focus and preparation of a soldier embarking on a military operation.

Le Duc Tho and the Vietnamese leadership immediately sensed Hun Sen's potential and invested in his development. His first political mentor was Ngo

Dien, Vietnam's ambassador to the PRK. Dien was a suave figure, standing out from the suited ciphers of the party bureaucracy in Hanoi. On his arrival in Phnom Penh in December 1979, Ngo Dien took charge of Hun Sen's political education. He received the foreign minister at his embassy each morning, schooling him in diplomacy and global politics.[25] At first, Ngo didn't let his young charge stray too far, accompanying him to press briefings and interviews with foreign journalists.[26] "Their relationship was like a body and its shadow," recalled Pen Sovan, the former prime minister. Ngo and his team of advisors dictated every decision made by Hun Sen's ministry, making sure they chimed with Hanoi's wider strategic objectives. Voeuk Pheng, a retired Foreign Ministry official, told me that the Vietnamese advisors "wanted all the officials, all the cadres, under their feet."

Hun Sen accepted these limitations and set about his education with rigor and discipline. Another who observed his early progress was Igor Rogachev, the director of Southeast Asian affairs at the Soviet Foreign Ministry. Rogachev first met Hun Sen during a fact-finding visit to the shattered Cambodian capital in February 1979, during a banquet that was held in the garden at the crumbling Hotel Le Royal, now dubbed the Sammaki, or "Solidarity." Sitting at a table in the overgrown hotel garden, the seasoned diplomat gazed across the chipped crockery at the world's least experienced foreign minister, his shirt hanging loosely from his thin frame. But as they spoke, Rogachev later told Elizabeth Becker, he was surprised by Hun Sen's sharp mind and probing questions. "I was impressed with him right away," Rogachev said.

Throughout the 1980s, during return visits to Cambodia, the Soviet diplomat would call on his young protégé and was ever more pleased with his progress: "I watched how he broadened his vision, not only on external affairs but internal affairs as well. He became an outstanding politician."[27] From the other side of the Cold War divide, Timothy Carney, a former US diplomat who met Hun Sen several times on visits to Cambodia in 1979 and 1980, recalled a green but self-confident leader surrounded by "clear fuddy-duddies" intoning Marxist-Leninist jargon. Meeting Hun Sen in the early 1980s, Bill Herod, an American aid worker with the Church World Service (CWS), was "quite taken with how bright he was, and what a quick study."

Hun Sen's keen intellect was matched by an equally combustible temper. In the early years he went everywhere armed, and reputedly shot out an air-conditioning unit in a fit of rage during a cabinet meeting in the early 1980s.[28] Another spiteful encounter took place in the early months of 1979. After receiving reports, later proven false, that his wife Bun Rany had been killed by the Khmer Rouge,[29] several sources claim that Hun Sen became engaged to a young woman who worked in his ministry. But when Rany returned to Phnom

Penh in February 1979 with the couple's infant son, Hun Sen broke off the engagement. "I don't think he really wanted to go back to the first wife, but there was pressure from the old [party] people and the specialists who worked in the ministry," said Kong Korm, an official who worked in the Foreign Ministry throughout the 1980s and later defected to the opposition. Korm said there was an acrimonious scene at the ministry when Hun Sen broke the news to the young woman. When she protested, he became enraged and threw his pistol on a table nearby. Soon afterwards Hun Sen shipped her off to serve at the PRK embassy in Hanoi.*

From its very first days in power, the PRK faced a fight for its survival. The aim of "building socialism," trumpeted in official propaganda, immediately took a back seat to feeding the population, fighting the civil war, and reconstituting a broken society. Improvisation was the order of the day. To stave off famine, the government disbanded the communal worksites and encouraged a return to the family economy of small rural landholdings, while a new program of partial collectivization—the gathering of peasant smallholders into *krom sammaki*, or "solidarity groups"—never really got out of first gear.

The authorities also turned a blind eye to the re-emergence of small-scale private enterprise. Slowly, Phnom Penh came back to life as the streets filled up with food sellers, bicycle repair-men, and other petty traders.[30] Until the introduction of a new Soviet-printed riel currency in March 1980, transactions were conducted in a mixture of Thai baht, Vietnamese dong, and gold retrieved from personal stashes buried during the civil war years. Smuggling across the Thai border thrived and the influx of consumer contraband—food, beer, clothing, motorcycles, and electronics—formed one of the country's few bridges to the West.

Throughout the 1980s, Cambodia remained closed to most of the noncommunist world. Foreign visitors invariably wound up at the Sammaki, an expatriot melting pot where Cuban diplomats and Russian KGB officers rubbed elbows with occasional aid workers and even the odd Western celebrity. (Julie Andrews visited on an orphanage tour in 1982.)[31] Most of the capital remained in a state of decay. Visiting for the first time in late 1980, Herod described

---

* Kong Korm's account is corroborated by a short biography of Hun Sen held by the Central Stasi Archives in Berlin. The woman's name is redacted in the file, but former prime minister Pen Sovan identified her as Pin Samnang, a villager from the Eastern Zone who fled to Vietnam and met Hun Sen sometime in 1978. Before returning to Phnom Penh with Samnang in January 1979, Hun Sen requested Sovan's help in tracking down his first wife, Bun Rany. When Rany returned to the city in February, Hun Sen asked Sovan to get his "second wife" out of sight. Sovan then sent her to the Cambodian embassy in Hanoi, where she served as a protocol officer.

Phnom Penh as a Spartan city with no power or running water, where people camped out in the empty shop-fronts along Monivong Boulevard, cooking on wood-fires. For another less charitable visitor, the city resembled "something between a refugee camp and a mammoth rubbish dump."[32]

The inner workings of the Cambodian regime were opaque. Like its "fraternal" counterpart in Vietnam, the KPRP ruled unchallenged, and mostly in secret. According to a constitution promulgated in June 1981, power was vested in the KPRP's 21-member Central Committee (led by an eight-member Politburo), whose policies were theoretically implemented by a network of people's committees stretching down to the provincial and district levels. For a communist party, however, KPRP had surprisingly few communists. One East German appraisal from April 1983 observed flatly that the number of party members, and their level of "political maturity," did "not yet correspond with the demands of the time."[33] When Ouk Bunchhoeun, by then the PRK's minister of justice, recalled that "there were no Marxist-Leninists" in the PRK, he exaggerated—but not by much.[34]

The regime also faced a mounting crisis of legitimacy. From its first days in power, the PRK defined itself by the fact that it had overthrown DK. One of its first acts had been to convene a five-day show trial which dramatized the crimes of the regime and sentenced Pol Pot and Ieng Sary to death in absentia. But once the euphoria of liberation had faded, many Cambodians began to see the Vietnamese and their 100,000-strong military garrison as a hostile occupation force. Their fears were encouraged by resistance propaganda, which depicted the Vietnamese invasion as the culmination of a centuries-long ambition to swallow Cambodian territory. The early 1980s saw a trickle of defections from the PRK, mostly by civil servants in western Cambodia who complained about the stifling oversight of Vietnamese advisors.[35] The party responded to anti-Vietnamese propaganda with a firm hand. Hundreds of suspected resistance agents were rounded up and jailed, usually without trial. The regime had no proper criminal code. Most crimes—even petty offenses— were seen as stirrings of "counterrevolution" and punished accordingly.[36]

At the same time, former Khmer Rouge were coming to dominate the upper echelons of the new government. The influence of Hanoi-trained revolutionaries like Pen Sovan, appointed prime minister in June 1981, waned as the decade went on. Having barely set foot in Cambodia since the 1950s, Sovan and his Vietnamese-trained comrades had few contacts on the ground. Former DK cadres, on the other hand, controlled extensive networks left over from the Pol Pot years. Among the most prominent was Interior Minister Chea Sim, who controlled appointments to the new police force and filled its ranks with relatives and colleagues. Former Eastern Zone cadres were appointed as provincial governors and party secretaries, and proceeded to give jobs to their own friends and family members. The importance of ideology began to recede next to the ability to mobilize support through patronage and personal connections. For all the corruption and inefficiency that resulted, this traditional system played a vital role in entrenching the regime's power.[37]

Given the regime's anti-Pol Pot stance, this reliance on recycled DK officials posed an awkward contradiction. The PRK squared the circle by heaping responsibility for Khmer Rouge atrocities onto "the reactionary Pol Pot-Ieng Sary clique," a code-phrase that effectively exonerated former Khmer Rouge serving in the new administration. The authorities also held out an olive branch to potential defectors, promising that "reformed" Khmer Rouge would be treated humanely and welcomed into government. The PRK and its Vietnamese backers were focused squarely on winning the civil war and gaining diplomatic recognition. In the shadow of these challenges, they were less concerned about the past crimes of its leadership than about whether they were loyal to the new government.

Those who failed to toe the official line faced excommunication. At the end of 1981, Prime Minister Pen Sovan was purged from the leadership and arrested. During his short time in power, he had grown uncomfortable with the PRK's smothering alliance with Vietnam. Sovan has since claimed Le Duc Tho reneged on a promise to respect the new government's independence. "Vietnam didn't come here to liberate us," he told me. "They just came to take our land. I didn't want to be subordinate to Vietnam." But unlike many other PRK officials, Sovan lacked the protection of a local power-base. On December 2, he was arrested, blindfolded, flown to Vietnam, and imprisoned at Dong Ha Prison outside Hanoi. There he was kept in a dark cell until January 1992, surviving on a daily ration of thin rice gruel and a single boiled egg. "Nobody could see me," Sovan said. "There was nothing at all. No sunlight, nothing, for eleven years." Inside Cambodia, the official story was that Sovan had "left the ranks of the revolution."[38]

Pen Sovan's purge was an early sign that the old band of Hanoi revolutionaries could no longer count on their backgrounds to get them ahead. The Fifth Party Congress of October 1985 marked a decisive turn against the Khmer Viet Minh. Four were dropped from an expanded, 31-member Central Committee, leaving just five as full members, while others were removed from key government posts, including the defense and planning ministries. For the dwindling core of Hanoi veterans, the best hope was to lie low and retain ceremonial positions in the party.[39]

One of the main beneficiaries of this development was Hun Sen. With the backing of the Vietnamese, the rugged rebel had enjoyed a rapid rise through the PRK's tangled state and party bureaucracy. He quickly stacked his ministry with young loyalists and, after his appointment as deputy prime minister in 1981, extended his realm of influence into the Council of Ministers, as the Cambodian cabinet was known. As foreign minister, Hun Sen had come to represent the public face of the PRK, communicating the government's positions in friendly foreign capitals and denouncing Western policy in bursts of colorful rhetoric. When Prime Minister Chan Si died in Moscow in late 1984, the 33-year-old was the most obvious replacement. On January 14, 1985, Hun Sen was appointed prime minister.

Hun Sen's ascent was marked by hard work, ingenuity, single-mindedness, and an uncanny ability to bend with the political wind. "Hun Sen is a man who can adapt himself to any situation, as long as he can win something," one former CPP official told me. "He doesn't believe in any ideology; he believes in himself, and he tries to turn any situation to his profit." For Kong Korm, Hun Sen was "a young person who bent and reflected to each situation for his own interests." Where figures like Pen Sovan bucked against Vietnamese control, Hun Sen made himself indispensable to the occupying power.

In the early 1980s, under Ambassador Ngo Dien's guiding hand, Hun Sen had signed a string of sensitive border pacts culminating in a controversial border delimitation treaty in December 1985. Hanoi hoped that the agreement would put to bed disputes over land and sea borders that had troubled its relations with Cambodia since independence. By any measure, however, the 1985 treaty was grossly unequal, "negotiated" at both ends by Vietnamese officials who utilized French colonial maps to the detriment of long-standing Cambodian claims. Hun Sen was widely criticized for his involvement in the border pacts. From the Thai border camps came accusations that he was a quisling, who had ceded Khmer land to the historical enemy. Similar concerns arose within his own party. But by defending sensitive border agreements at home and abroad, Hun Sen showed his overseers that he could be trusted to look out for their interests.[40]

Hun Sen's critics still speak darkly of his relationship with the Vietnamese. Pen Sovan claims that when he was arrested in 1981, Hun Sen was there to read out the charges. Sovan also accused Vietnamese agents of the death of Prime Minister Chan Si at the end of 1984, which smoothed Hun Sen's path to the leadership. According to Sovan's version of events, Chan Si, a student of his from Hanoi, was poisoned at a state function marking Vietnam's National Defense Day on December 22—a charge that has never been proven and remains doubtful.[41] To be sure, Hun Sen's rapid ascent would have been unthinkable without strong Vietnamese backing, but his close cooperation with Hanoi made sense for both sides. Hun Sen's political skills were crucial to a Vietnamese government that was trying to build up a viable client state in Cambodia. In return they gave their ambitious protégé what he craved most of all: power.

Hun Sen also chose his local allies well. Shortly after his appointment as foreign minister, he put out a call for young intellectuals and technocrats—basically, anyone who had studied overseas prior to 1975—and gave them jobs in his ministry. "Revolutionary" credentials were irrelevant. In contrast to figures like Heng Samrin and Chea Sim, who doled out jobs to flunkies and relatives, Hun Sen also "tried to recruit the best . . . all the people who could speak French or English or had high education," said Khieu Kanharith, one of his close allies and editor of the weekly party newspaper *Kampuchea*.[42] Soon Hun Sen was surrounded by lawyers, teachers, engineers, and diplomats—the best and brightest that a depleted Cambodia had to offer.

Hun Sen's Foreign Ministry, housed in a dilapidated building on the shady Tonlé Sap promenade, recreated the comradeship of barracks life; it was reportedly a relaxed place, with "eating, drinking, quarrelling, and a lot of messing around."[43] Many of those who came up in Hun Sen's ministry would go on to be appointed to high-ranking positions in government. Sok An, the ambassador to India in the late 1980s, was later installed in the Office of the Council of Ministers, where he became Hun Sen's grand vizier and *consigliere*; Cham Prasidh entered the Foreign Ministry as an interpreter in the early 1980s and was appointed Commerce Minister in 1994; Dith Munty became the president of the Cambodian Supreme Court. Another key figure was Hor Namhong, an experienced diplomat from the Sihanouk years, who succeeded Hun Sen as foreign minister in 1989.

In the more immediate term, these figures formed a crucial support network for Hun Sen as he found his feet in the international arena. On the road in the early 1980s—in Vietnam, Laos, Africa, the Soviet bloc—Hun Sen was accompanied everywhere by trusted senior diplomats and advisors. With the help of his young aides, Hun Sen's political education continued. They taught him basic French and English and produced summaries of foreign books that he avidly absorbed.[44] During the protracted peace talks of the late 1980s, the same small group was always at his side—interpreting, taking notes, offering quiet counsel.

Hun Sen also showed a talent for oratory. In an attempt to tweak his public speaking, he recorded himself speaking and then reviewed the tapes, making adjustments to his rhythm and intonation.[45] Voeuk Pheng, who went to work in the Foreign Ministry in 1980, said Hun Sen was able to soak up large amounts of information and then repeat it in fluent lectures later on. "He had no diploma, Hun Sen, but he had brains," Pheng said. "All the ministers respected him." Outsiders were equally impressed. In interviews with Western visitors, Hun Sen would typically speak for an hour and a half without notes, his aides scribbling away on either side. Then he would stop, light up a 555-brand cigarette, his favored variety, and field questions. Hun Sen "would lean back and chain-smoke and stare out the window or up at the ceiling," said Herod of CWS, who accompanied visitors to meetings with Hun Sen throughout the 1980s. "He would just blow smoke and give his answers. Nothing ever tripped him up."

Hun Sen's quick rise brought him into inevitable conflict with his older party colleagues—particularly Chea Sim, who had also established a large personal power base after 1979. The incipient rivalry between the two men could be traced along geographic lines. In his home province of Kampong Cham, Hun Sen had built a family empire, appointing his brother Hun Neng as provincial party secretary in 1985 and filling the administration with friends from the DK years. The prime minister had also gained a foothold in Svay Rieng due to the presence of another defector ally, Hok Lundy. In 1990, Lundy, later to become Hun Sen's feared national police chief before his death in a helicopter crash in 2008, was appointed mayor of Phnom Penh, bringing the capital and its resources into the prime minister's orbit.[46]

The Chea Sim wing of the party was strongest in Cambodia's second city, Battambang, where his nephew Ung Samy served as party secretary. Another of his allies headed the party administrations in nearby Banteay Meanchey and Siem Reap. Along with his control of the police—Sin Song, the interior minister in the late 1980s, was a close associate, while his brother-in-law Sar Kheng served as head of the Party Secretariat, which oversaw the security apparatus—Chea Sim was able to wield power through official and unofficial channels.[47]

Marx never had many foot-soldiers in the PRK, but by the mid-1980s, the nominally communist state had been subsumed under a tangle of personal patronage networks independent of central control. Older patterns of Cambodian politics began to reassert themselves. As under Sihanouk and Lon Nol, government posts began to be valued according to their potential to generate income, while the power of high-ranking officials depended on their ability to distribute those positions. As Evan Gottesman wrote in his detailed study of the PRK, "authority was handed down; money was passed upward."[48]

Those who couldn't play the patronage game saw their influence eroded. Pen Sovan and the rest of the Hanoi veterans suffered due to their lack of a personal power-base. Heng Samrin, who replaced Pen Sovan as the KPRP's general secretary in late 1981, also faded from view. By the end of the decade he had become little more than a communist waxwork, wheeled out to press the flesh in eastern-bloc capitals and deliver rambling speeches in a stilted socialist jargon soon destined, like the Soviet empire itself, for the dustbin of history.[49]

As politicians maneuvered in Phnom Penh, diplomatic initiatives to end the Cambodian civil war inched forward. Throughout the 1980s, the "Cambodian problem" centered around two conflicting imperatives: the threat of a return of the Khmer Rouge to power, and the need for a withdrawal of the Vietnamese occupation force. The PRK, with support from Hanoi and Moscow, refused to recognize the Khmer Rouge as a legitimate party, demanding diplomatic recognition and an end to Chinese support for Pol Pot as a precondition for the withdrawal of Vietnamese troops. For China, the US, ASEAN, and their allies, the Vietnamese military presence in Cambodia had to be addressed before any concessions would be made in relation to the Khmer Rouge. In the acrimonious atmosphere that prevailed, neither side was willing to give any ground. Both held out hopes that a battlefield victory would tip the balance in their favor.

But by the mid-1980s, a military solution had become remote. Despite significant gains during the 1984–5 dry season, when Vietnamese forces routed resistance bases in western Cambodia, the Khmer Rouge insurgency continued from new bases inside Thailand. The occupation of Cambodia was bleeding Hanoi white, while morale among the Vietnamese rank-and-file— "dressed in rags, puritanically fed, mostly disease-ridden," as Nayan Chanda described them[50]—was at an all-time low. The PRK also faced mounting discontent over the "K5 Plan," a scheme to construct a barrier of minefields and dikes along the Thai border in order to prevent the infiltration of resistance forces. Tens of thousands were drafted into the K5 construction teams, which endured harsh conditions in the forested border regions. Malaria was rampant and hundreds fell victim to landmines.[51] The return of forced labor brigades prompted uncomfortable comparisons with the DK regime, triggering further defections to the resistance zones.

On the other side of the front line, the noncommunist resistance was stagnating. Hampered by internal power struggles and heavy losses during the Vietnamese offensives of 1984–5, the KPNLF had ceased to be an effective military force. Many of its leaders seemed more interested in smuggling and black marketeering than fighting the occupation. Funcinpec, riven by its own leadership squabbles, was only marginally more effective. Timothy Carney, the former US diplomat, described the noncommunist resistance groups as "feckless" and "quasi-competent."[52] Only the Khmer Rouge were militarily viable, but in the short term the best even they could hope for was stalemate.

Superpower realignments eventually tipped the balance toward a diplomatic solution. In July 1986, Soviet leader Mikhail Gorbachev delivered a speech in the Pacific port city of Vladivostok that signaled Moscow's desire for a normalization of relations with China. Since the presence of Vietnamese troops in Cambodia had long been one of the chief impediments to normalization, the Soviets pressured Hanoi to reach a settlement. At the same time, regional diplomatic efforts—particularly by Australia and Indonesia—moved forward. By 1986, the outline of a potential settlement had taken shape. Though the specific plan was scuttled by Beijing and the Khmer Rouge before it could be discussed at an ASEAN foreign ministers' meeting that June, the promising blueprint envisaged a Vietnamese withdrawal in line with a cessation of Chinese support for the PDK, which would be backed by the deployment of an international peacekeeping force around Cambodia's land and sea borders.[53] One problem was that the Cambodian factions—the PRK and the three resistance groups that made up the CGDK—refused to meet. A CGDK proposal issued in March 1986 mooted the formation of a four-party interim government, but this was dismissed by Vietnam as "nonsense." The PRK controlled most of the country, it declared, and this *fait accompli* should be reflected in any future settlement.[54] The resistance groups continued to oppose any presence of Vietnamese troops on Cambodian soil, and refused to deal with the Phnom Penh regime on equal terms.

It took an unusual sequence of events to break the deadlock. In December 1987, Hun Sen met with Prince Sihanouk at Fère-en-Tardenois, a small town north of Paris. The grandeur of the converted thirteenth-century castle, built by a grandson of King Louis VI, was an apt setting for a meeting that was the culmination of years of backroom maneuverings. Jean-Jacques Galabru, a French diplomat who met Hun Sen in 1983, while Galabru was serving in Angola, acted as his go-between with Sihanouk; the diplomat's Cambodian wife, Pung Chhiv Kek, enjoyed close connections to Sihanouk's camp in Beijing. The meeting was opposed by most of the CGDK's superpower backers, who feared a Sihanouk–Hun Sen rapprochement would undermine the resistance coalition. The Chinese were particularly worried that their PDK proxies would be cut out of a political settlement. Even the French were cool to the idea, refusing to provide Hun Sen's delegation with cars and accommodation for the duration of its stay. (Transport was eventually provided by the Soviet embassy in Paris.)[55]

The meeting at Fère-en-Tardenois went well. Hun Sen clearly impressed the gray-haired monarch. As the French sociologist Serge Thion wrote, Hun Sen approached his meeting with Sihanouk like a long-lost son, flattering the prince with the assurance that his removal from power in 1970 was the root cause of Cambodia's current problems.[56] On December 4, the pair signed a communiqué pledging a political solution to the conflict involving all four

Cambodian factions. It was only a first step—Sihanouk backtracked soon afterward under Chinese pressure—but it marked a decisive turn toward a solution to the Cambodian crisis.[57] Sihanouk knew that he would eventually be forced to deal with the PRK, the only faction that held real power in Cambodia. Only pressure from his Chinese patrons, and the continued presence of Vietnamese troops in Cambodia, prevented him from severing his ties with the Khmer Rouge and cutting a deal directly with Phnom Penh.[58]

The next three years saw a flurry of meetings that edged the Cambodian factions closer to a settlement. Starting in July 1988, three rounds of talks in Indonesia—the so-called Jakarta Informal Meetings (JIMs)—brought the four groups into the same room for the first time. The JIMs proceeded in fits and starts, deadlocking on issues such as the disputed presence of Vietnamese settlers in Cambodia and the PDK's opposition to any use of the word "genocide" to refer to its past policies. In the improved regional environment, however, the question was less whether there would be a settlement and more the specific form it would take. In January 1989, Vietnam announced that it would withdraw its forces from Cambodia by September. The same month, Hun Sen traveled to Bangkok for meetings with Thai Prime Minister Chatichai Choonhavan, who famously pledged to turn Indochina's "battlefields into marketplaces."

As the Soviet empire began to crumble, the normalization of Sino-Soviet ties, and a gradual warming between Hanoi and Beijing, created the conditions for a resolution to the Cambodian problem. In November 1989, Australian Foreign Minister Gareth Evans issued a proposal for a UN-supervised interim administration of Cambodia pending elections. Sihanouk and Hun Sen both agreed, as did the Vietnamese. In July 1990, the US dropped its long-standing support for the CGDK and by the following month the permanent five members of the UN Security Council—the US, Britain, France, China, and the Soviet Union—had drafted a framework agreement that sketched out the basic elements of the peace accord that was eventually signed in Paris on October 23, 1991. Chinese and US pressure ensured that the Khmer Rouge remained a legitimate party to the peace plan—something that would create serious problems farther down the road. But with the Cold War beginning to thaw and the UN's blue helmets on the way, there was hope that peace was at last within reach.

On September 26, 1989, more than a decade after their arrival, the last Vietnamese troops withdrew from Cambodia. The occasion was marked by lavish Vietnamese-orchestrated celebrations across the country. In Phnom Penh, Soviet-built T-54 tanks rolled past the former Royal Palace, flanked by crowds clutching hundreds of small Vietnamese and Cambodian flags. Departing officers weepily embraced their Cambodian counterparts in the streets, as jeeps filled with cheering troops coursed past, flying red pennants bearing the words *quyet thang*, meaning "victory"—a generous assessment of the long occupation, perhaps, but one that unconsciously reflected Hanoi's relief at its extrication from the Cambodian quagmire.

Vietnam's "Vietnam" had taken a harsh toll. Around 23,000 Vietnamese soldiers lost their lives during the occupation—four times the number the US would later lose in Iraq and nearly half the number of American soldiers killed during the Vietnam War. An additional 55,000 were wounded.[59] Though it was never undertaken on humanitarian grounds, the Vietnamese invasion and occupation of Cambodia had delivered the country from one of the darkest periods of a dark twentieth century. Hanoi paid a high price in blood and treasure to help its Cambodian client state establish itself on the ruins of Pol Pot's rule. Without the protection of the Vietnamese troops, it's likely that the Khmer Rouge, fed and armed by China, would have returned to power, ready to restage the horrors for a second time.

Aside from the scattered bones of as many as 10,000 soldiers missing in the jungles of western Cambodia, the departing forces left little behind. A Cambodia–Vietnam Friendship Monument, built to commemorate the "fraternal" ties between the two countries, still stands in a Phnom Penh park along the thoroughfare once known as Lenin Boulevard—a controversial symbol of the Vietnamese occupation. At Tuol Tompong Market in the south of the city, nicknamed the "Russian Market" after its popularity with Soviet expatriates in the PRK years, it is occasionally possible to turn up some banknotes or postage stamps from that period, with their depictions of toiling peasants, drifting Soviet cosmonauts, and other antiquated revolutionary imagery. A careful observer might also spot the odd government seal or rusted street sign bearing the names of one of the old revolutionary heroes. But few other signs remain from Cambodia's socialist decade.

In large part, this was by design. As the country moved toward a peace settlement, the KPRP made concerted efforts to distance itself from Vietnam and its communist past. In April 1989, the regime rebranded itself the State of Cambodia (SOC), and adopted a new flag, national anthem, and coat of arms. Buddhism was reinstated as the national religion and party officials presided over religious ceremonies like the Water Festival, once associated with the monarchy. The SOC also reintroduced private property rights and passed a new foreign investment law. In anticipation of peace, the death penalty was abolished and political controls loosened.

Despite the KPRP's attempts to whitewash its communist past, the political legacy of the 1980s still charts a deep fault-line in Cambodian politics. The overthrow of Pol Pot became the party's foundation myth—a story of rescue and redemption that is reinforced annually with official pageantry marking January 7 as "Victory over Genocide Day." The party's critics, on the other hand, paint the overthrow of the Khmer Rouge as a foreign invasion that represented the culmination of Vietnam's insatiable desire to swallow Cambodian territory. The PRK was certainly a ward of Vietnam, but few non-Cambodian observers now credit the claims of a Vietnamese project to colonize Cambodia during the 1980s.[60] Even had it wanted to, Hanoi lacked the resources to engineer a full-blown "Vietnamization" of its western neighbor. Isolated internationally and counting the cost of a difficult military occupation, to say nothing of its own desperate economic situation, withdrawal soon became the overriding aim for Hanoi. Like their nineteenth-century predecessor, Emperor Minh Mang, the Vietnamese had tried—and failed—in their attempts to build a Cambodian party in their own socialist image.

CHAPTER THREE

The Wages of Peace

On October 23, 1991, the four Cambodian factions and representatives from 18 other nations gathered in the ornate surrounds of the Kléber International Conference Hall in Paris and signed an agreement aimed at ending the Cambodian civil war. The Paris Peace Agreements were a remarkable achievement, the product of long and often bitter negotiations. "A dark page of history has been turned," French President François Mitterrand announced in the glittering reception hall. "Cambodia is about to resume its place in the world."[1]

The signing of the treaty took place at a crucial historical juncture. The fall of the Berlin Wall and the crumbling of the once-mighty Soviet Union ushered in what many hoped would be a more cohesive, norm-based international order free from the paralyzing polarities of the Cold War. This was the era of US President George H. W. Bush's "new world order," and UN Secretary-General Boutros Boutros-Ghali's "Agenda for Peace." In 1989, the American political scientist Francis Fukuyama hailed the "end of history," arguing that the break-up of the Soviet Union marked "the end point of mankind's ideological evolution and the universalization of Western liberal democracy as the final form of human government."[2] In this new atmosphere, the UN would finally be able to fulfill its foundational promise as the embodiment of a singular "international community," intervening in the world's trouble-spots in order to spread the blessings of peace and liberal democracy. Cambodia, a perennial victim of Cold War realpolitik, would be a critical test.

The Paris Agreements created the UN Transitional Authority in Cambodia (UNTAC), which would take temporary control over the Cambodian state. For the mission's duration, sovereignty would be vested in a 13-member Supreme National Council (SNC) consisting of delegates from each of the four factions, with Prince Sihanouk serving as the body's "neutral" president. UNTAC had a daunting mandate. It was tasked with coordinating a ceasefire and the withdrawal of all foreign (i.e. Vietnamese) forces from Cambodia, followed by the disarming and demobilization of the four Cambodian armed factions. It would supervise the closure of the Thai border camps and the re-settlement of hundreds of thousands of refugees. Finally, it would create the "neutral political environment" necessary for the conduct of free and fair elections. To fulfill its mandate, UNTAC staff would be given sweeping vice-regal powers over key SOC ministries. UN Secretary-General Javier Perez de Cuellar described the Cambodian mission as "probably the most important and most complex in the history of the United Nations."[3]

The real aims of the Paris Agreements were mostly left unsaid. One of them was to extricate the major powers—especially China, the Soviet Union, and the US—from a Cambodian conflict they had stoked for more than three decades. In so doing, the treaty removed a major obstacle to Sino-Soviet detente and paved the way toward Hanoi's re-engagement with Washington. For the Chinese, Paris marked the end of Vietnamese hegemony over Indochina and gave Beijing the opportunity to re-establish a position of influence in Phnom Penh. The French had loftier aims; they would use the accord as a beachhead for a reawakening of cultural and political ties dating back to the colonial era—an ultimately futile push symbolized by the opening of the world's largest Alliance Française in Phnom Penh in 1989.[4] Of the permanent five members of the UN Security Council, which had drafted the framework of the accords, only Britain had no real skin in the game.

Another major player was Japan, which saw the Cambodian settlement as an opportunity to reclaim a leading role in Asian affairs. Tokyo would become a leading financial backer of the UNTAC mission, and its troop contribution would be the first overseas deployment of Japanese military personnel since the Second World War.

As a product of superpower compromise, however, the peace plan bore only a vague correlation with the political realities inside Cambodia. Having fueled the civil war for more than a decade, foreign powers suddenly decided that the fighting should end and that peace should prevail. The Cambodians had different ideas. Hun Sen saw no reason to give up power just because the "international community" demanded it. This was the same "international community," after all, that had voted to keep Pol Pot in the UN since his overthrow in 1979. As the only faction with any real claim to statehood, the SOC had the most to lose in the implementation of the accord. Even as they put pen to paper in the chandeliered hall on the Avenue Kléber, the SOC delegates viewed the Paris Agreements as merely a new and more sophisticated way of unseating them from power. To the extent that China, the US, and some of the ASEAN countries would have been happy to see the SOC ejected from office, it was not an inaccurate assessment.

The biggest point of contention, however, was the inclusion of the PDK. China had insisted that the Khmer Rouge be given a seat at the table as the price of ending their aid to Pol Pot. To secure the PDK's signature, all references to the "genocidal practices" of the Khmer Rouge regime had been scrubbed from the final treaty and replaced with a euphemistic phrase referring to "the policies and practices of the recent past." Many in Cambodia and overseas saw this as a moral outrage. Angry op-eds appeared in the *Washington Post* and the *New York Times*; the Italian journalist Tiziano Terzani said that the Paris treaty had created "an indecent peace."[5] But if the PDK's participation was indecent—if the Khmer Rouge leaders deserved to be tried for crimes against humanity, not feted in international conference halls—it also had a cold logic. The alternative was no superpower accord, no peace agreement, and no chance of ending the civil war. "It was as much as could be done at the time," said one American diplomat involved in the peace negotiations.

The dilemma was that the Khmer Rouge were even less likely to uphold the terms of the treaty than was the SOC. As Khieu Samphan put his signature to the Paris treaty, "Brother Number One" remained holed up on the Thai border, where he had spent most of the decade since his fall from power in 1979. In the intervening years Pol Pot's black hair became flecked with white, and he had fathered his first child, a daughter, on whom he lavished his attentions. But his political views remained as uncompromising as ever. At Office 87, his border headquarters a few kilometers from the Thai town of Trat, Pol Pot spent his time in the company of loyal disciples, holding forth on points of revolutionary doctrine, plotting his return to power.

The historian David Chandler wrote that of all Cambodia's prerevolutionary social institutions, Office 87—a cluster of buildings concealed by barbed wire fences and under 24-hour watch by the Thai military—most closely resembled a Buddhist monastery. Here the aging communist leader cultivated a revolutionary eschatology that he believed would lead to the cleansing of the Cambodian nation and the final elimination of the hated Vietnamese invaders.[6] Pol Pot rarely appeared in public, and moved along the border in four-wheel drives with tinted windows. But for Cambodians inside the country he was alive in every rumor and in every distant gunshot, a phantom presence who simultaneously threatened future miseries and promised deliverance from foreign invaders. He emanated a terrible power from afar.

Internally, the Khmer Rouge were divided on how to approach the peace settlement. On the one hand, the treaty offered the PDK a potential route to international legitimacy, via UN-backed elections. On the other, token adherence might be used as cover to advance revolutionary aims and lay the groundwork for a power grab once the UN was gone. For the time being, the Khmer Rouge remained well armed and economically self-sufficient. In October 1989, taking advantage of the Vietnamese military's withdrawal, PDK forces occupied Pailin, a northwestern town situated in rugged country rich with sapphires and rubies. By the time that China cut off its aid, the PDK were bringing in as much as $5 million each month from logging concessions and gem mining operations leased to unscrupulous firms connected with the Thai military.[7] Trucks laden with timber and gem-rich dirt rumbled back and forth across the border around the clock. Pailin became a frontier boomtown complete with Thai karaoke bars, 24-hour electricity, and even a small population of Burmese migrant workers. The rebel-held entrepôt ran on Thai baht and US dollars; "Hun Sen money" was not welcome.[8]

Also waiting in the wings was Prince Sihanouk, who had scores of his own to settle. During his years of exile, the prince had stewed over the coup that had removed him from power in 1970. Dividing his time between Beijing and Changsuwon, his sprawling palace in the alpine hill-country north of Pyongyang, Sihanouk dreamt of sweeping back to Cambodia to rescue his "children" and gather them in the embrace of a reconstituted Sangkum regime. Sihanouk, too, saw the coming international intervention as an obstacle—a rerun of the French protectorate, whose aims he would end up frustrating just as surely as he had those of the French colonial officials who placed him on the throne in 1941.

The Paris Agreements, brokered by foreign governments that had grown tired of their bloody Cambodian proxy war, thus created an accord which its main Cambodian signatories had little real intention of honoring. The tectonic pressure of shifting geopolitical interests was enough to get the Cambodian factions to the table, but as subsequent events were to show, it was not enough to force them to work together constructively. The ambitions of Sihanouk, Pol Pot, and Hun Sen all pulled in different directions. None of them was interested in reconciliation—only in using an "indecent peace" to prosecute the old war by different means.

A decade in the cockpit of international diplomacy had made a statesman of Hun Sen. By 1991, Cambodia's "puppet" leader had become far more polished. The scrawny political novice of the early 1980s had put on weight and now dressed in French double-breasted suits. Even Hun Sen's glass eye, part of a set of six he had custom made in Japan, looked more like the real thing. As the peace talks proceeded, the Western press suddenly began to take notice of the serious 37-year-old who strode confidently in and out of official meetings. In mid-1989, Hun Sen was the subject of profiles in the *New York Times* and the *Washington Post*, which charted his metamorphosis from "puppet" minister to key player in the Cambodian imbroglio.[9]

Hun Sen's opponents still saw him as a traitor and Vietnamese stooge, but what had been clear to Le Duc Tho and the Vietnamese leadership was now becoming clear to the rest of the world: puppet or not, Hun Sen was among the most astute and hardworking politicians involved in brokering a solution to the Cambodian conflict. During the peace talks of the late 1980s, he reportedly made do with as little as two hours sleep per night, a schedule that may have led to his hospitalization in Tokyo in 1991.[10] His international prominence was such that diplomats who once spoke of the PRK as "the Heng Samrin regime," after the party's cardboard general secretary, now started referring to it as "the Hun Sen government."[11]

With more exposure came more scrutiny. Many details from Hun Sen's past remained obscure, particularly his years with the Khmer Rouge. In 1989, Thach Saren, a former Lon Nol-era army commander, wrote a letter to the *Washington Post* accusing Hun Sen's troops of throwing hand grenades into occupied homes and slitting the throats of patients at two hospitals in Kampong Cham in 1973. He also accused Hun Sen of taking part in the massacre of rebellious Cham Muslims in September 1975, and commanding the cross-border massacre of Vietnamese civilians in 1977.[12] For David Roberts, Jr., a British critic, Hun Sen merited "a circle of hell only a short rung removed from that reserved for Pol Pot and his politburo."[13]

What role did Hun Sen play under the Khmer Rouge? In his early years, he served the revolution enthusiastically, probably more so than he has since been willing to admit. Hun Sen claims he remained in school until 1969, before joining the *maquis* at Sihanouk's request the following year.[14] But other sources suggest he left Phnom Penh much earlier to join the communists. According to Ben Kiernan's research, Hun Sen left the city in 1967 to become a courier for insurgents in Memot district, close to his hometown in Kampong Cham, before "organizing a youth movement" against land seizures in 1969.[15] A Vietnamese biography deposited in the Central Stasi Archives in Berlin claims that Hun Sen dropped out of school even earlier, in 1966.[16]

Hun Sen's official biography is notably silent about these early forays into political activity, an occlusion probably intended to counter accusations that he was ever an eager servant of the Khmer Rouge. The Cambodian leader has repeatedly denied having any sympathy for Pol Pot's cause. "I had simply responded to the appeal of Prince Sihanouk," he later told his biographers. "I realized only in 1974 that it was not Sihanouk but the Khmer Rouge who ran the show."[17] When ordered to put down the Cham rebellion in 1975, Hun Sen claims he told superiors that his regiment was riddled with malaria and that he was due back at hospital for treatment on his injured eye socket. In early 1977, as Pol Pot began ordering bloody raids into Vietnam, Hun Sen again says he made only "token" incursions, telling his bosses he lacked the military intelligence to proceed further.[18] It is hard to believe that Hun Sen's hands are entirely clean, but historians have found little hard evidence to contradict his claims.[19]

As his international profile rose, Hun Sen moved to distance himself from his communist past. In the late 1980s, he emerged as one of the PRK's most vocal advocates for economic liberalization and was a driving force behind the constitutional reforms of 1989. If the party didn't bend, Hun Sen realized, it would break, like its counterparts in Eastern Europe. A carefully managed tack toward the center, moreover, had many ancillary benefits. It would win his regime sympathy in the West, and bolster its political position ahead of the coming peace. A resurgent capitalism, Hun Sen argued in 1988, would help "develop the country, raise the standard of living of the people, and deprive the far-right of a weapon."[20]

Not everybody in Cambodia saw things the same way. Figures like Heng Samrin and Chea Sim took a harder line on political dissent. Despite the reforms, Chea Sim's Interior Ministry remained a "Stalinist bastion" independent of government or party control.[21] In May 1990, his police arrested seven government officials linked to Minister of Transport and Communication Ung Phan, a friend and ally of Hun Sen who had defected from DK in 1977, and imprisoned them on "antigovernment" charges. Ung Phan had taken advantage of the more liberal atmosphere by setting up a proto-political grouping—the Democratic Freedom Party—and attempting to rally support around a reformist platform.[22] The next month Khieu Kanharith, the editor of *Kampuchea* magazine and another close Hun Sen associate, was sacked for advocating pluralist reforms. The rift was only partly ideological. Hun Sen's rivals were resentful that their junior colleague had gained such international prestige. "They thought he was very well known abroad, too pro-Western and had made too many concessions to the enemy," one diplomat said. "They were jealous of his public relations."[23] They were further piqued that Hun Sen had nominated his own loyalists to all six positions on the SNC.*

By 1991, Hun Sen had also become a regular fixture on TV and radio. He began making trips to the countryside to drum up support ahead of the coming elections. Wearing sunglasses, safari suit, and cotton *krama* scarf, Hun Sen would borrow a bicycle or scooter and ride out to isolated hamlets, where state media captured him joking with old ladies and sharing his cigarettes with rice farmers. "He's really into the hard-sell style of politics—almost to the point

---

* The six delegates from the SOC were Hun Sen, Hor Namhong, Dith Munty, Tea Banh, Im Chhun Lim, and Sin Sen. Funcinpec was represented by Prince Norodom Ranariddh and Sam Rainsy, while Son Sann and Ieng Mouly were the two KPNLF delegates. Khieu Samphan and Son Sen represented the PDK.

of kissing babies," one foreign aid worker said in 1989.[24] It was classic populist electioneering in the Sihanouk vein—a style that Hun Sen would hone to a fine point over the coming decade.

After the signing of the Paris Agreements, Hun Sen got the chance to perform to a more difficult crowd. In March 1992, the Cambodian leader made his first visit to the US. Still seen by many Americans as a bloodstained Vietnamese marionette, Hun Sen nonetheless left a strong impression. He "seemed to be everywhere," wrote the *Washington Post*, "hosted by State Department officials, legislators, private organizations." Former Secretary of State Edmund Muskie described him as "a great salesman for his cause."[25] In Washington, Hun Sen had breakfast with George McGovern and former CIA head William Colby. He addressed the Asia Society and the Council on Foreign Relations, and, in New York, won over the editorial board of the *Wall Street Journal* by proclaiming his conversion to the free market creed. He also laid a plaque at the Tomb of the Unknowns at Arlington National Cemetery, recognizing US soldiers still missing in action in Cambodia, and the countless Khmer families who lost relatives "in some Cambodian place they know not where."[26]

Jeremy J. Stone, the president of the Federation of American Scientists, served as Hun Sen's official host. He recalled a smooth-talking politician, a cigarette perpetually in hand, who managed his varied meetings with aplomb. "Everywhere he was cool and often humorous," Stone wrote in his memoirs. "I fed him jokes for openers—but he improved on them. For a provincial from far-off rural Cambodia, he certainly was poised."[27] After lunching with Hun Sen, Stephen Solarz, a Congressman who had first encountered him during a visit to Phnom Penh in 1981, commented at the transformation of the "Cambodian bumpkin" he remembered. It was as if Hun Sen had been "shaped up by media consultants."[28]

In a sense he had. Despite his growing reputation as a reformist, Hun Sen's moves were always strategic. Multiparty democracy, like Vietnamese-style communism, was just another ill-fitting foreign suit, to be adopted and shed at will. "All my life I regarded myself as a pragmatic person," he told the *Washington Post* during his stop in the US capital. "I stayed under the so-called umbrella of Marxist-Leninism when I had to, but please don't think everyone . . . who goes to church has the same beliefs."[29]

But what *did* Hun Sen stand for? While the Fukuyamas of the West hailed the global triumph of liberalism, Cambodia had no history of democratic government or popular sovereignty. One appealing model was Singapore, where Lee Kuan Yew had used strong-handed methods to build a modern, prosperous, and tightly controlled island-state. Lee, like Hun Sen, had little tolerance for dissent. Along with Malaysia's long-serving prime minister Mahathir Mohamad, he rejected the idea of individual rights, arguing that

"Asian values" put a greater weight on collective prosperity. "Every time anybody wants to start anything which will unwind or unravel this orderly, organized, sensible, rational society, and make it irrational and emotional," Lee said of modern Singapore, "I put a stop to it without hesitation."[30]

History also weighed heavily on Hun Sen. He came of political age in a decade when his government was isolated and punished by an alliance of outside powers more concerned with Vietnam's occupation of Cambodia than the horrific crimes committed by Pol Pot. Years of Western double-standards had thus led Hun Sen to see human rights and democracy promotion as little more than moral flags of convenience for the advance of political interests. The idea of a universal democratic standard by which all nations could be judged, usually by leaders in Washington, London, or Geneva, was nothing more than a self-serving fiction. There were no international standards, Hun Sen would later argue, "except in sports."[31]

On November 14, 1991, Prince Sihanouk returned to Cambodia from Beijing after more than two decades in exile. He was accompanied by his wife, his son and an entourage that included a squad of stony-faced North Korean body-guards (a gift from Kim Il-sung) and four Chinese chefs. Standing alongside Prime Minister Hun Sen, he rode into the capital in a black 1963 Chevrolet Impala convertible—a favorite make from the halcyon days of the 1960s— along roads thronged with people.[32] Sihanouk's return provided a nostalgic respite from the political warfare that raged between the four Cambodian factions. After so many years of exile, the prince still retained his symbolic power. Many Cambodians, especially those of the older generations, saw Sihanouk as the nation's best and perhaps only hope for peace after decades of conflict. Standing on the banks of the Tonlé Sap, Sihanouk presided over the annual Water Festival—the first royal to do so since his overthrow in 1970. He watched a performance of the reconstituted Royal Ballet, and then participated in a ceremony in which white-robed Brahmin priests read the future of the crops in the wax of melted candles.

The tranquil atmosphere didn't last long. Two weeks after Sihanouk's homecoming, another famous exile made his return to Phnom Penh. Instead of cheering crowds, the PDK's Khieu Samphan was welcomed by a government-organized lynch mob that ransacked his apartment and cornered him in an upstairs room, along with PDK defense chief Son Sen, while Hun Sen materi-alized in an adjacent building with a megaphone calling for "calm." It was only after protesters began stringing up a wire noose in the street that police inter-vened and bundled Samphan, "his bleeding head ignominiously bandaged with a pair of Y-fronts," into a waiting car and put him on a flight back to Bangkok.[33] His return had lasted just eight hours.

The "spontaneous" attack on Samphan, who had returned to Cambodia to take his seat on the SNC, gave some indication of how the SOC was approaching the coming of free elections. Charles Twining, who had returned to Cambodia two weeks earlier as the head of a new US mission operating out of a suite at the Cambodiana Hotel, said the country's sudden opening had clearly "discombobulated" the SOC. Government institutions were weak, with just "two or three capable people" in each ministry. "The international presence coming in, which was supposed to create a level playing field, would be a threat to [the SOC's] survival, unless they found a way to play along with it."[34] Forced by the superpowers to accept multiparty elections, Hun Sen and his colleagues were determined to give themselves every possible advantage.

The first order of business for the SOC was to sweep away the last trappings of an unpopular communism. In August 1991, as Soviet power crumbled in Moscow, the government removed statues of Lenin, Marx, and Cambodian revolutionary heroes from ministry buildings and public places. References to Marx and Lenin were scrubbed from official documents, and the KPRP's red party insignia was exchanged for a blue logo featuring a *devada*, a Buddhist angel, sprinkling divine gifts.

The rebranding was completed at the Sixth Party Congress in mid-October, just before the signing of the Paris Agreements. The KPRP renamed itself the Cambodian People's Party (CPP), and announced the creation of a system of political pluralism. It released some 2,000 political prisoners—including those arrested during the Ung Phan purge of May 1990—and pledged to respect human rights and the formation of independent political parties.[35] While some optimistic observers spoke of a "Phnom Penh Spring," the CPP's makeover was never more than cosmetic. Privately, Hun Sen compared the reforms to the exchanging of a "red" shirt for a "blue" one.[36] He knew that whatever color it wore, the party still controlled an administrative network stretching down to the village level. The military and police, meanwhile, remained closely tied to the CPP's civilian leadership in Phnom Penh, united under the control of a political organization that retained its Leninist system of discipline.

All this put the CPP in a position to profit handsomely from the rapid transition to the free market. This proceeded in a similar fashion to what the Russians would later refer to as "grabitization." In haste, state-owned land and enterprises were sold off to government officials, foreign investors, and an emerging caste of oligarchs with close ties to the CPP. All pre-1975 land claims were annulled, reassuring investors that they would be safe from eviction if the old owners of their land returned. The aim was to put the commanding heights of the economy into friendly hands before the UN arrived to take over key government ministries. As the specter of political competition loomed, preferential access to this economic free-for-all—

a sort of licensed graft—became a crucial means of buttressing the regime's power.[37]

Phnom Penh became a boomtown. Wild speculation drove land values up to dizzying heights. Dilapidated villas that had lain vacant since the Pol Pot years were snapped up by government officials, who sold them off to Thai and Singaporean businessmen or leased them to international relief agencies scrambling for a foothold in the Cambodian "aid market."[38] Wealth suddenly appeared on the streets, standing out starkly against a bleached cityscape of splayed power cabling and grimy apartment blocks. The most jarring sight, one visitor wrote in 1991, was "the abundance of new Mercedes-Benzes and BMWs" that shared the pot-holed roads with the jerry-rigged motorbikes, ox-carts, and rattling *cyclo-pousses* left over from the prewar years.[39]

But Phnom Penh's patina of wealth concealed a desperate economic situation. Soviet and Eastern bloc aid, which previously supplied four-fifths of the government's budget, had come to an end in 1990, and virtually the entire Cambodian economy remained "off the books," yielding few revenues for the state. As officials feathered their nests, infrastructure crumbled, the salaries of civil servants went unpaid, and thousands were cast out of work as state-owned enterprises closed their doors. At first, brewing unrest was channeled by the authorities at approved targets like Khieu Samphan and Son Sen. But by the end of 1991, the protests had escaped the government's control, and began taking aim at the corruption of the SOC itself.

In December, emboldened by the arrival of a small advance team of UN civilian and military officials, thousands of students, civil servants, and laid-off factory workers took to the streets in Phnom Penh. An angry mob sacked a villa appropriated by Transport and Communications Minister Ros Chhun, a nephew of Chea Sim. As the *New York Times* reported,

> hundreds of people poured out of the slums and took revenge. They hauled the furniture out of the house and built a bonfire. Then they set fire to the Jeep parked outside. They threw stones through the windows and ripped new white tiles off the walls. The police were called, but most of them had not been paid in months, so they just watched.[40]

Tensions escalated the next day when police shot into crowds of demonstrators, killing at least six people and injuring many more. As protests swept through the tree-lined streets, the SOC authorities banned demonstrations and deployed the police. Ung Phan, who had formed a new political party after his release from prison, was attacked by unidentified gunmen as he was driving through the outskirts of Phnom Penh in January 1992. Two bullets grazed his back and a third lodged in his neck. He survived, but others were less lucky.[41]

The violence in Phnom Penh underscored the fragility of the political settlement that underpinned the Paris Agreements. As the protests and shootings spread, the UN's advance military mission, UNAMIC, remained silent. UNAMIC had no particular mandate to intervene to halt the deterioration of the political situation, but its inaction dimmed the hope of many Cambodian protesters that foreign nations were committed to change.[42] As a curtain-raiser for the main UN mission, it boded ill.

The first UNTAC personnel arrived in the tense Cambodian capital at the beginning of 1992. Before long, the streets were filled with a multinational contingent from the four corners of the globe. UNTAC employed 26,000 military, police, and civilian personnel from more than a hundred countries, who replaced the Vietnamese and Eastern bloc advisors who had by then returned to their own collapsing nations of origin. Few UNTAC staffers—"UNTACists," in Sihanouk's coinage—had any previous experience of Cambodia, and found themselves adrift in a scarred country still shaken by decades of war and revolution. The two sides "found no common language, literally or figuratively," wrote *New York Times* correspondent Henry Kamm. "The foreigners tended to treat ordinary Cambodians with amused, somewhat condescending indulgence, and were content to find congenial company among the other foreigners."[43]

Cambodia, isolated for a generation, suddenly found itself caught up in a maelstrom of high hopes and easy money. Villas and apartments, recently appropriated by senior government officials and their cronies, were rented out to the UN and international NGOs at astronomical rates. One ramshackle hotel in Stung Treng near the Lao border fetched $14,000 per month and provided only the barest amenities for UN staff.[44] UNTAC officials went about the country in a fleet of white cars, white helicopters, and white troop transports, pouring millions of dollars into a moribund economy that could scarcely digest them. In addition to their relatively high salaries, UNTAC's civilian workers were given a daily allowance of $130—equivalent to the average annual income in Cambodia—and their spending created runaway inflation.[45] As it plummeted in value, the Cambodian riel became basically worthless; before long, the US dollar had become the country's de facto currency.

Little of the money went toward alleviating the poverty and suffering of Cambodia's 8 million people, for whom UNTAC's arrival meant a spike in the cost of food and everyday necessities. HIV/AIDS also surged as the influx of foreign personnel spawned a flourishing brothel industry. By 1993, there were 20,000 commercial sex workers in Cambodia, up from just 6,000 a year earlier, and HIV/AIDS infection rates rose tenfold.[46] There were also regular reports of misbehavior by soldiers and police attached to UNTAC, including the sexual harassment of women, the mistreatment of locals, and scattered instances of theft and banditry. Resentment at the foreign presence was widespread.

The UN had its eyes fixed on a loftier goal. At the time, UNTAC was the largest peacekeeping operation ever mounted, a bold experiment in post–Cold War state-building that would eventually cost more than $2 billion. As a possible model for future UN operations, there was a lot riding on its success. To reward Japan for its generous financial contributions to UNTAC, control of the mission was given to Yasushi Akashi, a Japanese veteran of the UN system. Since joining the UN in 1974, Akashi had earned a reputation for his patience, tact, and aversion to confrontation. His steady climb through the UN hierarchy, according to one 1994 profile, was marked by an "absence of waves" as he moved between jobs and departments.[47] On paper, all this made Akashi an astute choice for the top job: as a fellow Asian, he was thought well placed to negotiate the tangle of Cambodian interests through a strategy of incrementalism and consensus-building. "My basic approach," he recalled later, "[was] to combine patient persuasion with sustained pressure."[48] Of course, this strategy assumed a great deal of good faith on the part of the Cambodians. It soon became apparent that a wide gulf separated Akashi's mandate from the realities on the ground.

The most obstructive of these realities was the Khmer Rouge. During 1991 and 1992, the PDK had remained divided on whether to take part in the peace process. According to Steve Heder, the movement initially planned to pay lip service to the Paris Agreements while working covertly to overthrow the SOC. In February 1992, Pol Pot declared that "the contents of the [Paris] Agreements are to our advantage," in the sense that they would impose constraints on Hun Sen. But by mid-year, when the hoped-for benefits failed to materialize, Pol Pot hardened his stance. Leaders who continued to advocate participation, including defense minister Son Sen, and the PDK's economic chief, Ieng Sary, were stripped of authority, and the Khmer Rouge embarked upon a campaign of obstruction. The PDK blocked UNTAC officials from entering its zones and refused to disarm or demobilize its forces in line with the peace plan.[49]

Australia's foreign minister, Gareth Evans, one of the key architects of the Paris Agreements, counseled Akashi to stay the course. The mission and its backers, he said, should "accentuate the positive, find the common ground, keep working away, and keep our fingers crossed."[50] But other than issuing resolutions and statements of "concern," there was little UNTAC could do. A series of economic embargoes targeting the PDK's export of gems and timber to Thailand had little effect on Pol Pot's finances.[51] One incident at the start of the mission would come to serve as a metaphor for UNTAC's unwillingness to confront the PDK. In May 1992, traveling near Pailin, Akashi and Lieutenant-General John M. Sanderson, the mission's Australian military head, came across a Khmer Rouge "roadblock"—a thin bamboo pole that had been laid across the road. Refused entry by the young PDK soldiers who manned the flimsy barricade, Akashi and Sanderson turned their convoy around.[52]

The "bamboo pole incident" caused a minor international sensation. Many observers argued that the UNTAC convoy had the right to force its way through the barrier, seeing its retreat as a symbol of the UN and Akashi's broader capitulation to the PDK. The incident prompted UNTAC's French deputy military commander, Brigadier-General Jean-Michel Loridon, to call for more muscular action against Pol Pot's forces. Sanderson refused, rightly pointing out that UNTAC lacked the mandate to engage in "peace enforcement" actions. Loridon was later dismissed for insisting that UNTAC let him deal with Pol Pot once and for all. For the Khmer Rouge, it was a handy lesson. Despite possessing all the outward trappings of power, UN member states were reluctant to take casualties. "The Cambodian people believed that the UN blue berets were like Jupiter threatening to unleash lightning against the Khmer Rouge," Sihanouk told the *Far Eastern Economic Review*. "What do the people see? When the Khmer Rouge advance, UNTAC pulls back."[53]

UNTAC faced similar challenges taking charge of the SOC's administrative apparatus. In many provinces, a handful of UN administrators—almost none of whom had any experience in Cambodia or any knowledge of the Khmer language—were expected to take control of a hostile and deeply rooted political system backed by a thuggish security force. Benny Widyono, UNTAC's provincial director in Siem Reap, the gateway to the temples of Angkor, described his first face-to-face meeting with SOC governor Nuo Som, whose province he was now, in theory, supposed to govern. "He stared at me, I stared at him, we stared at each other. Finally I blinked first. That was it."[54] Effective control, he later wrote, was "a myth."[55]

The PDK's refusal to disarm or cooperate with UNTAC gave the SOC leadership grounds for resisting the demobilization effort. The 126,000-strong SOC army was the one military force capable of opposing Pol Pot, and the government could credibly claim that Cambodians would be vulnerable if it was forced to disarm. In the end a token contingent of 42,368 SOC troops demobilized—in addition to 3,445 from Funcinpec and 6,479 from the KPNLF[56]—but its most effective forces remained active. This led, in turn, to further PDK foot-dragging and accusations that "*yuon*-TAC" was working covertly to aid the Vietnamese. Akashi was helpless. His mandate was stuck in a spiral of noncompliance on the part of the two most powerful Cambodian factions, and there was little he could do: the contradictions were embedded in the terms of the Paris Agreements, the success of which had relied on the good faith of the Cambodian factions.

By the end of 1992, the mission was threatening to unravel entirely. The Khmer Rouge began kidnapping peacekeepers, and, that December, forced UNTAC to withdraw its staff from Svay Loeu district in Siem Reap, close to the PDK stronghold of Anlong Veng. In April 1993, realizing that UNTAC was powerless to disarm the SOC, the Khmer Rouge formally withdrew from the election and closed their office in Phnom Penh. Speaking on PDK radio, Khieu Samphan decried the elections as "a theatrical farce to hand over Cambodia to Vietnam, the aggressor ... to legitimize the puppets Vietnam installed in Phnom Penh since 1979."[57] The announcement was the prelude to a wave of attacks throughout Siem Reap, which claimed the lives of two civilian police officers and injured another 16 peacekeepers.[58]

With two of the mission's three main aims—demobilization and administrative supervision—in disarray, UNTAC went all-in on the third. The holding of "free and fair" elections in May 1993 was suddenly elevated into the mission's core objective. But earlier failures meant that the political environment ahead of the election would be anything but "neutral." On the contrary, the atmosphere was marked by intimidation and violence. Of the 20 parties that registered for the election, the three largest—the CPP, Funcinpec, and the Buddhist Liberal Democratic Party (BLDP), Son Sann's successor to the KPNLF—all built their election campaigns on fear: fear of the Khmer Rouge, fear of a return to civil war, fear of domination by the Vietnamese.

The CPP's incumbency gave it a significant head start over its rivals. In 1992, the party had embarked on a nationwide membership drive, swelling its ranks to more than 2 million. In many areas enrollment was simply coerced. After arriving in a village, local authorities and CPP "grass-roots strengthening teams" would hand out party memberships to bewildered villagers, who were told that they were now expected to vote for the CPP.[59] The party's campaign pitch continued to focus on its opposition to the Khmer Rouge, and menacingly called on Cambodians to "vote for the party that has fed you all these years." State propaganda depicted Son Sann and Sihanouk's son Prince Norodom Ranariddh as PDK stooges, and TV broadcasts "exposed" the criminal activities of Funcinpec and BLDP members.[60] In an April 1993 speech, Hun Sen referred to the two parties as a "virus" spreading "seeds of war." Chea Sim accused the opposition parties of wanting to "kill their own citizens by leading them to the death pit of the genocidal regime."[61]

The CPP, backed by the full force of the SOC state apparatus, also waged an aggressive campaign of intimidation. As Funcinpec and the BLDP opened their first party branches in the provinces—some no more than shacks with a party sign erected outside—they came under immediate assault by CPP attack squads known as "A-Teams," operating covertly under the Ministry of National Security. Opposition activists, emboldened by the promise of UNTAC's protection, were subject to intimidation, violent threats, and assassination attempts. Ninety-six activists from the two parties were suspected killed by SOC/CPP death squads between November 1992 and January 1993; another 114 lost their lives between March and May.[62] UNTAC, which relied on the SOC to maintain a semblance of order throughout the country, was mostly powerless to stem the violence. While its Human Rights Component worked tirelessly to document killings and other violent abuses, the UN mission lacked the power to arrest and punish those responsible.

In the face of the onslaught, Funcinpec riffed on the theme of the civil war years, portraying itself as the party of Sihanouk and the monarchy. Although UNTAC had banned the use of the returned monarch's image during the election—as head of the SNC, Sihanouk was technically a neutral figure—Ranariddh campaigned in T-shirts printed with his father's portrait, leaving people in little doubt as to who they were voting for.[63] He also aped Sihanouk's political style, arriving in villages by helicopter, accompanied by a 30-piece marching band, at least until his choppers were grounded by the SOC aviation authorities.[64] The weaker BLDP, like its Lon Nol-era forebears, piled on the anti-Vietnamese polemics. Its party propaganda was filled with conspiracy theories about Vietnamese plans for "swallowing Khmer territory and committing genocide against the Khmers." One virulent November 1992 bulletin declared that "the *yuon* are an infectious invading germ . . . poisonous to all living things, both plant and human."[65]

This toxic narrative, peddled to varying extents by every faction bar the CPP, was to have tragic results. Since 1992, thousands of Vietnamese had migrated to Cambodia, drawn by the opportunities of the UNTAC boom. Most took up menial jobs as construction workers and prostitutes, but among the immigrants were many whose families had fished on the Tonlé Sap lake for generations before being expelled in the 1970s. Overall, the total number of ethnic Vietnamese in Cambodia probably remained lower than the pre-1975 population—one observer put it at around 200,000[66]—but the PDK continued to claim the presence of "millions" of illegal migrants, including Vietnamese soldiers who had remained behind, in mufti, in order to aid the CPP. For UNTAC, tasked with verifying the withdrawal of "foreign forces"—which the Khmer Rouge took to mean all ethnic Vietnamese—these claims were impossible to refute. When UNTAC failed to turn up hordes of phantom *"yuon"* colonists, the Khmer Rouge again denounced it as an agent of Hanoi. Nothing short of a UN-directed campaign of ethnic cleansing would suffice.

Where UNTAC "failed" to act, the PDK took matters into its own hands. On March 10, 1993, PDK soldiers descended on Chong Kneas, a floating village on the Tonlé Sap lake near Siem Reap, and massacred 33 unarmed Vietnamese fisherfolk, including more than a dozen children. The other three Cambodian factions showed little concern for the cold-blooded killings of unarmed civilians. Vietnam was, after all, "a very sensitive issue," one Funcinpec representative said. The BLDP issued a rote condemnation of the bloodshed, but followed it with calls for Vietnam "to immediately call upon her citizens currently living illegally in Cambodia to return to their homeland"—what it considered to be the main problem.[67]

Even the CPP, scared of demonstrating pro-Vietnamese sympathies, refused to deploy its police to protect ethnic Vietnamese civilians. In an interview with the *Bangkok Post*, Akashi quoted Hun Sen as saying that he did not want his government to be seen as "protectors of the Vietnamese," arguing that it would be "political suicide" in the run-up to the election.[68] In a replay of the pogroms of the early 1970s, nearly 200 ethnic Vietnamese were killed in the six months leading up to the May 1993 elections, while 20,000 more fled back to Vietnam, including many whose families had lived in Cambodia for generations.[69]

Again, UNTAC was found wanting. Despite the PDK's advance notice of the attacks, UN forces did nothing to protect ethnic Vietnamese communities, or to notify them of impending violence. UN Secretary-General Boutros Boutros-Ghali later took refuge in the letter of the Paris Agreements, arguing that protection was the responsibility of the local authorities—that is, the SOC—and that "appearing to make exception to the mandate" to protect the Vietnamese would have further discouraged the Khmer Rouge from participation in the election.[70] But by this point PDK cooperation was a hopelessly slim prospect, meaning that the Vietnamese were effectively sacrificed in a vain attempt to keep the mission on the rails. It was, as David Rieff later said of the UN mission to Rwanda, "a triumph of form over substance, legalism over reality, hope over experience."[71]

In this context, the peacefulness of the election—held over a week during May 23–28—came as a welcome surprise. The PDK, which had been threatening a violent campaign to derail the polls, mysteriously held its fire, and an astonishing 89.5 percent of Cambodia's 4.7 million registered voters bravely turned out to vote. In some provinces, so many people showed up on the first day of voting that polling stations stood nearly empty for the rest of the week. Widyono described the scenes that greeted him as Cambodian villagers, clutching their prized voter registration cards, lined up to have their say in the country's first multiparty election in a generation:

Dressed in their nicest clothes and beaming, they looked as if they were going to a carnival. Most came from up to twenty kilometers away—by foot, by bicycle, or trucks provided by the SOC or private companies. Whole families came, from grandmothers to nursing babies carried by their mothers. Most carried picnic baskets in anticipation of a long wait.[72]

The CPP expected an easy victory. Bantering with reporters after casting his vote in Kampong Cham, Hun Sen said his party had "done everything for the purpose and survival of the people" and was "very confident" of winning the election.[73]

But when the votes were counted, the victory belonged to Funcinpec. The party clinched 45.5 percent of the vote, followed by the CPP's 38.2 percent, and Son Sann's BLDP, which won 3.8 percent. The remainder of the vote went to a raft of small anti-CPP parties. In the 120-seat constituent assembly, Funcinpec won 58 seats, the CPP won 51, and 10 went to the BLDP, with the final seat taken by Molinaka, a royalist splinter party. UNTAC officials praised the conduct of the poll. Akashi declared the election "free and fair," and most other international observers agreed.[74] Despite all of its incumbent advantages—its strong networks of political control and its liberal use of violence—the CPP had failed to engineer victory. Its defeat represented a massive miscalculation of the desires of the Cambodian people. Taking advantage of the UN's secret ballot, they rejected the CPP and clung to what many saw as the one constant in an era of upheaval and suffering—a symbol of peace, tradition, and the hazily remembered golden age of the prewar years.

They voted for Sihanouk.

The CPP reacted to its defeat with complaints and threats. Even as the votes were being counted, senior officials complained about electoral irregularities. On June 10, Hun Sen launched a stinging criticism of the UN, accusing it and foreign nations of rigging the polls in Funcinpec's favor. In response to the UN's "massive fraud," he announced that the six provinces east of the Mekong River had seceded and declared an "autonomous zone." The secession, he said, was launched by CPP "dissidents" including the pugnacious National Security Minister Sin Song, an ex-DK cadre who joined Hun Sen in Vietnam in 1977, and Prince Norodom Chakrapong, a rebellious son of Sihanouk who had joined the CPP in 1991.

Throughout the secession zone the CPP unleashed its A-Team attack squads, which destroyed UNTAC offices and party branches and beat up opposition activists. Hun Sen claimed no hand in the creation of the "Samdech Eav Autonomous Zone"—cynically named after a popular honorific for Sihanouk—but offered to help "resolve" the situation. Five days later, he had convinced the secessionists to step down. After witnessing the CPP's show of strength, Prince Ranariddh agreed to share power with Hun Sen in an interim government pending the drafting of a new constitution. Both would serve as co-prime ministers, with Sihanouk as head of state.

Many observers have accused Hun Sen of engineering the secession in order to strong-arm Funcinpec into accepting a coalition deal. There is also evidence to suggest Sihanouk acquiesced to the secession, which gave him an opportunity to step in and "save" his country from partition, though Hun Sen eventually took most of the credit.[75] After the affair had passed, Sihanouk praised the secessionists for returning to the fold, and, in a characteristically Cambodian twist, elevated Prince Chakrapong to the rank of four-star general. Whatever its causes, the outcome represented a debasement of the democratic process. A coalition government was probably inevitable, given the fact that no party had the two-thirds majority necessary to form a government alone. Yet the CPP's theater of secession meant that winners and losers ended up with an equal share of the spoils.[76]

As the secession drama was playing out, Sihanouk convened a constituent assembly that annulled the 1970 coup and formally appointed him as head of state. The prince was ecstatic, and wrote to each of the assembly members to thank them for their "historic" decision. Three months later, on September 24, the assembly promulgated a new constitution, drafted by foreign experts and representatives from the four factions. In the spirit of the times, it was a liberal work of art, guaranteeing Cambodians a full panoply of civil and political rights. Sihanouk was restored to the throne with restricted powers—the constitution specified that "the king reigns but does not govern"—and the interim government became the Royal Government of Cambodia under the dual leadership of Ranariddh, who was appointed "first prime minister," and Hun Sen, who was appointed "second".

Having already chalked up the elections as a success, UNTAC had little inclination to oppose this convoluted power-sharing arrangement. Akashi more or less acquiesced, saying he "highly appreciated the efforts of Hun Sen" in ending the secession crisis, and UNTAC started packing its bags.[77] "Everybody was basically tired of the whole thing and wanted to create a fix that Cambodians could live with and get out," said Timothy Carney, the former American diplomat who headed UNTAC's Information and Education Division, "and the Cambodians were about ready to see the end of the foreigners, too."[78]

During the mission's final months, UNTAC was hit by a series of coordinated car thefts, carried out in daring night-time raids on UN compounds. No one knew for sure who was behind the burglaries, though some of the cars later showed up outside the homes of high-ranking CPP officials. When

UNTAC officers raided the house of a Cambodian official suspected of having stolen a Land Cruiser, they were held at gunpoint for seven hours. "We are fed up," said one UN official. "We are losing cars every night."[79] By September 1993, a total of 1,898 vehicles had been stolen, worth an estimated $15.8 million. This was followed by the theft of $1.3 million worth of satellite equipment and $23.9 million in computers and other supplies.[80] The thefts showed just how much contempt the Cambodian authorities had for the authority of the UN. "I present my apologies to the United Nations," Sihanouk said afterward. "We did not deserve $3 billion—our behavior is so bad, so bad."[81]

In Kratie, a sleepy provincial capital hugging the banks of the Mekong 200 kilometers northeast of Phnom Penh, there is still one faint echo from the UNTAC days. A few blocks back from the shaded river promenade, with its arching trees and stuccoed colonial-era buildings, stands an abandoned warehouse—little more than a large iron frame open on three sides to a grove of rustling coconut palms. Twenty years on, its rusty steel gate, slumping inward on its hinges, still bears a thin layer of sky-blue paint and, in two large white block letters, the UN's double-barreled acronym. In 1992 and 1993, the site served as the base of operations for UNTAC's Indian and Polish peacekeeping contingents. Today it's a lonely place, strewn with garbage, weeds, and empty Angkor Beer cans.

UNTAC notched up some undeniable successes in Cambodia. The mission brought some semblance of order to a shattered nation. It repatriated more than 360,000 Cambodians from the Thai border camps and helped reintegrate them into Cambodian society. UNTAC's Information and Education Division—one of the few parts of the mission that employed foreign Cambodia experts and Khmer speakers—played an important role in neutralizing the poisonous atmosphere that preceded the elections. In particular, Radio UNTAC successfully informed Cambodians about the secrecy of the electoral process, and gave airtime to opposition parties barred from the SOC-controlled state media. For the first time in many years Cambodians had access to an unbiased source of information.

UNTAC also prized open a space for the establishment of indigenous human rights groups and a vibrant press. Groups like the Cambodian Human Rights and Development Association and the Cambodian League for the Promotion and Defense of Human Rights—usually known by their French-language acronyms, ADHOC and LICADHO—were founded and began publishing detailed reports on government abuses, a level of scrutiny that had been unheard of under a succession of regimes. As international attention shifted to new global trouble-spots—to Somalia, Rwanda, and the fracturing former Yugoslavia—Cambodia offered a hopeful validation of the saving idea that peace could be engineered, democratic institutions molded, and human rights implanted in the DNA of nations emerging from periods of wrenching conflict. Before moving on to head the UNPROFOR peacekeeping mission in Bosnia, where his diplomatic diffidence was partly blamed for UN inaction during the genocidal massacres at Srebrenica in mid-1995,[82] Akashi described the Cambodia mission as "a striking demonstration to the world that an intractable conflict can be resolved and seemingly irreconcilable views can be reconciled." Cambodia, he said, would stand "as a model and a shining example for other UN member states."[83]

But the new dawn would turn out to be a mirage. Like its old warehouse in Kratie, UNTAC's democratic institutions weathered badly. Contrary to Akashi's hopes, Cambodia's conflict persisted and opposing political interests remained unreconciled. At its heart, the UN intervention had represented a slow-motion collision between the Kantian idealism of the post–Cold War era and the messy realities of Cambodian politics, where history, far from coming to its foreordained democratic end, ground onward into a new phase of struggle and political intrigue. UNTAC had succeeded in extricating outside powers from Cambodia's quarrels and putting power back in the hands of Cambodian leaders, but a glaring a question remained: what would they do with it?

CHAPTER FOUR

A False Dawn

New York City, October 1993. Cambodia's two prime ministers walked into the plush lobby of the Waldorf-Astoria Hotel on Park Avenue, took the elevator to the thirty-seventh floor, and each extended a hand to greet the US Secretary of State, Warren Christopher. The time and place of the meeting were highly symbolic. Throughout the 1980s, the New York hotel had played host to Prince Sihanouk's sumptuous soirées, at which he plied guests with champagne and petits fours while rallying support against the PRK. Now two former enemies, Prince Norodom Ranariddh and Hun Sen, returned as partners of peace, charged with safeguarding the UN's $2 billion-plus investment in Cambodian democracy.

In front of a large press contingent, Christopher presented Ranariddh and Hun Sen with the brass plaque that had once been attached to the front of the Cambodian Embassy on 16th Street, re-establishing a relationship that had been in a deep freeze since the US had run down its flag and evacuated Phnom Penh on April 12, 1975. When the ceremony was over, "everybody in the room broke out into applause," recalled Kenneth Quinn, then serving as US deputy assistant secretary of state.

> I thought it was a testimony . . . that, in fact, Cambodia somehow had been saved and—with all of the caveats to such a statement about all the problems that could obtain in the future—there was a moment there in which all the anguish, all of the sacrifice, all of the suffering of the past was somehow expiated.[1]

A similar sense of optimism prevailed elsewhere. In July 1994, Tony Kevin arrived in Phnom Penh and presented his credentials to King Sihanouk as Australia's new ambassador to Cambodia. Kevin had no previous experience in

Asia. His last posting had been in Warsaw, where he had seen out the collapse of communism and the shaky early presidency of the trade union leader and Nobel laureate Lech Walesa. Kevin's bosses in Canberra saw Cambodia in much the same way as they saw Poland and the other ex-communist countries of Eastern Europe. With communism crumbling, democracy would dawn. All Kevin would be doing in Cambodia, he was told, was "running an aid program."

The reality couldn't have been more different. Within days of Kevin's arrival in Phnom Penh, the Khmer Rouge ambushed a south-bound train in Kampot province, massacring 13 Cambodian passengers. They also took as hostages three foreign tourists—a Briton, a Frenchman, and an Australian. Despite heated negotiations to secure their release, the three men were executed two months later as the Khmer Rouge base at Phnom Voar came under attack from government forces. When the base was eventually overrun, their bludgeoned bodies were found in a shallow grave at the foot of a hill. The hostage crisis brought home to Kevin just how precarious the UNTAC settlement had been. "People in Canberra, and I suspect in a fair few other capitals as well, wanted to believe that UNTAC had solved all the country's problems," Kevin told me. "It was a completely false prognosis. I found myself in a very unstable and deteriorating political situation."

The new coalition government was highly volatile—a political Frankenstein's monster welded together from three factions that had been at war for more than a decade. First Prime Minister Ranariddh and Second Prime Minister Hun Sen headed a hybrid cabinet split awkwardly between their two sprawling party organizations: Funcinpec in control of 11 ministries, the CPP in charge of another 11, and Son Sann's BLDP, which ran third in the 1993 election, occupying the Information Ministry. Control of the important interior and defense ministries was split between Funcinpec and CPP co-ministers, and at the provincial level, governors from one party were paired with deputies from the other.

It was a bewildering arrangement—and one that concealed wide inequalities of power. After a decade of Vietnamese tutelage, the CPP remained a cohesive organization with political networks stretching far into the countryside. It continued to control the military, the police, the bureaucracy, and the courts. Funcinpec's power, in contrast, existed mostly on paper. Though the royalists were more urbane and educated than their CPP counterparts, they had spent much of their lives overseas and lacked the connections and political experience to wield power effectively. "It was very awkward," said Pou Sothirak, a former Boeing engineer and Funcinpec official who was appointed minister of industry in 1993. "Everybody knows you can't have one country, two systems."

Funcinpec's shortcomings reflected those of its leader. Physically, Prince Ranariddh was the spitting image of his father: he shared Sihanouk's cherubic grin and high-pitched voice, which frequently dissolved into peals of laughter. But there the similarity ended. Ranariddh lacked his father's exquisite political intuition. As prime minister, he was effete and ineffective, more interested in the perks and baubles of his office—an endless rota of gala dinners, receptions, and golfing jaunts—than the practical business of government.

As Sihanouk's second-eldest son, Ranariddh had enjoyed a pampered upbringing. Born in 1944, he grew up in a sumptuous villa close to the Royal Palace in Phnom Penh, where he attended the Lycée Descartes. He later studied law in France, earned his doctorate, and took a teaching position at a university in Aix-en-Provence. After Ranariddh joined his father's service in 1983, he enjoyed a frictionless rise. Three years later he was appointed commander of Funcinpec's armed force, the Armée Nationale Sihanoukienne, despite his evident lack of military experience. Later, when Sihanouk resigned from Funcinpec to head the Supreme National Council under UNTAC, Ranariddh added a third string to his bow: party leader and democratic politician. Victory at the 1993 election, a vote for father more than son, capped off his unlikely metamorphosis from law professor to national leader.

Ranariddh had the patrician airs of most royals. He thrived on the diplomatic cocktail circuit, and gave long, ebullient speeches at public functions. Next to Hun Sen, however, Ranariddh was a political amateur. Hun Sen had learned politics the hard way. Decades of civil war and struggle had made him a steely operator. In private meetings, diplomats noted Hun Sen's attention to detail and clear sense of purpose. Ranariddh's cabinet, on the other hand, was fashioned like a miniature royal court populated by returnee yes-men who rarely questioned his views. One Western diplomat described the first time he called on Ranariddh after his arrival in Cambodia in 1995: "He was nervous . . . he giggled a lot, and he wasn't well briefed. He had two or three sycophantic note-takers who didn't take a whole lot of notes but bowed and scraped every time he asked them a question. He was very much the *petit prince*."

To the extent that two mismatched leaders managed to forge a working relationship, it involved the division of corrupt spoils. As in the 1980s, political power in the new kingdom was counted out in currencies of loyalty and payola, a calculus that encouraged rent-seeking at the top—where officials creamed off aid money and took kickbacks from business deals—and at the grassroots, where poorly paid soldiers, police, and civil servants had no choice but to supplement their meager incomes by demanding bribes from the public. Funcinpec officials, arriving late to the party, scrambled to enrich themselves. Within the party, government jobs were literally bought and sold.

In return for their jobs, officials of both parties paid a portion of their illicit earnings to their bosses, a chain of graft that reached all the way up to the offices of the two co-prime ministers. "Every business deal must have a cut for the relevant minister (or Prime Minister) and every transaction involves a percentage for the relevant official in a situation where most government ministries are barely working," wrote Tony Kevin's predecessor, John Holloway, in a confidential cable in June 1994. Public servants, paid an average of $28 per month, were "only motivated to attend their offices at all by the possibility of making some extra money."[2]

One of the most lucrative sources of income was logging. In June 1994, Hun Sen and Ranariddh wrote to the Thai prime minister announcing that the Cambodian Ministry of Defense had been granted the exclusive right to export timber—in large part to secure the loyalty of powerful military commanders. The arrangement only came to light when a copy of the letter was leaked to the new finance minister, Sam Rainsy of Funcinpec, who raised loud protests in the media. Since the Defense Ministry was "shared" by the CPP and the royalists, it was obvious that the deal also had benefits for both prime ministers.[3] For Funcinpec, corruption was a cancer that would slowly bring the party to its knees. In 2010, Ranariddh admitted to me that his party abandoned its "basic values and origins and political approach" for the lures of easy money. "Most of our ministers applied a flexible theory," he said. "When they saw others get involved with corruption, they did so as well."

In the countryside, meanwhile, the fighting continued. In early 1994, six months after UNTAC's departure, government forces launched an offensive against the Khmer Rouge in western Cambodia, overrunning Pailin and Anlong Veng. But the victories were short-lived, and by April, both areas were back in PDK hands. The defeat was less a sign of Khmer Rouge strength than of the prodigious incompetence and corruption of the Cambodian military. Illegal logging was just the beginning. Cobbled together from the armies of the SOC, Funcinpec, and KPNLF, the Royal Cambodian Armed Forces (RCAF) was a factionalized force headed by a comically bloated officer corps numbering some 10,000 colonels and 2,000 generals. On paper the army consisted of 145,000 troops, but as in the Lon Nol era, as many as half were "ghost soldiers" whose salaries and rations flowed into the pockets of the top brass.[4]

In the military, promotion was granted as a reward for loyalty rather than for performance on the battlefield. In practice, this amounted to a license to loot the provinces and exploit the population. "People join the army to use their uniforms and weapons as a meal ticket," Holloway wrote in his 1994 cable.[5] Since 1992, UNTAC officials and human rights groups had accused senior Cambodian military figures of involvement in a systematic criminal campaign in western Cambodia, which included extortion, robbery, abduction, and the torture and execution of political opponents at secret detention centers. UN investigators claimed that a military intelligence unit known as S-91 was responsible for dozens of extrajudicial killings in 1993 and 1994.[6] With no recourse against arbitrary violence, many peasants reportedly feared government troops more than they did the Khmer Rouge.[7]

As the government offensives collapsed, King Sihanouk watched on from Beijing. Since his return to the throne, he had found himself in a figurehead position with little power, burdened again with the "terrible servitude and crushing responsibilities" that had prompted him to abdicate the throne in 1955.[8] But Sihanouk still hungered for power, and remained convinced he was the only figure who could unite Cambodia and prevent its slide back into chaos. At 71 years of age, and still full of energy, he wanted another chance to usher his people into a new "golden age" of peace and prosperity.

Sihanouk's initial strategy was to leverage his symbolic power to end the civil war and bring about national reconciliation. In January 1994, he had suggested that Khmer Rouge leaders like Pol Pot, Ieng Sary, and Nuon Chea should be given roles in government as an incentive to end the fighting.[9] After the failure of the government's 1994 offensives, Sihanouk summoned the American journalist Nate Thayer to Beijing and told him that if things got worse, he might be obliged to step in, assume power, and help "put an end to anarchy." Sihanouk proposed heading a new government of national reconciliation that would contain representatives from all four factions, including the Khmer Rouge. "How can I avoid intervening in a few months' time or one year's time if the situation continues to deteriorate?" he said.[10]

Hun Sen and Ranariddh both opposed the plan. Hun Sen wrote an open letter to the king arguing that the proposal was unconstitutional, and dismissed any idea that leading Khmer Rouge should be brought into government. According to Hun Sen, the only solution to the Khmer Rouge lay on the battlefield. Letting Sihanouk take power would be "a big blow to the achievement of the UN operation in Cambodia"—an act tantamount to a "cool coup d'état."[11]

Sihanouk's response was characteristic; he sulked, withdrew his plan, and complained that nobody appreciated him. "H.E. [His Excellency] Hun Sen and others want me to remain 'powerless.' I will no longer intervene in their affairs," the monarch wrote, saying he would instead stay in Beijing for cancer treatments.[12] The sudden withdrawal was vintage Sihanouk. But unlike in the 1950s and 1960s, when his dramatic reversals underlined his indispensability, the old God-King now found himself in a position of weakness. The government's final repudiation of Sihanouk came in July, when the National Assembly voted to outlaw the Khmer Rouge, spelling an end to the king's reconciliation bid. Later, Hun Sen would resurrect Sihanouk's peace plan, amnesties and all, in his own bid to end the civil war.

The episode was a vivid illustration of where the real power in Cambodia now lay. Since his return in 1991, the CPP had managed to confine the king in a constitutional straitjacket, restricting his room for political maneuver. "[Hun Sen's] letter is a warning to the king," one CPP official told Thayer. "The King must understand the message: 'Don't go too far. Be happy with being king.' "[13] As time went by Sihanouk would spend more and more time out of the country, watching Cambodian developments from an Olympian remove. Shuttling between his residence in Siem Reap and his opulent homes in Beijing and Pyongyang, the king retreated into more pleasurable diversions. In mid-1994, he put the finishing touches to a new film, *Peasants in Distress*, a typically florid romance set against the backdrop of the UNTAC mission. The king "may have lost touch with national politics," one observer noted pithily, "but he still has an eye for the camera."[14]

Within a year of UNTAC's departure, things were starting to unravel. The UN presence had helped foster an active civil society and rambunctious press, but the government still showed little tolerance for dissent. In late 1994, the media was chilled by a series of violent attacks on reporters investigating corruption at the highest levels of government. On September 7, Nuon Chan, editor of the *Samleng Yuvachun Khmer* ("Voice of Khmer Youth") newspaper, was gunned down in broad daylight in Phnom Penh by two men on a motorbike. Two months later, Chan Dara, a reporter for *Koh Santepheap* ("The Island of Peace"), was fatally shot while driving away from a restaurant in Kampong Cham. Both journalists had written extensively on corruption, and Nuon Chan had previously received warnings from the information and interior ministries about his paper's investigations of graft involving senior Funcinpec and CPP figures.[15] The government promised investigations, but no one was ever brought to justice. It was to become a familiar pattern.

One of the few to speak out against corruption was the new finance minister, Sam Rainsy. Along with his wife, Tioulong Saumura, the deputy governor of the Cambodian National Bank, Rainsy emerged as one of the government's few voices for reform, spearheading a campaign to root out corruption, centralize the budget, and introduce a modern system of revenue collection. Possessed of seemingly inexhaustible reserves of pluck and self-righteousness, Rainsy positioned himself as a gadfly and noble dissenter—one of the few incorruptible politicians in Cambodia.

Like Ranariddh, Sam Rainsy was the scion of an established political family. His grandfather had been a leading member of the Democrat Party in the 1940s and his father, Sam Sary, was a high-ranking member of Sihanouk's government. Described by *Time* magazine as "a suave, Paris-educated ladies' man,"[16] Sary served as deputy prime minister and represented Cambodia at the 1954 Geneva Conference, before falling out of Sihanouk's favor. In 1959, he was implicated in a right-wing plot against the government and disappeared after fleeing to Thailand, presumed killed by one of his foreign patrons.[17] In 1965, harassed by Sihanouk's police, Rainsy's mother, In Em, took the family to live in Paris, where Rainsy would remain for the next 25 years.

Rainsy later described Sary's disappearance and the family's flight to France as a traumatizing experience, and a formative one. Even though he was just ten years old at the time, he recalled the strong influence of Sary's anticommunist politics. "My father was in favor of a strict neutrality—that Cambodia should not move closer to the communist world," Rainsy told me in 2009. "This has marked my background and my conviction that communism is oppressive: that freedom is essential and that we have to fight for [it]." Later on, during a student trip to London in 1968, Rainsy encountered the writings of the Anglican American pastor Frank Buchman, who had founded the Moral Rearmament movement in the late 1930s. Buchman's revivalist doctrine preached the importance of having a "clear moral perspective" on life. In his memoirs, Rainsy recalled being seized by Buchman's almost mystical belief that moral clarity could not only benefit individuals, but could release entire nations from "their prison cells of fear, resentment, jealousy, and depression."[18]

As Rainsy embarked on a successful career as an investment banker in Paris, politics began to exert its gravitational pull. In 1981, he and Saumura became founding members of Funcinpec, and at the start of the 1990s, abandoned their professional careers and returned to Cambodia to prepare for the UN-organized elections. But nothing prepared Rainsy for what he would encounter as finance minister. After a life of economic modeling and Japanese stock assessments, Rainsy found himself in charge of a system hovering on the verge of financial anarchy. The lack of effective regulations made Cambodia a paradise for money launderers and organized crime syndicates. As Rainsy put it, "The whole of Cambodia is a big casino."[19]

The new finance minister took his campaign abroad. In fluent French and English, he urged Cambodia's foreign donors to withhold development aid until the government improved transparency, democratic accountability, and respect for human rights. At an international donor meeting in Paris in March 1995, he distributed a 13-page document detailing the "institutionalization" of high-level corruption and called for an aid freeze until the government established "greater transparency in public decision-making."[20] He took particular aim at the intimate nexus between the government and a new class of crony-tycoons that had emerged since the free market reforms of the late 1980s.

One of Rainsy's main targets was Teng Bunma, a Sino-Khmer tycoon who controlled a portfolio of investments including hotels, manufacturing concerns, a daily newspaper, and vast tracts of real estate in several countries. Bunma was an apt symbol of the new Cambodia, driving about Phnom Penh in four-wheel drives accompanied by a phalanx of bodyguards armed with automatic rifles and grenade launchers.[21] He would later attain global notoriety by shooting out the $3,000 tire of a Royal Air Cambodge airliner on the tarmac at Pochentong airport, apparently angered by the "insolent" attitude of the cabin attendants.[22]

Rainsy and other critics accused Bunma of gold smuggling and customs fraud, and placed him at the center of a wide circle of drug traffickers who were using the country as a transshipment point for heroin from the Golden Triangle. The US State Department later banned him from entering the country because of his links to narcotics, though no evidence was ever made public. Whatever the nature of his dealings, Bunma had a chummy relationship with government leaders, deluging them with gifts and personally under-writing the military budget. He served as an advisor to Chea Sim, and was a benefactor of both prime ministers, presenting Hun Sen with a bullet-proof Mercedes limousine and Ranariddh with a $1.8 million King Air 200 light aircraft. In late 1995, Bunma was elected president of the Cambodian Chamber of Commerce.[23]

Rainsy's anticorruption crusade put him on a collision course with the two prime ministers. In October 1994, after a showdown with Teng Bunma over a Phnom Penh market development that had dispossessed local vendors, Rainsy was dumped from the cabinet. The following May, he was unceremoniously expelled from Funcinpec, and then stripped of his seat in parliament. The vote that removed him from the National Assembly in June 1995 was a travesty of democratic procedure. Son Soubert, then the assembly's vice-president, recalled: "It was completely illegal. They didn't even give him the chance to present his case. After the proclamation by the vice-president, they switched off all the microphones so he couldn't say anything."

Sam Rainsy's anticorruption crusade incensed the government, but it had little impact on the donor countries that had bankrolled the UNTAC mission. In June 1992, as UNTAC was getting under way, the major donor nations and development agencies had gathered in Tokyo for a Ministerial Conference on the Rehabilitation and Reconstruction of Cambodia. At the meeting, Koji Kakizawa, Japan's Vice-Minister for Foreign Affairs, described the world's commitment to establishing a "truly durable peace" in Cambodia.[24] For William Draper III, administrator of the UN Development Programme, Cambodia remained "a critical test for the post–Cold War world."[25]

To maintain UNTAC's momentum, the new UN Secretary-General, Boutros Boutros-Ghali, asked foreign governments for $590 million to fund Cambodia's reconstruction. The donors went on to pledge $880 million. They also established the International Committee for the Reconstruction of Cambodia (ICORC), a foreign aid "club," chaired by the World Bank, which would meet annually to assess Cambodia's needs and coordinate international aid contributions. When ICORC met for the first time in Paris in September 1993, donors pledged another $120 million.

The influx of development aid filled the vacuum left by the drop-off in Soviet-bloc aid at the end of the 1980s, and re-established Cambodia's long-standing reliance on outside support. Vietnamese and Soviet assistance had guaranteed the survival of the PRK throughout the 1980s, just as the French had helped preserve the kingdom from Vietnamese and Thai encroachments in the nineteenth century. In a similar way, China had helped safeguard and support Pol Pot's revolution. Unlike Cambodia's past patrons, however, these foreign donors claimed to represent a loftier set of principles. In place of the socialist brotherhood they spoke of democracy; instead of the *mission civilisatrice*, there was the exalted tongue of human rights.

None of these concepts was taken too literally. The superpowers that had framed the Paris Agreements hadn't paid $2 billion to bring democracy to Cambodia. They had paid $2 billion to get it off the agenda. "It wasn't to establish democracy," said Charles Twining, who became ambassador when the US mission was upgraded in 1994. "It was to stop the fighting."[26] If the country moved in the direction of democracy, all the better—but this was never a central objective. "The big story out of every annual World Bank meeting was corruption," said another Western ambassador posted in Cambodia at the time. "There were no real sanctions in spite of all the threats. Most of us were happy just to see the country stable and with reasonable fiscal discipline at the center."

After UNTAC's departure, foreign nations doubled-down on their Cambodian gamble, pledging $770 million in aid in 1994, followed by $520 million the year after. They issued lukewarm condemnations of Rainsy's expulsion from the National Assembly and other human rights violations, but satisfied themselves with vague promises from the government that it would combat corruption, overhaul the country's financial system, and end human rights abuses. All of these goals were vague and aspirational, a utopian horizon-line toward which Cambodia would drift, donors hoped, if the winds of international support stayed strong.

In truth, neither of Cambodia's prime ministers had much interest in liberal values. Hun Sen lashed out at even mild criticisms from the West, accusing foreigners of trampling on Cambodian sovereignty. Ranariddh held similar views. In a revealing manifesto published in mid-1995, the law professor argued that democracy in Cambodia was "just a phrase to be talked about in idle gossip" and stated that "discipline is more essential in our society."[27] The "Ranariddh doctrine" provided the blueprint for an accelerating government crackdown on political dissent. In July 1995, the government passed a new Press Law which criminalized the publication of any information that harmed "national security" or degraded the authorities. More attacks followed. In October, a mob of villagers from Kraingyov commune in Kandal province, where Hun Sen had sponsored rural development projects, ransacked the offices of Sereipheap Thmei ("New Liberty") after the paper published a story critical of the prime minister's efforts. Hun Sen later applauded the actions of the villagers, denouncing their critics as "Khmer Rouge."[28] In September 1995, Frederick Z. Brown, a professor of Southeast Asian studies at Johns Hopkins University, told a US Congressional Subcommittee that the noisy Khmer-language press spawned by the UNTAC mission had "been pretty much cowed into submission."[29]

After Sam Rainsy's expulsion from the National Assembly, opposition lawmakers clammed up for fear of losing their seats (or worse), and the parliament rapidly devolved into a rubber-stamp for CPP-tabled legislation. At the same time, CPP leaders tried to buy off opposition members with bribes and government posts. The first party to fold was the BLDP. After the 1993 election, the party had split following a power struggle between Son Sann, the BLDP's founder, and Information Minister Ieng Mouly, who formed a breakaway faction and aligned himself to the CPP. "I needed the support of Hun Sen to make a big splash," Mouly later said. "I couldn't say no."[30] In late September 1995, as the Son Sann faction of the BLDP prepared to hold a national congress, two men on a motorbike threw grenades at the party's headquarters and at a nearby Buddhist pagoda that was housing delegates from out of town. No one was killed in the attack, but 30 people were wounded. As the casualties arrived at Calmette Hospital, staff refused to treat them, fearing official retaliation. They were left bleeding in the halls.[31]

Similar tactics were employed against the new Khmer Nation Party (KNP), founded by Sam Rainsy in November 1995. The KNP's platform, which combined liberal rhetoric with warmed over references to the Vietnamese threat, immediately attracted strong support, and by March 1996, the party claimed to have 100,000 members.[32] At first the authorities refused to recognize Rainsy's party as a legal entity. KNP activists were harassed by government goon squads and Rainsy received a string of death threats. When the KNP tried to open three provincial offices in Sihanoukville, police tore down party signs and shot at activists who tried to replace them. Three party members were killed during May and June, including Thun Bun Ly, the editor of the KNP-aligned newspaper *Oddomkete Khmer* ("Khmer Ideal"), who was gunned down just hours after attending the opening of a Sihanoukville party office.[33]

As foreign criticism mounted, Hun Sen challenged the authority of Western states and human rights groups to dictate how Cambodia should conduct its business. "I am fed up with the world expressing alarming fear over Cambodia's internal affairs," he said in a barnstorming speech in late 1995. "Let me say this to the world: whether or not you want to give aid to Cambodia is up to you, but do not discuss Cambodian affairs too much." In response to US critics he threatened anti-American demonstrations and called for reparations for the B-52 bombings of the 1960s and 1970s. ("How much?" he asked. "Only about $20 billion.")[34] Hun Sen would later denounce donors for treating Cambodia like "a parrot." When governments sought the reform of Cambodia's political system, he accused them of "neocolonial" designs.[35]

Beneath his bluster were memories of devastating war and a lingering bitterness about the hypocrisy of the foreign nations that had kept Pol Pot in the UN until 1991. Throughout Cambodia's modern history, the US and other Western governments had flouted democratic norms when it suited them. Why should it be any different for Cambodia? As far as Hun Sen was concerned, the past actions of foreign powers indemnified him from criticism of any kind.

After two years in office, Prince Ranariddh was in a precarious position. His imaginary empire was eroding away on every front. Cut out of national decision-making, royalist ministers found themselves sitting in empty offices, "shuffling meaningless documents, attending vacuous meetings, reading newspapers."[36] Other Funcinpec officials were growing unhappy at the fact that their bosses had fewer jobs to distribute than their CPP counterparts did. The party's crisis reached a peak in November 1995, when Funcinpec's Secretary-General, Prince Norodom Sirivudh, was arrested in connection with an alleged plot to assassinate Hun Sen. The charges against Sirivudh were dubious. Speaking with a journalist at a cocktail party, the jovial prince had reportedly "joked" about attacking Hun Sen's motorcade with a grenade launcher. A few days later Sirivudh awoke to find his party chatter splashed across the front page of the *New Angkor* newspaper. Hun Sen went on the warpath; troops were deployed and Sirivudh was arrested at tank-point.

The National Assembly convened for a closed-door session and stripped the prince of his parliamentary immunity. The vote was a unanimous 105 for and zero against; at Ranariddh's request, every Funcinpec member present voted to condemn Sirivudh, who was locked up pending trial. Ranariddh argued later that he denounced his colleague and uncle "to save the Kingdom of Cambodia."[37] But the Sirivudh affair showed just how powerless Ranariddh had become, and how far he now had to bend in order to appease Hun Sen. In the weeks that followed, King Sihanouk brokered a compromise arrangement whereby Sirivudh (his half-brother), would be allowed to go into exile in France and avoid prison.

Joke or not, Hun Sen wasn't taking any chances. For much of the past year he had remained cooped up in his heavily fortified compound at Tuol Krasang, close to the town of Takhmao, ten kilometers south of Phnom Penh. Hun Sen reportedly worked late into the night, chain-smoking 555-brand cigarettes, trusting few people outside his family and a close circle of advisors. In a 1995 cable from the US embassy, Twining described Hun Sen's "near-obsession" with security. Even before the Sirivudh affair, he traveled about the country with around 60 armed bodyguards—more than any other government official.[38]

By 1996, Hun Sen's personal bodyguard unit had grown into a small personal army of more than 1,000 men backed by tanks, armored personnel carriers, and helicopters. Up to 800 of these troops were based at Tuol Krasang—dubbed the "Tiger's Lair" by foreign journalists—who were supplemented by several hundred more men based at a special CPP complex located behind his villa in the capital. Technically part of RCAF's elite Brigade 70, set up in October 1994 to guard the government leadership, Hun Sen's bodyguards existed outside the military chain of command. In return they received salaries of around $300 per month—far in excess of the $13 received by normal soldiers.[39] In part, Hun Sen had built up his forces as insurance against his co-premier, who commanded a formidable personal security force of his own.[40]

Hun Sen's bodyguards also offered him protection against challenges from within his own camp. Despite the CPP's outward appearance of unity, its internal balance of power remained in flux. Though the 1993 election had marked a distinct shift from the Chea Sim faction of the CPP to a younger group of officials close to Hun Sen, his party rivals still retained much of their power.[41] Chea Sim continued to control the National Assembly, and his brother-in-law Sar Kheng remained in charge at the Ministry of Interior. Both were closely linked to the RCAF commander-in-chief, General Ke Kim Yan, who had risen up through the military ranks in Battambang and was related to Sar Kheng by marriage. This web of alliances, rooted in the security forces and the provincial administrations in Prey Veng and Battambang, posed a potential rearguard threat to Hun Sen.

The discontent in the CPP came briefly to the surface on July 2, 1994, when armored personnel carriers carrying around 300 troops based in Prey Veng were deployed westward toward Phnom Penh. Around 30 kilometers from the capital, the column was stopped by government forces and forced to return to barracks. Not a single shot was fired, but soldiers were deployed in Phnom Penh and the government immediately announced that it had quashed an attempted coup. The plot was spearheaded by General Sin Song and Prince Norodom Chakrapong, who had languished on the political fringes since leading the secession of Cambodia's eastern provinces in 1993. They found another willing co-conspirator in Sin Sen (no relation to Sin Song), who had commanded the feared "A-Team" attack squads during UNTAC. He, too, was apparently piqued at having been sidelined in the new government.[42]

The aim of the coup attempt was never entirely clear. But the foiled plot had significant political aftereffects. In the immediate aftermath, Hun Sen moved quickly against his factional rivals. Sin Song and Sin Sen were taken into custody. After an armed stand-off at a Phnom Penh hotel, Chakrapong was allowed to go into face-saving exile in Malaysia. Instead of deploying CPP forces to quash the coup, Hun Sen used Funcinpec and KPNLF men, and failed to notify Sar Kheng at the Ministry of Interior—both moves that suggested a lack of trust in his own party's forces.[43] During the Sirivudh assassination "plot" in 1995, he would again work around Sar Kheng.[44]

Implying their involvement in the coup, Hun Sen insisted to Chea Sim and Sar Kheng that he be allowed to nominate the next chief of the national police, a powerful institution which had been under Chea Sim's control since 1979. The figure he chose was Hok Lundy, his old ally from Svay Rieng, who, after his appointment in September 1994, would report directly to Hun Sen. At the same time, Hun Sen's small security detail began to expand into a personal army which lay outside the control of any state institution. It was a decisive turning point. Backed by ruthless force, Hun Sen now had the clout to reshape the Cambodian political landscape to his liking.[45]

For many Funcinpec officials, Sirivudh's arrest was the last straw. In January 1996, the party held a closed-door meeting in Sihanoukville and resolved to press for a larger share of power and begin building up its military wing.[46] Characteristically, Ranariddh overcompensated. At the next Funcinpec party congress in March, he launched a blistering attack on the CPP, denouncing the coalition government as a "slogan," or an "empty bucket" that was beaten in the name of democracy. If the CPP didn't make more concessions, Ranariddh threatened to dissolve the National Assembly and hold a new election "before the end of 1996."[47]

The Funcinpec leadership failed to anticipate Ranariddh's outburst. "It came out spontaneously," one former royalist minister told me. "He couldn't bite his tongue." The CPP responded by accusing Funcinpec of using the issue of power-sharing as a pretext to create "political instability" and confuse public opinion. CPP-controlled media outlets excoriated Ranariddh and began speaking of a "royal plot" against Hun Sen. In a speech on April 27, Hun Sen ominously pledged to use force against any "coup to destroy the Constitution."[48] In contrast to Rainsy and Ranariddh, who both held dual French-Cambodian citizenship, Hun Sen painted himself as a true Khmer, a son of the soil who stood by the people and wouldn't board a plane to Paris at the first sign of trouble. In a similar vein, he threatened to pass legislation disqualifying dual nationals from public office. He warned his opponents, "Don't say you are Khmer when it is easy and American when it is difficult."[49]

Just as the coalition began to fracture, a volatile new compound was added to the mix. On August 9, Hun Sen announced that Ieng Sary, Pol Pot's brother-in-law and the former Khmer Rouge foreign minister, had defected to the government, bringing with him not only a large portion of the Khmer Rouge fighting force—including the commanders Y Chhean (in charge of Division 415) and Sok Pheap (Division 450)—but also the gem and timber-rich areas around Pailin. The Khmer Rouge had been in a slow decline since the departure of UNTAC. After the movement was outlawed in mid-1994, the Thai government had finally begun cracking down on exports from Khmer Rouge zones, choking off its finances. All the while, a steady trickle of defections turned into a cascade, as soldiers and their commanders, worn out from decades of fighting, cut deals with the government.

Ieng Sary had always been the most flexible and slippery of the Khmer Rouge top brass—the one who most easily shed old revolutionary convictions and adopted new guises. Sary had a taste for the finer things, like lobster thermidor, cognac, and French perfume, which he indulged even as Cambodia suffered through years of civil war. Throughout the 1980s, he had enjoyed prominence due to his close ties with Beijing, and had consequently lost influence when China cut off its aid in 1990. The Khmer Rouge leader in Anlong Veng was also suspicious of the great wealth he had amassed from Pailin's gem mines and timber concessions.[50] Faced with the enmity of his old comrades and recognizing that their days were numbered, Sary put out feelers to the government. On August 7, after word of the negotiations leaked out, Khmer Rouge radio denounced Sary as a "traitor" who had embezzled millions in Chinese aid and collaborated with the "Vietnamese aggressors, annexationists, and race-exterminators."[51]

The defection dealt the Khmer Rouge a body-blow. Sary took more than 3,000 soldiers over to the government, delivering two base areas—Pailin and Malai—that years of armed offensives, including another RCAF loot-and-pillage mission during the 1996 dry season, had failed to secure. In return, Sary received a royal amnesty that overturned the death penalty handed down by the PRK in 1979. His forces were incorporated into the national army, and Sary was allowed to retain control of Pailin, where he returned to augmenting his vast and hidden wealth. Now just 2,000 Khmer Rouge remained in Anlong Veng, a remnant of bedraggled diehards professing loyalty to a triumvirate of Pol Pot, Nuon Chea, and Ta Mok, a one-legged military commander who had earned the nickname "The Butcher" during the purges of the Eastern Zone in 1977 and 1978.

Pol Pot continued to live a will-o'-the-wisp existence along the Thai border. After the government offensives of 1994, he had relocated to Kbal Ansoang, perched on the crest of the Dangrek Mountains eight kilometers north of Anlong Veng. As his movement crumbled, Pol Pot retreated into the past, restaging his old revolution in a new form. Buddhist pagodas and markets that had opened in Khmer Rouge areas were shuttered. Trade with neighboring areas was banned. Local farmers were rounded up and subjected again to the miseries of collectivization. In this way, Pol Pot tried to mimic the austere conditions that had led to his seizure of power in April 1975. Facing defeat, he hoped to conjure a repeat of the movement's lone triumph.

Ieng Sary's defection also played into the fragile balance of power in Phnom Penh. For Funcinpec and the CPP, an alliance with the defecting Khmer Rouge forces suddenly loomed as a rich prize, one that might tip the scales of power decisively in their favor. In late 1996, both prime ministers paid visits to Pailin to woo Sary's support. Hun Sen's trip in October was a highly publicized affair in which the two former enemies grasped each other's hands like long lost comrades and prayed together at a local pagoda. Hun Sen then laid on a feast at which government soldiers and their Khmer Rouge counterparts ate, drank, and danced the Lambada—a surreal coda to years of tense and grinding conflict.[52]

As 1997 dawned, Hun Sen's relationship with Ranariddh continued to deteriorate. Horse-trading and alliance-building proceeded at a frenzied pace, as both parties cast an eye toward national elections due in mid-1998. Ranariddh announced the formation of a new political alliance with Rainsy and Son Sann's faction of the BLDP, which he dubbed the National United Front (NUF). Two years after throwing Rainsy out of his party, Ranariddh now described him as "respected" and "beloved."[53] Rainsy didn't much trust the prince, but described him as "the lesser of two evils" next to Hun Sen, who was "like someone from a different planet," a "wild man" who trampled on democratic norms.[54]

The Ranariddh–Rainsy–Son Sann alliance represented a potentially formidable challenge, resurrecting the anti-Vietnamese and anticommunist alliance of the 1980s. The royalists, for all their failures, still drew on a deep well of support for Sihanouk, while the KNP's popularity was soaring on the back of Rainsy's anti-Vietnamese agitations and the party's roots in Cambodia's nascent labor union movement. As the political temperature rose, threats flew back and forth between the two prime ministers and skirmishes broke out between their personal bodyguard armies. In February, factional forces clashed in Battambang, leaving 14 CPP and two royalist soldiers dead. The two sides hovered on the edge of open warfare.

On the morning of March 30, 1997, Im Malen and two of her sons left their home in Phnom Penh and joined a group of KNP supporters in a march on the National Assembly. Malen was then 55 years old. A nurse who ran a small clinic and pharmacy, she had been a member of Sam Rainsy's party since 1995 and admired the leader for standing up to the sorts of official corruption she had encountered while working at the Ministry of Health in the 1980s. The rally on March 30 was similar to others Malen had previously attended. Several hundred people gathered at the KNP party headquarters and then proceeded on foot toward the parliament. Malen walked behind Rainsy as the crowd marched down leafy Street 240 behind the Royal Palace, coming to a stop in the park across the road from the National Assembly. It was a hot morning; the building's spired roof rose to a pinnacle against a blue sky. Protesters held blue banners emblazoned with the words "Down with the Communist Judiciary!"

Rainsy began to speak, denouncing corruption in the courts. At around 8:25 a.m. he finished his speech and handed the microphone to a female garment worker. A few seconds later there was a deafening explosion. Malen was thrown to the ground as three more blasts ripped through the crowd. "At first I didn't realize I'd been hurt," Malen told me. "I saw Mr Sam Rainsy, he escaped and got up. But what had happened to me? When I touched my back I felt a lot of blood." Malen looked around. The dirt around her was streaked with red. Torn placards covered mangled bodies. Malen tried to get up but her legs didn't respond. The police stood back. Why weren't they doing something? One of her sons appeared. He had a gash on his cheek but seemed otherwise unscathed. He picked her up and took her by cyclo to hospital, steering the rickety pedicab through the traffic after its driver had fled the scene in fear.

In the space of 15 seconds, four American-made M33 fragmentation grenades had transformed a peaceful gathering into a scene of carnage. Sixteen people were killed in the grenade attack and more than one hundred were injured. Some of the worst carnage took place around a sugarcane cart, where people had gathered to slake their thirsts in the rising morning heat. The target of the attack was Rainsy, who survived when one of his bodyguards shoved him to the ground and took the full force of the blast, which killed him instantly. After escaping the park, Rainsy held an impromptu press conference during which he pointed the finger squarely at the second prime minister. "Hun Sen is behind this," he declared, his suit still covered with blood and broken glass. "He is a bloody man. He will be arrested and sentenced one day."[55]

Hun Sen immediately denounced the grenade attack, but then went on to insinuate that Rainsy and the KNP had staged it themselves in order to smear the government. The police, he said, should "drag the demonstration's mastermind by the neck to court."[56] At the rally, however, eyewitnesses reported the presence of around 15 heavily armed members of Hun Sen's bodyguard unit, who were not usually deployed on such occasions. Not only did the troops fail to help the wounded; they also let the assailants pass through their cordon and flee to the CPP compound behind Hun Sen's nearby villa, blocking those who tried to pursue them. Similar claims were later echoed by UN investigators and human rights groups.[57]

To satisfy international demands for an investigation, the government formed a committee filled with squabbling Funcinpec and CPP officials. Few people expected much to come of it, but there were hopes for a proper investigation from another direction. During the attack, Ron Abney, an American citizen who headed the local office of the International Republican Institute, had been injured by a piece of shrapnel. Under US law, the Federal Bureau of Investigation was authorized to probe any terrorist attack that killed or injured US citizens abroad. The FBI decided to become involved. It dispatched a team headed by Agent Thomas Nicoletti, who arrived in Cambodia on April 17. Within a month Nicoletti and his team had interviewed several dozen sources and identified three suspects. Again, all the signs pointed to Hun Sen's bodyguards.

For US officials, however, the case posed a political conundrum. Putting Hun Sen's men on trial in an American court could have explosive diplomatic ramifications. Kenneth Quinn, who succeeded Twining as ambassador in 1995, was particularly uncomfortable with pointing the finger at the CPP. He had a close relationship with Hun Sen dating back to the peace talks of the early 1990s, and after documenting communist atrocities on the Vietnamese border in the mid-1970s, shared his deep disdain for the Khmer Rouge. Like many other diplomats posted in Cambodia at the time, Quinn saw Hun Sen as a man who could get things done in Cambodia. Quinn spoke with Hun Sen in Vietnamese and felt they had a good rapport. As he later said, Hun Sen "had a lot of power and influence . . . Therefore, he was somebody, along with others, who you would hope to shape."[58]

Where the grenade attack was concerned, Quinn was anxious about the US burning its bridges with the CPP or getting sucked into Cambodia's internecine political struggles. Declassified files released under Freedom of Information laws and published by the *Cambodia Daily* in 2009 showed that at least one FBI official shared his concerns, fearing that the probe could embroil the agency in a combustive political fight and jeopardize its relations with the CPP.[59] So the FBI decided to pull the plug. Before he could complete his investigation, Nicoletti was ordered out of Cambodia. Rising political tensions between the CPP and Funcinpec had made his work difficult. Quinn also warned Nicoletti that his life had been threatened, reportedly by the Khmer Rouge. The withdrawal was supposed to be temporary, but Nicoletti was never sent back to finish the job.

Nicoletti later confirmed that his team had gathered "substantial" though incomplete evidence pointing to the involvement of the CPP's security apparatus in the grenade attack.[60] Declassified files provided further confirmation: key witnesses interviewed by Nicoletti all told similar stories about Hun Sen's bodyguard soldiers, their deployment, and the fact that assailants were allowed to escape into the nearby military compound.[61] But the results were never publicly released. When the FBI reported to the Senate Foreign Relations Committee in November 1998, as it was required to do by law, it assigned no blame.[62] According to additional files obtained by the *Cambodia Daily*, the most sensitive allegations were whited out of the FBI's report after consultation with the Justice Department and the US embassy in Phnom Penh.[63] Congressional Republicans and Rainsy allies cried foul, but the bureau was not forthcoming. In 2005, the case was quietly closed.[64]

Im Malen, meanwhile, never walked again. Now a withered 71-year-old with short-cropped sliver hair, she moves about in a wheelchair donated by a Christian NGO. Lacking an income of her own, Malen has been forced to survive on the charity of family and neighbors and a small monthly pension from Sam Rainsy's party. Each year, like many others, she attends the annual ceremony commemorating those who died in the grenade attack, which transformed a call for impartial courts into a symbol of Cambodian injustice. "We didn't have any arms," she said. "We just came with paper banners."

The grenade attack prompted a steep deterioration in the political situation. By the middle of 1997, Tony Kevin recalled, Phnom Penh "was on a hair-trigger, just waiting for something to set it off." Senior officials from both parties traveled through the city with motorcycle outriders armed with AK-47s and rocket launchers. Their homes were watched around the clock by armed guards, who eyed passers-by warily from machine-gun nests and barricades of sandbags. The government had virtually ceased to function, as the two premiers plotted their next moves from fortified compounds.

The final end-game revolved around the unfolding drama in Anlong Veng. After Ieng Sary's defection, the remaining Khmer Rouge were still divided over whether to keep up the fight or to seek accommodation with the government. The allegiance of those allegedly wishing to defect now became the subject of a new political courtship. In the meantime, Hun Sen redoubled his attacks on the royalists, attempting to bribe Funcinpec members of parliament to oust Ranariddh as first prime minister and put a more "friendly" figure in his place. In April, 12 renegade parliamentarians split from the party and declared for the CPP. The next month, troops loyal to the CPP seized a Polish arms shipment supposedly destined for Ranariddh's bodyguard unit, triggering further fusillades of accusations.[65]

As Funcinpec and the Khmer Rouge neared a political deal, the movement imploded. At midnight on June 9, seized by a final reflex of paranoia, Pol Pot ordered the killing of his defense chief Son Sen, accusing him of treason. Son Sen was assassinated along with his wife, Yun Yat, and 12 other people, including several small children, whose bodies were then run over with trucks.[66] Pol Pot's "night of long knives" threw a diminished movement into turmoil. Angered by the brutal killings, Ta Mok rallied his forces at Anlong Veng and led a rebellion against Pol Pot, who was captured as he tried to escape into the jungle with a handful of supporters.

Six weeks later, Pol Pot was put on trial by Ta Mok and "sentenced" to life imprisonment for the killing of Son Sen and other crimes against the leadership. The outdoor trial north of Anlong Veng was a bizarre spectacle, a phantasmagoric throwback to the grim mass meetings of the DK years. Groups of peasants raised their fists in unison, chanting "Crush! Crush! Crush! Pol Pot and his clique!" as cadres lined up to denounce their old boss through a crackly loudspeaker powered by a car battery. Nate Thayer, the one foreign journalist invited to the trial, later described the Robespierre of Cambodian communism as a stooped shadow of a figure, drained of the charm and magnetism that had beguiled generations of disciples: "Slumped in a simple wooden chair, grasping a long bamboo cane and a rattan fan, an anguished old man, frail and struggling to maintain his dignity, was watching his life's vision crumble in utter, final defeat."[67]

After Pol Pot's arrest, Funcinpec and the remaining Khmer Rouge resumed their alliance talks. On July 4, news leaked out that the two sides had reached a deal.[68] Hun Sen took decisive action. At dawn the following day, his forces unleashed a lightning strike against the royalists. Pochentong airport was secured. Tanks growled along the capital's wide boulevards. Gas stations were set ablaze and buildings across the city were damaged as the two sides traded artillery and tank fire. Thousands of residents fled the city in panic, while rattled opposition members rushed to board flights out of the country or sought sanctuary at the homes of Western diplomats.

Hun Sen, vacationing at the Vietnamese beach resort of Vung Tau, returned to Phnom Penh to "take control" of the situation. After his arrival, the fighting came to a quick end. By the afternoon of July 6, the Funcinpec headquarters and Ranariddh's residential compound were both in CPP hands. Victory was followed by a wave of looting. Frightened civilians looked on as the military and police combed the city for booty, carting off cars, motorbikes, televisions, and other appliances from shattered shop fronts. The halls at Pochentong airport were picked clean, right down to the departure ramps. The fighting caused an estimated $50 million in damage and gutted a tourist industry just recovering from years of chaos.

As calm returned, Hun Sen stood alone. Prince Ranariddh had flown to France the day before the CPP offensives, and as Phnom Penh burned, he appeared on French TV showing journalists his rose garden in Aix.[69] Meanwhile, his party was being shattered by a ruthless campaign of arrests and extrajudicial killings that continued long after the fighting was over. "Bodies were turning up all over the place," recalled one UN investigator.[70] In a report issued a few weeks later, the UN Centre for Human Rights documented 41 politically motivated executions.[71] Most of the victims were senior Funcinpec military officers. Ho Sok, the head of Ranariddh's personal bodyguard unit, was tortured and executed in the ministry grounds on July 7. The following day, General Chao Sambath, whose villa had been the scene of fierce fighting, was shot along with Kroch Yoeum, another senior commander.

The CPP forces acted with calculated brutality. UN investigators found the victims stripped of most of their clothes, handcuffed and blindfolded, with one or two bullets in the head. Other prisoners were tortured until they confessed to having links to the Khmer Rouge and other "charges." Some of the worst tortures were carried out by members of Brigade 911, an elite RCAF paratroop unit trained by the Indonesian special forces. According to the UN's report, around 33 Funcinpec officers were taken to the Brigade 911 headquarters outside Phnom Penh, where they were subject to harsh interrogations. "The torture involved beatings with a belt, the wooden leg of a table, a wooden plank, kicking with combat boots and the knees, punches in the face and the body and blows to the blade of the upper part of the nose with the edge of the hand. . . . An iron vice was also used on several detainees, to squeeze their fingers or hands until they responded satisfactorily."[72]

One Funcinpec general who escaped the CPP's dragnet was Nhek Bun Chhay, who made for the old royalist strongholds in the west and established an "army of resistance." By August, Bun Chhay's forces were holed up at O'Smach on the Thai border, grimly struggling to repel government forces.

The UN, the Western press, and most foreign observers denounced the violence of July 5–6 as a coup d'état. From Bangkok, where the opposition had regrouped, Ranariddh lobbied the UN to withhold recognition of the new status quo in Cambodia. In Phnom Penh, the CPP followed up its military offensive with a public relations blitz. On July 9, it released a 27-page "White Paper," likely prepared ahead of time, arguing that Ranariddh had pursued a "strategy of provocation" by bringing Khmer Rouge soldiers into the city and scheming to overthrow Hun Sen. In this context, the violent removal of Ranariddh was a simple law enforcement operation, a pre-emptive assault undertaken in the interests of national stability.[73] During a news conference, a triumphant Hun Sen compared Ranariddh to the boxer Mike Tyson, who would resort to biting when he couldn't win: "He failed, and his only choice was to flee and cry 'coup!' "[74] If there had really been a coup, Hun Sen later said in a televised address, "the name Funcinpec would not exist and there would be no other parties."[75]

Hun Sen was hardly a victim, of course. Eyewitnesses reported that his troops were on the move at dawn on July 5 and had struck their Funcinpec targets with an efficiency and coordination that suggested careful preparation. In the weeks prior to the clashes, Hun Sen had boosted the size of his body-guard to 1,500 men, and had equipped them with heavier weapons.[76] During the fighting there were virtually no CPP casualties. But it was also true that Ranariddh's actions had done much to ratchet up the tension. One former royalist minister recalled that Ranariddh had surrounded himself with "dare-devil" army men who fed him the idea that the power he craved could be acquired through force of arms. In reality, the fighting was the culmination of months of mutual escalation between two rival centers of power bent on maximizing their own control. "It was a mini-civil war," said Gordon Longmuir, then Canada's ambassador to Cambodia. "It was no coup, not in the ordinary sense."

Coup or not, Hun Sen's act of *force majeure* left the Paris Agreements in tatters. On July 11, 1997, five days after the fighting had ended, foreign embassies in Phnom Penh received a letter from the Cambodian parliament. To help repair the damage caused by the fighting, it read, "We appeal to you to give us humanitarian assistance, either financial or material." The smoke had barely cleared on a city looted and destroyed by Hun Sen's troops. Now he was asking for help to pay for the damage. Diplomats were astounded. One European envoy described the demand as "insulting."[77] Foreign investment stalled. Some governments suspended aid. Cambodia's seat at the UN was vacated under American pressure and the country's long-awaited admission into ASEAN was postponed.

The reaction was especially strong in Washington, where conservative figures lined up to put their boots into "Saddam Hun Sen."[78] Dana Rohrabacher, a Republican Congressman representing a large Khmer diaspora community in California, denounced the violence and criticized Ambassador Quinn for trying to appease Hun Sen. Quinn and the State Department, he said, had failed in their responsibility "to deter Hun Sen and his forces from violence." Rohrabacher's aide Al Santoli, an author and decorated Vietnam veteran, went further, attacking Quinn for kowtowing to "a little murderous dictator."[79] These critics in Congress combined the democratic triumphalism of the post–Cold War years with a hangover from the US humiliation in Vietnam. Hun Sen, in their view, was a dictator and a war criminal. Not only had he been installed by communists, but he had been installed by *Vietnamese* communists. Rohrabacher later dubbed him "a new Pol Pot."[80]

Aware of his government's need for foreign aid and legitimacy, Hun Sen went to great lengths to maintain a mirage of constitutionality. In Washington, the CPP assembled a crack team of lawyers and corporate strategists to counter the criticisms coming from Congress and advance its own version of events. (The party would eventually spend $550,000 on Beltway spin-doctors.)[81] In Phnom Penh, the coalition government was kept intact; Hun Sen remained "second" prime minister. Ranariddh was removed and replaced with a pliant Funcinpec colleague named Ung Huot, who had directed the party's 1993 election campaign. Human rights groups would be permitted to continue their work and an election would be held as planned in mid-1998. King Sihanouk, overseas at the time of the fighting, had initially described his son's ejection from power as "illegal and unconstitutional" but now, seeing the futility of further opposition, backed the status quo, undercutting Funcinpec's campaign against Hun Sen.[82]

Most international observers saw through the ruse. With Ranariddh out of the country and other Funcinpec officials scared for their lives, elections would mean little. Brad Adams, a UN lawyer based in Phnom Penh, told a US Congressional Committee:

> Hun Sen has staked out a clear strategy: create the appearance of a consti-
> tutional, multi-party government and political system, such as by placing a

malleable figure such as Ung Huot in the position of first prime minister, hold elections next year without any semblance of a real opposition, exercise control over all levers of government, dominate the electronic media, and wait for the international community to hold its nose and declare the elections minimally free and fair.[83]

But Cambodia's foreign backers saw few other options. Diplomats deplored Hun Sen's bloody takeover, but many of them also saw the CPP as vital for political stability. "Is this not better than getting back into the sterile game of propping up Ranariddh?" Tony Kevin wrote in a confidential cable shortly after Hun Sen's power-grab. "It seems to me that this would simply help to prolong the long war—and for what?"[84] Engineering a new election seemed like the best way to restore order and a functioning government. "Let's be realistic," one French diplomat told Philip Gourevitch of *The New Yorker*. "We get Hun Sen elected, not free and fair like in other countries, but OK good enough. Then we can have legitimacy, diplomacy, investment, order, and these people can get on with their lives."[85]

In the diplomatic frenzy that unfolded in late 1997 and early 1998, securing the return of Ranariddh—the crucial ingredient for a minimally credible poll—became the overriding aim. Eventually, a solution of sorts was brokered by Japan. Under Tokyo's plan, the CPP held a bogus trial at which Ranariddh was found guilty on a raft of prefabricated charges and sentenced to 30 years jail. He was also ordered to pay $54 million in compensation for damage from the fighting and looting, even though this was almost entirely carried out by the CPP's forces. Then Sihanouk stepped in and offered his son a royal pardon, which allowed him to return in time for the election. On March 30, Ranariddh flew back to Phnom Penh and hunkered down at the Hotel Le Royal, where he resumed plotting Hun Sen's demise—this time at the ballot box.

The CPP could afford to make some concessions. It still controlled the police, the military, the courts, and most of the print and broadcast media. Its opponents were scattered and fearful. Unlike five years earlier, the 1998 election would be administered by a newly formed National Election Committee (NEC) stacked with CPP appointees.[86] If foreign governments wanted another election, Hun Sen would give them one—with all the trimmings.

Still, the CPP left nothing to chance. It launched more forced voter registration drives, and pressed local officials to take oaths in support of the party. As one human rights worker in Battambang told Human Rights Watch, "they make people take an oath by drinking water with a bullet in it from an AK-47. Those who drink this must promise to vote for the CPP. If they break their promise, those people will be killed by the bullet they drink." In Phuong, a

58-year-old activist for the KNP—recently renamed the Sam Rainsy Party (SRP) to protect it from CPP infiltrators—was shot and killed along with his four-year-old daughter in Prey Veng. Elsewhere, homes belonging to Funcinpec activists were burned to the ground. Around 40 opposition activists were found dead in the run-up to the election.[87]

When Cambodians finally went to the polls on July 26, the result from 1993 was reversed: the CPP won 41.4 percent of the vote, followed by Funcinpec with 31.7 percent, and Rainsy's SRP with 14.3 percent. Two new BLDP splinter groups, the Son Sann Party and the Ieng Mouly-led Buddhist Liberal Party, both failed to win a seat and sank from view.[88] Hun Sen got exactly the result he wanted. International observers noted the killings of opposition activists, the CPP's wall-to-wall media domination, and its control of the National Election Committee. And they signed off on the process anyway. Observing events, Stephen Solarz said the election might one day be seen as a "miracle on the Mekong," an assessment that he was later forced to qualify.[89] As an exercise in democracy it was a mirage, of course. But it *was* something close to a miracle that despite CPP intimidation, Funcinpec and the SRP had together won more of the popular vote than Hun Sen. Cambodians had again used the secrecy of the ballot to signal their discontent.

This time it was the opposition's turn to cry foul. Rainsy and Ranariddh alleged ballot-stuffing and complained about the NEC's quiet adoption of a new voting formula which had magically increased the CPP's share of National Assembly seats. Since the CPP had failed to win the two-thirds majority required to form a government alone, a joint Funcinpec–SRP boycott could hold Hun Sen hostage until an agreement was reached on a new coalition. In mid-August, the two parties launched a campaign of street protests calling for a new election. The park in front of the National Assembly, the site of the previous year's grenade attack, was turned into a tent-city dubbed "Democracy Square."

The high-spirited protests lasted two weeks before the police were deployed. Democracy Square was forcibly cleared and bulldozed, while protesters hurled rocks and crude Molotov cocktails. Monks marched through the city, defying the orders of their superiors to remain in their *wats*. In response, the CPP mounted its own "spontaneous" demonstrations, populated by plain-clothes thugs, many of them belonging to a pro-Hun Sen front group known as the Pagoda Boys' Association. Armed with sticks and rocks, they drove protesters off the streets and beat up those who refused to budge.[90] By the time the demonstrations came to an end, dozens of protesters had been beaten and several shot.

As the situation simmered in the capital, Sihanouk again stepped in to mediate. A few days before the newly elected parliamentarians were to be sworn in at Angkor Wat, he called the three parties to his Siem Reap residence to end the political deadlock. The talks went well. But on September 24, as the parliamentary motorcade made its way through Siem Reap to the swearing-in ceremony, a rocket whizzed out of the bushes on the side of the road, narrowly missing Hun Sen's passing car. When police investigated, they uncovered four B-40 rocket-propelled grenades concealed in the brush, wired for remote detonation. Three of them had failed to fire; the one that did smashed into a house across the road, killing a 12-year-old boy and injuring three members of his family.

It was never clear who was the target of the rocket attack. The government denounced it as an attempt to assassinate Hun Sen, again leveling a finger at the opposition. The prime minister later claimed the rocket missed his car by "just 20 centimeters."[91] Rainsy and Ranariddh fled the country, fearing arrest or retaliation from Hun Sen's men. Opposition supporters accused the CPP of staging the attack to provide a pretext for cracking down on prodemocracy demonstrators, and others blamed the Khmer Rouge or rogue royalist elements. As the years went by Hun Sen would repeatedly accuse the SRP of involvement in the attack, a Damoclean threat that could be conjured up whenever the situation demanded it. But the mystery of the rockets was never properly investigated.[92] Like so many collateral bystanders, Sor Chanrithy, the young boy killed in the explosion, was quickly forgotten.

Political negotiations resumed, and in November 1997, Sihanouk finally arranged a deal for the formation of a new government. Ranariddh walked out on his alliance with the SRP and again joined hands with Hun Sen, who became sole prime minister in a new government. Ranariddh agreed to accept the post of National Assembly president in exchange for amnesties for Funcinpec commanders who took part in the July 1997 clashes. The other two exiled Norodoms, Sirivudh and Chakrapong, were also pardoned for their earlier misdemeanors and allowed to return to Cambodia. Chea Sim, forced to vacate his old post at the National Assembly, was installed at the head of a newly created Senate, a legislatively unnecessary body designed to provide jobs and sinecures for members of his entourage. As so often in Cambodian politics, old grudges were put on ice and enemies became allies overnight. Champagne flowed in Phnom Penh as the deal was signed. Politicians who had been at war with each other just a year before smiled and raised a toast to the new coalition government.[93] It was as if nothing had ever happened.

By the end of 1998, little remained of the Khmer Rouge. After his "trial," Pol Pot was confined to a wooden hut in Anlong Veng, a ward of his own collapsing revolution. A stroke had left him mostly bedridden, passing his time by listening to Khmer Rouge and Voice of America broadcasts on a small transistor radio. In

October 1997, the enigmatic leader had finally broken his silence in an interview with Nate Thayer, the first he had granted since 1979. For two hours, Pol Pot reflected on his legacy, reminiscing about his childhood and his years in Paris. On the 1975–9 period, Pol Pot was unrepentant. He admitted that his movement had made "mistakes," but shifted responsibility to a familiar scapegoat. Tuol Sleng, the Khmer Rouge-era prison known as S-21, was a "Vietnamese exhibition"; death and starvation was caused by "Vietnamese agents" who withheld rice from the people. To the last, he depicted Cambodia as an innocent victim of nefarious foreign forces. "If we had not carried out our struggle," he told Thayer, "Cambodia would have become another Kampuchea Krom in 1975." After the interview was over, Pol Pot rose, and, hobbling back to the Toyota that brought him from his house arrest, turned to one of his guards. "I want you to know," Thayer heard him say, "that everything I did, I did for my country."[94]

Thayer's interrogation was the closest Pol Pot would ever get to a real trial. His health declined rapidly. In March 1998, when government forces overran Anlong Veng, the remaining Khmer Rouge fled north into a sliver of territory along the Thai border and Pol Pot was confined to a three-room hut. It was here, on the evening of April 15, 1998, that he died, just as the news broke that his captors had agreed to turn him over to an international tribunal. The cause of death was heart failure. On April 17, 23 years to the day after his movement's triumphant march into Phnom Penh, journalists were allowed in to see a bloated corpse laid out on a bare mattress.*

The next day, Pol Pot's body was taken to a dusty forest clearing, dumped onto a pile of old tires and burned, along with his last remaining personal effects—a mattress and wicker chair—and a few handfuls of flower petals, a nod to the Buddhist rituals that the Khmer Rouge had done their best to eradicate. As Seth Mydans wrote in the *New York Times*, "There were no words of eulogy and no tears as the flames crackled and grew ... As the tires and the kindling burned away, Pol Pot's blackened skeleton remained within the orange flames, its right arm and fist raised upward."[95] It was a fittingly anonymous end for the architect of the Khmer Rouge horror, attended by just a handful of low-ranking soldiers. None of his family, nor any senior members of the movement, was present.

---

* Since Pol Pot's death, rumors persist that he either committed suicide or was poisoned by former colleagues to prevent him from being arrested and put on trial in an international court. In January 1999, Nate Thayer wrote in the *Far Eastern Economic Review* that Pol Pot committed suicide by taking an overdose of valium and the powerful antimalarial drug chloroquine. But no autopsy was performed before the body was cremated and little other corroborating evidence has since come to light. Philip Short, the author of a biography of Pol Pot, has described rumors of suicide as "bunkum."

"Pol Pot has died, like a ripe papaya," Ta Mok chillingly told a Cambodian reporter. "Now he's finished, he has no power, he has no rights, he is no more than cow shit. Cow shit is more important than him. We can use it for fertilizer."[96] Like his former boss, Ta Mok trod a path of escalating paranoia, seeing "enemies" around every corner. On December 25, Khieu Samphan and Nuon Chea abandoned Ta Mok's border hideout and surrendered to the government. Three months later "The Butcher" was captured by Cambodian troops, officially bringing an end to the strange revolution of the Khmer Rouge. Seven years later, Mok would die in prison awaiting trial. What the UN had been unable to do via resolutions and mandates had been accomplished through arms, amnesties, and political deals. Cambodia was finally at peace.

Pol Pot's grave remains in the hills north of Anlong Veng, marked by a simple mound of earth, a low roof of rusting corrugated iron, and a hand-stenciled sign. The surrounding jungle has long been cleared. Day laborers working on a Thai border casino lounge in hammocks in a grove of scrawny trees as stray dogs poke about in the dirt. The ghost of *Angkar* still exercises a magnetic pull in this forgotten corner of Cambodia. On a small wooden platform above the pyre there are two tins of burnt-out joss-sticks.

Locals often come to pray at the grave, in the hope that Pol Pot's spirit will bring good luck or reveal magic numbers that will fetch them riches in the Thai lottery. Others nurture a genuine sympathy for the departed tyrant and his revenant plea that Cambodia's road to hell was paved, as always, with the noblest of intentions. Khim Suon, a hunched 56-year-old woman, spends her days in a small wooden hut selling tickets to the cremation site and keeping the grave swept and planted with flowers. She described Brother Number One as a patriot: "Pol Pot tried to protect the nation," she said. "He did not kill people. What the people say is not true."

CHAPTER FIVE

Potemkin Democracy

As Cambodia turned its back on the twentieth century, there were many reasons to be hopeful. For the first time in half a century, it was a country at peace. It had a government that was more open and tolerant than those in neighboring Vietnam and Laos, where the hammer and sickle still flew proudly, or in Burma, inching into the twenty-first century under a stifling military junta. Cambodia had a democratic constitution, a vibrant civil society, and a press that appeared to enjoy more freedoms than in many other Asian countries. With the onset of peace, guns began disappearing from the streets. Foreign investment resumed and tourists returned to the temples of Angkor in greater numbers than ever. At the end of 1999, unprecedented crowds turned out in Phnom Penh for the Water Festival and its traditional boat races and fireworks. There were cheers and an air of celebration as King Sihanouk opened the festivities and the long boats sliced through the brown waters of the Tonlé Sap.

But years of civil war had left the country in a desperate state. Life for rural Cambodians remained nasty, brutish, and—by regional standards—short. A Cambodian born in 1998 could expect to live 53.5 years, the shortest lifespan in Asia. Just a short drive outside Phnom Penh, an island of affluence in an ocean of poverty, clean water and electricity were rare. Nearly two-thirds of the population were illiterate, while infant and maternal mortality rates were among the highest in the region—indicators more comparable to the war-torn states of sub-Saharan Africa than to the economic tigers of Southeast Asia.[1]

The Cambodian political class, distracted by the civil war and by the division of power and its spoils, had paid little attention to most of the country's problems. In 1998, 43 percent of the national budget went toward the bloated army and overstaffed police force, while health, agriculture, education, and rural development combined accounted for less than a fifth.[2] There was more wealth sloshing around the cities and towns, but most of this was controlled by politicians and their well-connected friends. When the National Assembly convened in November 1998 to approve the new CPP–Funcinpec coalition deal, Michael Hayes of the *Phnom Penh Post* noted the hungry villagers who were squatting in front of the Royal Palace begging for rice, while nearby "the street in front of parliament was Cambodia's largest parking lot for luxury Mercedes Benz, BMWs, and Landcruisers."[3]

War also cast a long shadow. During two decades of conflict, Cambodia's armed factions had planted millions of landmines, which continued to extract a bloody toll in rural areas. As old Khmer Rouge zones opened to the outside world, human rights workers reported discovering isolated villages populated nearly entirely by landmine victims. In the early 1990s, NGOs and government agencies had begun the painstaking work of clearing the 4–6 million mines believed to infect Cambodia's soil, but thousands of villagers lost lives and limbs trying to reclaim farms abandoned during wartime. Mines claimed 1,715 casualties in 1998, a terrifying echo of war that failed to discriminate between man or woman, soldier or child.[4] The war left Cambodia with one of the highest proportions of amputees in the world—around one for every 290 people.[5]

Other scars were less visible. Chhim Sotheara, a foreign-trained psychiatrist who began working among the Cambodian population in the mid-1990s, noticed surprisingly high levels of depression, anxiety, and psychosis—all typical responses to prolonged trauma. He also noticed something else. The nightmare of the Khmer Rouge seemed to have reinforced the most conservative and deferential strains of Cambodian culture. For many Cambodians, particularly those in rural areas, Pol Pot's disastrous attempt to overturn a feudal system only seemed to prove the wisdom of the old codes of conduct, the *chbap*, which taught them to accept their lot and defer to those with authority. Sotheara would later coin a phrase for Cambodia's cultural response to trauma. He called it *bak s'bat*, or "broken courage." Those who suffer from it "tend to be mute," he told me, "not speaking, not hearing, not seeing . . . They are very respectful of authority, submissive to authority. They know what is right and wrong, but they dare not stand up."

This reflexive deference was also encouraged by a political system that provided no effective check on the actions of the powerful. On July 6, 1999, the actress Piseth Pelika was shot three times by unidentified assailants in Phnom Penh and died in hospital a week later. The French newsweekly *L'Express* later reprinted excerpts from what it claimed was Pelika's diary, alleging that she was Hun Sen's mistress. The publication also claimed that Bun Rany, in a fit of jealousy, had ordered the shooting of her young rival. Rany denied the claims and threatened to sue *L'Express* for defamation, but no charges were ever filed. Neither was there a serious investigation.[6]

On December 5, six weeks after *L'Express* published its explosive allegations, the karaoke singer Tat Marina was eating lunch with her niece at a
market stall in Phnom Penh when a luxury four-wheel drive pulled up nearby.
A woman got out of the vehicle, walked up to Marina, and yanked her to the
ground. Along with one of her bodyguards, she kicked the young woman in
the chest until she fell unconscious. As she lay prone, one of her attackers
opened a bottle of nitric acid and tipped it over her head. The singer awoke,
kicking and screaming as the acid ate into her flesh. Marina, just 16 years old
at the time of the attack, was left severely disfigured. As she later told journalists from a hospital bed in Ho Chi Minh City, "I look like a ghost, so I hate
myself, detest myself. Everyone is afraid of me, including my three-year-old
niece. She stopped calling me mom. She will only touch my fingers."[7]

It was hard to imagine what could possibly have justified such an inhuman
attack. Eyewitnesses quickly identified Marina's attacker as Khoun Sophal, the
wife of a government official who was having an affair with the teenaged
singer. A court ordered Sophal's arrest, but, as so often, nothing happened. The
police claimed Sophal was nowhere to be found, even though she was reportedly living at home as if nothing had happened. A decade later Sophal and her
husband Svay Sitha divorced, and Sitha admitted his wife's responsibility for
the attack on Tat Marina.[8] But as in the Piseth Pelika case, no charges were ever
laid against Sophal—or anyone else.

The cruelty and callousness that allowed jilted wives to order and commit
such brutal attacks on young women also had its echo in history. As the historian Michael Vickery has written, patterns of sudden and extreme violence had
deep roots in Cambodia, especially against those groups and individuals
defined in some way as enemies. Though cruel violence found its fullest
expression under Pol Pot, it long predated Democratic Kampuchea, stemming
from cultural notions of face, honor, and revenge, in which personal grudges
(*kum*) could elicit a disproportionate and overwhelming response.[9] In peace-
time, too, the pattern persisted. People like Khoun Sophal continued to
commit the most appalling acts of personal violence, seemingly untroubled by
remorse and unchecked by effective legal restraints. For Singapore's longtime
prime minister, Lee Kuan Yew, Cambodia's leaders were "utterly merciless and
ruthless, without humane feelings". The historian Margaret Slocomb likened
them to mythical gods:

> They do what they like, they exist on another higher plane, they believe
> they have rights which usurp the true rights of the masses, they sit up there
> in Valhalla, eat grapes, love their wenches, count their money, and occa-
> sionally hurl down thunderbolts to remind the masses who they are.[10]

By the end of the 1990s, things were turning out well for Hun Sen. The 1998 election had worked its democratic alchemy, giving his seizure of power a pluralistic sheen. Shortly afterward he flew to New York to reclaim Cambodia's seat at the UN, and, in April 1999, after nearly two years' delay, the country was finally admitted into ASEAN. For Lee Kuan Yew, the calculation of outside powers was simple: "no country wanted to spend $2 billion for another UN operation to hold fair elections."[11] For Hun Sen, Cambodia's admission into ASEAN was a long-awaited trophy of international acceptance, the sort of recognition he had craved for more than a decade.

In February 1999, foreign donor governments convened a summit in Tokyo and pledged another $471 million toward Cambodia's development. This time, however, they imposed conditions. With the war over, the Cambodian government was now expected to get serious about reform. Hun Sen thanked the donors for their generosity and reeled off an impressive list of planned reforms, pledging to fight corruption and illegal logging, demobilize the bloated armed forces, and modernize Cambodia's financial management systems.[12] Nothing much happened. The coming years would see the creation of a dizzying mirage of strategies, action plans, councils, coordination bodies, monitoring mechanisms, and reform benchmarks—and very little real progress. Corruption still infected every sphere of Cambodian society.

In mid-1999, Western governments that had poured millions into ridding Cambodia of deadly landmines were shocked to learn of significant corruption in the Cambodian Mine Action Centre (CMAC). Established in 1993, the government's demining office had been hailed as a poster-child of international partnership, and had succeeded, with Canadian assistance, in training up skilled teams of Cambodian deminers. This pleasant image was clouded when it emerged that around $90,000 in demining funds had been channeled into a slush-fund controlled by CMAC's director, Sam Sotha. Donors soon learned of a scheme in which demining teams were sent to clear land owned by military commanders and government officials in exchange for kickbacks. Around $500,000 in mostly donor funds had been used to clear a plantation owned by Chhouk Rin, the former Khmer Rouge commander who had ordered the execution of the three Western tourists seized from a train in 1994. Tens of thousands of dollars had been misappropriated in other ways.[13] An outcry followed and Sotha was removed from his post. Six weeks later, it turned out that he had in fact been promoted, becoming Hun Sen's "Advisor on CMAC Affairs and Land Mine Victim Assistance."[14]

Similar allegations of corruption were later leveled at a $42 million military demobilization initiative run by the World Bank. Under the plan, 30,000 RCAF soldiers would be discharged and given cash payments of $240 and other goods as a starter-kit for life outside the army. However, it turned out that the army had inflated its manpower with tens of thousands of "ghost soldiers," whose military supplies, in time-honored fashion, flowed into the pockets of high-ranking officers. The World Bank later discovered that troops were bribing their officers to get them back into the service and make them eligible for more handouts.[15] In June 2003, the World Bank halted the demobilization project after detecting misprocurement on a $6.9 million contract to provide motorbikes. The Bank then threatened to cut off funds unless the government repaid some $2.7 million that had been creamed off the contract.[16]

Each corruption scandal followed a similar pattern: more finger-wagging from donors, more government promises, and more fruitless monitoring schemes. The World Bank and foreign governments would withhold funds for a time, Cambodian officials would commit to some new target or reform, and before long the money would be flowing again. Because warnings and "concerns" were not backed by meaningful sanctions, Hun Sen and his government either ignored them or played for time, carefully cultivating the impression that a breakthrough lay just over the next horizon. All the while the aid rolled in: $548 million was promised in 2000, followed by $556 million in 2001. At the June 2002 donor meeting, World Bank Country Director Ian Porter reported that progress over the past year had "not been adequate." He said donors were particularly concerned about the "slow pace" of judicial and legal reform. They then went on to pledge $635 million in aid, about $150 million more than the government had requested.[17]

It wasn't hard to manipulate foreign governments. Hun Sen had always sensed that the international commitment to democracy was more rhetorical than real. After having invested more than $2 billion on the UNTAC mission, and a couple billion more in the years since, the donors weren't about to abandon Cambodia. The name of the game now was preserving "access." Western officials felt they had no choice but to continue assisting Hun Sen if they wanted to maintain some say over the country's human rights record and political future. And for that they needed a mirage of reform that would allow them to stay engaged, to keep vital development programs running, and to secure Cambodian cooperation on issues like counterterrorism and drug trafficking.

Despite the violence and corruption of Cambodian political life, most diplomats in Phnom Penh saw Hun Sen as the one man in Cambodia who could get things done. Charles Ray, the ambassador who would go on to spearhead the US re-engagement with Cambodia in the mid-2000s, recalled that Hun Sen "always kept his word . . . If he said he'd do something he'd do it. If he didn't want to do it, he would either avoid the issue, or just look you in the face and say, 'Hell no.'" His successor, Joseph Mussomeli, had a similar view:

"Whenever there was a problem I would go see him and we would work it out." As in any country, having the prime minister's ear was the crucial prerequisite for a successful mission. Hun Sen might be ruthless and unpredictable, but in a country that had never known universal rights or any sort of popular sovereignty, diplomats saw him as the only figure of any consequence. Again, Hun Sen had made himself indispensable.

After the reckoning of July 1997, a triumphant Hun Sen had symbolized the new status quo by ordering the erection of a small statue of a revolver pointing skywards with a knot in its barrel. The statue was designed to commemorate a weapons amnesty, but Hun Sen ordered that it be placed in the sunbaked traffic circle in front of Funcinpec's headquarters in Phnom Penh, where it stood as a constant reminder of the party's defeat.[18]

Funcinpec might be finished as a military force, but the issue of guns and who controlled them remained a pressing concern. July 1997 had been a crucial test of loyalties. Commanders aligned with the Chea Sim–Sar Kheng faction of the CPP had refused to take part in the fight against the royalists, forcing Hun Sen to rely on his private bodyguard unit, the French-trained *gendarmerie* (military police), Khmer Rouge defectors, and loyal factions of the security forces.[19] The subsequent decade saw a slow settling of accounts. Those who had supported Hun Sen in his hour of need were rewarded with promotions and riches; those who had refused sooner or later had their barrels tied.

Huy Piseth, the head of Hun Sen's bodyguard unit, and his deputy, Hing Bun Heang, rose magically through the ranks. The top echelons of RCAF were stacked with Hun Sen loyalists. Chap Pheakedei, the commander of RCAF Brigade 911, which had carried out the violent interrogation of captured Funcinpecists, got his general's stars and won a spot on the CPP Central Committee.[20] Hun Sen also commanded the personal loyalty of the *gendarmerie* (under Sao Sokha) and the national police (under Hok Lundy)—an axis of power that provided a bulwark against any future armed challenge.[21] The verdict of one top CPP official was that "no one can challenge Hun Sen. The only way to keep Hun Sen down is for those inside the party to soften him up from within."[22]

Funcinpec, meanwhile, wasn't faring well. Despite polling surprisingly well in 1998, the party's perennial problems soon resurfaced. Sihanouk's legacy was further leeched of political capital as royalist officials resumed feathering their nests. Unlike Hun Sen, who made frequent excursions to the countryside, Ranariddh and his officials rarely left town, neglecting the party's rural support base. Without firm leadership, old concerns of income and prestige returned to the fore. Senior officials complained about the loss of high-ranking posts. Reports of rampant corruption, including the auctioning-off of provincial governorships and senate seats, further undermined morale.[23] What did Funcinpec stand for? Nobody in the party had a convincing answer.

Left outside the tent was Sam Rainsy, who settled back into the well-worn role of agent provocateur. Rainsy's eponymous party now held 14 parliamentary seats and many outside observers considered him to be Cambodia's best democratic hope. It was an impression Rainsy was careful to cultivate. After setting up his own party in 1995, Rainsy had focused his lobbying efforts on Western donor governments. Foreign envoys remembered him as a constant and irritating presence at diplomatic cocktail parties, where he buttonholed diplomats and tried to enlist them in his crusade. Rainsy had cleverly tapped into the post–Cold War zeitgeist, with its hopes for a "new world order" based on democratic principles and liberal norms, and he spoke its language well. For former Australian Ambassador Tony Kevin, Rainsy "was always feeding off the international enthusiasm for the things that he espoused . . . It gave him the opportunity to cast a much longer shadow in Cambodia than he would have otherwise been able to cast."

Rainsy drew his strongest support from the US, where the presence of politically salient Cambodian diaspora communities made Hun Sen-bashing a profitable pastime for Congressmen like Dana Rohrabacher. In addition to receiving financial support from Khmer communities in California and Massachusetts, the Cambodian opposition enjoyed the political backing of the International Republican Institute (IRI), an arm of the National Endowment for Democracy set up by the Reagan administration in 1983 to promote the global spread of democracy. Unlike other US-funded democracy promotion groups, which claimed to be neutral and nonpartisan, the IRI made no attempt to hide its preference for the SRP. Funding, advice, and technical assistance were channeled solely to Rainsy's party, which the IRI described, in Burma-fashion, as "the democratic opposition."[24] During a visit to Washington in September 2002, Republican Senator John McCain, IRI's chairman, presented Rainsy with the IRI-Heritage Freedom Award, describing him as "a genuine hero."[25]

In truth, Sam Rainsy had many guises. At international donor meetings, he was the Western-educated technocrat, making principled calls for fiscal responsibility. To his friends in Washington, he was the democratic dissident and freedom fighter, a Khmer avatar of Vaclav Havel or Aung San Suu Kyi, who stood with humility on the right side of history. But in front of a Cambodian crowd—whether in suburban Long Beach or rural Kampong Speu—he struck a more traditional pose. Like his father, Rainsy was a patriot, fighting to free his country from the clutches of the historic enemy: Vietnam.

This was the predominant theme during Rainsy's election campaign stops in 1998, when he gave fiery speeches branding Hun Sen a "Vietnamese puppet" and pledged to "send the *yuon* immigrants back."[26] Rainsy's speeches drew little distinction between illegal immigrants, the Vietnamese government, Vietnamese business interests, and ethnic Vietnamese who had lived in Cambodia for generations. All were simply *"yuon."* At the postelection Democracy Square rallies, Rainsy denounced the CPP as *yuon* and *thmil* (unbelievers), and told a crowd that he would "not form a coalition with one who has a *yuon* . . . head and a Khmer body," a statement that could easily have come from Pol Pot.[27] At one demonstration a riled-up mob scaled the Cambodia-Vietnam Friendship Monument near the Royal Palace and tried to set it on fire, while chanting anti-Vietnamese and antigovernment slogans.[28] During the postelection protests, at least four ethnic Vietnamese were killed by angry mobs.[29]

All the while, the pro-SRP press churned out stories scapegoating the Vietnamese for everything from outbreaks of food poisoning in Phnom Penh to a fuel leak on a plane scheduled to carry Sihanouk to Beijing in 2000.[30] Rainsy wasn't the only figure to employ racial rhetoric, but for a self-proclaimed liberal democrat it was particularly problematic. To many otherwise sympathetic foreign observers, it sent the message that he was more interested in playing the firebrand than in working constructively with the government. "The impression you had [of Rainsy] was very little flexibility, very little compromise," recalled another former diplomat. "It was hard to take him seriously sometimes." But Rainsy's anti-Vietnamese baiting reflected a basic political calculation. When it came to mobilizing ordinary Cambodians, folktales about Vietnamese avarice were much more potent than anything contained in the Universal Declaration of Human Rights.*

Rainsy's political strategy was also conditioned by the political climate in which he was forced to operate. After 1998, CPP repression prevented the SRP from

* Sam Rainsy and his supporters frequently deny that the word *yuon* has derogatory or racist connotations. In a series of newspaper op-eds in 2014, Rainsy argued that the word has been used to refer to Vietnam and its people for more than a thousand years. Indeed, it's fair to grant that the word *yuon* is used in a wide range of contexts in Cambodia, many of them harmless. (For instance, *samlor m'chou yuon*, "sour Vietnamese soup," is a popular and tasty Cambodian dish.) But the etymology of the word is only part of the story. More important is the way in which a string of Cambodian regimes has stoked ethnic animosities for political gain, a tactic that has historically resulted in anti-Vietnamese discrimination and violence. In an interview in April 2014, Rainsy described accusations of racism as a "foreign-entertained controversy" ginned up by "experts" ignorant of Cambodia's history. For Rainsy and many other Khmers, the country remains as it was in the nineteenth century—a nation on the brink of extinction, comparable to the Palestinian territories under Israeli occupation, or Poland before the partitions of the late 1700s. It's hard to deny that Vietnam has a strong presence in Cambodia today, which has its share of negative impacts, from deforestation to illegal migration. But this can best be explained by the lack of transparency and rule of law, rather than racial conspiracy theories. Today, ethnic Vietnamese make up around 5 percent of the Cambodian population, according to the US Central Intelligence Agency.

establishing any effective presence in the countryside, home to some 85 percent of the electorate. In rural areas, far from the haven of Phnom Penh, being a Rainsy supporter was a dangerous occupation—a fact that became increasingly clear as Cambodia prepared for commune elections scheduled for February 2002. These local government polls were the cornerstone of a UN- and donor-driven "decentralization" plan, designed to devolve power to local levels of government. The communes had been under firm CPP control since the 1980s and played a huge part in the lives of ordinary people. CPP commune authorities appointed village chiefs, who together controlled everything from land transactions and marriage licenses to the registrations of voters at election time. This gave many rural Cambodians the impression that it was the party that provided them with basic services, rather than the government, a point that was driven home by the CPP's ubiquitous blue party billboards, present in nearly every village in Cambodia. More decentralization, theoretically, meant more democracy.

It was another mirage. The CPP agreed to reforms to keep the donors happy, and then simply worked around them. A new commune election law, drafted in consultations between UN officials and dissimulating Cambodian bureaucrats, had little effect on the conduct of the poll, which proceeded along familiar lines. SRP activist Phoung Phann was shot dead at his home in Kampong Cham. The corpse of the Funcinpec candidate Ros Don turned up near a roadside in Siem Reap, his head bludgeoned in. Police marked his death as "accidental." Human rights groups could find no hard evidence linking the killings to top levels of government, but they spread fear in the run-up to the poll.[31]

At the same time the CPP made efforts to soften its image. After its defeat in 1993, the party had gotten into the "hearts and minds" business. Its national patronage networks were converted into organs of Western-style electioneering. At election time, flocks of party activists, wearing white T-shirts and baseball caps with the party logo, trooped through dusty villages, handing out rice, sarongs, dried noodles, and packets of MSG. Ok Serei Sopheak, a former resistance fighter brought on as a CPP electoral strategist in 1998, told me that the loss five years prior had jolted party leaders into action. Winning elections meant winning votes, he told me, which in turn meant "giving what people want in their daily life."

The result was a program of rural construction which recycled crony money into schools, roads, wells, and Buddhist temples that were presented as gifts from Hun Sen and other senior officials. The party patronage machine was well oiled. In the run-up to an election, tycoons and government officials would make compulsory donations to party "working groups" at each level of government, which sponsored development projects and coordinated campaigns. Meanwhile, individual officials were assigned responsibility for delivering the vote in certain provinces, districts, and communes. Ministers sponsored schools. Generals paid for wells. The fact that infrastructure projects were often built with international aid money was generally irrelevant. If Hun Sen cut the ribbon on a project, it became a "Hun Sen project." When an agency like the World Food Programme donated rice, village and commune officials presented it as a gift from the party.

The CPP's vote-harvesting scheme was anchored by the person of the prime minister, now a dominant presence in the media. Like Sihanouk, Hun Sen ruled from the rostrum, using school graduation ceremonies and rural ribbon-cuttings to manipulate the chessboard of Cambodian politics. Hun Sen's speeches were a masterful brew of strongman posturing and frothed-up populist appeal. Unlike many of his foreign-educated opponents, he spoke in a language ordinary people could understand. Audiences of rice farmers would chuckle and laugh as he joked, or jibed, or summoned up the spirits to curse his enemies. He might quote the old Khmer proverb about the ants and the fish, which devour one another when the water levels rise and fall. Or he might mention the "necktie fortune-tellers" who came from abroad, lectured Cambodians about democracy, and then disappeared again.[32]

Watching Hun Sen work the crowd on a trip in Siem Reap, Ambassador Ray was reminded of a Chicago ward politician making his rounds: "He would take his shoes off, roll his pants legs up and wade out into a rice paddy with the farmers and sit in their huts with them . . . He was at ease in crowds." The whole exercise—from god-like helicopter descent to the distribution of gifts—drew heavily on Sihanouk's modus operandi. The main difference was that Sihanouk had inspired genuine devotion in his "children." Hun Sen's visits were more staged. And they were always accompanied by a hint of menace.

When asked about his political philosophy, Hun Sen once said that it was to "know reality."[33] And indeed, his firm grasp on the fears and yearnings of rural people allowed him to exploit them to great political effect. The CPP's campaigns teased out the instinctual conservatism of a population traumatized and worn out by decades of conflict. Constant references to Pol Pot kept people in fear, grateful for the peace, stability, and basic development brought by the CPP's rule. Hun Sen reminded people not to take these things for granted. The country was only ever a whisker away from chaos. Only a vote for the CPP, delivered loyally at each election, could protect the country from slipping back into the abyss.

With memories of war still fresh, it was a winning strategy. The CPP dominated the 2002 commune poll, winning 68.4 percent of the seats and retaining all but a handful of the country's 1,621 commune chief positions. As the results rolled in, international observers from the donor countries signed off on the process in the usual hollow language of "progress" and "challenges." The UN Development Programme (UNDP), which had helped devise the commune election law and was eager to declare its intervention a success, declared that the National Election Committee had "produced a credible election under difficult circumstances."[34] Those difficult circumstances, of course, were a direct outgrowth of CPP policy. But by the bloody standards of past elections, donor agencies could claim a marginal improvement.

Shortly afterward, in an address to the National Press Club in Washington, Rainsy made an impassioned call for "international standards in Cambodia," lamenting that the world always seemed to accept state-sponsored intimidation, violence, and electoral manipulation, "so long as it is always a little less than the last time."[35] In response, Hun Sen shot back: "What are international standards? I don't understand. International standards exist only in sports."[36]

For Funcinpec, the 2002 commune elections were a disaster. Concerned about its "lapdog" status, Ranariddh had rearranged the deck-chairs, welcoming Prince Sirivudh back as secretary-general and shuffling his cabinet. The new-look party hoped to win 40 percent of the vote.[37] When it failed to achieve even half that amount, Funcinpec began to disintegrate. Royalist officials resigned, spawning a school of electoral minnows like the "Hang Dara Movement" and the "Norodom Chakrapong Khmer Spirit Party." The more principled members of the party joined Sam Rainsy or entered civil society. Among the most prominent of these was the Funcinpec senator Kem Sokha, who quit the party in late 2002 and became the founding director of the Cambodian Center for Human Rights, set up by IRI with $450,000 in USAID funds. Many more royalists joined Hun Sen, who guaranteed them government posts and secure perches in the party's patronage tree. "I lost faith in the Funcinpec leadership," said one former royalist minister who defected to the ruling party. "It was so bad already, I didn't want to get my name tainted."

Besieged by inducements and threats, Funcinpec stumbled in the national elections held in July 2003. The party won just 20.8 percent of the vote, slipping back to third place behind the SRP, which won a respectable 21.9 percent. Now the CPP was truly dominant, winning 47.3 percent and boosting its share of National Assembly seats to 73 out of 123. But since the CPP still fell just shy of the two-thirds majority required to form a government, Ranariddh and Rainsy were given another chance to pressure Hun Sen with the threat of political deadlock. The election was followed by nearly a year of stalemate and political gymnastics as Sihanouk and the three parties attempted to hammer out yet another coalition deal. As in 1998, Ranariddh and Rainsy joined hands—this time they called themselves the "Alliance of Democrats"—and pressed for concessions. Chief among their demands was the reform of the NEC and the sharing of power at the village level. More provocatively, they called for Hun Sen and his powerful right-hand man, Sok An, to step down. Rainsy proposed a new coalition be formed under Chea Sim, presumably hoping to divide the CPP along factional lines.

Rainsy's strategy was never likely to succeed. Hun Sen laid out the usual assortment of carrots and sticks. To lure them back into government, he promised new jobs for Ranariddh's men at every level of government. Some Funcinpec officials could literally not afford to stand on principle. During the 2003 election, CPP-aligned tycoons had bankrolled the campaigns of a number of royalist politicians, saddling them with debts and obligations that they could only pay back by securing lucrative government posts. Steve Heder described the party as "a partly-owned subsidiary of the CPP and its tycoons," a fact which alienated the younger, more idealistic politicians in the SRP.[38] As the negotiations dragged on, Cambodia effectively had no functioning government. But since the government did so little for the people in any case, most of the country barely noticed.

Om Radsady was not a man given to extravagance. He lived modestly and drove a beat-up old car. Everyone who knew him described him as generous, humble, and warm-hearted. In fact, if there was one Cambodian politician who could convincingly claim to be uncorrupted by his office, it was Radsady. Radsady, who had served as a member of parliament with Funcinpec from 1993 to 1998, often ate at a small restaurant a short walk across the park from the National Assembly building, near the Kabko Market. It was a popular place, which served simple Khmer dishes and chipped pots of jasmine tea under brightly colored plastic awnings.

At noon on February 18, 2003, Radsady had just finished a meal at his usual spot when an unknown assailant walked up and shot him several times in the chest. After walking away, the killer calmly returned to take Radsady's mobile phone, to provide "evidence" for later claims that the killing was motivated by robbery. The killer escaped on a motorbike. Radsady died four hours later. Ira Dassa, Keith Schulz, Evan Gottesman, and Brad Adams, four legal consultants who had worked with Radsady during his time in parliament, penned a moving eulogy in the pages of the *Phnom Penh Post*: "It's hard to imagine a more unlikely target for an assassin's bullet ... The irony that someone as gentle and open to discussion as Radsady was silenced in such a violent way is beyond contemplation."[39] Two soldiers were arrested and confessed to the "robbery." Rights groups claimed they were scapegoats; even the Ministry of Interior didn't believe the official story. It formed an emergency committee to investigate the killing further, but little progress was ever made.[40] In October, the two were sentenced to 20 years prison for the shooting. One SRP lawmaker described the trial as "a show."[41]

Om Radsady's lunchtime killing was just one of a string of political homicides that marked the run-up and aftermath of the 2003 election.[42] Two weeks earlier, the monk Sam Bunthoeun, who had agitated against a voting ban for monks, was gunned down outside Wat Lanka. In October, with the three main parties locked in coalition talks, motorcycle assassins shot Chuor Chetharith, the news director of Funcinpec's Ta Prohm radio station, not long after Hun Sen criticized its "insulting" broadcasts. A few days later, armed thugs wounded karaoke star Touch Srey Nich, who had performed in a song that was used in Funcinpec's election campaign. The highest profile victim was Chea Vichea, a popular trade unionist and SRP supporter who was shot in early 2004 while buying a newspaper outside a *wat* in Phnom Penh. (The Sam Bunthoeun and Chea Vichea cases are explored further in Chapter 10.)

It was against this menacing backdrop that Prince Ranariddh again agreed to enter government with the CPP. The arrangement, signed by the two parties in June 2004, was a rerun of the 1993 and 1998 coalition deals, but this time on terms even less favorable to Ranariddh's camp. To keep the royalists happy, more than 160 new positions were added to the bloated cabinet, which now totaled 7 deputy prime ministers, 15 senior ministers, 28 ministers, 135 secretaries of state, and 146 undersecretaries of state scattered across 26 ministries. Hundreds of additional posts were created at the district and provincial levels.[43] To sweeten the deal for Ranariddh, the CPP also tossed in a brand-new French Aérospatiale Alouette II helicopter and returned a private jet that had been seized by the authorities in July 1997.[44] Sam Rainsy, once again, was left at the altar.

Just one obstacle for Hun Sen remained. The CPP–Funcinpec deal required a tricky legislative workaround known as a "package vote," which would allow the National Assembly to approve the new legislative and executive appointments with a single show of hands. This was contrary to the Constitution (which required two separate votes), and an amendment would be necessary before the vote could take place. The package vote was opposed by the SRP and more staunchly by Sihanouk, who had grown frustrated at being sidelined and ignored during the postelection negotiations. The king's proposal for a three-party agreement was dismissed, as was his suggestion for a popular referendum on the package vote. The 81-year-old monarch eventually threw up his hands in disgust. In early 2004, he branded the deadlock "a ridiculous comedy" and flew to Beijing for medical treatment.[45] Political leaders refused a further royal summons to North Korea in May to break the political impasse.

As an embittered Sihanouk retreated to the lakes and vales of Changsuwon, refusing to return and sign the package vote amendment, he dispatched an open letter calling on acting head of state Chea Sim to follow his "conscience" in deciding whether to sign the bill—something that was largely taken for granted. But the Senate president, to widespread surprise, also chose to abstain. Hun Sen, enraged by Chea Sim's defiance, took decisive action. On July 13, scores of riot police commanded by Hok Lundy surrounded Chea Sim's home in Phnom Penh and escorted him under armed guard to the airport, where he was put on a plane to Bangkok.

The official story was that Chea Sim had left the country for "medical treatment." Few believed it. Rainsy and others said Hun Sen had presented him with a choice: sign the package vote amendment or leave town.[46] The decision was made for him. With Chea Sim out of the way, Funcinpec's Nhek Bun Chhay—deputy president of the Senate and next in line as acting head of state—stepped in and signed the controversial amendment. The National Assembly convened and a new government was formed. SRP lawmakers boycotted the vote in protest. From his aerie in the North Korean hills, Sihanouk denounced the new government as an "anti-Constitutional, anti-Democratic, anti-Royalty 'Coup d'État.' "[47]

Chea Sim's forced departure formed a bizarre coda to a year of stalemate. It was also a rare public display of the rift within the CPP. If the party had learned anything from its Vietnamese mentors, it was the importance of maintaining a fierce internal discipline and presenting an unbreakable front. But in 2004, as during the "coup" attempt of 1994, divisions briefly emerged into the open. The disagreement, as ever, was about power and privilege. Chea Sim was apparently unhappy with the new coalition deal, which had left many of his protégés out in the cold.[48] Nine days later, he returned to Cambodia, and the same armed reception that had seen him off. The humiliating episode capped off the erosion of his power since the mid-1980s, and cemented Hun Sen at the apex of both party and government. After suffering a stroke in late 2000, the 71-year-old party president no longer had the vim or clout to oppose his energetic younger rival.

Chea Sim wasn't the only one fuming over the new power-sharing pact. Speaking to Voice of America after the formation of the new government in mid-2004, Sam Rainsy denounced Ranariddh's shift "from white to black" and accused him of taking bribes from the CPP to join government. Ranariddh responded that he had joined the coalition in order "to serve the nation" and save it from paralysis.[49] Whatever his motivation, the deal was strongly criticized within Funcinpec, and more party members resigned in protest. Once a robust source of opposition, the party had now become little more than an empty shell of patronage, clinging barnacle-like to Hun Sen's steaming ship of state. Mu Sochua, who served as Funcinpec's minister of women's affairs before quitting and joining the SRP in August 2004, said the party no longer had any clear strategy or political platform. "I didn't see the prince moving further," she said. "It was so painful how Rainsy had to beg the prince to put national interests first."

On October 7, 2004, King Sihanouk announced that he was abdicating the throne. At first it was hard to tell if he meant it. Threatening to quit had been a signature move since Sihanouk's early years in power, and many people assumed he was hoping for a national outpouring of support that would "force" him to remain on the throne. But this time Sihanouk wasn't bluffing. He was plagued by health problems, including cancer and hypertension, and was worn out by years of political wrangling with Hun Sen, who had effectively elbowed him from center stage. Frustrated and defeated, Sihanouk had decided to go out on his own terms.

His successor as king was Norodom Sihamoni, his son by Queen Monineath, a 51-year-old, Czech-educated former ballet dancer who had served as Cambodia's ambassador to UNESCO. The graceful ascension ceremonies, a paean to age-old Hindu and Buddhist tradition, gave another brief respite from the contortions of Cambodian political life. On October 28, under a full moon, Brahmin priests offered prayers to the *devadas*. The next day, Sihanouk and Monineath bathed their son with water taken from Phnom Kulen in Siem Reap, where King Jayavarman II first proclaimed the independence of the Khmer Empire from Java in the ninth century. The new king, clad in a white jacket laced with gold thread, was borne through the gardens of the Royal Palace on a golden palanquin. Surrounded by silk-clad guards, Buddhist monks, and women carrying miniature silver trees, the king entered the royal throne room, where he was greeted by the prime minister, Cambodian officials, and foreign diplomats.

After elaborate rituals in which the shaven-headed Sihamoni lit candles amid the ministrations of a Brahmin *baku*, a vestige of Cambodia's Indic heritage, he addressed the assembly. "As from this happy and solemn occasion," he promised, "I shall devote my body and soul to the services of the people and the nation, pursuing the exceptional work accomplished by my august father, grandfather, and great-grandfather." Palace heralds blew three bursts on conch shells and fireworks burst above the city, casting a colorful reflection on the churning confluence of the Mekong and the Tonlé Sap.[50]

The coronation ceremonies gave an illusion of continuity, but in truth Sihamoni's coronation marked a deep rupture. Sihanouk's abdication was a tacit acknowledgment that he no longer had the energy for the political fray. For the CPP, it was a moment of quiet victory. Since Sihanouk's return to Cambodia in 1991, Hun Sen and the CPP leadership had seen the wily monarch as the greatest long-term challenge to their power. The king was too symbolic to be challenged directly, and too revered by the party's rural base. And so the party did the easiest thing, and simply claimed Sihanouk's legacy for itself.

In November 1991, it organized a lavish welcoming ceremony for Sihanouk. After years of excoriating Sihanouk as a feudal reactionary, the CPP started asserting that it was the "little brother" of his Sangkum regime.[51] At the monarch's suggestion, Kampong Som returned to its pre-1970 name of Sihanoukville and the boulevards of the capital regained their Sangkum-era titles, including the only Mao Tse Toung Boulevard in the world outside of China.[52] Cambodia's flag, official crest, national anthem, and army uniforms were all modeled after those of the 1950s and 1960s. But while Hun Sen gladly adopted the trappings of Sihanoukism—just as he adopted the trappings of democracy—he never relinquished the reins of power. Sihanouk's ambitions would be confined to the ceremonial roles laid down in the 1993 Constitution. The "Father of the Nation," as he was now termed, was to remain strictly "above" politics.

What resulted was an understated game of cat and mouse, in which Sihanouk sought to extend his power and the CPP sought quietly to rein it in. When the CPP–Funcinpec coalition fell apart in early 1996, the monarchy came under attack as part of a supposed royal "plot" against Hun Sen, and the CPP press published articles criticizing Sihanouk and justifying the 1970 coup. Speaking to *Le Monde* during a trip to France in April of that year, Sihanouk remarked that he was "surrounded by spies" in Phnom Penh.[53] While the king was away, Hun Sen took the opportunity to establish diplomatic relations with South Korea. A relationship with Seoul was clearly in Cambodia's best interests, but it was also a calculated repudiation of a promise Sihanouk had once made to Kim Il-sung that as long as he lived, Cambodia would never recognize South Korea. Shortly afterwards the king lashed out at "the rapaciousness of small local tyrants" scheming to win "absolute power while making a reign of terror."[54]

The factional fighting of July 1997 marked a sharp decline in Sihanouk's influence. Prince Ranariddh and his father were never close, but the relationship between the two deteriorated as Ranariddh moved into direct confrontation with Hun Sen. Resentful and determined to strike out from his father's long shadow, Ranariddh frequently ignored the wishes of the king. From Sihanouk's perspective, Ranariddh, the royalist *dauphin*, had been a great disappointment. Tony Kevin recalled that Sihanouk "despised his son—despised him. There was no great love for Ranariddh ever." Funcinpec's poor performance in the 2003 elections only deepened the monarch's disenchantment. To Sihanouk's dismay, Cambodian voters no longer associated the party with his legacy—only with the corrupt and ineffective royalist party establishment.

Frustrated and bitter, Sihanouk spent most of his time in Beijing, dispatching caustic missives back to his homeland. Through a "Monthly Documentation Bulletin" issued by the Royal Palace, the king kept up a written commentary on Cambodian affairs. The bulletin was a blend of royal correspondence, scrapbook reminiscences, and political musings, all written out in an elegant French longhand punctuated with exclamation points and emphatic underlinings. Sihanouk's commentary was boisterous and ironic, but beneath the surface it was laced with the pride and sorrow of a king who knew his best days were behind him. One moment Sihanouk would shower Hun Sen with sarcastic praise, describing him as "our Great Leader, 'clairvoyant, intelligent, perspicacious, exceptional.' " The next he would grow melancholy, scrawling laments and sour commentary in the margins of clipped newspaper reports:

A political candidate is shot dead—"Again, an assassination."

Ship registrations are sold by corrupt officials—"This is scandalous and miserable."

A woman poisons her husband with battery acid—"Another scene of violence and cruelty. We are in full decadence, alas!"[55]

Many of Sihanouk's criticisms appeared under the pseudonym Ruom Rith, a supposed childhood friend of the king's who began "corresponding" with him in the mid-1990s from his home in the Pyrenees in southern France. Rith, who was around the same age as Sihanouk and "shared" his distinctive writing style and nostalgic bent, rarely pulled his punches. His letters denounced government corruption and ventriloquized Sihanouk's well-known views on issues like poverty, political violence, and the "super-rich mafias" who backed Hun Sen.[56] Angered by the interjections of his fictional interlocutor, Hun Sen would call him out in public speeches. "Who is Ruom Rith?" he asked in 2003, after a particularly scathing series of messages. "How does he know how to write such smart letters, as if he lived here and knew everything that goes on?"[57] Hun Sen knew perfectly well who Rith was, of course, but never directly accused Sihanouk of responsibility for the letters. Neither would Sihanouk admit it. He responded by politely apologizing for his "friend's" excesses.

At times, the jousting between Hun Sen and Sihanouk took on an almost playful tone. They had a clear mutual respect. Sihanouk admired Hun Sen's political ability, while Hun Sen recognized the symbolic power of the monarchy and flattered Sihanouk by imitating many of his political tactics, from his theatrical rural excursions to the crafty manipulation of his political foes. Chhang Song, who served in Sihanouk's administration in the 1960s and later became a senator under Hun Sen, said the latter grew "more and more" like Sihanouk as time went by, while Sihanouk frequently described Hun Sen as his "true political son." One former Asian diplomat recalled Sihanouk saying, "I wish Hun Sen was my son. Ranariddh is my Kim Jong-il."

On certain issues, however, the two men clashed. In 2002, they started sparring publicly over the issue of the royal succession. According to the Constitution, there was no heir apparent to the Cambodian throne. When a king died or abdicated, his successor was to be selected from among members of the three royal blood lines by a nine-member Throne Council, a body that included the prime minister, the presidents of the National Assembly and Senate and their four deputies, and the leaders of the two Buddhist sects. But the law regulating the council's activities had never been passed, and Sihanouk, dogged by ill-health, worried that if he died suddenly the CPP might manipulate the process to put a "puppet king" in his place.

In 2002, Sihanouk called for the government to pass a law regulating the procedures for succession. Hun Sen refused, and Sihanouk again threatened to abdicate. When one member of the royal family suggested that the next king be elected by popular referendum, Hun Sen warned royalist politicians not to "wander too far" lest they "stumble into Hell."[58] He claimed a central role in returning Sihanouk to the throne in 1993, and said he would also determine who would succeed him. "I have no right to be the king," he boasted in a 2002 radio address, "but I have the right to create a king."[59] As the issue festered, Sihanouk issued a press release accusing Hun Sen of turning Cambodia into a "beggar nation" dependent on foreign handouts. Hun Sen shot back with a criticism of the Royal Palace's $5 million in annual expenditures.[60] Some members of the royal family worried that if the clashes continued, Hun Sen might abolish the monarchy in a fit of pique, something he had reportedly considered doing in July 1997.[61]

Eventually Sihanouk decided to step aside voluntarily, hoping to retain some say in who would take the throne. Before his abdication, he worked tirelessly with Hun Sen and other officials to anoint a successor. It had long been assumed that this would be Ranariddh, his second-eldest son, but Hun Sen controlled the Throne Council and wouldn't countenance a political prince taking the throne. Prince Sihamoni, on the other hand, was an attractive option. Unlike Ranariddh, he had no heirs and no apparent political ambitions. He was also the preferred choice of Monineath, his mother, who hated Ranariddh and was known to exercise a strong influence over her husband. When the Throne Council met on October 14 to nominate Sihanouk's successor, it took just 40 minutes to reach its decision.

Sihamoni suited every party—except one. Publicly, Ranariddh had supported his half-brother's accession, but it was clear he was angry at being overlooked. In a cable from the US embassy, Ambassador Ray described Ranariddh's "childish and petulant" behavior in the lead-up to Sihamoni's coronation. On October 28, Ranariddh found the palace gates closed in his face when he attempted to follow the new king's motorcade into the grounds. In rage and embarrassment, Ranariddh ordered the dismissal of the palace's head of security. The man had merely been doing his job; according to palace protocol, only the king, prime minister, and visiting heads of state were permitted to use the entrance. A few days later, Ranariddh failed to attend a Buddhist coronation ceremony for royals. One source close to the palace also recalled that in the first days of Sihamoni's reign, Ranariddh addressed him as "my cousin" rather than using kingly honorifics—a *faux pas* that scandalized the royal family. "Rather than raising his stature, [Ranariddh] is increasingly making himself a laughing stock," Ray wrote. "King Sihamoni's reserved and respectful behavior, by contrast, seems quite regal indeed."[62]

As Sihanouk entered a mournful retirement, his stream of commentary continued, much of it now posted on his website. His correspondence even saw the appearance of a new pen-pal alter ego, a certain "Ruom Rith, Jr." But the old monarch now spent the majority of his time outside the country, ostensibly for medical treatment, and he slowly faded from Cambodia's political life. Nominating Sihamoni as his successor was to be his last significant political act. It ensured the survival of the monarchy into a limited and uncertain future, but also gave Hun Sen and the CPP what they had always wanted—a king who would steer clear of politics. Sihamoni inhabited the Royal Palace, but it was Hun Sen, unbound for the time being by effective opposition, who would rule.

With Sihanouk out of the way and the royalists neutralized, Hun Sen turned his sights on his last real rival, Sam Rainsy. As the price of its access to lucrative government positions, Prince Ranariddh had agreed to aid the CPP in its efforts to split and sideline the SRP. One official described the strategy as "squeezing their membership at the bottom and scaring their leadership at the top." By late 2004, the CPP's attention had turned to the SRP's "shadow" cabinet, which monitored government ministries and collected sensitive information on their activities. A particular target was Cheam Channy, the SRP's shadow defense minister, whose wide network of military informants was proving a particular embarrassment for Hun Sen. But while SRP shadow interior minister Ou Bun Long fearfully jumped ship to Funcinpec, Channy refused to turn. So Hun Sen's military intelligence chief Mol Roeup cooked up a story that Channy's informants constituted a "secret army" seeking the overthrow of the government.[63]

Rainsy, meanwhile, was being squeezed in the courts. Hun Sen sued him for defamation after Rainsy accused the prime minister of responsibility for the March 1997 grenade attack, and Ranariddh filed a separate suit challenging claims he had taken bribes to join the new government. On February 3, 2005, the National Assembly voted to suspend the parliamentary immunity of both Rainsy and Channy, as well as their party colleague Chea Poch, who had also accused Ranariddh of pocketing payoffs. Rainsy and Poch fled the country; Channy was snared and locked up in a military prison.

The trials that followed were episodes in crude political theater. In August, a military tribunal found Channy guilty of trying to form an "illegal army" to topple the government and sentenced him to seven years' jail. No evidence was presented to substantiate the accusations and Channy pleaded to the judges that he had "never done anything even close to what the charges against me say."[64] Four months later, Rainsy himself was found guilty of criminal defamation and sentenced in absentia to 18 months in prison. From his bolt-hole in Paris, the SRP leader thundered that Cambodia was becoming "more and more like a fascist state" and slammed Funcinpec for doing "whatever the CPP tells them."[65]

The attacks on the SRP were accompanied by the opening of a second front against Cambodian civil society. In October 2005, police arrested Mam Sonando, an independent radio broadcaster, and Rong Chhun, the head of an independent teachers union. Both were accused of criticizing a new supplemental border treaty with Vietnam, which, like its predecessor treaties in the 1980s, had been widely attacked for ceding territory along the country's eastern border. Three more arrests followed. Yeng Virak, an activist with the Community Legal Education Center, was detained on New Year's Eve and hauled before an ashen-faced judge at the municipal court, who fumbled through papers bearing the stamp of Hun Sen's lawyers. "The investigating judge was so pale, he was like he had almost fainted for handling these cases," Virak later told me. While he was being questioned, a police officer poked his head through the door and asked the judge if Virak's wife could come in and say goodbye to her husband. The judge hadn't yet announced whether Virak would be jailed and tried, but it was now clear that everybody was reading from a prepared script. The decision to lock him up had already been made.

Civil society leapt to the defense of the five dissidents. Rights activists formed an Alliance for Freedom of Expression and yellow ribbons were handed out and worn in solidarity. Western diplomats made public statements conjuring up the specter of Burma-style isolation and pariah status. Since UNTAC, Cambodia's flourishing civil society had been mostly insulated from government attacks. Now Hun Sen had apparently crossed a red line. "It is bad news for Cambodia, and will affect it both in the field of tourism and in garment exports," predicted one foreign diplomat.[66] US Ambassador Joseph Mussomeli was more outspoken: "When governments are afraid they do stupid things," he told the press, "and to do this is really stupid." Cambodia, he later said, had to "decide whether it's going to be a real democracy or whether it's going to move inexorably toward a one-party state."[67]

As international pressure mounted, Hun Sen appeared to relent. A few days after Mussomeli spoke out against at the arrests, American officials learned that Hun Sen was willing to release the group of activists. All he needed, Mussomeli later told me, was "a pretext to back down. We were eager to help him find one." The timing was propitious. Two weeks later, US Assistant Secretary of State Christopher Hill was scheduled to visit Phnom Penh to inaugurate a new $47 million US embassy compound in Phnom Penh. When Hill arrived, he met Hun Sen and warned him that if he didn't release the shackles, people in Washington would soon start seeing Cambodia as "another Burma."[68] After the meeting with Hill ended, Mussomeli said, "Hun Sen immediately informed us that he would release the three activists as a 'gift' for the new embassy. They were released within an hour."

Overnight, the political climate thawed. Sam Rainsy sent letters to Ranariddh and Hun Sen expressing regret for his "defamatory" comments and promising to stop blaming Hun Sen for the 1997 grenade attack. In return, he received a royal amnesty and was mobbed by supporters at the airport when he returned on February 10, 2006. Cheam Channy was released from prison, and the charges against the five civil society leaders were dropped after they wrote their own letters of "apology." Observers scrambled to explain the government's apparent about-face. Had Hun Sen capitulated to Western and US pressure? Had he finally decided to loosen his grip? The reconciliation had gone farther than even many government critics had expected. Rainsy himself hailed a "new chapter in Cambodian history" and said his country's politicians were finally "seeing the light."[69]

But had anything really changed? Despite the threats of foreign governments, there had been little cost for Hun Sen, who presented the release of the dissidents as an act of generosity. This, too, was a mirage. Instead of advancing democratic principles the outcome had reinforced the notion that democracy was an indulgence of those in power. "Just as the human rights activists were arrested with impunity," the Cambodian development specialist Sophal Ear wrote, "they were also released with impunity."[70] Hun Sen's political timing, as always, was exquisite. He reaped political benefits twice, first in the repression and then in the loosening. Yeng Virak described it as a "win-win" strategy: "Not 'you win, and I win,' " he said. "It's like, 'I win now, and I win later.' "

CHAPTER SIX

The Peasant King

We heard Hun Sen's helicopter long before we saw it—a sleek black dragonfly roaring over the tree line. Old peasant women shielded their faces with *kramas* as the craft turned, banked in a blue sky, and descended in a maelstrom of dust. As soon as it touched down, a door swung open and Cambodia's prime minister stepped into the sunshine. Hun Sen was dressed in gray military pajamas, and wore gold glasses perched beneath neatly parted hair. The screech of the rotor blade gave way to triumphant music as Hun Sen smiled and walked forward into a confected carnival scene celebrating his arrival. "Welcome Samdech Hun Sen!" a voice intoned over the music, employing his official honorific. "Long Live Samdech Hun Sen!" Students and rural folk who had waited for hours under plastic marquees rose respectfully for the Cambodian national anthem, a scratchy recording made in Sihanouk's time. Monks droned and chanted. Hun Sen mounted the stage and gripped the lectern. The master of ceremonies announced, "We are all very fortunate to live in the Samdech Techo era!"

In the Svay Antor district of Prey Veng, a hot dry heartland stretching from the Mekong to the Vietnamese border, Operation Hun Sen was more exciting than anything that had happened in a long while. All morning local people had bumped along dusty village roads to see the prime minister cut the ribbon on a new Buddhist *wat*—a candy-colored structure rising from a nearby hill. Security was tight. Police and other heavies with curly earpiece radios set up a cordon, using airport hand-scanners on grizzled rice farmers and barefoot children in Angry Birds T-shirts. One district official stood nearby, wearing a white CPP baseball cap and holding a two-way radio. He explained that the trip took a week for local authorities to prepare, during which marquees were assembled and billboards of Hun Sen were erected. "Prime Minister Hun Sen came once before, in 1998," he remembered, "and every commune got a school."

Pich Ran, a 62-year-old rice farmer with a mouth half-full of gold teeth, drove his beat-up Daelim scooter six kilometers to attend the event. "I wanted to see him for real, not only on TV," he said as we crouched in the shade, waiting for Hun Sen to descend. When I asked Ran about what the prime minister had done for the local area, he reeled off the usual list: schools, pagodas, roads, hospitals. Ran seemed like a true believer. He explained that Hun Sen's immense wealth stemmed from all the good he did for the people. "He's built a lot of pagodas and he respects the monks," Ran said. "According to Buddhist beliefs, when you do something there are consequences. Hun Sen is richer because maybe in the past he did good things. And the poor people maybe did bad."

Hun Sen spoke for over an hour. His bodyguards killed time by posing for photos in front of his helicopter, while other onlookers squatted beneath the sugar palms, snacking on lotus seeds and bags of green sugar cane juice. We all listened as an amplified Hun Sen started off with one of his favorite themes: his own life story. "I have some very pleasant memories of Prey Veng," he informed his audience. "I also stayed and lived in a pagoda . . ." This thought progressed naturally to a discussion of his own modest achievements in the field of pagoda-building. Hun Sen said that the CPP supported every one of Cambodia's pagodas—all 4,676 of them. And then there were schools. In Prey Veng alone there were 259 "Hun Sen schools."

Warming to his theme, Hun Sen announced a donation of large wax candles for Bon Tean Var Sa, an annual rainy season festival, traditionally patronized by the monarchy, in which Buddhist monks kept candles burning continuously for three months. He then discoursed on Thai politics and the recent developments on the Korean peninsula. His speech finished in the usual way. After running through a list of requests from community leaders for schools, pagodas, and other vital services, he triumphantly delivered his catchphrase, *choun tam samnompor*, meaning "granted according to your request."

Turning to the line of officials seated on the stage behind him, Hun Sen told the people whom to thank for the generous donations. Interior Minister Sar Kheng, sitting stiffly, had paid for the renovation of the pagoda, now a freshly painted riot of pinks and greens. A high-ranking general would pay for a brick wall. A nearby school building was generously donated by the National Police Chief, Neth Savoeun, who sat sweating in a uniform covered with medals. At Hun Sen's "request," the people of Prey Veng got all of these things—a miraculous intercession that, like all the prime minister's speeches, was broadcast out on state television. "I don't give 'air promises,' " Hun Sen said. "I give you reality."

The ceremony climaxed with the cutting of a ribbon and the distribution of additional gifts—books and pencils for students, wads of cash for scouts and teachers and health workers. There was more fanfare. Pop songs blared and slogans extolled the "heroic Samdech Techo era." Cambodia's prime minister then walked through the crowd, his hands pressed together in a *sompeah* of greeting, and returned to his helicopter, which crouched in the sun, its rotors sagging like giant black antennae. He gave one last wave before the door snapped squarely shut. Then the great beast whined, rose on a storm of dust, and bore the Peasant King, retinue and all, back to Olympus.

As Hun Sen marked his twentieth year in power in January 2005, few real sources of opposition remained. His rivals were cowed and his grip on the levers of power seemingly secure. At the CPP's annual congress that month, when the party expanded its Central Committee from 153 to 268 members, Hun Sen filled the vacancies with a new generation of loyalists who shored up his position in the party. The same happened later in the year when the party added eight new seats to the Politburo, making it a body of 28 members now mostly loyal to Hun Sen.[1] Then, in November, the party named Hun Sen the sole prime ministerial candidate for the 2008 national election. Unlike in 2003 and 2004, when rumors swirled that the party might choose a different candidate, Hun Sen was now the undisputed party leader.

By now, Cambodia's prime minister was an all-pervading presence in the media, his ribbon-cuttings and rural speeches cramming the airwaves. At donor fora he used the buzz words of "sustainability" and "capacity building." On his rural speaking-tours he threatened opponents, dispensed folktales, lambasted the UN, and kept farming communities up to date on his political feuds and other passing obsessions. "I know all," he warned opponents in a 2006 address. "Even if you farted, I would still know. You cannot hide from me."[2]

The core of Hun Sen's power was the Council of Ministers, run with many-armed effectiveness by Senior Minister Sok An, who had worked under Hun Sen at the Foreign Ministry during the 1980s. With the decline of Funcinpec, Sok An was given control of so many authorities, committees, and commissions that he was likened to a Hindu god with 48 arms.[3] The CPP's bureaucratic Kali oversaw financial reform, demobilization, rural electrification, and the management of the Angkor temples. He was silver-tongued during the donor aid conferences. He controlled the national petroleum authority, a technological development body, and the task force for the trial of surviving Khmer Rouge leaders. If something was important, Sok An had a hand in it.

With Sok An running the government, Hun Sen focused on the wider political game. When not overseas, he remained at the Tiger's Lair, obsessively plotting the downfall of those who still dared defy him. In this he suddenly found an unlikely ally in Sam Rainsy. In March 2006, during the short period of reconciliation that had followed Rainsy's return from exile, the SRP sponsored a constitutional amendment reducing the two-thirds majority required to form government to a simple majority of 50 percent. Rainsy explained that the amendment would remove an outdated restriction and hopefully put victory within closer reach of his own party. But there was also another motive. "I wanted to get rid of Funcinpec," he told me. "The CPP used Ranariddh to create problems for me ... They had some influence because they used the two-thirds majority; so I said, to hell with the two-thirds majority." The amendment duly passed, and the CPP no longer had any need for a coalition partner. Funcinpec and its leader were suddenly surplus to requirements.

The purge began immediately. Hun Sen fired Funcinpec's co-interior and co-defense ministers, giving the portfolios solely to his own men. Ranariddh responded by resigning his post as National Assembly president, supposedly to concentrate on party matters, and retreated to the lecture halls of Aix. The CPP–Funcinpec coalition, a partnership only ever held together by threats and inducements, had finally collapsed. Along with it went the remainder of the royalists' unity. Rainsy's amendment had spelled the end for Norodom Ranariddh; it also allowed Hun Sen to sweep away the last pretenses of power-sharing.

Funcinpec collapsed into in-fighting. The prince's dwindling camp faced off against a faction of CPP accommodationists led by Nhek Bun Chhay, whom Hun Sen had rewarded with an appointment as deputy prime minister. The two sides traded accusations of treachery and vied for control of the party. Hun Sen, professing to be incensed that Ranariddh's mistress, a former royal ballet dancer, had used her influence to get friends and family into lucrative posts, called for Ranariddh's removal and said he would only work with Bun Chhay's wing of the party. In a speech, he warned recalcitrant royalists to "prepare their coffins."[4]

In October 2006, Funcinpec's leadership voted to remove Ranariddh as president and replace him with Keo Puth Reasmey, Cambodia's ambassador to Germany and the husband of Sihanouk's youngest daughter. Bun Chhay's bodyguards stormed Ta Prohm, the remaining pro-Ranariddh radio station, which fearfully adopted a CPP-friendly line. Ranariddh, who had spent most of the year overseas, announced the formation of his own Norodom Ranariddh Party (NRP), but his political comeback swiftly ground to a halt in the courts. By year's end he faced one lawsuit from his ex-wife, accusing him of adultery— recently outlawed under a monogamy law tailor-made for Ranariddh—and another from his old party comrades, who accused him of embezzling some

$3.6 million from the sale of the party's former headquarters. In March 2007, from his self-exile in Malaysia, Ranariddh watched as a court found him guilty of the embezzlement charge and sentenced him to 18 months' jail. It was a virtual rerun of Rainsy's exile and conviction in 2005–06. Only the charges differed.

The royalist movement limped in several pieces toward the national election scheduled for mid-2008. With Funcinpec in decline, Rainsy grew bullish about his own prospects of challenging Hun Sen. "In 2008, there will be only two major parties competing against each other," he predicted, "the CPP and SRP—and I put them in that order out of politeness."[5] Held over a month in July, the 2008 election campaign was the most peaceful since 1993. The parties staged colorful processions through Phnom Penh and the provincial towns, the CPP in white, the SRP in blue, the Funcinpecists in swarming royal yellow. Political songs blared from pick-up trucks that rolled down boulevards and dusty backstreets. The Human Rights Party (HRP), formed by Kem Sokha in 2007 after his departure from the Cambodian Center for Human Rights, was represented by a green disk on a gold field. Lon Nol's son Lon Rith even flew in from Fullerton, California, to take his chances at the head of a resuscitated Khmer Republican Party, working out of a tumbledown townhouse where portraits of the old Marshal gazed down from mildewed walls.

On election day, July 27, Cambodians trooped out to *wats*, schools, and other polling stations to cast their votes. On the surface, the process looked peaceful and orderly. But, as ever, this impression was a mirage. Standing under gray skies in a Kampot schoolyard, Van Dara, a local SRP candidate, complained to me about subtle pressures exerted by the CPP officials at the village level: "In 80 percent of polling stations, the commune chief was hanging around. The presence of local authorities is like a threat to the local people." Other monitors recorded small but significant numbers of voters whose names were missing from electoral lists. Most were opposition supporters.

Before the election, journalists and other political observers had speculated about a surge in support for Sam Rainsy's party. But as evening fell, and results began coming in from the provinces, everything pointed to Hun Sen. The official count gave the CPP 58.1 percent of the vote—its largest victory yet. This translated into 90 seats in the National Assembly, compared to the SRP's 26. Not all of this was due to electoral manipulation. Many voters were genuinely satisfied with the stability and development brought by CPP rule. Then, just three weeks before the election, Hun Sen claimed a diplomatic victory when Prasat Preah Vihear, a graceful eleventh-century Angkorian temple perched on a cliff along the Thai border, was inscribed on UNESCO's World Heritage list. The long-awaited listing, made over the objection of Thai nationalists who claimed sovereignty over the temple and its surrounding territory, prompted an outpouring of national pride which Hun Sen rode triumphantly to the polls. The image of the temple featured prominently in the CPP's election campaign.

Prince Ranariddh, meanwhile, had reached the end of the line. Fifteen years after leading the royalists to a stunning electoral victory, his new party won just two seats. Funcinpec won another two. In October, Sihanouk's *dauphin* received a royal amnesty and returned to Cambodia. Speaking to journalists gathered around a dinner table at a Phnom Penh hotel, Ranariddh announced his retirement from politics and said he now wanted to "serve my nation" in another capacity.[6] By engineering Ranariddh's return home, Hun Sen had extracted another quid pro quo: the prince's exit from the political arena.

With Ranariddh off the scene, Sam Rainsy was now ambiguously placed. While his party had just made its largest electoral gain to date, most of the old royalist vote had gone to Hun Sen. The SRP's constituency remained overwhelmingly urban; it had failed to make much headway in the CPP's rural heartland. Rainsy protested that the election result had been skewed by intimidation and voter-list manipulation. Again, international monitors complained of "shortcomings," made "recommendations" for future elections, and applied a reluctant stamp of approval. Again, most of the tampering had taken place long before election day. An EU election monitor in rainy Kampot pinpointed the dilemma. "The elections were free," he told me, "but free for dependent people."

For the first time since the signing of the Paris Agreements, the CPP was in full control of Cambodia. Sihanouk and Ranariddh had retired and Rainsy—spit out like Sihanouk's proverbial cherry pit—was cast back onto the political margins. It had taken 15 years, but the CPP had finally wrenched back the control it had been forced to cede during the UNTAC mission.

Hun Sen had always regarded the UN with contempt. In 2001, he called the UNTAC elections the "worst elections the world has seen in the 21th century," and said Cambodians alone were responsible for the peace that followed.[7] Three years later, he dropped the annual commemoration of the October 23 signing of the Paris Agreements from Cambodia's crowded roster of national holidays. The CPP had finally repudiated a UN intervention for which it had never asked and a democratic project it had always viewed with suspicion. A mirage of democratic constitutionalism obscured a system that operated much as it always had: through the manipulation of money and personal connections. Hun Sen's Cambodia appeared to have reached its apotheosis.

In late 1993, shortly after retaking the throne, Sihanouk had given Hun Sen the title *samdech*, meaning "lord" or "prince." His title quickly sprouted branches and grew into *Samdech Akka Moha Sena Padei Techo Hun Sen*, a page-consuming epithet which ascribed to him the qualities of "Illustrious Prince, Great Supreme Protector, and Famed Warrior." It must have been satisfying for Hun Sen. Since his earliest years in politics, Cambodia's leader had been driven by a deep craving for legitimacy. Hun Sen lacked the divine right of Cambodia's royals and the instant brand recognition of its old political families. He was self-made, and had risen by dint of his sheer ruthless pragmatism and single-minded dedication to the weighing and accumulation of power. When the facts didn't fit his vision of reality, well, so much the worse for the facts.

But simply being in charge was never enough. Each of Hun Sen's victories—over local rivals, over factional foes, over the "international community"—only stoked his hunger for more and greater successes. Year by year, state propaganda described Hun Sen in increasingly superhuman terms—as a military genius, a political mastermind, and "a human being with a golden heart."[8] The trappings of his rule became increasingly royal. He presided over ceremonies traditionally associated with the monarchy. He began awarding his own "royal" ranks. When they ruled over Cambodia, the Angkorian God-Kings took names that ended in the Sanskrit term *varman*, meaning "armor." Sihanouk similarly claimed to have united his people under the "shade" of the Cambodian monarchy. Now it was Hun Sen who stepped into the role of benevolent protector and bringer of peace, raining benisons on a grateful people.

Like the rulers of Angkor, Hun Sen dramatized his great merit through the building of roads, bridges, pagodas, and other infrastructure works. Schools were a particular specialty. The first "Hun Sen school" was built after the 1993 election; by 2010, the prime minister and first lady had bestowed 3,458 schools (totaling 17,931 classrooms) on communes across Cambodia.[9] Schools and other infrastructure works were paid for by the government officials, deep-pocketed tycoons, and other "meritorious benefactors," or *saboraschon*, who accompanied Hun Sen on his rural excursions. (In 2013, state media even reported on the construction of a $700,000 Hun Sen school in Mali in West Africa.)[10] In exchange for rendering unto Hun Sen, Cambodian elites were granted preferential treatment and their place in a taxonomy of florid Sanskrit ranks. Tycoons received the title *oknha*, awarded to anyone who contributed more than $100,000 to "national reconstruction."[11] In premodern times, the *oknha* were envoys appointed by the king, expected to perform a wide variety of duties, take elaborate oaths of loyalty, and present him with regular gifts.[12] The *oknha* performed a similar function under Hun Sen, supporting him with cash and loyalty in return for access to a continuing flow of riches.

Hun Sen's quasi-royal pretensions were bolstered by a burgeoning personality cult, which ran the gamut from gold watches and clocks with the PM's portrait (available in military or civilian flavors) to the ubiquitous party bill-boards, which featured portraits of the "three Samdechs": Hun Sen, Heng Samrin, and Chea Sim. He also appeared frequently in Dear Leader mode, waving out over highways or cradling sheaves of golden rice. The story of Hun Sen's rise from humble beginnings became a bedrock of party mythology. Portraits of Sihanouk, Monineath, and King Sihamoni hung as always from the walls of businesses and government offices, but the prime minister dominated everywhere else. In some government offices and military-owned businesses, the king's image would be eclipsed by a larger portrait of Hun Sen, in army fatigues or mortarboard, striking a strongman pose or accepting one of his countless honorary degrees.

Hun Sen had even begun composing songs. In emulation of Sihanouk, the "songman of Cambodia" was said to jot down lyrics whenever the inspiration seized him—in helicopters, on overseas trips, during late-night work sessions—which were set to music by his aides. At the height of his late 1990s creative "peak," Hun Sen's catalogue ran to dozens of cassette tapes that were sold in markets and beamed out over state radio. To compete with Sihanouk's bursting songbook, Hun Sen produced "The Life of the Pagoda Boy," which told of his difficult early years. Then there were the paeans to Hun Sen's personal charity projects, including a song titled, "In the Shade of the Palm Trees of Kraingyov Development Center."[13]

Moving with the times, the party also began producing karaoke videos praising the prime minister's far-sighted agricultural policies (say) or the boundless charity of Hun Sen and Bun Rany. In one video a singer crooned, "Mother Bun Rany gives us opportunity and destiny, and Father Techo is highly superior and elicits our great gratitude." Another praised Bun Rany as a "great model person," a woman who is "actually made of diamonds and gold."[14] Eventually even Cambodian history was revised and refashioned to support the glorious "Samdech Techo era." After Sihanouk's abdication in 2004, a forgotten legend re-entered public circulation in service of the Hun Sen myth. Between his speeches and ribbon-cuttings, Cambodians began hearing an old tale about a humble temple servant who rose, like their own prime minister, to become king.

By the end of the fifteenth century, a hurricane of change was blowing through the Cambodian kingdom. Angkor was in decline. To the west a new rival had risen, the Siamese kingdom of Ayutthaya, which fanned aggressively out into territories once held by the Khmer empire. In 1431, Siamese troops had swept into Cambodia, plundering Angkor and carting thousands of Khmers westward as prisoners of war. The defeat shook Angkor to its foundations. As the population shrank, the empire's reservoirs and grand irrigation works dried up and were reclaimed by the jungle. A few years later, the royal family abandoned the city and shifted the capital south to Phnom Penh. Kings whose ancestors had commanded a vast empire fought to keep death and chaos at bay.

In 1486, King Thommo Reacha I died and his shrinking kingdom passed to his son, Srey Sukonthor. Sukonthor became an archetypally vain and paranoid ruler. Like many future Cambodian leaders, he was superstitious, prey to mystical reveries and dreams that he sifted over for signs of blessings and premonitions. One night in 1508, the king woke in a sweat. In a dream, he had seen a fire-breathing dragon drive him from his wooden palace and lay waste to the kingdom. At this sign he fell into a depression that none of his aides could dispel.

Sukonthor was soon bewitched by a second vision—this time of two dragons, breathing fire as they circled the head of one of his trusted military commanders, a man named Kan. Kan was of lowly origins, a member of the temple-slave class whose sister served in the king's harem; he was loyal to his monarch and had risen quickly. After the king's nightmare, messengers brought reports of other dark signs from across the kingdom. Summoning his soothsayers, Sukonthor learnt he would be overthrown by a man born, like Kan, in the Year of the Dragon. The portents left no room for doubt. The king schemed to have Kan lured into a fishing boat and killed.

Kan's sister overheard the king's plan, and alerted her brother to the trap. The young commander escaped and fled eastwards to raise an army. In 1512, with tens of thousands of men at his back, Kan returned seeking revenge against Sukonthor. The king fell, cut down by one of his aides, and Kan took power for himself. For the first time in centuries, a commoner sat on the Cambodian throne. Kan took the royal name Srey Chetha, though he is popularly known today as Sdech Kan, or "King Kan." The Khmer chronicles remember Kan as a strong, wise, and benevolent ruler. During his short reign he brought order and prosperity to the realm, and introduced the first Cambodian currency, the *sloeung*, a gold coin inscribed with a scaled dragon.

Just four years into his reign, a new war broke out after Sukonthor's brother Chant Reachea returned from Ayutthaya with Siamese troops to avenge his sibling's death. The ensuing war dragged on for nearly a decade, turning Khmer against Khmer and unleashing another round of bloody retribution. Sdech Kan's forces fought bravely but were gradually overrun. In 1525, Chant Reachea's soldiers cornered the usurper in Pursat and beheaded him, and the rightful heir was restored to the throne. The rebel's reign had lasted just 13 years.[15]

The tale of Sdech Kan is scantily documented, part of the diet of legends and fables that Cambodians consume during childhood. Historically, it has been treated as a cautionary tale—an example of the dangers that can follow the usurpation of the natural social order. But in recent years the story has been revived by a new official cult extolling Kan's achievements and linking them with Prime Minister Hun Sen, who, by subtle implication, is presented as the reincarnation of the lost king. Like many Cambodians, Hun Sen encountered the Sdech Kan tale during his primary school years,[16] and seems to have grown genuinely to identify with it. In rural speeches he has linked Kan's legend to his own well-known life story. Both men were born in the Year of the Dragon, and Kan's origin as a "temple-servant" roughly parallels Hun Sen's time as a pagoda boy. Like Kan, Hun Sen retreated eastwards from an enemy—the Khmer Rouge—and then returned to wreak vengeance on his enemies.

The Sdech Kan tale has far-reaching political significance. As the story of a commoner who rose to topple an unjust king, it provides historical justification for Hun Sen's overthrow of Prince Ranariddh, his eclipse of the Cambodian monarchy, and its replacement with his own stable "reign." In one 2006 speech, Hun Sen praised Kan as a hero-king who "liberated all outcasts under his area of control" and upended Cambodia's hierarchical social structures. Sdech Kan was also a military man, fielding an army of 190,000 soldiers, a force "larger than that of the former State of Cambodia's forces."[17] In the foreword to a 2006 book on Sdech Kan, funded by Hun Sen, he redefined the usurper as "a brilliant hero" of world-historical standing who prefigured Marxist class struggle and the notion of individual rights that inspired the French Revolution.[18] This bizarre revisionism has identified sixteenth-century Cambodia as both a military powerhouse and—a more jarring claim—the global birthplace of democracy. Sdech Kan's death then kicked off centuries of instability that lasted until the late 1990s, when Hun Sen defeated the Khmer Rouge and finally united Cambodia under a single government.[19] Sihanouk and his achievements remain objects of secondary official praise, but it was only Hun Sen—the Peasant King reborn—who brought true peace and unity to the realm.

According to the Swedish political scientist Astrid Norén-Nilsson, the Sdech Kan myth has been disseminated widely by the joint efforts of academics, businessmen, and CPP-controlled media outlets. Obsequious tycoons have commissioned statues of Kan bearing what is clearly the prime minister's face.[20] Hun Sen has funded research into the location of Sdech Kan's supposed capital, which was identified as a temple site in Kampong Cham that has become the subject of extensive redevelopments and infrastructure works.[21] A book on Sdech Kan was published in 2006 and the National Bank of Cambodia has issued commemorative coins modeled on the sixteenth-century *sloeung* currency.[22] A dramatic retelling of the story has even been staged by performers attached to Hun Sen's personal bodyguard unit.[23]

Hun Sen is not the first Cambodian leader who has looked to history for validation. Sihanouk rooted his rule in the Angkorian era, finding in its great temple-building sprees a model for the "socialism" of his rule. Democratic Kampuchea, too, harked back to Angkor's mass-mobilization of human resources, a foreshadowing of its own monstrous forced labor practices. One CPP official described Hun Sen's adoption of the Sdech Kan myth as an expression of his pride that "a normal peasant like him became much more powerful than the king himself." By rooting Hun Sen's rule in Cambodian traditions of kingship, the Sdech Kan story depicted him as the legitimate leader of the country, displacing the legitimacy of Sihanouk and the Cambodian royals once and for all. In another sense, it was an attempt to give his rule an aura of predestination, to fully subsume his country's social and political life within a self-sustaining cosmology of power.

The Peasant King eventually even got his own "palace"—a massive block of concrete and jet-black glass set on Russian Federation Boulevard near Phnom Penh's Art-Deco railway station. The Peace Palace, as it soon became known in English, was unveiled in time for the 2012 ASEAN summit and housed Hun Sen's offices and the Council of Ministers.[24] Built in a neofascist idiom of dominating size and symmetry, the Peace Palace spoke of remote and unaccountable power. Towering over passers-by, it was the perfect embodiment of political life under Hun Sen's reign.

On January 7, 2009, the CPP marked the thirtieth anniversary of the fall of Pol Pot with a lavish ceremony at the Olympic Stadium in Phnom Penh. Fifty thousand people crammed the concrete bleachers as dancers danced, singers sang, and a brass band marched around the 400-meter running track. A well-rehearsed crowd held up colored cards that formed swooping doves of peace and the words *prampi makara*—"January 7." The old party troika of Hun Sen, Chea Sim, and Heng Samrin marked their three-decade dominance of Cambodian politics by cruising the arena in a black Mercedes convertible to the blare of triumphant anthems and a pattering of unspontaneous applause. As always, Victory over Genocide Day brought out its share of detractors who claimed that the fall of Pol Pot wasn't a liberation at all, but rather an occupation by the Vietnamese. Hun Sen wasn't having any of it; those questioning the legitimacy of January 7, he said in a speech, were "animals" and apologists for Pol Pot.[25]

For Hun Sen, the continuing presence of an opposition, however marginalized, remained an affront. Like past Cambodian leaders, his worldview had little place for political opponents or "international standards." The national interest was identified exclusively with his own party's myths and patrimonial systems of control. In this scheme, there was no middle way. Anyone outside the official consensus was considered an unpatriotic wrecker or a stooge of foreign interests; any institution not harmonized with the CPP and its founding myths posed threats to a hard-won peace. Hun Sen's control would only be secure when it managed to subsume and neutralize all alternative sources of power.[26]

For the moment, a mirage of pluralism remained. Human rights monitors working for groups like ADHOC and LICADHO continued churning out reports bravely outlining the government's violation of local laws and UN human rights conventions, but it seemed to make little difference. Hun Sen's system was engineered to absorb and neutralize criticism. The critics were now a harmless part of the scenery, as politically inert as rice paddies or sugar palms.

Sam Rainsy and his party tacked between narrowing political horizons. After the CPP's resounding victory in the 2008 election, lawmakers from the SRP and what was left of Funcinpec were again lured with cash bribes and posts in government. Anchored by the Peasant King and the mythology of January 7, the CPP presented itself to defectors as a big tent in which officials from every party were welcome—as long as they accepted Hun Sen's primacy and divested themselves of old political ambitions. In mid-2009, Rainsy's party produced a recorded telephone conversation in which a CPP commune councillor offered an SRP counterpart "$700 or $800" cash in exchange for voting against his own party in district elections.[27] The party claimed it was just one of dozens—maybe even hundreds—of similar incidents.

Those who refused to be "harmonized" faced the courts. As violence receded in Cambodian politics, government critics were subjected to the tactic of "lawfare," in which accusations of defamation or incitement were leveled by powerful people and then rubber-stamped by pliant judges. Throughout 2009, journalists, human rights defenders, and opposition figures were slapped with lawsuits and hauled into court. One of those was Mu Sochua, the most prominent woman in the SRP, and one of its most charismatic parliamentarians. As minister of women's affairs under Funcinpec, the Berkeley-educated Sochua had campaigned tirelessly against human trafficking and child abuse, and fought to secure living wages for female workers. She also helped draft a law against domestic violence that was passed in 2005.

In April 2009, during a speech in Kampot, Hun Sen referred to Sochua as *jeung klang*, or "strong legs"—a term with demeaning connotations when used toward women. Sochua responded by suing Hun Sen for defamation. What happened next was like something straight out of Franz Kafka's novel *The Trial*. Hun Sen's lawyers decided that suing the prime minister for defamation was itself an act of defamation. Sochua's suit against Hun Sen was thrown out; instead, she was tried, found guilty, and ordered to pay 8.5 million riels

($2,125) in fines and 8 million riels ($2,000) in "compensation" to Hun Sen. She refused to pay, until the National Assembly voted to deduct it from her salary. Sochua never seriously expected to win the case, but without access to most TV stations and newspapers, the legal campaign was one of the few ways she had left to challenge the CPP and advance the rights of women. Hun Sen was reportedly enraged that Sochua dared to challenge him. "He has a need for total control," she told me later. "If you look further into it, it's a lack of self-confidence."

On the whole, however, the SRP was struggling by 2009, riven by internal disputes and under siege from the authorities. With most avenues for organized activism closed off, Rainsy fell back on attacking Hun Sen's main political vulnerability: his ties to Vietnam. In October of that year, he trooped down to Svay Rieng with a contingent of party officials and journalists and joined local villagers in pulling up half a dozen temporary demarcation posts along the Vietnamese border. Later he produced maps alleging Cambodia had lost land in the various border agreements signed on Hun Sen's watch. As always, the allegations that the government had sold Cambodia out to the Vietnamese cut a little too close to the bone. Charges swiftly followed and Rainsy was sentenced to 12 years of imprisonment. Before the verdict came down, he boarded a flight to France, where he began petitioning foreign governments and filing fruitless legal cases against Hun Sen in foreign courts. Lacking the means to escape overseas, two rice farmers who had taken part in Rainsy's stunt were arrested and jailed.

As foreign governments had come to accept Hun Sen, Rainsy's pitch to foreign donors and overseas constituencies was having less and less effect. His friends in the US Congress remained as outspoken as always, but they no longer had as much say over an American policy now more concerned with the rise of Chinese influence than with evangelizing democracy abroad (see Chapter 11). Donor aid continued to flood in, despite Rainsy's calls for foreign governments to turn off the tap and impose sanctions on Hun Sen.

The inability to capitalize on Funcinpec's collapse in 2008 showed that by tuning its message to the international zeitgeist, the party had failed to gain much ground in the countryside, where the CPP's machinery of patronage hummed as efficiently as ever. A public opinion survey conducted by the International Republican Institute (IRI) in mid-2009 showed that despite high levels of corruption, 79 percent of Cambodians felt their country was headed in the "right direction." More than three-quarters of these respondents put this down to the building of new roads; 61 percent cited the opening of schools. One IRI official told me that despite winning the SRP international attention, legal battles had "steered the party way off message." "They talk about party leaders being persecuted on the basis of esoteric rights that many Cambodian people have very little ownership of," the official said. "They've adapted to appeal to outside constituencies rather than Cambodian voters."

But still the party forged on. Mu Sochua campaigned tirelessly through the villages of Kampot. The party bolstered its youth wing and began merger talks with Kem Sokha's HRP, hoping to establish a unified opposition front in time for the 2013 election. In July 2012, the two parties came together to form the Cambodia National Rescue Party (CNRP), whose name cleverly echoed the Khmer phrase *sangkruos cheat* ("national rescue" or "salvation") contained in the name of the Front that helped topple Pol Pot in 1979.

Despite remaining in self-exile abroad, Rainsy stayed upbeat about his prospects, arguing that demographic changes would create an inevitable groundswell of support for his party. As he told me by phone from Paris in late 2009:

> In a typical family, you have the grandfather, who votes for Funcinpec; you have the father, who votes for the CPP; and you have the children, who when they reach voting age will vote for the SRP ... It will take less time than one might imagine now, because of the progress of technology, information, communication, and education.

To Rainsy, the pattern was obvious: "History is accelerating." But could anybody say which way it was moving?

On October 15, 2012, just two weeks shy of his ninetieth birthday, Norodom Sihanouk died of a heart attack in Beijing. The last message posted on his website was a short typed missive under the heading "How Norodom Sihanouk of Cambodia Employs His Time," in which the ailing monarch listed the routine of injections, examinations, and Chinese herbal treatments that consumed the final years of his life. Amid the rota of doctors' visits, he also found time to post scans of several pages of an unpublished memoir, *Le Calice jusqu'à la lie* ("The Cup to the Dregs"), covered with feisty underlinings and annotations.[28] Right to the end, Sihanouk was actively engaged in shaping his legacy, smoothing the edges of a storied and controversial career.

Cambodia was shaken by his death. Hun Sen immediately flew to Beijing, where he tearfully embraced members of the royal family and knelt down in front of Sihanouk's casket. In Phnom Penh, mourners converged spontaneously on the Royal Palace. They wore white—the traditional shade of mourning—and came clutching lotus flowers, candles, black ribbons, and portraits of the beloved "King Father." Some of them had traveled hundreds of kilometers. When Sihanouk's body returned from China two days later, thousands lined the streets to see the gold funeral cortege on its stately procession to the Royal Palace. Some wept openly as the coffin arrived outside the mustard-colored palace walls, covered with flowers and draped with Cambodia's blue royal standard. Buddhist monks formed a saffron guard of honor. Crowds remained outside the palace well into the evening, setting fire to biers of incense that sent plumes of fragrant smoke billowing into an inky night sky.

The public outpouring was a reminder that for much of the population, particularly the older generations, the monarchy retained its emotional grip. Sam Sokhan, a 78-year-old Buddhist nun with a shaved head, served in a village militia regiment during Sihanouk's "royal crusade" for independence in the early 1950s. She recalled how under the guidance of *Samdech Eav*—"Monsignor Papa"—the soldiers in her regiment confronted the French and "scared them back to their own country." "I hope he gets reborn soon," she told me as she waited in the sun for Sihanouk's coffin to pass. "I pray for the king in heaven. And when he gets there I hope he takes a look back at the people."

The scenes in Phnom Penh formed a neat symmetry with those that had greeted Sihanouk on his return from exile 21 years earlier. On that sunny day in November 1991, Hun Sen had escorted the silver-haired prince home from Beijing and then rode into town with him from the airport. As they moved along the crowded streets, the young prime minister, wearing a loose-fitting navy blue suit and sunglasses, basked in Sihanouk's reflected glory. After playing a key role in the peace talks that brought his exile to an end, Hun Sen would always claim credit for Sihanouk's return. In 2012, the prime minister drove along the same roads, at a discreet distance behind Sihanouk's funeral carriage, in a Mercedes with blacked-out windows. But the political symbolism was unmistakable. Again, Hun Sen had brought Sihanouk home.

The Royal Government spared no expenses bringing the curtain down on Cambodia's last God-King. While Sihanouk's body lay in state at the Royal Palace, the government built a $1.5 million crematorium, topped by a golden spire 47 meters high. It was erected on the *veal mean*, the open area next to the palace where royal funerals have traditionally taken place. A new annual public holiday was announced to mark his passing and the government reinstated the annual celebration of the signing of the Paris Agreements, abolished in 2004 but now hailed, in a subtly backhanded compliment, as Sihanouk's shining achievement.

On February 1, 2013, the first royal funeral procession in half a century bore Sihanouk's casket through the streets of Phnom Penh, while loudspeakers rigged across town broadcast eulogies of the King Father. Three days later, on the sultry evening of February 4, dignitaries including French Prime Minister Jean-Marc Ayrault and Prince Akishino of Japan filed into the lavish pavilions on the *veal mean*. As darkness fell, Sihanouk's crematorium blazed with thousands of tiny lights as King Sihamoni, Queen Mother Monineath, a teary-eyed Hun Sen, and his wife Bun Rany entered its inner chamber to ignite the casket. Half an hour later the former king was engulfed in flames, ascending in a cloud of smoke as officers of the Royal Cambodian Armed Forces sounded a deafening artillery salute.

Despite his colossal stature, Sihanouk's passing had little political significance. There was plenty of emotion near the *veal mean*, but no calls for freedom or justice—only a shared immersion in the rhythms of Buddhist ritual and a nostalgia for the remembered, or misremembered, "golden age" that had preceded the storm of civil war and revolutionary violence. Each night of the funeral, thousands of mourners crowded outside the blazing entrance of the *veal mean*. Sidewalk vendors, industrious as ever, hawked commemorative photos tracing Sihanouk's long career, from images of the haughty young monarch of the 1940s, swaddled in gold cloth, to Sihanouk's official portrait in suit and tie, taken at the cherubic peak of his power in the mid-1960s. Some even sold photos of Sihanouk in the black pajamas he wore during his propaganda tour of the Khmer Rouge "liberated zone" in 1973. "In [Sihanouk's] time, all of his children were very happy and educated," said Saem Yeam, a 77-year-old who sat patiently in the crowded park as the royal smoke rose a few blocks away. "Everything was being developed. Everything was perfect."

Sihanouk's lavish funeral was a fitting farewell for a towering political figure. In its tightly scripted pomp, it was also a victory lap for Hun Sen and the CPP: the culmination of the party's long effort to bind the monarchy in ceremony, shackle it with praise, and assert itself as the sole protector and heir of the royal legacy. From beginning to end, the proceedings were closely controlled. Government dignitaries and tycoons enjoyed front-row seats, while members of the royal family were relegated to the edge of the funeral complex. Sam Rainsy's request to return to Cambodia and pay his respects to the King Father was refused. Barriers kept ordinary mourners far from the *veal mean*.

The party's true attitude toward Sihanouk, of course, was much more ambiguous. A month earlier, when the CPP had met for its annual January 7 celebrations marking the fall of the Pol Pot regime, attendees honored Sihanouk with a minute of silence, while the CPP "martyrs" who died battling the Khmer Rouge were given two minutes.[29] For more than 20 years the party had worked hard to neutralize Sihanouk's political potency and appropriate his legacy. Now it had just about succeeded. Sihanouk was gone, and the monarchy had expired as a political force in Cambodian politics.

While Sihamoni performed the king's traditional duties, Hun Sen left little doubt as to who was the true heir. In a speech shortly after the cremation, Hun

Sen claimed the lighting of the casket had been delayed because Sihanouk's spirit was waiting for the prime minister to light it himself. In the small funerary chamber, away from the prying television cameras, Hun Sen claimed a "miracle" had occurred. As the prime minister said in a speech to Buddhist nuns and city officials a few days later, King Sihamoni and his mother tried three times to set the casket alight, but each time the flame failed to catch. Then the supreme patriarchs of the two main Buddhist sects tried. They too failed. "For the fifth time, it was me alone," Hun Sen told his audience. "I brought forth the fire and the flame finally ignited . . . Now I have to inherit the task of protecting the monarchy." He was anointed, he proclaimed, by a "miracle of the late King Father's sacred power."[30]

As Cambodia's last God-King passed on, its first genuinely constitutional monarch remained a forlorn figure. Norodom Sihamoni was always a reluctant king, plucked from an artistic European milieu to serve the Cambodian throne. At the age of nine, he was sent by Sihanouk to Czechoslovakia, where he completed primary and high school and went on to study classical dance at Prague's Academy of Musical Art. Sihamoni still speaks fluent Czech, and has said his time in Prague "belongs to the happiest in my life."[31] After the Khmer Rouge takeover in 1975, he returned to Phnom Penh with Sihanouk and became a prisoner with his parents in the Royal Palace. Along with his brother Narindrapong, he was forced to wear black and put to work weeding the palace gardens and sweeping out the Throne Hall.[32] After the Khmer Rouge collapse, Sihamoni served for a short time as his father's secretary in Pyongyang and then moved to Paris, where he taught classical dance and, in 1993, became Cambodia's ambassador to UNESCO.

Until then, Sihamoni had led a relatively happy life. Unlike his half-brother Ranariddh, he had never craved the royal limelight. For a lifelong bachelor with no children—Sihanouk once noted delicately that his son "regards women as his sisters"[33]—Europe represented freedom, a chance for Sihamoni to pursue a life away from the restricting social mores of his native country. "I don't want to be king," he said in 1995. "I want to consecrate my life to culture, to choreography, to film. The throne does not interest me. I have never wanted to be king . . . If I were asked, I would say no."[34] But when the moment came nine years later, Sihamoni reluctantly accepted the burden. Within the royal family, he would always say he took the throne only out of love for his father.

Unlike Sihanouk, the new king had no aptitude for the trench warfare of Cambodian politics. His coronation in October 2004 had elicited some brief hopes of an activist reign, but Sihamoni was no match for Hun Sen. A month later, the CPP shot down plans for a new public forum in which people could air their grievances directly to the new king.[35] Within a year the die was cast. In October 2005, Sihamoni docilely put his signature to the controversial border treaty that Hun Sen had brokered with Vietnam—one that Sihanouk himself described as "suicide" for Cambodia.[36] Sihanouk might have handled the situation by throwing up his arms and jetting off to Pyongyang or Beijing in protest, but his son stayed in Phnom Penh and signed the bill. His coopera- tion sent the message that the king would not obstruct CPP policies, however controversial. Like the remaining monarchs of Europe, he would play a strictly constitutional role.

For a second time, Sihamoni became a prisoner in his palace. The man holding the keys this time was an unlikely figure. Kong Sam Ol, the Minister of the Royal Palace, was an agronomist who had graduated from the University of Georgia in the 1960s and was later hailed as one of the brightest young officials in the Lon Nol government. A slick, gray-haired figure with red-framed glasses, Sam Ol survived the Khmer Rouge and served as minister of agriculture during the 1980s. Just before Sihanouk was crowned king in 1993, he was appointed as Minister of the Royal Palace, a post that he has since used to bring the palace under the party's firm control. One former Asian diplomat described Sam Ol as "a very dedicated CPP man," put in place to "manage" the king. Throughout the 1990s, Sam Ol vied with Sihanouk's minders for control over the royal schedule and appointment book. He eventually gained the upper hand after the abdica- tion, when the king's squad of grim North Korean bodyguards returned home and were replaced by Cambodian guards taking their orders from the CPP.[37]

Sam Ol shadowed Sihamoni's every move. He accompanied the king on most of his trips overseas and closely chaperoned him on his sojourns beyond the palace walls. He lurked in the background of royal photographs. At his request, Sihamoni granted audiences and royal honors to tycoons and other ruling party flunkies. One source close to the palace said the king clashed with his minister "on a weekly basis" over these impositions, but had no real power to refuse his requests. Sam Ol was also the brains behind Sihanouk's tightly scripted funeral. During the procession he sat on a float behind Hun Sen, barking orders into a two-way radio, while his daughter's construction company was contracted to build the royal crematorium.[38]

King Sihamoni played his constitutional role to the letter, putting his royal rubber-stamp to amnesties and appointments requested by Hun Sen, and furnishing the CPP leadership with royal titles and honors. While Sihamoni continues to cut ribbons, sign papers, and perform the ceremonial duties of kingship, the weak and downtrodden retain an unfailing sense for where the real power lies. In the old days, they gathered outside the gates of the Royal Palace, holding portraits of the king, begging on the monarch's mercy. More recent years have been marked by a stranger sight: clusters of poor rice farmers sitting in the park outside Hun Sen's mansion near Phnom Penh's Independence Monument, clutching portraits of the prime minister and first lady, gazing up at walls bristling with CCTV cameras. With little place else to turn, they are forced to put their faith in the Peasant King.

In Prey Veng, the mid-morning sun beat down. After Hun Sen had departed, lifted back to a vast and distant realm, the stage was dismantled and the crowds began to disperse. A few villagers hung around, lounging in the shade on motorbikes. It was hard to know what most thought of Hun Sen's fabulism. Few dared to openly criticize the prime minister, but the praise for his achievements often sounded hollow and formulaic. Some people who were denied entrance to Hun Sen's speech joked among themselves about the self-importance of the whole affair—from the party officials with identification badges to the stern police who refused to let them pass. When Cambodia held commune elections in June 2012, many people in Prey Veng had voted against the CPP, which explained Hun Sen's helicopter visit—one of five pagoda-opening excursions he made to Prey Veng in the first half of 2013. "They can't say they hate Hun Sen," said Sa Teun, an activist for the newly formed CNRP who was blocked from attending the prime minister's speech. "The mouth and the heart are different."

Ninety minutes away by road, the provincial capital of Prey Veng slumbered in the midday heat. Its red roofs crouched amid the tamarind trees and coconut palms. Its broad cracked streets were untroubled by traffic. At Wat Sang Semei, a young Buddhist monk reflected on the political situation in his province. While more people were voting against the CPP, the basic calculation for most rural Cambodians, especially the older generations, remained much the same. "People are afraid to speak of politics in Cambodia—even monks," said 32-year-old Chan Sothea. "We are so poor we don't talk a lot about politics. We don't have any money so we just think with our stomachs. It's a big problem in this country."

For most Cambodians, this is nothing new. Politics has traditionally been the business of powerful people in distant places, far beyond the orbit of agricultural life. Hun Sen's political success stems from the fact that he has dealt with Cambodia as it actually exists—as a poor, overwhelmingly rural society, haunted by the past, accustomed to living within the margins of basic subsistence. People are genuinely grateful for the schools and roads and pagodas that the CPP brings them, but the party has discouraged them from demanding anything more substantial. The CPP's rule has emphasized those elements of Khmer culture that prize security, dependency, and deference to the powerful—a mentality best summed up in the imperative *doch ke doch aeng*—"do like others do."

To a great extent, Hun Sen's political strategy since the early 1990s had been a success. For most rural Cambodians politics remained a case, to paraphrase the German playwright Bertolt Brecht, of "rice first, then democracy." But for all their seeming strength, Hun Sen and his system were rent by contradictions. Despite carrying him through repeated cycles of Cambodian history, and underpinning an unprecedented era of peace and economic growth, Hun Sen's intellectual framework was still built around the imperatives of survival. Over 30 years, the pragmatism of a rural guerrilla fighter had turned into the tactical obsession and occasional paranoia of a leader increasingly isolated from the reality of most ordinary people.

Perhaps it was inevitable. As his power and stature rose, Hun Sen's old circle of trusted advisors—men like Sok An, Cham Prasidh, and Hor Namhong—had been replaced by a younger caste of sycophants, who filtered the country's realities and told the prime minister what they thought he wanted to hear. In 2013, Phoeung Sophoan, an official in the Ministry of Land Management, announced plans to build a new, 35,000-hectare capital city in honor of Hun Sen. At a preposterous cost of $80 billion—seven times Cambodia's GDP—"Samdech Techo Hun Sen Dragon City" would spread out to the north of Phnom Penh, an Asimovian fantasy of towers and shimmering arcades culminating in a 600-meter skyscraper. At its tip Hun Sen would have a private office, closer to Olympus than ever. "In the 12th century we had Suryavarman II who built Angkor Wat," this would-be Cambodian Speer told the *Cambodia Daily*. "Now we are in the Samdech Hun Sen period."[39] The project had little hope of ever being built, but it showed the extent of the flummery that now surrounded Cambodia's leader.

In large part, too, Hun Sen was constrained by a political system that had no clear purpose beyond its own perpetuation. Political stability rested not on any deep social or political consensus, but on a tenuous pact between the country's elites, whose loyalties had to be constantly renewed through fresh distributions of profits and patronage. There was no goal beyond the endless branching and twining of patronage strings, no objective beyond the capturing of fresh resources to swell the system further. Despite the democratic mirage that had settled over the country in the early 1990s, little had changed in the way political power operated. The king still "ate" his kingdom, just as he did in the times of the Angkorian Empire.

Under Hun Sen, however, the system approached the outer limits of its logic. Despite entrenching himself in an unparalleled position of power, Hun Sen's reliance on the Cambodian elites meant that even had he wanted to, he had little real power to rein in corruption and other abuses. Land, forests, and natural resources were all fed into a machine that produced little for ordinary people. Cambodia's health, education, and justice systems were neglected—its future mortgaged—in order to keep the Ponzi scheme of patronage afloat. The Cambodian contradiction was cast into sharp relief after the CPP's landslide election victory in 2008. This was the moment when Hun Sen and his government might have started building a legacy by focusing on the needs of Cambodia's poor. Instead, it marked the beginning of an era of Big Money.

CHAPTER SEVEN

Hunsenomics and Its Discontents

Just before dawn each day, thousands of foreign tourists leave their guest-houses and hotels in Siem Reap, Cambodia's main tourist hub, and make their way out of town. An exodus of buses, cars, and sputtering tuk-tuks crawls past hotels and service stations, still glowing in the murky morning light. A few kilometers outside town the road enters an enveloping rural darkness, skirting a broad moat dotted with lotus flowers. Visitors alight near an ancient lime-stone causeway bridging the water. After crossing and entering a small stone entranceway, it looms suddenly and majestically into view: Angkor Wat, Cambodia's symbol and talisman, its five sandstone towers backlit by the first fiery streaks of morning.

An image of this wondrous temple-city has graced the flag of every Cambodian regime since independence. It has also driven a recent surge in tourism to Cambodia. Around 4.2 million people visited the country in 2013, with a trip to Angkor Wat and its surrounding temples often at the top of their list.[1] The tourism boom has transformed the gateway town of Siem Reap from a dusty township in one of Cambodia's poorest provinces into a touristic oasis of cocktail bars, restaurants, massage parlors, and cerulean hotel swimming pools.

To cope with greater visitor numbers, access to the Angkor temples has been greatly streamlined. Tourists are greeted at the entrance gate by smiling staff who photograph them and print their faces on a personalized ticket: either a US$20 pass, which grants a single day's access, a $40 pass for three days, or a week-long pass for $60. The process is so quick and professional that few visitors think to ask where their money goes. Most probably assume it goes toward preserving temples and monuments for future generations.

The truth, as so often in Cambodia, is more tangled. Each ticket to the Angkor Archaeological Park features the name of a company, Sokha Hotels Ltd. Sokha Hotels is a subsidiary of Sokimex Group, a petrol conglomerate owned by Sok Kong, an *oknha* tycoon close to Prime Minister Hun Sen. In May 1999, the Cambodian government awarded control of Angkor ticketing to Sokha Hotels. No competing bids were taken. In a sweetheart deal, Kong was asked to pay the government a flat fee of $1 million each year and pocketed everything above that. The deal was renegotiated the following year, again in secret, and has been renewed every five years since.[2] In 2005, a Siem Reap tourism operator that tried to bid for the ticketing contract was knocked back, and officials at the Apsara Authority, the government's official temple management body, reportedly said they had "no choice besides Sokimex."[3]

Sokha Hotels is admirably efficient in its handling of the ticketing operation, but without an open bidding process there is no way of knowing whether the government might have received a better deal. Son Chhay, a parliamentarian from the Cambodia National Rescue Party, has been investigating the Angkor ticketing scheme since the early 2000s. An affable man with thick-rimmed glasses and a lingering drawl from his years living in Australia, Chhay says the public remains in the dark about the Angkor ticket revenues. In 2005, Sok Kong told the local press that 15 percent of ticket proceeds were going to Apsara, with the remainder split 80–20 between the government and his company.[4] But Sokimex releases no official profit-loss statements. Nor does it publish detailed information about its contract with the government. "We raise this problem and they respond that [Sokimex] has been doing a good job, so they will keep on doing it," Chhay said, sitting in his office at the National Assembly in Phnom Penh, a framed painting of Angkor Wat gracing his wall. Even today, the amount of money being raised by the Angkor temples—Cambodia's national treasure and pride—remains a closely guarded secret.

According to his own investigations, Chhay estimates that about 80 percent of visitors to Cambodia visit the temples, most of whom shell out for a three-day or seven-day pass. Even assuming each tourist spends just $30 on tickets, the total annual revenue from the temples could well approach $150 million. Apsara does occasionally release annual revenue figures—it claimed $51 million was raised from ticket sales in 2012[5]—but without further details it's impossible to know if this was the full figure, or where this money ended up. Chhay argues that as much as $120 million could be disappearing into private pockets. Some of the money undoubtedly goes to Apsara for conservation, staffing, and park maintenance, but again, there's no way of knowing how much. Most major temple conservation projects are funded by foreign governments, and Chhay says he has found no evidence that ticket proceeds have been used for this purpose. "Maybe [Sokimex] pays a couple of local people to guard the temples—you can see a number of people there—but they pay them something like $30 a month," he said. "That's peanuts."

For Sok Kong, the Angkor ticketing concession is just one part of a sprawling business empire rooted in the fertile ground where business and politics meet. In the 1980s, the Vietnamese-speaking Kong got his start supplying the Cambodian government with rubber products, military uniforms, food, aluminum, and medicine imported from Vietnam.[6] When subsidized Soviet fuel imports were cut off in 1990, he founded Sokimex, which became the main supplier of fuel to the Cambodian military.[7] In 1996, Sokimex purchased the state oil company, Compagnie Kampuchea des Carburants, for $10.6 million (another closed bid) and took over its fuel storage depots in Phnom Penh and Sihanoukville.[8] The company now runs a national distribution network that includes five storage terminals and a fuel import jetty in Sihanoukville able to handle 46,000-ton oil tankers.[9] The only petrol firm boasting better connections is Kampuchea Tela Co., Ltd., which is partially owned by Hun Sen's daughter Hun Mana. Between them, the two firms control the lion's share of the domestic petrol market.

Kong reportedly earned Hun Sen's gratitude during his seizure of power in July 1997, when Sokimex kept the CPP's forces supplied with free fuel.[10] The rewards quickly followed. After the lucrative Angkor concession in 1999, Sokha Hotels was awarded the right to develop the site of an old French prison in central Siem Reap, where it built a five-star resort.[11] Later, it received similar rights to the abandoned colonial hill-station at Bokor Mountain in Kampot, where a rococo hotel-casino complex opened its doors in 2012. Sokimex has also expanded its portfolio to include garment factories, rubber plantations, property developments, and a small private airline.

The rise and rise of Sokimex is a typical example of the political favor and secrecy that characterize capitalism, Cambodia-style. Over the past two decades, those who supported Hun Sen's rise have been rewarded with access to the impoverished country's resources: land, forests, fisheries, mining concessions, air routes, ship registrations, stadiums, prisons, courts, hospitals, agribusiness concessions, and ministry buildings. The main beneficiaries have been a handful of Cambodian and Sino-Khmer tycoons who emerged from humble beginnings and rose in parallel with Hun Sen. Madame Lim Chhiv Ho, the head of the powerful Attwood Group conglomerate, once sold noodles at the Russian Market. Oknha Sam Ang and Madame Chhun Leang, the husband-and-wife founders of the Vattanac Bank (and owners of a White House-sized mansion on Norodom Boulevard) arrived in Phnom Penh on bicycles in 1979.

Hun Sen's old foreign ministry allies from the 1980s have been similarly well rewarded. Deputy Prime Minister Sok An, Hun Sen's bureaucratic Kali, built a fortune through his control of the Council of Ministers and his links to prominent Sino-Khmer business families, whom he meets for daily meetings at luxury hotels around Phnom Penh. Another former aide, Cham Prasidh, served as minister of commerce from 1994 until 2013, and remains a close ally of the prime minister. His wife, Tep Bopha Prasidh, a formidable businesswoman, is also friends with Bun Rany and owns shares in several leading corporations. Son Chhay estimates each family to be worth more than $1 billion.

Today, Cambodia's economy is controlled by this new quasi-palace elite: a sprawling network of CPP politicians, military brass, and business families arranged in vertical *khsae*, or "strings," of patronage emanating from Hun Sen and his close associates. Given the dearth of trust in Cambodian society, political and financial ties are frequently consummated by marriage. Of Hun Sen's six children, five have been married off in politically auspicious arrangements. Hun Sen's youngest daughter Hun Mali is married to Sok Puthyvuth, a son of Sok An. Sok An's other son is married to Cham Krasna, a daughter of Cham Prasidh. Hun Sen's nieces and nephews are similarly enmeshed. In this way, oligarchs are linked to ministers, police chiefs to party power-brokers. Money circulates within a nexus of political and economic connections in which allies are not just friends, but family, too.[12]

As Hun Sen's rule has taken on dynastic overtones, his own sons have been maneuvered into key positions. The heir apparent is his eldest son, Hun Manet, who graduated from the US military academy at West Point in 1999. Manet (born 1977) now serves as a four-star general in the Royal Cambodian Armed Forces, the commander of his father's bodyguard unit, and the head of a national counterterrorism task force set up with US support in 2008. Hun Sen's second son, Hun Manith (born 1981), also educated in the US, has been promoted to the rank of brigadier-general. The youngest of the three, Hun Many (born 1982), has been groomed for a political career. He heads the Union of Youth Federations of Cambodia, a CPP-aligned youth organization, and was elected to parliament in the 2013 election.

Crowning this tree of elite family connections are Hun Sen and Bun Rany. No one knows the true extent of the Hun family's wealth—one expatriate businessman pegged it at "several billion" dollars—but the "royal" couple sit at the point where all the most lucrative strings of patronage converge. Hun Sen's personal business interests are opaque, hidden under the names of his relatives and children or concealed behind shell companies that publish no annual reports. During an audit of Canadia Bank, which counts Hun Sen's daughter Hun Mana among its roster of shareholders, one foreign auditor recalled that staff at PricewaterhouseCoopers were warned off sending financial confirmations—third-party requests often made during financial audits—to the prime minister or members of his family.[13]

The Cambodian first lady occupies a particularly important place in the constellation of power surrounding her husband. As chair of the Cambodian Red Cross (CRC), the largest charity organization in the country, Bun Rany controls what might be termed the "humanitarian wing" of the CPP. The CRC's website is a spectacle of self-regard, featuring pictures of Bun Rany— pink lipstick, sculpted black hair, diamond earrings—presenting gifts to grateful villagers. Though the CRC claims to be neutral and independent— two core principles of the International Committee for the Red Cross, founded in 1863—critics allege that it operates as little more than a front for the CPP. After all, Cambodians don't need to be told who Bun Rany represents when she turns up in their village to hand out medicine or sacks of rice. The same is true of her daughter Hun Mana, whose Bayon Foundation offers another "charitable" channel for party patronage.

Meanwhile, the CRC's board of directors is packed with crony tycoons closely linked to the CPP, and Bun Rany has been known to openly stump for the party during Red Cross charity drives.[14] In May 2013, to mark World Red Cross Day, the CRC held a pre-election fundraising event in Phnom Penh at which oligarchs and politicians pledged $14 million in charitable donations. The biggest donation ($3 million) came from the Booyoung Group, a South Korean development firm. Phnom Penh governor Kep Chuktema donated $300,000. Sok An, whose wife serves alongside Bun Rany as the CRC's second vice-president, donated $15,000. At the same ceremony, Bun Rany was also granted the title *samdech*, the first time it had been awarded to a woman, and appended it to her pre-existing title, "Most Glorious and Upright Person of Genius." In bestowing the title, Royal Palace Minister Kong Sam Ol (a *samdech* himself) announced that Rany is "a great leader, is highly respected by people, and deeply honors the monarchy."[15]

Hun Sen is unabashed about the extent of his family's wealth, which he trumpets as a sign of karmic legitimacy reinforcing his status as a *neak mean bon*—a man of merit. In one barnstorming March 2013 speech, Hun Sen bragged about spending "hundreds of millions" of his own money on charity projects—an almost inconceivable sum in rural Cambodia. "I don't even use the national budget," he said.[16] On another occasion he channeled the trickle-down bromides of Reaganomics, urging his audience to "make the bosses rich." "If a country has no millionaires," he argued, "where can the poor get their money from?"[17]

Hun Sen's rise over the past two decades has been accompanied by the rise of what might be termed Hunsenomics—a blend of old-style patronage, elite charity, and predatory market economics. Since the transition to the free market in 1989, Hunsenomics has succeeded in forging a stable pact among Cambodia's ruling elites, but has otherwise done little to systematically tackle the challenges of poverty and development. As Cambodia emerges from an era of conflict and enters an era of globalization, it does so not on the basis of individual rights or representative government, but, as ever, at the whim of powerful men and women.

From the viewing deck on the thirty-second floor of the Canadia Tower, Cambodia's first skyscraper, Phnom Penh spreads outward toward a ribbon of smog and dust lining the horizon. Far below, the Central Market, a yellow Art-Deco ziggurat built by the French in 1937, extends its four arms at the center of radiating boulevards. Ant-like traffic crawls along in the heat, bottlenecking at the major intersections. Like Siem Reap, Cambodia's once-sleepy royal capital is a boomtown, marching along the same dynamic path trodden three decades ago by Bangkok, Jakarta, and other groaning Asian megacities. As if to dramatize its emergence, Phnom Penh is starting to rise. The Canadia Tower, completed in 2010 as the headquarters of Canadia Bank, has already been surpassed in height by the 39-story Vattanac Capital Tower, built by the family-run Vattanac Bank. The city skyline, once an undulating line of palm trees and golden spires, is now bisected everywhere by modern high-rise towers, filled with office space and apartments.

The changes are just as visible at ground level. At a plush coffee shop on the city's breezy riverside promenade, young middle-class Cambodians sip cappuccinos while chatting on iPhones and tapping away at laptops. A cavernous interior, all dark hues and exposed brick, echoes with the comforting sound of grinding coffee beans and hissing steam. Cambodians have been caffeine addicts since French times, preferring their brew rich, iced, and sweetened with dollops of condensed milk. But when it opened in 2009, Brown Café and Bakery was something different from the city's street-side coffee shops. It was Cambodia's answer to Starbucks—a Western-style chain, selling cakes and pastries and elaborate caffeinated concoctions. Before Brown opened, the one or two modern coffee shops in Phnom Penh were patronized mostly by expatriates. "I thought there was a market for that, for good coffee and good ambience," said Hok Kang, one of the four young entrepreneurs behind Brown.

Kang and his partners hit upon the idea for Brown in early 2009. Two of them flew to Bangkok to learn about baking and pastry-making, while Kang, an architect, scouted locations and sketched out a design for the first store, which opened on Samdech Pan Street, near the Royal Palace. The then 31-year old, who speaks in accentless English, picked up while studying at Washington University in St Louis, Missouri, said he wanted Brown's stores to feel relaxed and slightly worn—a comfortable place for young people to meet for lunch or spend a few hours working. The first outlet was an instant hit, and eight more branches quickly followed. All have been a roaring success among an emerging middle class willing to pay the same for a cappuccino—two or three dollars— as they would pay in many Western countries. Following Brown's success, international chains have stampeded into the Cambodian market. In Boeung Keng Kang, Phnom Penh's leafy district of NGO offices and expat bars, there are now coffee shops on nearly every corner, including leading chains from South Korea, Thailand, Australia, and the UK. Few of them are ever empty.

To keep ahead of the competition, Brown has plans to open two more stores in the capital, and an additional outlet in Siem Reap. If the brand continues to take off, Kang hasn't ruled out taking it abroad—to Vietnam, maybe, or Burma—which would be a remarkable story for a homegrown chain. The four Brown partners, all aged in their thirties, are part of a generation of young Cambodian entrepreneurs with the savvy and start-up cash to take advantage of the opportunities of a booming economy. Kang, whose parents founded ISI Steel, a leading producer of roof sheeting and steel pipes, said it took just six months for Brown to move from sketchpad to reality. Four years on, the chain employs 450 people, and has gained a local following for being Cambodian owned and run. "Business can move very fast," Kang said over coffee—a $2.40 Americano—at Brown's airy riverfront store, an artfully converted colonial warehouse built in the 1890s. "If you have an idea and you work hard for it, I think it's possible to start something here."

The success of Brown speaks to the social and economic changes that have gripped Cambodia's capital during a recent surge in economic growth. Between 1998 and 2007, Cambodia's gross domestic product grew by nearly 10 percent per year—the sixth fastest growth rate in the world.[18] After a short downturn during the global financial crisis of 2008–9, the upward trend resumed. In 2004, one out of every two Cambodians was living in poverty, according to the World Bank; by 2011, the figure had dropped to one in five.[19] In two decades, Cambodia's per capita income has almost quadrupled, rocketing from $240 in 1993 to more than $1,200 in 2018, and spawning a small middle class with the disposable income to spend on cars, motorbikes, and consumer electronics like smartphones and iPads. Cambodia is now on the verge of admission into the World Bank's club of "lower middle-income" countries.[20]

In many ways, this is a remarkable accomplishment. When Cambodia's civil war ended in the late 1990s, roads and infrastructure remained in a state of near-collapse and economic indicators, especially in the areas that had seen the heaviest fighting, languished at pre-1970 levels. But Hun Sen's Cambodia has come full circle, from battlefield to marketplace: today it is one of the most open economies in Asia, where starting a business is relatively easy and foreign-owned firms can operate without a local partner. The dollarized economy, an unintended legacy of the UNTAC years, reduces the risk of exchange rate fluctuations. The government has made other efforts to woo overseas business. Since 1999, it has hosted a twice-yearly Government Private Sector Forum attended by Hun Sen and his cabinet, at which investors can air concerns directly to ministers. "They've taken away the exchange rate risk, they've taken away the foreign ownership risk, there's a large pool of cheap labor," said one foreign business figure with ten years' experience in Cambodia. "You've got a compelling country to do business in."

Cheap labor, untapped markets, and open economic policies have attracted large inflows of foreign investment from China, Taiwan, South Korea, Malaysia, Vietnam, and Thailand, which have poured billions into the garment, construction, and tourism sectors—the main drivers of the recent growth. Garment manufacturing in particular has been a success: since 1994, the country has built an industry with an export value of $10 billion as of 2018, most of which is exported to the US and the European Union. The garment sector now employs some 800,000 people and accounts for close to 80 percent of Cambodia's exports; dozens of apparel factories dot the outskirts of Phnom Penh.[21] In the center of town, meanwhile, a large foreign expat community and open visa policies have drawn young entrepreneurs who have opened sophisticated bars and restaurants that have turned the capital of one of Asia's poorest countries into a regional gastro-hub, with better variety (and better prices) than many larger cities in the region. In a very real sense, Cambodia's prospects today are brighter than at any other point in its history.

But while Hunsenomics has promoted growth and openness in the visible sectors of the economy, its most lucrative activities remain off the books. Vital sectors like banking, import-export, agribusiness, and natural resource extraction are still dominated by vested interests that operate in an economic netherworld lying beyond the reach of effective regulation. Companies linked to tycoons and politicians import beer, cigarettes, and gasoline minus the VAT and import duties—a phenomenon that costs the government millions in lost revenue each year. Millions more drain out of the formal economy via mining, forestry, and economic land concessions that are handed out with little or no financial or environmental oversight. Much of the wealth sloshing around in Phnom Penh—from its skyscrapers and lavish mansions to the sports cars and luxury SUVs that choke the streets—is a financial mirage. Officially, it doesn't exist.

The story of Hunsenomics began in the late 1980s, when the CPP cast off its communist trappings and began its "transition" to the free market. In reality, it was more of a sudden lurch, prompted by the abrupt cutoff of aid from the

Soviet Union. Economic controls were abandoned overnight; state enterprises were sold off to politicians and cronies at a heavy discount. As noted in Chapter 3, liberalization was pursued less for the sake of economic competition than as a way of thwarting political competition by transferring the economy into friendly hands. In June 1989, Hun Sen told a visiting Vietnamese delegation that privatization of state-owned enterprises was vital, "because if we leave them with the state, we will face problems when the three [opposition] parties come and spend money that belongs to our factories."[22] The logic was simple: enemies would be starved of funds; friends would be showered with gold.

Hunsenomics has since evolved in reaction to outside pressures and the demands of foreign aid donors. With donor governments and international financial institutions like the World Bank and International Monetary Fund pressing Cambodia to improve governance and fight corruption, Hun Sen's government has learnt the utility of keeping two sets of books. On one side of the ledger there are the public statements of Cambodian ministers, who present their mirage of "good governance" and public financial management reform. On the other is the submerged economy, made up of patronage strings that bind party, government, business, and military into tight networks of mutual dependence. The result has been reform à la carte: as Caroline Hughes has argued, this bifurcated system churns out laws and reforms designed to appease donor constituencies while resisting any changes that would throw light on its own opaque operations.[23] Under Hunsenomics, reforms in the visible economy, like macroeconomic policies to stabilize the exchange rate and rein in inflation, often produce real results. Anything touching on the shadow state, however, stands little chance of success.[24]

The effect of Hunsenomics has been to concentrate Cambodia's wealth in relatively few hands. Poverty reduction, creditable compared to the near-famine state of past decades, has been slow relative to economic growth. The gap between rich and poor is among the widest in Asia, a reality that is immediately apparent to any visitor encountering the designer boutiques and SUV snarls of Phnom Penh at peak hour.[25]

Under Hunsenomics, areas of government that do not provide opportunities for illicit revenue generation—areas like education, health, and rural development—have been neglected. Tax revenues have stagnated as wealthy elites pump millions into CPP election campaigns and Red Cross charity drives, which have kept the patronage machine humming while doing little to improve the real quality of the country's schools or medical clinics. In the same manner, government employees like police officers, soldiers, teachers, and healthcare workers remain so poorly paid that many are forced to demand bribes and "fees" from the people who can least afford it. This, too, serves a purpose. By keeping salaries and horizons low, Hunsenomics keeps most of the population yoked to the wheel of patronage, dependent on a drip of charity from above.

Few of the benefits of Cambodia's economic boom have trickled down to villages like Trapaing Prolit, a dusty hamlet sitting in a landscape of rolling hills and black-earthed cassava fields along the Thai border. The jungle that once covered this remote area of Battambang is long gone, sold by the Khmer Rouge to Thai logging companies in the 1990s, but a few scraggly patches of young forest remain, growing like crowns on otherwise bald hills. Seng Cheun, now in his forties, settled here as a farm laborer about seven years ago, fleeing a life of poverty in Kampong Cham. At the time, this was Cambodia's frontier. Land was cheap, and there was plenty of work for those willing to clear the remaining jungle or work for local landowners.

Cheun, a lean former soldier with thick black hair and a body covered with magical tattoos thought to impart luck on the battlefield, has done well. He has a brick home—a rarity in the village—with a small porch and a row of potted plants. He also has a small generator that powers a couple of strip lamps and a television. But life remains hard. Cheun suffers from a chronic stomach illness, and with six children to support he can't afford to rest and get treatment. "Because we're poor I have to force myself to work," he said, as one of his daughters swung in a hammock nearby.

Most Cambodian villages provide only the most grudging, marginal sustenance to their inhabitants. The main drivers of economic growth—garments, tourism, and construction—are concentrated in Phnom Penh, Siem Reap, and the larger provincial towns, and about 90 percent of the country's poor live in rural areas. While the statistics show a sharp fall in the poverty rate over the past decade, millions of rural poor, like many in Trapaing Prolit, sit on a knife-edge. The World Bank acknowledges that if the 2011 poverty line of 5,326 riels ($1.33) were raised by just 30 cents, the poverty rate of 20.5 percent would double.[26] The trick to the poverty numbers game, clearly, is in how low one sets the bar.

Agriculture, the engine of the rural economy, has lagged far behind the urban industries. As a country of rich farmland and plentiful water resources, Cambodia has huge potential as a producer of rice: 80 percent of the country's cultivated land is still given over to paddy fields,[27] which has left deep impressions on rural society. The Cambodian countryside glows emerald green at the end of the monsoon as the first rice seedlings, painstakingly transplanted into the muddy soil by hand, emerge from the flooded rice paddies. For 9 million Cambodians—nearly two-thirds of the population—life is dictated by the cycles of the wet season crop, which begins with the planting of rice seedlings in July and August, and finishes with the harvest at year's end. In food security terms, too, rice is of crucial importance, providing three-quarters of the energy intake of the average Cambodian citizen.[28] The country's reliance on the staple is so strong that it is inscribed in the Khmer language, in which *bai*, the word for "rice," means "food" as well.

Rice production unsurprisingly forms a central part of the Cambodian government's development strategy. In 2010, Hun Sen set a goal for Cambodia to export 1 million tons of milled rice by 2015. But Cambodia's rice industry, and its agricultural sector more generally, remains a case of unfulfilled expectations. Despite paddy rice production more than doubling from 3.4 million tons in 1998 to 9.3 million tons in 2013, agricultural products make up just 3.7 percent of total exports by value. By 2013, the government had fulfilled just 378,856 tons of its rice export target.[29] In part this was due to the shortage of government capital to buy unmilled paddy rice, but it was worsened by high electricity and transportation costs—the latter exacerbated by bribe extraction on the highways and informal "customs fees" at the country's border crossings. Much unmilled rice instead ends up being smuggled into Thailand or Vietnam and milled there.[30]

Another reason for the sluggish growth of the agricultural sector is corruption in the Ministry of Agriculture, Forestry, and Fisheries (MAFF). Hun Sen and Prince Ranariddh fought for control of the ministry after the 1993 and 1998 elections, and it's not hard to see why. As the ministry with the power to grant forestry and agribusiness concessions, MAFF has long been a conduit for speculative land deals and agribusiness ventures that have been made with little or no thought for the long-term health of the rural economy. In the past decade these deals have involved the forced eviction of thousands of rural poor from their farms—a human rights nightmare that has undermined rural development and driven away prospective foreign investors (see Chapter 9). "They get scared off," said one foreign business figure. "[MAFF] is full of cronyism and corruption."

Because Hunsenomics provides few incentives for sustainable agricultural development, Cambodia's land and water resources remain drastically underutilized. Just a third of Cambodia's total land area is currently under cultivation, a much lower proportion than in neighboring countries.[31] Only 18 percent of this land was irrigated as of 2005, compared to 33 percent in Thailand and 44 percent in Vietnam, and due to poor maintenance, only a fifth of irrigation systems were fully functional.[32] As a result, rice yields per hectare lag far behind the likes of Vietnam and Thailand. While most Cambodian farmers cultivate paddy rice once per year during the rainy season, some farmers in Vietnam's Mekong Delta region can produce more than three crops annually. As in ancient times, agricultural output is acutely vulnerable to variations in weather, and many rice farmers can do little more than what they have always done: pray for rain.

The precarious nature of the crop cycle leaves many rural people living in fear that a sudden shock, such as floods, drought, or expropriation, could reduce them to destitution. A great fear—the greatest, perhaps—is illness. Virtually nobody outside the city has health insurance and the government provides only the most limited subsidies for healthcare. In the case of an accident or sudden sickness, villagers are forced to take their chances in the country's parlous hospitals and medical clinics—ramshackle facilities where it is not uncommon for medical staff to demand unofficial cash "fees" in exchange for treatment. To meet these costs villagers are often forced to borrow money from predatory moneylenders or sell what for many is their only asset—their land.[33]

Ros Peun and his wife, Soun San, have a large wooden house in Trapaing Prolit. Enjoying pride of place on the wall, close to portraits of the late King Father Sihanouk and Queen Mother Monineath, are old photos of their daughter Peun Say. One of them shows a pretty young woman on her wedding day, wearing a light blue dress. In another, the same woman stands next to her younger brother holding a leather handbag, the pair of siblings superimposed on a colorful stock-image of London's Tower Bridge. Peun Say died three years ago, at the age of 20, after complications with her pregnancy—a death her parents blame on the parlous state of the Cambodian health system.

Ros Peun, an animated bundle of weather-beaten features and wiry black hair, says his daughter was at the end of her second trimester when she experienced a sudden excruciating headache. At the district health center, a badly resourced concrete building in Sampov Loun, doctors said they lacked the equipment to conduct the proper tests and sent her to nearby Thailand. On the way, Say began to shake and then lost consciousness. Her symptoms were consistent with the onset of eclampsia, a condition in which pregnant women experience violent seizures. With proper care, the condition can be resolved in its early stages. But in Peun Say's case it was too late for the doctors to do anything. She died the next morning.

The ordeal left the family 440,000 riels ($110) in debt—a significant sum in rural Cambodia. Neighbors pitched in to help the family with hospital costs, but to pay them back Ros Peun was forced to sell two of his four hectares of cassava fields. Today, he laments the fact that there is so little information available for first-time mothers, and no subsidies that could have allowed his daughter to see a doctor earlier on. "She had no money," he said, "so she just waited and waited until something bad happened to her."

The ordeal of childbirth is known in Khmer as *chhlong tonle*, or "crossing the river," a phrase that encapsulates the very real dangers that still face mother and child. These include the low quality and high cost of healthcare, demands for "fees" from medical staff, and the drastic shortage of midwives and skilled birth attendants. Five Cambodian women still die in childbirth each day, according to the UN, and maternal mortality forms a dark counterpoint to the blessings of Cambodia's economic boom, actually increasing from 440 deaths per 100,000 live births in 2000 to 460.8 in 2008. By 2015, the figure had dropped to 161, according to the UN,[34] but giving birth is still feared by women in rural areas, where maternal mortality rates are three times higher than in the city.[35] In Trapaing Prolit, up the road from the house where Peun Say used to live, Pheap Sophany awaits her own perilous river-crossing. Eight months pregnant, she has only visited the doctor a couple of times, and worries about what will happen when she enters labor. "I think about where I will go," says Sophany, a 22-year-old with brightly painted nails. "I think about the safety. I'm very frightened."

Like agricultural development, healthcare occupies a marginal position in the scheme of Hunsenomics. According to the World Health Organization, the Cambodian government spent just $11.50 on healthcare per person in 2011, compared to $38.30 in Vietnam and $152.30 in Thailand.[36] In theory, the government offers free healthcare to the poorest members of society, and claims 3.8 million poor Cambodians accessed such services in 2012.[37] But few people in Trapaing Prolit seemed to have benefited from the program. Set Sam, the village chief, said just 30 of the village's 150 families were judged poor enough to receive official "poverty cards" making them eligible for free health-care. The expectant mother Peun Say was excluded, even though she had no money to pay for checkups; so was Seng Cheun, the ex-soldier suffering from stomach problems.

The etiolated state of the Cambodian healthcare system means that those who can afford it look elsewhere for treatment. High-ranking government officials and expatriates fly to Singapore or Thailand. The middle classes often board the daily buses from Phnom Penh to Ho Chi Minh City, where they can obtain affordable care at Vietnam's state-run hospitals. Everybody else relies on inconsistent private hospitals and clinics, handouts from foreign NGOs, or Khmer traditional medicine. With nowhere else to turn, the poorest are susceptible to the claims of mountebanks and mystical healers promising cheap and instant cures. In October 2013, people from across the country converged on a small village in Kampong Cham where a two-year-old boy by the name of Kong Keng was reputed to possess magical healing powers. Hundreds of pilgrims camped out, burning incense and making small offerings, hoping for an "audience" with the celestial toddler. "We came from Koh Kong province after we saw the Magic Boy on TV," one pilgrim told the *Cambodia Daily*. "It took days."[38]

Back in Trapaing Prolit, Cheun and his wife sat in front of their nice brick home, speaking in hopeful tones about an NGO-run hospital in Battambang that offered medical treatment free of charge. There were also rumors going around of American doctors offering checkups far away to the east along the Mekong—hundreds of kilometers distant. "When people hear about this sort of thing," Cheun said, "they come from every corner of the country."

To escape the stagnating rural economy, increasing numbers of Cambodians have left their villages in search of work. Thousands of young men have been lured by illegal labor brokers into Thailand, where many are put to work on fishing boats in squalid conditions. Young women often seek work as maids in Malaysia and other countries, but the poor regulation of the sector, which is similarly rife with bogus "agents" and brokers, has resulted in frequent cases of abuse by foreign employers. Despite the risks, seeking informal work overseas has become increasingly common. In 2011, the International Organization for Migration reported that Cambodia was the sixth greatest point of origin for trafficked people worldwide.[39] The following year more than 123,600 illegal migrant workers were repatriated to Cambodia, according to government figures. Most worked in Thailand, but some returned from as far afield as Japan, South Africa, and Fiji.[40]

Many more have migrated internally, drawn toward the booming industries in Phnom Penh and Siem Reap. Opportunities for the rural poor in urban centers consist mainly of low-skilled or casual jobs. Men can find work as laborers, tuk-tuk drivers, or security guards. Women, overwhelmingly, have gone to the garment factories. Like thousands of others, Yem Sreyvy came to the city seven years ago from her village in Prey Veng and got a job as a seamstress. Eventually her six sisters followed her, as well as a brother, who landed a job as a mechanic. "My neighbors were mostly farmers, and some made *kramas* [cotton scarves]," the 31-year old said, sitting cross-legged on the floor of her small room on the outskirts of the city. "Many farmers didn't have much land for crops or planting rice. It couldn't support their living."

Sreyvy works at the Conpress Holding Garment Factory north of Phnom Penh, where she takes home $68 per month working six 11-hour days per week. Most of her remaining time, including Sunday, her day off, is spent here, in a concrete, furniture-less room—a tiny space she shares with three other women. In the corner are a television, two small gas cookers, and a small mirror. A fan of ripening bananas hangs from a nail. The building contains another dozen rooms, each housing three or four women, linked by a stairwell with bare concrete walls. Sreyvy's hours at work are long and tedious, especially when garment orders are due and the Chinese managers press seamstresses to work overtime. But she needs the money to help support her six-year-old daughter, who lives back in her home village. Due to high transport costs, she only travels home once or twice a year, at the Khmer New Year and during Pchum Ben, the annual festival when Cambodians light incense and pray to their ancestors. This month she sent just $10 to her family.

In a neighboring room, 27-year-old Choeun Ran explained that so many youngsters from her village in Kampong Thom have gone to the city in search of work that few remain. "When we have a celebration, no young people are there. Mostly they are very old, and they look after their grandchildren," she said. Garment work offers little escape from the cycles of poverty. Despite recent wage increases, unions and labor advocates argue that wages remain below the cost of living. Small hikes in garment wages are often matched by an immediate increase in rent by landlords.

After eight years in the capital, Ran said she can only earn enough money to pay her living costs and send small amounts home, and there's very little left over to do what she really wants, which is to start a business or buy some land back in her village. Women can earn more money by working as "beer girls" at restaurants or bar girls in Phnom Penh's red-light districts—but these industries carry great social stigma and leave young women vulnerable to sexual abuse or exploitation. "It's very difficult to save money to go back home or go somewhere else," Ran said. "The salary is very small, and the money goes with eating."

There are few ladders out of poverty under Hunsenomics. Education, the most obvious route upward, is as infected with corruption as everything else. In a system so starved of funds that classes are often run without textbooks or stationery, the one consistent lesson that all Cambodian children learn is that everything—even good grades—has a price. At 12 years of age, Sor Sopheavy is already well versed in the art of the underhand payment. Each day she comes to school with 1,500 riels (about $0.37) for her teacher, which allows her to attend a private class he holds each afternoon after school. "If we come to extra classes we will get the questions and answers for the exams," she said, slinging her satchel over her shoulder. "I'm not happy with this. I know the teacher probably paid 100 riels to print the answer sheet and they make us pay 1,500."

It's a common story at the Hun Sen Bun Rany Wat Phnom High School in the center of Phnom Penh. Even here, at a "Hun Sen school" where the prime minister personally bestowed new buildings in 2003,[41] poorly paid teachers are forced to supplement their income by accepting per diem "tips" in return for additional private tuition and extra credits on exams. "If we make a mistake the teacher will give us extra points," said Chuon Phanmey, 17, a grade 11 student. "If students don't go to the extra classes they only get graded on their paper; they get nothing extra." In the worst cases—and things are generally worse in rural areas—small payments can buy the manipulation of marks and grades, cash-for-answers schemes, and other cushy treatment from teachers.

Like many of his classmates, Kimkuong Chandan, an 18-year-old in his final year at Russei Keo High School in the city's north, has paid for good grades. He studies hard, hoping to pursue a career as a civil engineer, but it's frustrating to see lazier students outscore him by slipping payments to their teachers. For $15 or $20, paid discreetly a few days before the exam, he can at least keep up with his classmates. But he said that this schoolyard graft has a leveling effect, discouraging hard work and promoting low expectations among the brightest students. "I also pay money, but at the end I get the same score as someone who never comes to study and just pays," said Chandan, sitting under a tree in the school yard, near a rusty basketball ring.

Not all teachers accept "tips" and payments, but their low salaries—starting at just $50 per month for primary school teachers and $120 at secondary level—puts many teachers in the position of having to choose between their ethical commitment to their students and the imperative of survival. "Many bad things happen in the education system, and I've also joined in. I'm not happy about it, but I have to live," said one teacher at Russei Keo High School, who spoke on condition of anonymity, concerned he would be disciplined for admitting to taking payments. Such schoolyard bribery was rare two decades ago. During the 1980s, teacher salaries were minuscule, but they received food allowances, and, in rural areas, land and housing. Payoffs only became commonplace with the onset of the free market. "In 1993, the corruption started and has gotten bigger and bigger," the teacher told me. "The Education Ministry knows about this, but they just close their eyes . . . They have no ideas of how to stop it."

As with healthcare, Cambodians continue to be let down by their education system. In 2010, public spending on schooling was among the lowest in ASEAN: at 2.6 percent of GDP, only Burma spent less. Since 2000, education spending has risen steadily in absolute terms, but as the number of students has grown, education funding has dropped from 14.6 percent of the budget in 2000 to just 7.2 percent in 2014.[42] Meanwhile, the construction of "Hun Sen schools" has been undertaken for political, rather than pedagogical, reasons.

After they are unveiled by the prime minister, the paint peels and classrooms molder. In its annual report for 2012–13, the Ministry of Education stated that a fifth of all Cambodian public schools lacked "good walls." Almost half had no access to running water and nearly a third didn't have a toilet. Faced with overburdened teachers and collapsing classrooms, almost 60 percent of Cambodian students fail to graduate beyond the ninth grade.[43] Instead, many choose to go to work, helping their parents on the land as young people have done in Cambodia for generations. In 2012, the International Labour Organization reported that Cambodia had more than 429,000 child laborers, 383,000 of them in rural areas.[44]

As government education funding has tailed off, the private sector has picked up the slack. The best high schools in Cambodia, like the Lycée René Descartes and the International School of Phnom Penh, are private institutions restricted to those few who can afford the annual fees. Smaller private language schools are a common sight in Phnom Penh and the large provincial towns, but their flashy names and logos gave a misleading impression of the quality of education on offer, which often leaves much to be desired.

The crisis in the public schools has even provoked anger at the top. In early 2013, during a workshop when the EU announced €37.2 million ($50.3 million) in education support funding for 2014–16, then education minister Im Sethy tossed out his prepared speech and attacked his colleagues in the Ministry of Economy and Finance for making such small allocations for education. "The Finance Ministry doesn't know how to make policy at all," Sethy said, pointing an angry finger at a finance official sitting on stage. He then thanked the EU for its contribution.[45] But instead of helping to drag Cambodia's education system upward, donor handouts have reduced the government's need to provide funds itself, meaning that the sector, and millions of Cambodian students, are more dependent on outside help than ever.

Aside from the burden of extracurricular "fees," Cambodia's education woes have longer-term implications. Cambodia is a young country: 65.3 percent of the population is below 30 years of age, according to the UN Development Programme.[46] From an early age, an entire generation has been habituated to a system in which hard work and initiative are disincentivized and self-reliance is frustratingly self-defeating. For the 13 percent of Cambodians who pursue education beyond high school, the situation continues: a majority of tertiary institutions are private and unregulated. There are frequently shortages of computers, libraries are badly stocked, and students lack access to important online resources such as academic journals. There is little reward for succeeding, and few consequences for failing. The best institutions in the country, such as Pannasastra University and the Royal University of Phnom

Penh, set more exacting standards for students, but many other private institutions leave their graduates with few skills other than how to work the system.

Despite the rapid growth of the economy, few of the 250,000 graduates who enter the workforce every year have the skills required by potential employers. In the garment factories there are few if any Cambodian managers. Other business owners frequently speak of managerial vacancies being kept open for months due to the lack of qualified candidates. Unable to rely on the education system, employers instead have to invest considerable time and money in bringing staff up to their required standard. Senaka Fernando, a chartered accountant who first came to Cambodia from Sri Lanka in 1994 to open a local office for Ernst & Young, said graduates in his in-demand field are so ill-equipped that they have to be retrained from scratch: "They'll have a bachelor's degree in accounting, [but] you put them to work and they don't even know how to do basic bookkeeping." The French oil giant Total, meanwhile, runs its own courses for engineers.

The social implications of the growing reservoir of restless youth can be seen each day in the local media, which has documented the recent surge in gang violence and drug use—especially crystallized methamphetamine, or "ice." Economically, too, the effects of the education crisis could be catastrophic. Without improvements in the quality of schooling, the system threatens to strand Cambodia at its current stage of development—as a factory floor of international capital.

Oknha Mong Reththy leans back in his chair and casts an eye over a career's worth of trinkets and mementoes. Sitting on a wooden cabinet in his air-conditioned office are the rubber sandals that he wore after the fall of the Khmer Rouge in 1979. "I cut the car tire myself," he says. On the other side of the room is a black-and-white photo of a thinner Reththy in the robes of a Buddhist monk, taken in the mid-1960s when he lived at Wat Neakavoan along with a young temple boy named Hun Sen. Behind glass doors are the fruits of his lifetime association with the prime minister, including state medals stored in wooden display boxes, which Reththy wears in the official portrait on his website, above a flowery passage praising him for the "simplicity of his heart, normality of his thought, hardworking of his legs and hands, gracefulness of his consciousness, wisdom of his brain, socialization of his body, and his smile."[47]

Few of these are immediately evident—except perhaps the smile, which arises under arching eyebrows and shortly-cropped black hair. The 55-year-old Reththy is in an expansive mood, proud to speak of his business successes and close partnership with the prime minister. Dubbed "Hun Sen's money man" by

US officials, Reththy has had a career which nicely illustrates the circular principles of Hunsenomics. Since the 1990s, he has contributed millions toward the construction of Hun Sen schools, and his Samnang Khmeng Wat (Pagoda Boy Construction) company has an exclusive contract for the prime minister's charity projects, which include schools, roads, bridges, drainage dikes, and religious facilities.[48] Like Sok Kong of Sokimex, he has benefited from these close ties: his Mong Reththy Group boasts extensive interests in rubber and palm oil plantations, livestock, and real estate, as well as a private port (named after him) close to Sihanoukville. In 1996, Reththy underwent the Cambodian tycoon's rite of passage and was anointed an *oknha* by King Sihanouk; in 2006, he was elected a senator for the CPP.

Loyalty has also purchased protection. In April 1997, when officials in Sihanoukville seized seven tons of marijuana disguised as a rubber shipment with documentation bearing the stamps of one of Reththy's companies, Hun Sen publicly defended his friend, warning that anyone attempting to arrest him had better "wear a steel helmet." The investigation then came to a convenient end when Ho Sok, the Funcinpec official leading the drug probe, was murdered during the showdown with the CPP in July 1997.[49] The environmental group Global Witness claims that the Oknha Mong Port has been used as "a gateway for large-scale smuggling," including by senior members of Hun Sen's bodyguard unit.[50] When asked about the allegations, Reththy dismisses them as the fabrications of political enemies. "We are pure gold," he says, quoting a Khmer proverb. "We're not afraid of any fire."

Despite being an *oknha* and senator who has built more than 3,000 schools bearing Hun Sen's initials, Reththy insists he has received no personal favors or tax breaks. "It's not a business, it's just like a charity," Reththy says of his school-building partnership with the prime minister. "We just want to help the nation . . . The children don't have schools. If you don't construct schools, how can they study? And the poor people, when their houses have been hit by a storm, if you don't reconstruct their houses, where can they stay?"

Reththy's comments hint at the central paradox of Hunsenomics. On one hand, Cambodia's economy continues to surge. With each passing year, more international corporations are moving into the country. In car manufacturing, there is Ford and Tata; in insurance, Prudential and Manulife. A country that had no paper currency four decades ago now has a flourishing retail banking sector, while investment funds raise capital for further entrepreneurial ventures. The economy is slowly starting to diversify away from low-skilled garment production into more sophisticated forms of industry, such as vehicle manufacturing, electronics, and sporting equipment.[51] The most positive sign, perhaps, is the recent surge in investment from Japan, which typically holds its firms to higher standards of transparency than the Chinese, South Korean, and other Asian firms that have previously been the handmaidens of Hunsenomics. Hungry for the legitimacy and prestige that comes with Japanese investment, Hun Sen has bent over backward to accommodate Japanese firms, even handing out his personal phone number to CEOs and directors.[52]

But as entrepreneurship and investment flourish in the visible half of the economy, the shadow economy continues to elude any attempt at control. Consider the Cambodian government's highly publicized attempts at cracking down on corruption. These have arisen almost entirely as a response to foreign donor demands that the country improve transparency and combat graft. Cambodia first announced to donors that it had drafted an anti-graft bill in 1994, but it was 16 years before it was signed into law—and then in much-diluted form.

In 2001, after seven years of inaction on corruption issues, frustrated foreign governments tabled the passage of an anticorruption law as a reform "benchmark"—one of several changes it requested of the Cambodian government in exchange for their aid disbursals. When government and donor officials met for their regular Consultative Group aid conference in Phnom Penh in 2002, the law had not yet appeared. Hun Sen told his audience that he was committed to finalizing the draft before the end of June 2003. That deadline came and went. At the next meeting, in 2004, Sok An reassured donors the law would be resubmitted to the National Assembly for passage "as a matter of urgency." Again, they waited in vain. By 2006, the law was "in its final stages"; 2007 brought more unexplained delays, but still the government said it was "committed without any hesitation."[53] Donor representatives protested at the lack of action, but stuck safely to the realm of "concerns." Between 2002 and 2007, foreign governments promised more than $3 billion in aid. This was topped up by a $951 million pledge in December 2008, by which time the government had announced that the anti-graft legislation was now ready to go, but would need to await the passage of an updated Penal Code.[54]

Cambodia's Anti-Corruption Law was finally passed in March 2010. It was riddled with loopholes. Key elements of a confidential early draft were dropped, including an entire chapter with provisions for the development of a "corruption-free personnel recruitment system for government" and a code of ethics for civil servants. Key sections were broad or vaguely defined. One article banned the giving of gifts or bribes in exchange for favors, but exempted any gift given "in accordance with custom and tradition"—a caveat that could be taken to mean just about anything. The verdict of one international corruption expert was that the law was "far too obviously open to abuse."[55] When the National Assembly met to vote on the law, opposition delegates walked out in protest.

The Anti-Corruption Law, of course, was another well-engineered mirage. Donors wanted a piece of paper, so the government gave them one. Everything was done in ostentatiously public fashion. The government set up an Anti-Corruption Unit (ACU) under the Council of Ministers and installed as its chairman Om Yentieng, a long-time advisor and satrap of the prime minister whom environmental campaigners had previously linked to a number of "highly dubious" mining projects.[56] The ACU then moved into a prominent compound on Norodom Boulevard in Phnom Penh and announced that it would begin collecting mandatory asset declarations from government officials.

That's as far as anything went. The law didn't require spouses and family members to make declarations of assets, and what information it did collect remained closed to the public. The executive branch was in firm control of the ACU, leaving little hope that probing questions would be asked of Hun Sen and other senior officials. On April 1, 2011, an absurd piece of theater ensued in which Hun Sen appeared before a pack of journalists and TV cameras and publicly "declared" the 4.6 million riel ($1,150) monthly salary he drew as prime minister. "Today," he told the media, "I have fulfilled my obligation under the Anti-Corruption Law."[57] He then got up, entered his black, bullet-proof Mercedes-Benz, and glided off to his next appointment.

The ACU is not entirely toothless. Since 2011, it has effectively investigated and prosecuted a number of mid-level corruption cases. But on the whole it has left the government's foundations of patronage and power untouched. Like the courts, it has become a handy way of removing factional rivals and other small fry who have embarrassed the authorities or fallen out of political favor, leaving the big and politically protected fish to swim free. While there are many able technocrats and officials within the Ministry of Economy and Finance who have successfully enacted reforms and promoted development in the visible economy, more fundamental reform remains anathema. Any serious attempt at dismantling the patronage state would risk undercutting the very foundations of the CPP's support. Today, Cambodia remains imprisoned by the founding logic of Hunsenomics, which was to promote the consolidation of the party's power above all else.

This may well be the defining tragedy of contemporary Cambodia: that the same leaders who have helped usher the country into a historic period of peace and development have also been those most responsible for corruption, widening income inequalities, urban land-grabs, and the steady stripping of the country's natural resources. Grateful for their liberation from chaos and civil war, many ordinary Cambodians nonetheless find themselves in the grip of all the old curses.

CHAPTER EIGHT

"A City With No Smoke and No Sound"

The police came at dawn, with truncheons and tear gas. Roused by her grandson, Noch Chhoun barely had time to get out of her home before the fighting started and the bulldozers arrived, demolishing her house and burying her family's possessions under an avalanche of rubble and splintered wood. "If I didn't wake up I would have died there," the 72-year old said, standing outside the forlorn shack she now occupies at a resettlement site on the outskirts of Phnom Penh, a flimsy assemblage of thin wooden poles, blue tarps, and strips of corrugated iron.

On January 3, 2012, Chhoun and several hundred others were violently evicted from Borei Keila, a derelict former sporting complex in central Phnom Penh. The eviction followed months of standoffs between residents, city authorities, and security guards in the pay of Phanimex, a well-connected Cambodian firm with permission to develop the site. Eventually the police were ordered in, firing rubber bullets and tear gas in a bid to dislodge the recalcitrant residents, who responded by hurling bricks and setting tires alight. When the people retreated the bulldozers came, smashing down dozens of wooden homes and leveling two concrete apartment blocks. All that remained were smoking heaps of debris, which weeping residents picked over for clothes and other belongings.

"Our property was totally destroyed. We couldn't bring anything with us," said Chhoun, a feisty old lady in a gray singlet and floppy white fisherman's hat. The displaced families were then trucked 45 kilometers out of town, dumped in an open field, and left to fend for themselves. Another woman, Sok Saroeun, wiped away a tear as she described her arrival at the desolate resettlement site. "Before we came it was still forest here," she told me. "The families who didn't have tents slept under the sky."

A year later, around a hundred families still eke out an existence at a sunbaked resettlement zone known as Srah Po village. The small community sits within sight of Cambodia's precolonial capital, Oudong, a hilltop bristling with historic stupas and spires where pilgrims pray for blessings and good fortune. Here lie the remains of long-forgotten kings, interred in ornate reliquary houses. Oudong also boasts an urn said to contain the ashes of the Buddha. Srah Po's own existence is far less charmed. With the assistance of foreign charities, evictees have built rudimentary homes of thatch and corrugated iron. People have planted some scrawny trees and collect water at newly dug wells—another gift from the NGOs—but they live without power, drainage, or proper toilets. Stagnant water gathers in the gutters, overflowing into rivers of mud and effluent in the monsoon season.

The biggest problem, however, is jobs. After the eviction, Phanimex officials handed out starter-kits for a new life—basic building materials, small amounts of cash, and a few sacks of rice—but people had few ways of sustaining themselves beyond that. At Borei Keila, most of Srah Po's residents had lived off the city, selling noodles or fruit in the streets or working as moto-taxi drivers. Some of the men have since returned to Phnom Penh, where they scrounge a living and send a few dollars back home. Those who remain have nothing to do but await NGO handouts and maybe sell some basic goods—dried fish, prawn snacks, slices of sour green mango—that bring them a few thousand riels per day.

Vich Kimen knew better than to protest. Two weeks before the eviction of Borei Keila, he packed his things and set off for the resettlement site. With the help of his children, Kimen laid down a slab of concrete, erected a roof of wood and corrugated iron, and reassembled the small barbershop he had run at Borei Keila. He installed a wooden door and painted it dark blue. Inside he decorated the walls with photos of Cambodian fashion models and a few of his own paintings: two raunchy nudes, and another of a scaly green dragon and golden garuda flapping about a burning red sun. A small Sony TV and electric fan sit on his dusty cabinet, patiently awaiting the time when the village is hooked up to the power supply. "They're just for display," he said with a wry grin. Unlike most of the other families at Srah Po who fought the eviction, Kimen was one of the few to save his possessions from the bulldozers. "I felt making demonstrations was hopeless," he told me. "When I saw the people burn tires and try to get compensation, I knew we wouldn't get anything."

The story of Borei Keila is the story of Cambodia's capital writ large. The housing complex was built in the high noon of Prince Sihanouk's rule, to house athletes visiting for the First Asian Games of the New Emerging Forces, or GANEFO, a showcase of non-aligned solidarity that was held in Phnom Penh in late 1966. (The name Borei Keila roughly means "sports center.") Like the nearby Olympic Stadium, a modernist masterpiece completed two years earlier, it represented the future-leaning face of Sihanouk's Phnom Penh. Its buildings were clean and symmetrical, set amid landscaped grounds and broad ornamental ponds, including a light-filled café, a gymnasium, and eight gleaming apartment blocks capable of housing 1,000 athletes.[1] When civil war flared up in the early 1970s and Phnom Penh swelled with refugees, the complex was appropriated for use as a field hospital. Later, in the ghost capital of the Khmer Rouge, it hosted political training sessions.[2]

When Phnom Penh was repopulated after 1979, the old land records had disappeared and people settled wherever they could find vacant land or housing. After a few years as a police training facility, the old athletes' village was opened up to residents. By then it was in a decrepit state, its ponds filled with muck and its flagpole-lined entrance strewn with garbage. But people happily occupied the old athletes' apartments, modifying them to suit their needs; others erected shacks on the surrounding land. They came, like thousands of other migrants from the countryside, in search of opportunity, earning a living as market vendors and moto-taxi drivers, hairdressers and construction workers. As the years went by, the homes became more permanent. They were reinforced with brick and metal sheeting, and decorated with potted plants and spirit houses. Soon enough homes and apartments at Borei Keila were being bought, sold, and rented out.

It was only a matter of time before the site attracted the attention of developers. In 2003, Phanimex, a firm owned by a businesswoman named Suy Sophan, expressed an interest in acquiring the site. As part of a widely publicized program of "slum upgrades," Hun Sen announced that Phanimex would be granted rights to develop part of the area in exchange for building ten new apartment blocks to accommodate the 1,776 families who would be displaced. Anyone who owned a home at Borei Keila, or had rented for at least three years, was eligible for a new apartment. The city trumpeted the settlement as a symbol of the government's commitment to the urban poor. Land rights activists were optimistic that the authorities recognized the need to balance development against the interests of the city's poorest residents. But in April 2010, after constructing eight of the ten buildings, Phanimex reneged on the agreement. The government did nothing. Suddenly, 384 Borei Keila families were left without housing. Most claimed they had lived in the area since the 1990s. Some had documentation proving their ownership or residence; others didn't, or, like Noch Chhoun's family, lost their documents when their homes were later demolished. The city then ordered them to leave, accusing the families of building illegal "temporary shelters" in a bid to obtain free housing.[3] When the people refused to budge, the authorities resorted to force.

There was nothing particularly unique about Borei Keila. A raft of similar disputes have occurred across Phnom Penh over the past decade, as political stability and economic growth have pushed up land values and triggered a frenzied grab for inner-city real estate. Since 1999, an estimated 150,000 people have been displaced from Phnom Penh—around 11 percent of the city's current population.[4] Accompanying the wave of evictions, 54 resettlement sites now dot the outskirts of the city—dumping grounds for the displaced. These scattered colonies are plagued by poor infrastructure and a lack of social services. They very often lack proper sanitation and access to clean drinking water. Few are technically in the city at all: on average, they are 20 kilometers away, in a semirural no-man's-land far from most urban amenities. Communities that live beyond the city's water and electricity supplies are forced to pay between 4 and 16 times more to secure these from private suppliers.[5]

Over the past 20 years, Phnom Penh has been physically and socially transformed by urban land evictions and modern developments that have replaced "informal" city settlements with all the trappings of the rising Cambodian middle class: malls, hotels, gated communities, and the sprawling villas of the wealthy. Today, the center of the city is populated by middle-class Cambodians and expatriates. Surrounding them is an outer ring inhabited by the displaced urban poor. Along with thousands of migrants who have flooded into the city from the countryside in search of jobs in garment factories or on construction sites, they form a new proletariat consigned to the periphery of Phnom Penh's urban revolution.

In many ways, Cambodia's capital is a success story. When the Khmer Rouge abandoned Phnom Penh in January 1979 they left behind an urban husk, a phantom-city of abandoned buildings and collapsing infrastructure. The Australian journalist John Pilger, visiting in August of that year, likened Phnom Penh's desolation to "the wake of a nuclear cataclysm which had spared only the buildings."[6] During their time in power, the Khmer Rouge had unspooled decades of human and social development in a graceful city that had been known in the prewar years as the "Pearl of Asia." After the liberation, as hungry families trickled back into the derelict capital, they brought village life with them: chickens and cows roamed the city streets while people camped on the floors of shop-houses and strung their laundry from the balconies of peeling colonial villas. Most of the city's streets remained unpaved and muddy, troubled by few motorbikes and even fewer cars.

Under the PRK, all property remained in the hands of the state, which organized housing for civil servants but otherwise let people take up residence wherever they could find the space. New arrivals set up shelters in public parks, while cyclo drivers and construction workers often slept in the street. Political leaders, naturally, occupied the choicest locations. In 1979, Hun Sen moved into a property fronting the Independence Monument in the center of the city, where his imposing mansion stands today. "There were so many houses in Phnom Penh—everybody could choose one," he later recalled. "I could get 300 houses if I wanted."[7] Little changed until 1989, when the government reintroduced private property rights. The new land registration system, however, was chaotic. In theory, anybody could apply for titles to land they had occupied throughout the 1980s, but practice, as so often, differed wildly. Those with money or connections were able to satisfy land registration requirements and obtain formal title deeds, but the rest of the population lacked the knowledge or resources to navigate the complicated registration process.

With economic liberalization came a boom in urban development and construction. Today's Phnom Penh is a city in the midst of constant change and regeneration: buildings rise and fall, sped by a combination of lax planning codes and cheap construction labor. First-time visitors to the city are often surprised to encounter air-conditioned supermarkets, 24-hour convenience stores, and designer clothing boutiques. On Monivong Boulevard, well-dressed young Cambodians speed along on scooters, weaving in and out of the slower vehicles. They scoot past 1960s-era apartment blocks, now faded to a sepulchral gray, which are slowly making way for new buildings of glass and steel. Farther along, at outdoor Chinese restaurants, diners sit on plastic chairs under neon signs where animated fish flip and neon crabs snap their claws.

To the south and east lies the symbolic center of the city—the Royal Palace, situated at the point where the "four arms" of the Mekong, Tonlé Sap, and Tonlé Bassac converge. Each night the square in front of the palace fills up with snack vendors and fortune tellers. Others sit with small cages full of birds, which for a fee can be set free to earn spiritual merit. Farther along Sisowath Quay, the riverfront promenade, Cambodia's booming tourist and expat scene declares itself in a string of sidewalk bars and restaurants, offering cold beer, cheap massages, and a wide range of cuisines. After witnessing the horrors of the "Killing Fields" or S-21 prison, with its rows and rows of mute black-and-white interrogation portraits, it can be hard to discern signs of Phnom Penh's traumatic past in its bustling present. The city fizzes with life.

Nowhere is the changing face of Phnom Penh more apparent than on Koh Pich. Diamond Island, as it is called in English, made international headlines in November 2010, when a stampede on a narrow bridge during that year's Water Festival left 353 people dead.[8] In the years since, the small lemon-shaped island, sitting at the point where the Mekong and Bassac Rivers converge, has become a window into Phnom Penh's future. Fifteen years ago there was nothing here but farmland, where around 300 families grew eggplants and other vegetables to sell in the city's markets. In March 2004, the Overseas Cambodia Investment Corporation (OCIC), a firm controlled by Canadia Bank with links to Hun Sen's family, announced plans to clear the island, reinforce its banks, and create "Diamond Island City"—a Western-style entertainment and housing complex. The farmers were offered small compensation payments and moved on.

OCIC's vision was a paradise for the wealthy: ordered, paved over, ringed by wide smooth roads, a monument to a new mode of Cambodian middle-class living. Today, Diamond Island boasts a driving range (the "Elite Golf Club"), a water park, wedding reception halls, and luxury condominiums. Future plans include a gem-shaped observation tower and a forest of high-rise apartments. La Seine, a luxury housing development, features a fake French colonial clocktower, and developers have laid out parks dotted with scrawny saplings and classical statuary. The pièce de résistance, unveiled in March 2012, was the $5 million Koh Pich City Hall, a tacky mock-classical reception complex complete with chandeliers, stained glass windows, and opera boxes. Hun Sen has also announced plans to build a 554-meter skyscraper, an absurd and probably infeasible prestige megaproject that, if it ever comes to fruition, will be more than four times taller than the city's next highest building.[9]

In Elite Town, another of the planned luxury developments on Diamond Island, wealthy buyers have forked out between $232,000 and $1.08 million for modern townhouses built on streets named after famous American universities: Stanford, Princeton, Yale, Harvard. Berkeley Street, the main drag, is lined with bright yellow condominiums, some half-finished, others with SUVs parked in the driveway. Skinny trees cast small circles of shade, and lonely dogs scamper across the tarmac. Similar satellite city projects have sprung up over the past decade. Grand Phnom Penh International City, built from reclaimed wetlands in the city's north, is a secret garden of gated neoclassical mansions, shady streets, water fountains, and manicured lawns, which residents enter through what looks like a replica of Berlin's Brandenburg Gate, crowned with rearing bronze stallions. There's also an 18-hole golf course designed by Nicklaus Design, a firm owned by the American golfer Jack Nicklaus, where high-ranking officials drive and putt their worries away. Prime Minister Hun Sen, in true "Dear Leader" style, is said to have shot a number of holes in one here.[10]

Seven satellite city projects are scheduled for completion in the next 10 to 15 years, covering nearly 8,000 hectares, or about 12 percent of the city's total land area.[11] Phnom Penh has also seen a proliferation of mall-style shopping. When the eight-story Sorya Mall opened its doors in 2003, few of Phnom

Penh's residents had seen escalators, let alone modern shopping centers. In mid-2014, Japanese retail giant Aeon unveiled its Aeon Mall, Cambodia's first international-standard mega-mall, which included 100,000 square meters of restaurants, luxury boutiques, and cinemas. For the new Cambodian middle class, living and consuming have moved from the streets to private, air-conditioned interiors. Layers of security divide Phnom Penh's suburban future from the disordered bustle of the Cambodian street—the honking traffic, wagon vendors, and other sidewalk businesses that are the source of most of the city's ramshackle charms. In 2005, one city official described the urban ideal as a "city with no smoke and no sound."[12]

It's a vision Phnom Penh Municipality has come a long way toward realizing. Over the past decade most of the city's streets have been sealed and resurfaced. Overgrown public gardens have been tamed and lined with neat flowerbeds. The riverfront, once a ribbon of dirt where people sold cans of beer by candlelight, is now a handsome promenade lined with palms and streetlamps. Like Bangkok and Jakarta in the 1970s, Phnom Penh is marching toward a clean, sanitized modernity. "I am so proud that from bare hands and ghost city we have come this far," Hun Sen said during the ground-breaking of a highway overpass in late 2012. Looking back to 1979, he said, "there were sections where people [could] sleep for a week without any car to disturb them. Now Phnom Penh is a city of heavy traffic."[13]

Many of these developments have been overwhelmingly positive. But the city's growth has been unplanned and chaotic, the result of a system of economic incentives that marries the maximum of rapacity with the minimum of regulation. The profit motive reigns unbounded, to the detriment of the old, the jerry-rigged, and the informal. City officials often refer to the urban poor and their settlements with the Khmer word *anatepadei*, meaning "anarchy." The word fills official statements and crops up in the speeches of municipal officials, who denounce "slums" (*samnang anatepadei*, "anarchic constructions") as "illegal" settlements standing between Phnom Penh and its modern, developed future.

Once, Boeung Kak was a lake. Now it's an expanse of sand, dotted here and there with the shells of old buildings awaiting demolition—the first stage in its planned transformation into a futuristic matrix of leafy streets and luxury condominiums. When the Phnom Penh city authorities first announced plans to develop the lake in 2007, leasing it to an obscure company called Shukaku, Inc., the only thing standing in its way were the 4,000 families who lived around its edges. Many had called the area home since the 1980s, when parts of the lake's shores were a public park. Boeung Kak was also the location of a strip of cheap tourist guesthouses and bars, where people could drink beer and eat shrimp as the sun set over the water.

Residents in one of the city's prime undeveloped areas now faced a looming collision with one of the captains of Cambodian industry. Lao Meng Khin, a powerful tycoon and CPP senator, had set up Shukaku as a front company for Pheapimex, a powerful conglomerate owned by his wife, Choeung Sopheap, which controls 7.4 percent of Cambodia's total land area through a string of controversial logging and economic land concessions.[14] The decidedly un-Cambodian name—*shukaku* means "harvest" in Japanese—was clearly chosen to deceive. Shukaku had no permanent office address. Its lease was negotiated in secrecy, with no input from any of the people who would eventually be affected by it. In some ways it was no wonder: Shukaku's plans for the lake envisioned the largest displacement of people since the Khmer Rouge emptied Phnom Penh in April 1975.

What happened next followed a familiar script. Water and electricity were cut. Residents received eviction notices. Then, on one morning in August 2008, they woke to the sound of a large iron pipe pumping a sludge of sand and water into the lake. Rather than opt for a mass eviction, Shukaku let the rising waters do their work for them, flooding residents' homes with mud. As the waters crept upward, homes and businesses that had stood by the lake for years were gradually abandoned and demolished. In desperation many people accepted cash compensation payments of $8,600—an amount that fell far below the market value of the land. Others forewent cash and accepted compensation housing at a relocation site 25 kilometers from town, far from schools, jobs, and healthcare. Real estate agents estimated that the 133-hectare lakeside site could be worth more than $1.3 billion on the open market, and maybe twice that once developed. Shukaku paid just $79 million for its lease.

Lakeside resident Tep Vanny, then 27, remembers receiving a letter from the authorities informing people about the Shukaku lease and promising them they would not be affected by the project. "But they cheated us," Vanny told me later. "The municipal government sold the land illegally to the private company without coming to negotiate with the villagers who live here." Boeung Kak soon became a flashpoint for the rising discontent about urban land evictions. Residents from the lake, led by a hardy band of local women, took their grievances to the street, staging noisy protests outside City Hall that often culminated in violent crackdowns by riot police. Later, they were joined by evictees from Borei Keila and other urban communities.

In the forefront of the anti-eviction protesters was Vanny, a self-described housewife with long black hair and intense mahogany eyes. Born into a poor family in Kampot, Vanny settled at Boeung Kak with her husband in 2004.

Four years later, when the sand-pumping began, Vanny threw herself into the fight for the residents' land. She led marches on City Hall and tussled with riot police. In mid-2011, as the activities of Vanny and her fellow protesters began attracting international attention, Hun Sen announced that 12.44 hectares of the Boeung Kak development zone would be carved off for the remaining families, but many claimed they were excluded and protests continued. At a peaceful protest in May 2012, a mixed force of gendarmes, riot police, and district security guards arrested 13 women, including a 72-year-old grandmother. For Vanny, catapulted from a quiet home life to the frontlines of a struggle against arbitrary government power, her month in custody was surreal. "I used to watch Chinese movies where people were treated unjustly," she said of her time in prison, "but I couldn't believe it was happening to me."

The trial of the "Boeung Kak 13," as they became known, took place two days after their arrest. They faced charges of "cursing public authority" and encroaching on public land. The women stood trial at 2 p.m.; by half past five, they had each been sentenced to two and a half years' prison. "They brought us to the court just for a legal procedure, but not for justice," Vanny said, her eyes flashing. "They court did not follow the law—they just followed the authorities." The city reacted to the international backlash by redoubling its pressure on the protesters. It described Boeung Kak as "an insecure place, shelter for criminals, gangsters, drug dealers, prostitutes and terrorists."[15]

Under international pressure, the Boeung Kak 13 were released on appeal in June 2012, but the protesters continued to face the threat of arrest. In September, a Boeung Kak community leader by the name of Yorm Bopha was arrested and later sentenced to three years' jail for assaulting two men, despite thin and contradictory witness testimony.[16] The protests snowballed. Amnesty International declared Bopha a prisoner of conscience. Protesters burned fake $100 bills and hurled chili peppers at the municipal court in an attempt to put a curse on the judiciary. Later, they symbolically burned sarongs outside the CPP headquarters on Norodom Boulevard and dragged puppets representing corrupt government officials through the dunes of Boeung Kak. The disappearance of Boeung Kak lake had become the focus of an increasingly potent popular movement against urban land evictions.

The residents had a strong case. The legality of Shukaku's lease hinged on Boeung Kak's status under a new Land Law passed in 2001. The law defined Boeung Kak as "state public land," a category of land with a public interest use—including roads, schools, hospitals, and natural resources such as forests, lakes, and rivers—which cannot be legally transferred unless it has lost its "public interest value." In August 2007, to get around the law, the government arbitrarily reclassified the lake as "state private land," thus retrospectively legalizing its lease to Shukaku. The legal conjuring act was conducted without due process. As one land rights activist told me at the time, "we have no clue whether Boeung Kak has been properly inventoried as state public property. They pick and choose what is state private land and what is state public land in a manner that is convenient to them."

But the reclassification created legal complications. Under the Land Law, residents living on state private land for five years prior to 2001 had the right to apply for legal title to the land. By reclassifying the lake in order to provide cover for an illegal lease, the government now arguably activated residents' property rights. Either the lake and its surrounds were state public land, and the Shukaku lease was illegal, or it was state private land, and the residents could claim ownership. Legally speaking, the city couldn't have it both ways. But with the waters creeping upward, the law would eventually become moot.

In this sense the Boeung Kak case reflected a wider failure. In 2002, the World Bank and other major donors had set up a program known as the Land Management Administration Project (LMAP), which aimed to create an efficient and transparent land administration system in Cambodia and to "reduce poverty, promote social stability, and stimulate economic development." The $38.4 million project envisioned the creation of hundreds of thousands of land titles in Phnom Penh and elsewhere around the country. But from the beginning LMAP struggled to fulfill its mandate. While nearly a million titles were handed out across the country between 2002 and 2009—a creditable achievement—it refused to issue titles for disputed land, leaving conflict resolution to the Cambodian courts, which ruled inevitably on the side of big business.

LMAP's backers were taken in by the mirage. The World Bank and the other donors involved in the project seemingly made little attempt to assess the government's capacity or willingness to implement LMAP faithfully. Promises were simply taken at face value. Like the World Bank's demobilization program (see Chapter 5), LMAP became just one in a series of problematic attempts by donors and development agencies to relieve poverty and promote transparency via "technical" reforms. Far from reducing poverty and promoting "social stability," the application of the World Bank's market template had nearly the opposite effect. David Pred, an American lawyer advocating on behalf of the Boeung Kak residents, argued that the Bank was "asleep at the wheel for seven years," while the government manipulated LMAP to serve elite business interests.

In September 2009, land rights activists filed a formal complaint with the World Bank's official "inspection panel" in Washington, arguing that it had failed to uphold its own safeguard policies. Eighteen months later, as the last residents were being evicted from their homes, the panel handed down its decision. It concluded that the Boeung Kak families had, in fact, been denied access to due process of adjudication and that their eviction had, in fact, represented a violation of World Bank safeguards. The Bank promised redress. "We are deeply troubled and frustrated about the people who are being forced from their homes," said World Bank President Robert Zoellick. "We have repeatedly called on the Government to end the evictions. We are seeking a positive Government response."[17] They didn't receive one. When the World Bank had raised preliminary concerns back in late 2009, the government responded by pre-emptively cancelling the LMAP project, with Hun Sen claiming donors had insisted on "too many conditions."[18] The Bank responded by freezing its funding to Cambodia, but for most of Boeung Kak's residents, it all came much too late. The lake was already gone.

Cambodia's greatest living architect still lives in the home he built nearly half a century ago, an angular structure of red brick and concrete rising from behind a fence covered in bougainvillea. Like many of Vann Molyvann's designs, the house is a seamless blend of modern and traditional forms. During the 1950s and 1960s, Molyvann was Prince Sihanouk's court architect and senior town planner, presiding over the transformation of Phnom Penh into a modern capital. Today, the Molyvann name is attached to some of the city's most striking buildings, from the fan-shaped Chaktomuk Theater, where Pol Pot and Ieng Sary were tried for genocide in 1979, to the Olympic Stadium, perhaps the landmark of the "Khmer modern" school. Such designs privileged the needs of water, natural light, and ventilation—the hallmarks of the local context and climate. An elevated V-shaped roof, still seen on many old villas around the city, has become Molyvann's trademark, a coded signature of his initials—VMV—written in zigzags of concrete.

On a bright sunny morning in February 2013, Molyvann shuffled into the cool downstairs of his home wearing a gray suit-jacket over a pinstriped black shirt, spectacles hanging from his neck. Then 86 years of age, the master architect was too frail to climb the wooden stairs into the top story of his home—an airy space with an audacious swooping ceiling—so we sat downstairs at his dining room table, surrounded by wooden shelves lined with books on topics ranging from Angkorian history and the art of the Renaissance to ancient Tunisia and nineteenth-century Paris. From time to time, Molyvann glanced up at the shelves, his eyes darting owl-like behind his glasses, and asked an assistant to fetch another tome. "The red book," he instructed in Khmer, extending a finger, and then changing his mind. "No, the black one."

With black book in hand, Molyvann's eyebrows twitched as he tirelessly hunted down a phrase. To explain his architectural philosophy, Molyvann quoted extensive passages from his treatise, *Khmer Cities*—an answer to the uncontrolled development that he says is slowly gnawing away at Phnom Penh's heritage. "During the present government era there has been no urban planning about Phnom Penh. It is very *grave*," he said, pronouncing it the French way. "They have no planning—no economic plan, no urban plan, no financial resources to develop the plan."

Born in Kampot in 1926, Molyvann was one of the first Cambodians to earn his *baccalauréat* from the Lycée Sisowath in Phnom Penh. After graduating, he won a bursary to pursue his studies in Paris, where he studied architecture at the École Nationale Supérieure des Beaux-Arts, exposing himself to the work of the Swiss-born modernist Le Corbusier. "I was not a direct student under Le Corbusier, but he was really my master," Molyvann said. When the young architect returned to Cambodia in 1956, Prince Sihanouk appointed him head of the city's urban planning and housing department. The prince was the perfect patron, giving Molyvann free rein to experiment with a new vernacular—a striking hybrid form that encapsulated the hope and optimism of an ancient civilization taking its first steps as a modern nation-state.

Over the next 15 years, Phnom Penh doubled in size as swamps were drained and land was reclaimed from the Tonlé Bassac.[19] It became a garden city dominated by the eaves and spires of its Royal Palace and the daring, jagged visions of Molyvann and the Khmer modernists. When Lee Kuan Yew visited Cambodia in April 1967, he was impressed. Cruising along in one of Sihanouk's Mercedes convertibles, the Singaporean leader reportedly turned to his host and mused, "I hope, one day, my city will look like this."[20] After the cataclysms of the civil war and the Khmer Rouge, invocations of prewar Phnom Penh—the "Pearl of Asia" and the "Paris of the East"—would be accompanied by bittersweet backward glances.

Molyvann fled to Europe shortly after Sihanouk's overthrow in 1970; when he and his wife returned to their old home on Mao Tse Toung Boulevard in 1993, he found a set of water skis that had lain undisturbed for more than 20 years. Since then, Molyvann has watched his creations disappear one by one, overtaken by uncoordinated urban development and runaway land speculation. The Preah Suramarit National Theater, inspired by the American master Frank Lloyd Wright, was a magnificent triangular structure rising like the prow of a ship from a garden of palms and blooming frangipani. After being damaged by fire in 1994, the theater lay derelict and was finally torn down in 2007 by the Royal Group, a leading conglomerate.[21]

After years of fruitless lobbying, Molyvann has given up hope that Phnom Penh's heritage will survive the city's relentless surge toward the future. "Nobody cares. We don't have any system for the preservation of these monuments. We have laws for expropriations, laws for building permits and so on, but don't want to apply them." Molyvann is particularly worried about the fate of what he sees as his crowning achievement: the National Sports Complex. He lays out documents showing the construction of the Olympic Stadium, and black-and-white photos of the complex's inauguration in 1964. In 2000, part of the complex was sold to a private developer who has filled up its vital hydraulic system, designed to prevent flooding, with shoddy constructions.[22] Though still widely used, the 60,000-capacity stadium has fallen into disrepair, its concrete bleachers chipped and its railings rusted. Trash fills the old moats. "I don't want to speak about this, please," he said, gathering up his photographs. "It's very *triste*, very sad for me."

Phnom Penh's development encapsulates all the pathologies of Hunsenomics. Major projects are initiated at the whim of senior officials and tycoons. Often, they are announced in speeches by Hun Sen before they receive any planning approval, making a mockery of what few processes exist.[23] Each project is its own island. Little thought is given to wider issues like parking and traffic, which continue to worsen as an expanding middle class indulges its taste for sports cars and luxury SUVs. Most major urban planning initiatives, like flood mitigation programs, are funded and carried out by donor countries. In 2005, French consultants drafted a 2020 Master Plan, laying out a rational growth plan for the Cambodian capital. The municipality thanked them for their efforts and then left the Master Plan to gather dust.

On January 6, 2009, city officials marched into the Renakse Hotel, an elegant, shabby, mustard-stuccoed colonial building across from the city's Royal Palace, and started stripping the premises. Mattresses, crockery, furniture, and guests' luggage were all hauled out, right in front of Kem Chantha, who had managed the hotel since the late 1980s. The hotel premises were owned by the CPP, and once housed the Kampuchean United Front for National Salvation that helped overthrow Pol Pot in 1979. (The word *renakse* means "front.") But even though Chantha had a valid lease and had invested hundreds of thousands of dollars restoring the building, the party ordered her to vacate in mid-2008 on the grounds that the building was over a hundred years old and posed dangers to public safety—two claims that later turned out to be groundless.[24] When the issue went to the courts, the judges produced a ruling in favor of the party. Despite being offered $200,000 in compensation Chantha refused to leave, saying the amount was far below what she had invested. The city sent in the goon-squad. A year or so later it emerged that the Renakse and several adjoining government buildings had been granted to none other than Pheapimex—the same firm behind the Boeung Kak development.[25]

The seizure of the Renakse was a textbook case of the controversial practice of "land swaps," in which state properties in prime locations are gifted to private business figures, sometimes in exchange for building replacement offices on distant plots of land worth a fraction of the value. Ministries, government offices, hospitals, prisons, universities, state-owned villas, even parts of the Royal Palace[26]—all have been "swapped" over the past decade. The year 2005 brought a bumper crop. In January, the city's police headquarters was swapped with a location nine kilometers outside town. Then, in February, the north Phnom Penh campus of the Royal University of Fine Arts and the Monivong Hospital went.[27] Shortly afterward the police station in Siem Reap was swapped, just two years after it was built.[28] (The old town prison had already been handed to the Sokimex Group in 2000.) "The decisions [to sell public land] seem to be dictated by money and political expediency," Miloon Kothari, the UN's special rapporteur on adequate housing and housing rights, said during a visit to Phnom Penh in mid-2005. "There seems to be a frenzy, a momentum to grab up anything you can."[29]

Under the Land Law, state public properties could not be transferred to private hands unless they had lost their "public-interest use." But without a legal mechanism to control such transfers, rulings were made at the whim of city officials. Even after a "subdecree on state land management" was passed in November 2006, banning the sale, exchange, or transfer of state public land, the rules were routinely flouted. The swapping frenzy reached its apotheosis in 2010, when nearly the entire Siem Reap provincial government was exchanged with a local construction company and relocated 16 kilometers beyond the town limits. (The new location was so inconvenient the offices were later moved back to town.)[30] Hun Sen has made repeated calls for an end to the transfer of public buildings, but the practice shows no signs of letting up; it seems that there are too many powerful interests with skin in the game.

Land evictions and "swaps" have been key factors in the concentration of valuable urban land in the hands of the rich. In many cases, land is put to no productive use; it is merely scraped clean and left to accumulate value for its owners. Nearly six years after it was shuttered, the old Renakse Hotel rots and slumbers behind blue metal sheeting. The land where Molyvann's National Theater once stood remains empty, a disturbance of fenced-in dirt and weeds. Dey Krahorm, a nearby urban poor community violently evicted the same month as the Renakse, experienced a similar fate. At the time of the eviction one city official described the destruction of 150 families' homes as "an effort to clear the area for development,"[31] and the development company, 7NG, said it wanted the land for a housing project. Today, where a vibrant community once lived, all there is to "development" is a few volleyball courts and a fashion boutique.

As Phnom Penh continues to grow, the lack of planning threatens to unleash urban chaos. The city has experienced spiraling land prices, worsening traffic, and flooding due to improper drainage. When the monsoon comes, a third of the city is inundated. In 2009, the northern district of Russei Keo was frequently under water for weeks at a time. While Phnom Penh has benefitted from a $350 million Japanese-funded flood mitigation project, its gains have been undermined by the filling of lakes by property developers. Vann Molyvann warned that the filling of Boeung Kak has eliminated one of the city's main rainwater catchments and will only exacerbate the monsoon flooding. "The whole district will be flooded," he said, pointing to a map of the lakeside. "It is very dangerous what they are doing."

The other scourge is traffic. As the Cambodian middle class has grown, cars have emerged as an important indicator of status. Over the past five years, the number of cars on the road has doubled.[32] Such status markers are especially important for government officials, who often receive a freshly imported Lexus—the brand name printed in large letters on the side—as a perk of office. Public amenities such as roads and overpasses, however, have barely kept pace with the boom in vehicle ownership. Oversized cars are often parked on footpaths, or two- or three-deep into busy roads. Leafy backstreets, crammed with parked four-wheel drives, have become bottlenecks.

Cambodia's social problems can be seen in microcosm on its roads. Like the country as a whole, the country's road traffic operates less by the existing laws (which are ignored by just about everybody) than by a loose convention: small gives way to large, or suffers the consequences. As a result, Cambodians see little benefit in following road rules or making allowances for other road users. Large 4WDs roar down narrow back streets, horns blaring and headlights flashing. People drive drunk, or drive while texting. Frequently, they drive on the wrong side of the road. A recent study by Handicap International-Belgium found that less than a third of drivers even understand the concept of speed limits, which don't exist in any case.[33] What laws do exist are enforced so selectively that few people see fit to follow them. Traffic police, crouched behind parked cars on busy thoroughfares, jump out to shake down unsuspecting motorists for bribes, whether or not they've committed an offense, while vehicles with military and state license plates breeze past unmolested.

When accidents happen, which is about as often as one would expect, the less wealthy and "connected" party is invariably at fault. Very often the perpetrator simply leaves the scene, or buys their way out of trouble. On the night of August 3, 2008, a middle-aged crane operator named Sam Sabo was puttering along Sothearos Boulevard on his motorbike. Not far from the walls of the Royal Palace, he was run down by a black Cadillac Escalade driven by Hun

Chea, one of Hun Sen's nephews, who had been speeding at more than 100 kilometers per hour. The force of the impact shattered Sam Sabo's scooter and tore off the man's left arm and left leg. Hun Chea tried to drive away but the accident had shredded a tire. Traffic police arrived at the scene, saw who was at the wheel of the flailing vehicle, and fled in fear. Next a group of military police came, removed the SUV's license plate, and, according to the *Phnom Penh Post*, comforted Hun Chea and told him the accident wasn't his fault. Hun Chea walked away. Sabo was left bleeding to death in the street. His family was later paid $4,000 after they promised not to file a complaint in court.[34] In an irony that was blacker than the Cadillac's paintjob, Sabo was hit and killed just meters from the Ministry of Justice.

Phnom Penh is no longer the wild city it was in the 1990s, but cases like Hun Chea's, involving a volatile mix of alcohol, fast cars, and firearms, still surface regularly in the news. Inefficient and corrupt law enforcement, combined with fear of blowback from the top, prevents most of the cases being prosecuted properly. In December 2001, Hun Chea and Hun To, another mega-rich nephew of the prime minister, allegedly took part in a shootout at a Phnom Penh shopping center. The pair were jailed briefly but a city court later released them, saying investigators had insufficient evidence.[35] Hun To is particularly notorious for his violent antics. He lives in a lavish, palm-shaded villa on Mao Tse Toung Boulevard, guarded around the clock by surly guards in black military pajamas. The front yard is filled with expensive cars, including a black Lamborghini and a black Rolls-Royce Phantom. In 2012, an Australian newspaper accused Hun To of involvement in drug trafficking, a claim he vehemently denied.[36]

Then there was the case of Nim Sophea (also known as Nim Pisey), another of Hun Sen's nephews, who allegedly killed two people with an assault rifle in October 2003, after a drag-race through the city ended with one car slamming into a parked truck.[37] Sophea was arrested for murder, but the courts watered down the charge. In a closed March 2004 trial hearing, he was found guilty on the lesser charge of "unintentional murder" and sentenced to just three years' prison, half of which was suspended.[38] The next case to be heard that day was of a man accused of stealing 2,700 riels (about $0.67). He was sentenced to four years in prison after his relatives were unable to pay the $1,000 required for his release—a sad symbol of the double standards applied in the city's courts.[39] Then, in August, Sophea walked free on appeal, having served just ten months of his truncated sentence.[40] For years, Hun Sen has made public calls for parents and police to crack down on misbehaving rich kids—his own children have a reputation for being well behaved—but his appeals have done little to stem reports of violent incidents.[41] In August 2012, Sophea's brother Nim

Chantana (aka Nim Pov) was suspected of firing a gun in a restaurant in Koh Kong province. Police declined to investigate.[42]

The transfer of valuable inner-city land from the poor to the rich is just one part of a municipal campaign to "beautify" the city and purge it of unattractive architectural and human elements. In 2012, the municipality branded Phnom Penh "The Charming City," a designation that was strung up over some of the city's main thoroughfares. This superficial initiative was never intended to improve the lives of ordinary people. Quite to the contrary: in pursuit of this charm, "undesirables" such as beggars, drug users, street children, and sex workers are routinely taken off the streets. These campaigns typically accelerate before visits by foreign dignitaries. Ahead of an EU-ASEAN Ministerial Meeting in May 2009, around 25 street people were rounded up by police and sent to Prey Speu, a government "rehabilitation" center run by the municipal Department of Social Affairs.[43] Similar sweeps took place ahead of ASEAN Summit meetings in late 2012, when street peddlers and beggars were sent to Prey Speu and the authorities cracked down particularly hard on anti-eviction protesters.[44] One municipal spokesman said the roundup was necessary to make a good impression on world leaders. He explained, "If the leaders from across ASEAN and the world see beggars and children on the street, they might speak negatively to the government."[45]

Prey Speu is one of around a dozen "social affairs" and drug rehabilitation centers run by various arms of the Cambodian government. The Social Affairs Ministry has repeatedly claimed that poor homeless people stay at its centers "on a voluntary basis," receiving vocational training and other forms of treatment. But human rights groups have described the centers as little more than de facto prisons, reporting beatings, grossly unsanitary conditions, and the sexual abuse of detainees. In late 2008, Cambodian human rights workers visiting Prey Speu found messages scrawled on the walls of two rooms. "Detained in a miserable prison," wrote one former detainee. "Pity me, help me," wrote another. A third had etched the words "Hell life," in English, into the wall.[46]

Conditions in government-run drug rehab centers, often run by the *gendarmerie* (military police), are frequently appalling. Only a tiny fraction of individuals commit themselves voluntarily to these centers; the majority are detained arbitrarily by the authorities or, in the case of drug users, at the request of relatives. In a 2010 report, Human Rights Watch (HRW) described the "treatment" on offer at rehab centers as "ethically unacceptable, scientifically and medically inappropriate, and of miserable quality."[47] As in China, Vietnam, and many other Asian countries, drug users face "cold turkey" treatments backed up by grueling physical exercise routines, which supposedly help drug users "sweat out" addictive substances. Detainees have described being beaten for the smallest infractions. For the city authorities and the staff at these centers, drug addiction is less a medical condition requiring treatment than a sign of moral weakness that can be purged through brutal military-style rehabilitation. Needless to say, the relapse rate is high.[48]

Detained sex workers face similarly harsh conditions. Neary, a transgendered sex worker interviewed by HRW, recalled an incident that allegedly took place in April 2009 in central Phnom Penh:

> Three police officers beat me up seriously at Wat Phnom commune police station after I was taken from the park. One of the police officers pointed his gun at my head and pulled the trigger, but the bullet did not fire. They kicked my neck, my waist, and hit my head and my body with a broomstick.[49]

Like the young women who work in garment factories, many sex workers move to Phnom Penh from rural areas in search of economic opportunity, joining a new urban underclass living on the city's geographic and economic fringe. The government makes few provisions for this floating population of seamstresses, bar girls, and construction workers, who do not figure in official statistics. Very little housing is provided, and no welfare support; in order to access the opportunity of the Cambodian capital, people are forced to rely on their own resources.

Ham Chantha looks much older than his 49 years. For two decades he has lived in shacks on construction sites around the city. His current digs—a workers' camp of corrugated iron shacks with wooden walls held together with rope—sit in the shadow of the half-completed Sokha Phnom Penh Resort, a towering Sokimex project across the river from central Phnom Penh, where he has worked pouring concrete foundations. Chantha, a laconic man with gray hair and sunken cheeks, recounts a familiar story. In 1993, drawn by the UNTAC boom, he moved to the city from his village in Prey Veng, where he lacked the land to support a family. Since then, he has lived and worked on construction sites, one of the thousands of laborers who have transformed Phnom Penh into a modern city. Workers at the Sokha site earn $5 per day ($7 for supervisors), enough for Chantha to provide for his wife and their three-year-old grandson—whose mother works in a garment factory—but little more. "My children are still in the provinces," he said, "but I never send money to them because my work takes money from hand to mouth."

Back across the river, Diamond Island was under lockdown. Its main road was blocked off by city police. Private security guards in tan safari suits waved SUVs through the barricade and on toward the entrance to a vast reception hall. Rising from a sea of flowers, a giant pink love-heart proclaimed the marriage of Hun Chan Makara, a niece of Prime Minister Hun Sen, to Bun Eang Chhoung, the son of a wealthy Sino-Khmer gold trader. After passing through metal detectors, guests accumulated at large round tables inside the hall, a vast hangar with sails of pink bunting drooping from the ceiling. Pink lights illuminated a pink stage, where a wedding band casually worked their way through a list of Cambodian pop standards. As at a sporting event or political convention, three large projector screens provided live coverage of the red carpet entrance where SUVs and Mercedes-Benzes disgorged wealthy guests. Men in suits and women in diamonds bowed to the happy couple and placed cash-stuffed envelopes in a large box.

The bride walked down the red carpet, diamonds binding her hair and gracing her neck. Her dress was a perfect white. Waiters bore waves of seafood, suckling pig, and abalone; in the center of each table stood a large bottle of Chivas Regal 18YO. When the bride's uncle finally arrived, fashionably late, guests crowded along the red carpet to offer their respects. Prime Minister Hun Sen walked slowly down the carpet with Bun Rany, her face frozen into a smile above a large diamond necklace. Cambodia's first couple moved slowly, stopping now and then to shake hands or greet children. After the prime minister's party was seated, the cake was cut and guests crowded the front of the stage. The wives of government officials lined up and performed the *ramvong*, the circular Cambodian folk dance, spinning their wrists as the band broke into "Let's Twist Again" and "Sunshine Day." And so another elite Cambodian coupling was consummated, in lavish style.

Strangely, most guests paid little attention to the prime minister and his group once they were seated at a table near the stage, under the stern eye of bodyguards with earpiece radios. Hun Sen, in a bright blue shirt, sat sipping red wine, with Bun Rany to his left. At his right hand was the foreign minister, Hor Namhong, hunched over his plate. Across the table was another couple: a tall man in a black suit with an open-necked shirt and a woman with dyed black hair, her face painted a ghostly white. They were Senator Lao Meng Khin and Choeung Sopheap, the baron and baroness of Boeung Kak lake. They gazed at the prime minister, their bodyguards hovering, the *ramvong* circling hypnotically on the dance floor. Then they raised their glasses, smiling across the table as the band played on.

1 "Brother Number One": Pol Pot, Cambodia's Robespierre and the architect of the Khmer Rouge revolution, photographed shortly after taking power in Phnom Penh in April 1975.

2 Women toil on a communal worksite in Democratic Kampuchea.

3 Supporters of the Vietnamese-backed Kampuchean United Front for National Salvation celebrate the collapse of Democratic Kampuchea in Chhbar Ampov, Phnom Penh, on January 25, 1979. The sign in the photo reads, "Bravo, Cambodia is fully liberated!"

4 The new masters of Cambodia: Heng Samrin (center) and Pen Sovan (left) greet a state media delegation from the Mongolian People's Republic at Pochentong International Airport on March 15, 1979. Two years later, Pen Sovan would be appointed the first post-Khmer Rouge prime minister of Cambodia, before being purged, arrested, and imprisoned in Vietnam.

5 The world's youngest foreign minister: Hun Sen, then 26 years old, meets with a Mongolian delegation in Phnom Penh on March 15, 1979.

6 Chea Sim, the PRK's Interior Minister, with Cambodian schoolchildren, c. 1984.

7 Echoes of a nightmare: a classroom-cum-torture chamber at S-21 prison, photographed shortly after the fall of Phnom Penh in January 1979.

8 Cambodian peasants carry international food aid back to their farms via the "land-bridge" connecting Nong Chan refugee camp on the Thai border to the interior of the country, December 1979.

9 Like father and son: Sihanouk and Hun Sen toast their landmark meeting at Fère-en-Tardenois, near Paris, in December 1987. The meeting between the two men helped pave the way towards a diplomatic settlement of the Cambodian conflict.

10 Hun Sen swimming at Teuk Chhou Resort during a tour of Kampot province in January 1989.

11 A Vietnamese tank rolls past the Royal Palace in Phnom Penh on September 25, 1989, part of state-sponsored celebrations marking the Vietnamese withdrawal from Cambodia. An estimated 23,000 Vietnamese troops lost their lives during the decade-long occupation.

12 From left to right: Chea Sim, Sihanouk, and Hun Sen celebrate shortly after the prince's return to Phnom Penh on November 14, 1991, a month after the signing of the Paris Peace Agreements.

13 Cambodia collides with the new world order: a UN helicopter takes off near a temple complex in Kampong Cham on March 1, 1992. At a total cost of more than $2 billion, the UNTAC mission was the largest peacekeeping mission mounted to that point and was seen as a "critical test for the post-Cold War world."

14 With friends like these…: First Prime Minister Norodom Ranariddh and Second Prime Minister Hun Sen attend a Funcinpec congress in Phnom Penh on March 21, 1996. Despite Funcinpec's victory in the UN-organized 1993 election, royalist officials quickly found themselves with little effective power—"shuffling meaningless documents, attending vacuous meetings, reading newspapers."

15 Former DK foreign minister Ieng Sary in his fiefdom of Pailin in October 1996, during a ceremony finalizing his defection to the government—a move that spelled the beginning of the end for the Khmer Rouge revolution.

16 "Utter, final defeat": Pol Pot during an interview with a Thai journalist at Anlong Veng on January 4, 1998. Pol Pot spent his last months in custody, a miserable ward of the movement he helped establish. He died in April 1998, just as his captors reached a deal to hand him over to an international tribunal.

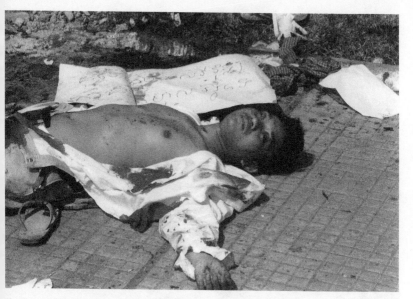

17 The bloody aftermath of the grenade attack that tore its way through a Khmer Nation Party rally in front of the Cambodian National Assembly on March 30, 1997, killing sixteen people and injuring more than 100. Nobody has ever been brought to justice for the attack.

18 A government soldier walks past a burned-out tank at a street corner in Phnom Penh on July 7, 1997, two days after Hun Sen ousted his coalition partner, Prince Ranariddh, in bloody street battles.

19 The reluctant king: Great Supreme Patriarch Tep Vong, the CPP-appointed head of the Cambodian Buddhist monkhood, bathes Norodom Sihamoni during his coronation as king on October 29, 2004, two weeks after Sihanouk's abdication.

20 Sam Rainsy, the main political challenger to Hun Sen, had many faces: gadfly, technocrat, democratic reformer, old-style Cambodian nationalist.

21 Deputy Prime Minister Sok An, the former diplomat and aide who later became Hun Sen's grand vizier and *consigliere*. His control of the Council of Ministers and literally dozens of other offices allowed him to amass a large personal fortune.

22 The new royal couple: Prime Minister Hun Sen and his wife Bun Rany cut the ribbon on a school for blind and deaf children in Phnom Penh on April 6, 2011.

23 Mourners converge on the Royal Palace in Phnom Penh shortly after the death of Norodom Sihanouk on October 15, 2012, two weeks short of his 90th birthday. The former king's passing sealed the end of the monarchy's involvement in Cambodia's political life.

24 Angkor Wat: Cambodia's symbol and talisman—and a major tourist drawcard. An estimated 4.2 million foreigners visited Cambodia in 2013, many drawn to witness the wonders of the country's powerful premodern empire.

25 Garment factory workers travel home after a shift in Russei Keo district on the outskirts of Phnom Penh on September 7, 2010. With around 400 factories employing some 475,000 workers, the apparel sector is Cambodia's largest industry, earning $5.5 billion annually and making up the lion's share of its exports.

26 Cambodia's new rich: the Norodom Boulevard mansion belonging to Oknha Sam Ang and Madame Chhun Leang, founders of the Vattanac Bank.

27 Development and displacement: sand and water inundates the lower floor of a building awaiting demolition on the edge of Boeung Kak lake in Phnom Penh on December 25, 2010.

28 A man sits beside a bulldozer in a rubber plantation clearing at the heart of Prey Lang forest in Kampong Thom province in June 2013.

29 Tep Vanny, a Boeung Kak resident and anti-eviction activist, confronts police during a protest at Phnom Penh's Independence Monument on April 22, 2013.

30 The mirage of justice: Kaing Guek Eav, alias Comrade Duch, confers with his defense lawyer during closing arguments in the first trial at the ECCC, Cambodia's war crimes tribunal, on November 26, 2009. Duch was eventually sentenced to life in prison for his role as the head of S-21 prison, where he oversaw the interrogation, torture, and execution of at least 12,272 people.

31 Accused war criminal and former DK Social Affairs Minister Ieng Thirith (center) attends her husband's funeral in the former Khmer Rouge stronghold of Malai on March 21, 2013. In September 2012, judges at the ECCC ruled that Thirith was unfit to stand trial due to age-related dementia, and released her from custody.

32 A Buddhist monk watches on as a mob sets fire to a military police truck during riots following national elections on July 28, 2013, which saw a surge of support for Sam Rainsy's Cambodia National Rescue Party—and widespread accusations of vote-rigging by the ruling CPP.

33 Cambodia's future prime minister? Sam Rainsy greets supporters at a CNRP forum in Kampong Chhnang province in March 2014.

CHAPTER NINE

The Scramble for Cambodia

The photograph presented an idyllic scene: an English garden with a gravel path and hedges trimmed square. Superimposed in the center, under an arch of pink roses, was a 13-year-old girl in red Hello Kitty pajamas. Heng Chantha seemed tall for a girl her age. The seventh of ten children born into a large farming family in Broma, a poor village in the backwoods of Kratie province, Chantha had been forced into adulthood at an early age. Each day she worked hard with her parents on the farm and helped her sisters prepare daily meals. When she could find the time she studied at a nearby pagoda. This grainy photo, snapped on a camera phone and set in a gold plastic frame, was now a valued family possession. A year after it was taken, hundreds of soldiers and military police stormed into Broma to evict villagers from land belonging to a foreign rubber company. As she ran to hide, Chantha was hit by a stray bullet and killed.

For miles around Broma the land is barren, scraped clean by bulldozers belonging to Casotim, the firm holding a 15,000-hectare rubber concession in the area. The village itself, on the edge of the concession area, is spread out along muddy roads that wind their way through the chewed-up landscape. Since the concession was granted in 2010, Broma's thousand-odd families have been fighting with Casotim for farmland they claim was included in the plantation zone; a month before the raid 700 people had blocked a national road to protest the arrest of one of their community representatives.

The soldiers arrived on the morning of May 16, 2012. Chantha's mother, Houy Lai Han, was planting beans when she saw them marching through the village. From what she could recall, a group of villagers confronted the armed men, and tried unsuccessfully to block their way. The soldiers responded by firing warning shots. As the crowd swelled there were more shots, and the troops started advancing toward Lai Han's small home, a cramped heap of wood and corrugated iron strung with blue tarps. Lai Han and her children ran and hid, but Chantha sought cover away from the others, behind a wooden ledge near the family's home. As a soldier approached, Chantha got up to see what was happening, and the soldier fired a shot. The girl fell to the ground. "She said that she'd been injured," her mother recalled, "and then she couldn't speak anymore." Chantha was rushed to hospital, but died on the way. A few days later she was buried in a lonely spot on the family's farm, under a roof of red corrugated iron, where a rusty tin of old joss-sticks was now lodged in the dirt near a row of flowers.

For farming families like Chantha's, peace was supposed to be a blessing—a respite from years of violence and political chaos. Instead the end of Cambodia's civil war brought a new wave of social dislocation. Just as Hunsenomics has transformed life in the cities, it has fundamentally altered age-old patterns of rural life. Like the Scramble for Africa, the subdivision of the continent by European colonial powers in the late nineteenth century, Cambodia's land, forests, and natural resources have been parceled out and sold to the highest and best-connected bidders. Rivers have been dammed, forests have been felled, and millions of hectares have been leased in mining and economic land concessions, the latter mostly for plantations of crops such as rubber, sugar, and cassava. Since 2000, the resulting land disputes have affected more than 700,000 people, sometimes escalating into violent confrontations with the authorities.[1]

Heng Chantha was the latest in a long line of victims. A month before her death the prominent environmentalist Chut Wutty was shot and killed during an altercation with military police in the Cardamom Mountains, where he had dedicated his life to fighting illegal loggers. Before that, security guards employed by the agro-firm TTY opened fire on villagers trying to prevent the clearing of cassava fields in Snuol district, not far from Broma. Five protesters were injured, one critically.[2] During the Broma raid, the military evicted hundreds of families in an operation the rights group LICADHO later described as "a textbook case of excessive force."[3]

The government immediately dismissed Chantha's killing as an unfortunate accident and ignored calls to investigate. Then they went further, accusing the Broma residents of plotting to "secede" from the nation. Provincial governor Sar Chamrong told the media that villagers had armed themselves with "axes, knives, hoes, crossbows, and arrows" in an attempt to form some kind of breakaway state. This ludicrous allegation quickly sprouted branches. The authorities launched a manhunt for suspected "secessionists"; police arrested Mam Sonando, one of Cambodia's few independent radio broadcasters, an old foe of Hun Sen whose advocacy group, the Democrats Association, had strong support in Broma. In October, Sonando was sentenced to 20 years' jail for masterminding the "plot." (He was freed five months later.) After the eviction soldiers were stationed in Broma to secure the area and keep an eye on the remaining residents.

Chantha's parents never lodged a complaint about her death. There wasn't much point. "I'm not sure which soldier shot her," her mother said during my visit to Broma in late 2012. "So I begged them to give some money so my family could hold a funeral ceremony." The governor gave the family $2,000 in compensation, but the cash didn't last long. Sitting in the cramped hut she then shared with her husband and nine remaining children, Lai Han pulled out the photograph of Chantha amid her background of flowers. Her eyes moistened at the memory. "I'd prefer to live without food than to have food and lose a family member," she said. Not long after my visit, newspapers reported that Chantha's family had gone. The military had made life difficult for them in Broma, so they sold their remaining land and sought a fresh start in Siem Reap[4]—just one of thousands of poor rural families uprooted by the great Scramble for Cambodia.

More than anything, one is struck by the emptiness. After an hour bumping along narrow tracks through dark forest undergrowth, the lack of trees comes as a shock. Suddenly there's blue sky above. Suddenly, the hot beating glare of the Cambodian sun. This is where Ba Heak works, in the midst of a shadeless expanse. His work begins when the trees are already gone, felled and trucked to unknown destinations. He then begins bulldozing the earth, pushing the remaining roots and branches into piles to be burnt. Heak's job is to make the land *sa'aht*, "clean," a term used by people here to refer to land that's been flattened and prepared for agriculture. "First they cut all the trees down, and then I come to scrape the land clean. After that maybe I'll get sent to another area," the 31-year old told me, standing in the shadow of his bulldozer, a hulking gray beast bearing a sticker from Phnom Penh's United Mercury Group, along with its slogan: "The Relentless Pursuit of Excellence."

Heak receives $9 for every hectare he clears, which is pretty good money considering he can manage three or four per day. He sends most of his earnings to his wife and child in Kampong Speu, some 270 kilometers away. Heak's days are long. With nothing to protect him from the sun, he spends his downtime snoozing in a hole he has dug in the shade between the bulldozer's two large caterpillar tracks. A creased brown moonscape stretches in every direction, littered with burnt tree stumps and piles of smoldering wood that give off a fragrant silver-blue smoke. Fringes of forest tickle the horizon.

This clearing lies at the heart of one of Cambodia's most significant forests. Prey Lang, as it is known locally, is the largest primary lowland evergreen forest remaining in mainland Southeast Asia—a zone of 3,600 square kilometers sprawling across four provinces in the country's north. Prey Lang is a crucial biodiversity area that is home to dozens of endangered plant and animal species. Its role in regulating the flow of water and sediment south to the Tonlé Sap lake basin is so vital that Cambodian environmentalists sometimes describe it as a "second Amazon." The forest also supports some 10,000 families—mostly members of the Kuy indigenous minority—who practice rotating slash-and-burn agriculture and harvest forest products like vines, rattan, and liquid tree resin, a special product used for waterproofing wooden boats and making paints and varnishes.

Despite Prey Lang's ecological significance, the Cambodian government has yet to declare it a protected area. Since the late 1990s, firms linked to high-ranking government officials have been granted logging concessions in and around Prey Lang, on the pretext of clearing land for agro-plantations. In 2007, the London-based environmental watchdog Global Witness reported in detail on one particular project, the Tumring Rubber Plantation, a 4,359-hectare concession used as cover for the extraction of huge amounts of timber. Global Witness linked logging proceeds to relatives of Prime Minister Hun Sen, his bodyguard unit, and authorities at every level of government.[5]

The Tumring logging operation finished up in 2006, but it wasn't the first or last venture of its kind. In 2010, the Ministry of Agriculture, Forestry, and Fisheries (MAFF) leased a 6,044-hectare plantation in Kampong Thom province's Sandan district to a Vietnamese rubber firm called CRCK, not far from where the Tumring operation had been. The loggers soon got to work, striking new roads through the forest. Standing in the CRCK plantation clearing, Mao Chanthoeun, an activist with the Prey Lang Community Network, which patrols the forest and documents logging activities, told me that the trees were felled several months ago, but that fires to clear roots and scrub had raged just the night before. When network activists protested against the felling, the authorities said they'd suspend their work. "But they didn't stop," she said, smoke curling upwards from charred logs nearby. "They cut trees night and day."

Kuy tribespeople living around the CRCK plantation all had a similar story. "They destroyed our cashew nut trees," said Chea Sot, a man in a faded T-shirt who lost a hectare of cultivated fields to the bulldozers. Local officials arrived, took his name, and promised to compensate him for the loss of his crop. Nothing happened. "The company got my land, but they didn't give me anything back. There was no compensation at all." Kun Thea, from the same village, said her family relies on the tapping of resin, which they sell or barter in Sandan town. "We have no rice fields," she said from her perch on a mound of earth near a felled tree, where more local people sat and surveyed the scene. "We need oxen or buffalo to help cultivate the land, but we don't have any. That's why we need the trees."

There is evidence that CRCK's logging operation extends far beyond the official plantation boundaries. According to Chhim Savuth, a wiry former soldier who has fought illegal logging in Cambodia since 2002, the company fells logs as far as 20 kilometers away and then trucks them back within the concession in order to conceal the illegal harvests. "This company gets very good access. They destroy more forest than other companies, right in the middle of the jungle," Savuth said, as we bumped along the muddy road from the provincial capital of Kampong Thom to Sandan, occasionally passing a large truck filled with timber planks. The local authorities have even provided battalions of police and military police to help guard the plantation area. "They all get money," he said, staring intently ahead as he piloted the battered Toyota Camry through the mud, "from the low level up to the high level."

In early 2012, the Cambodian government drafted a subdecree that would extend protected status to Prey Lang.[6] Passage of the law would be a step forward, but it's unclear what difference it would make. Legal protections have done little to prevent the Boeung Per Wildlife Sanctuary, a 242,500-hectare protected area just to the west of Prey Lang, from being obliterated by illegal loggers. According to the human rights group ADHOC, nearly half of the area has been granted to rubber companies, the biggest of which are owned by the casino and logging magnate Try Pheap and An Marady, another *oknha* tycoon.[7] As in Prey Lang, Savuth says these two firms fell trees in surrounding areas and then launder them through their concession lands. He even suspects that Try Pheap Import Export Co. Ltd. has driven into Prey Lang, removed trees, and transported them back to Boeung Per for processing. One Environment Ministry official said the concessions were granted in "degraded forest" areas.[8] But Savuth said the firms single out valuable "luxury" trees like Siamese rosewood, a richly hued hardwood that can fetch tens of thousands of dollars per log from buyers in Vietnam and China. "With the value of these logs there would be no need for the Cambodian government to borrow money from foreign countries," he said, urging the car onward. "When I see the loss caused by deforestation, I feel almost crazy."

If there was one upside to Cambodia's decades of upheavals, it was that the country's abundant forests remained mostly intact. During the Sihanouk era, forest cover actually increased, and extended over more than three-quarters of the country by the time the Khmer Rouge came to power in 1975.[9] Subsequent spells of war and isolation meant that the country largely avoided the severe deforestation experienced by Indonesia, Malaysia, and Thailand during their respective economic booms. All this changed at the end of the 1980s, however, with the advent of Hunsenomics.

The Cambodian government, facing economic collapse in 1990, kick-started logging operations in order to earn hard currency to fund its ongoing war against the Khmer Rouge; by 1992, forestry revenue made up four-fifths of the government's foreign exchange earnings.[10] The same was true for Pol Pot's men, based in their heavily forested strongholds along the Thai border. Selling off logging rights to Thai firms helped to fill the breach left by a falloff in Chinese aid—a process that accelerated further after Thailand declared a domestic logging ban in January 1989, pushing timber dealers over the border into Cambodia. Before the ink was dry on the Paris Peace Agreements, the two sides were competing to strip Cambodia's forests bare.

The pattern continued after the coalition government took office in 1993. Hun Sen and Prince Ranariddh quickly agreed on a joint forestry "policy," signing Cambodian forests away to Thai and Malaysian logging firms, while keeping taxes low to maximize the informal profits that flowed back their way. Logging cash was spread around to maintain the loyalty of the military, fund the civil war, and grease the wheels of patronage. Logging and conflict formed a particularly destructive cycle: as Global Witness observed, logging was used to fund military campaigns, which were then used as a pretext for more logging.[11] This free-for-all took place beyond the reach of any competent restraining authority. Mok Mareth, a secretary of state in the Ministry of Environment, admitted in 1994 that his department was "powerless" to act. "The situation is really very delicate. My officers cannot get to the remote rural areas and can only speculate as to what is really going on," he told the *Phnom Penh Post*.[12]

For Cambodia's international backers, the forestry sector would emerge as a key test of reform and "good governance" initiatives. Development consultants then saw timber as the country's most valuable natural resource, and pressed the government to reform its forestry management system. But Cambodian political leaders relied heavily on logging as a source of patronage, and zigzagged around donor recommendations. Between 1992 and 1996, log export bans were declared on five separate occasions, but within weeks or months they were lifted on various pretexts and it was back to business as usual.[13]

By the time the Khmer Rouge imploded in the late 1990s, the Cambodian government had quietly granted between 30 and 40 logging concessions to local and foreign-owned companies, covering 7 million hectares of forest—around 39 percent of the country's land area.[14] Only a fraction of the profit was reaching the state's coffers. In 1998, a forestry report funded by the World

Bank estimated that as much as 95 percent of the past year's timber production had taken place off the books.[15] By another estimate, the state was losing around $100 million per year in duties and taxes.[16] Donors started to lose patience. In 1996, the International Monetary Fund froze a $20 million tranche of funds in response to the mismanagement of forestry revenues. The World Bank withheld $15 million.[17]

At the Tokyo aid summit in February 1999, forestry issues topped the agenda. The outcome was the creation of a Forest Crimes Monitoring Unit to help build the government's "capacity" to fight illegal logging, and Global Witness was appointed as an independent forestry monitor. To placate the aid-givers, Cambodian officials conjured up their mirage. They passed a new Forestry Law requiring logging concessionaires to produce sustainability and environmental impact plans, and Hun Sen vowed clampdowns on those breaking the rules. "If I don't take away your concessions and close down your factory I will cut my throat," he said in December 2001.[18] Shortly afterward the government announced moratoria on the harvesting and transportation of logs. Noncompliant concessions were cancelled, and the concession system was eventually abandoned altogether.

It looked a lot like real change. But as with the LMAP land titling program described in Chapter 8, hope and reality soon parted ways. The truth was that Hun Sen probably couldn't have stopped logging even if he had wanted to. Profits from the sale of timber, like other forms of illicit income, were the glue that held the CPP patronage state together. Logging generally increased in the run-up to national elections, when the CPP campaign machine slipped into high gear. The rest of the time, access to the slush fund helped keep powerful interests happy and bought the government the loyalty it needed to secure its hold on power, and hence on further resources. The vicious cycle of Hunsenomics brooked no reforms—just the creation of new mirages to distract donors from the workings of the shadow state.

The work-around of choice was economic land concessions (ELCs): long-term leases of land for agricultural plantations. ELCs were first introduced in the early 2000s as part of a government scheme aimed at boosting rural development through large-scale agribusiness ventures. The catch was that while commercial logging was now banned, exceptions could be made for companies planning to plant rubber, cashews, cassava, or other crops in designated ELCs. So exceptions were made everywhere. MAFF would grant concessions to favored local companies, sometimes working in partnership with a foreign agribusiness firm. The loggers would then move in and fell the commercially viable trees in and around the concession area, and the company would fire-hose the local authorities with kickbacks. More money went upwards.

Sometimes a plantation would be established on the cleared land, as in Prey Lang. Sometimes the concession was simply abandoned once the timber had been sold.

Soon ELCs were being minted with abandon. The Land Law passed in 2001 capped the size of ELCs at 10,000 hectares, but the limit was often ignored. Some companies simply sliced up large concessions into a series of smaller adjacent plots with near identical names. The use of ELCs as logging cover took place with the active involvement of the very authorities charged with policing forest crimes. In August 2003, Agriculture Minister Chan Sarun established the Forestry Administration (FA), a mirage-like body which theoretically had greater powers to enforce the Forestry Law passed in 2002. In practice, it simply provided a new channel for patronage.

Shortly after its creation, Chan Sarun and the FA's Director General Ty Sokhun convened an auction for around 500 jobs in the new administration. The pricing scheme took into account both rank and geographic location. In those provinces with rich forestry resources, the payoff necessary to secure a top job could be as high as $30,000. Successful candidates were then required to pay as much as half their income to their superiors.[19] The burdens of bribery forced many FA staff into debt, creating an even greater motive for them to squeeze money from their positions. Far from tackling forest crime, the new system actually incentivized the felling of trees.

Global Witness, the group chosen to oversee Cambodia's forestry management efforts, quickly made powerful enemies by documenting the extent of official involvement in the timber trade. On the evening of April 30, 2002, Eva Galabru, who headed the group's Cambodian operations, was attacked as she arrived at her office in Phnom Penh. As she got out of her car several men, at least one of them masked, pushed her to the ground. Then they kicked and beat her. The following day she received an anonymous email with a single threatening word: "QUIT."[20] The government eventually fired Global Witness as its forestry monitor, while Hun Sen castigated the organization for its "hostile, untruthful, unjust, and destructive attitude."[21]

From its London "exile," Global Witness kept publishing damaging reports that exposed high-ranking involvement in illegal logging and natural resource extraction. *Cambodia's Family Trees*, a report released in 2007, blew the lid off operations in Prey Lang and for the first time named close associates of Hun Sen—including his first cousin Dy Chouch, Dy Chouch's ex-wife Seng Keang, and Khun Thong, an in-law of Agriculture Minister Chan Sarun—as the heads of the Seng Keang Import Export Co. Ltd., which it described as the most powerful logging syndicate in Cambodia. The report was immediately banned in Cambodia. Hun Sen's brother Hun Neng, the governor of Kampong Cham, said that if any Global Witness staff returned to Cambodia he would "hit them until their heads are broken."[22]

Global Witness's "name and shame" approach unfortunately had little real effect. In 2010, in response to bad publicity about logging, Hun Sen fired Ty Sokhun from his position as head of the Forestry Administration. Sokhun was kicked upstairs, becoming an undersecretary of state at MAFF. Hun Sen said he should treat it as a learning experience. Technically, it was a promotion.[23] And the logging continued. By 2010, Cambodia's forest cover had dropped to 57 percent, down from 73 percent two decades earlier. These were the FA's own statistics; the real figure was probably much lower.[24]

For the past decade, conservation and forestry management have remained understandably high on the donor agenda. But progress toward reform "benchmarks" has been a mix of intermittent crackdowns and holographic management schemes that never seem to emigrate from PowerPoint presentation to reality. In 2008, the World Bank terminated its $5 million Biodiversity and Protected Areas Management Project (BPAMP) after the government opened the project area to mineral exploration rights by Indochine Resources, a little-known Australian mining firm. Indochine was given the right to prospect across 180,000 hectares of Virachey National Park, and neither the Bank nor the Ministry of Environment had been consulted.[25]

The decision threatened to undermine BPAMP's main objective. Since 2000, the project had made steady progress toward the creation of "an effective national protected areas system" for Cambodia.[26] BPAMP focused on improving management procedures in Virachey, a 333,000-hectare area in Cambodia's northeast "Dragon's Tail"—the secluded point of Ratanakkiri province where the borders of Cambodia, Vietnam, and Laos converge. Of the 23 protected areas created by royal decree in 1993, Virachey was among the most important; it included a crucial watershed supporting the Mekong River and vast tracts of semi-evergreen and deciduous forest that were home to endangered cat and primate species. It also contained the remote Veal Thom grasslands, which one ecologist described as "a secret world of golden light and open vistas carved out of the middle of the jungle, an immense area of rolling amber hills."[27] If BPAMP managed to establish effective management structures in Virachey, they could then be extended to protected areas nationwide.

For a while things seemed to be going well. Then, during a routine surveillance flight in May 2004, World Bank officials were shocked to discover a large-scale logging operation in the heart of the Virachey sanctuary. Glenn Morgan, one of the Bank representatives on the flight, said the logging was taking place on an "industrial and commercial scale" with paved roads running in and out of the area.[28] While BPAMP and ministry officials had been setting up ranger patrols, ecotourism ventures, and other "best practice" park management procedures, $15 million worth of timber had been brazenly harvested and trucked over the Vietnamese border.[29] The Bank demanded an investigation. In March 2006, just before that year's donor aid summit, Hun Sen announced that key officials in Ratanakkiri had been removed from their posts. In November, seven people, including Ratanakkiri's governor Kham Khoeun and the director of Virachey, were found guilty of involvement in the Dragon's Tail logging operation and sentenced to lengthy jail terms.

But the mirage was thick in Virachey. Of the seven only one, the provincial police chief, was ever arrested. After being fired, the others had gone into hiding. The government had a good idea where they had gone—Khoeun was known to have friends and business interests over the border in Laos—but they made no real attempt to track them down. The truth is that responsibility for the Virachey logging scheme extended much further up the chain than Ratanakkiri. Kham Khoeun reportedly enjoyed the protection of Bou Thang, a high-ranking member of the CPP Central Committee who belonged to the same Tumpoun ethnic minority group as Khoeun. In 1973, Thang, a Hanoi-trained communist, had mutinied against the Khmer Rouge and led hundreds of minority peoples over the border into Vietnam. After the fall of Pol Pot in 1979, the Vietnamese put him in charge of Cambodia's northeast provinces and he had maintained a strong influence in Ratanakkiri ever since. Thang personally appointed the province's governors, who, according to the dictates of patronage, paid him for the privilege. One source of income was logging.[30]

When the World Bank woke up to what was happening in Virachey, the government cast about for a way to deflect attention from the system as a whole. "They had to save face. They found scapegoats," said Graeme Brown, an Australian forestry specialist who was working in Ratanakkiri at the time. "There is no way that the logging in VNP was not known about at national level."

When information about the Indochine Resources exploration deal emerged in mid-2007, the World Bank finally pulled the plug on BPAMP. In its final assessment report it cited the project's "positive institutional impacts," including the passage of a new Law on Protected Areas, drafted with the Bank's assistance. As usual, the law adhered to the best international standards. It divided up each of Cambodia's protected areas into four conservation areas, including a "sustainable use zone" that could be used for commercial activities like mining once the proper zoning had taken place. As with illegal logging, however foreign legal consultants made the mistake of assuming Cambodian officials had any real incentive to enforce the regulations.

It seemed the World Bank still hadn't learnt its lesson. Its final assessment was that improvements in national park management remained a technical matter, requiring the "continued strengthening of the [Environment] Ministry's managerial and coordination skills."[31] But legal and technical tinkering did little to alter the fundamental reality: the government's aim wasn't conservation; it was economic exploitation. The Bank wasn't responsible for the deforestation, of course, but the road to environmental neglect had been paved with its own optimistic assumptions. In its entire project assessment report, the words "patronage" and "corruption" were each mentioned exactly once.

In the years since the Indochine deal, dozens of licenses to explore for bauxite, gold, and copper have been awarded in the same ad hoc fashion as Cambodia's forest and land concessions—many of them in protected areas.[32] The same has been true for perhaps the country's most valuable resource: its oil and gas deposits. Questions still remain about the extent and commercial viability of Cambodia's reserves, thought to exist both offshore and under the Tonlé Sap lake, but the interest of foreign firms like US oil giant Chevron and France's Total indicates the country could be in for a future windfall totaling in the billions.

In 2014, Cambodia faces the same issue it faced with forestry two decades ago. If managed well, oil and gas revenues might be enough to wean the government off foreign aid and lift countless Cambodians out of poverty. But so far it looks like business as usual. In 1998, Hun Sen shifted control of oil revenue management from the Ministry of Industry, Energy, and Mines to a new Cambodian National Petroleum Authority (CNPA), later placed under the control of his economic gatekeeper, Sok An. The CNPA's activities are cloaked in secrecy. "Key positions are populated by his [Sok An's] in-laws," said one foreign NGO worker with knowledge of the institution. "It's pretty clear what's coming." Under Sok An, the CNPA refused to disclose details of its agreements with foreign oil companies and has baulked at revealing the signature bonuses these firms have paid to secure exploration rights, payments that can sometimes run into the tens of millions of dollars.

The larger the figure, the larger the potential for "irregularities." In 2006 and 2007, the Indonesian oil firm PT Medco Energi Internasional announced that it had paid the government $7.5 million in signing bonuses after securing exploration rights for two oil blocks, but only a fraction of this figure appeared in the government's annual financial reports.[33] Around the same time, Jeffrey Bruhjell, president of the Vancouver-based Indocan Resources, told the *Bangkok Post* that the company had backed out of Cambodia after high-ranking officials in the Cambodian government demanded "large sums of money as bribes."[34] In the mining sector there have also been questions about payments made by foreign companies. In 2007, the water resources minister Lim Kean Hor described a $2.5 million payment from the Australian mining giant BHP Billiton, intended for a social development fund, as "tea money"— Khmer slang for a bribe.[35]

In response to criticisms, the government has taken steps to improve transparency and publish more information about oil and mineral exploration agreements. In 2010, it began disclosing some signature bonuses and other payments, and vowed to comply with the Extractive Industries Transparency Initiative, an international set of benchmarks for resources management. There is still time for concrete improvements. The mineral sector currently accounts for just a tiny fraction of government revenues, and oil is not expected to start flowing before 2016. But so far the government's promises have a familiar hollow ring.

After two decades of Hunsenomics, Cambodia's land is concentrated in fewer hands than ever. In 2012, the human rights group LICADHO reported that 22 percent of Cambodia's surface area—around 3.9 million hectares—had been granted in ELCs, mining concessions, and other allotments. A map accompanying LICADHO's findings resembled a patchwork of colored concession blocks covering around 53 percent of the country's arable land.[36] Few parts of the country have been left untouched. Take Koh Kong, a southwestern province of pristine coastland and dense jungles. Since 2007, the province's coastal estuaries and marine areas have been devastated by large-scale sand mining operations run by Ly Yong Phat, another big-time senator-tycoon. US officials have described Phat as the "King of Koh Kong." The initials of his LYP Group are attached to nearly everything in the province: roads, bridges, construction firms, power-stations.[37] LYP's headquarters are located in a kitschy hotel-casino complex on the Thai–Cambodian border, a short drive from Koh Kong Safari World, another LYP enterprise. (Come for the baccarat, stay for the boxing orang-utans.)

Since dredging operations began in 2007, LYP has exported vast amounts of sand to Singapore, where it is used for land reclamation and construction. On one visit to coastal Koh Kong in 2009, I observed LYP's dredgers operating around the clock, scooping up sand and piling it onto barges belonging to a Hong Kong-based partner firm. The vessels chugged offshore and dumped their loads into a bulk carrier bound for Singapore. At the height of the operation in 2009, Global Witness estimated that 796,000 tons of Cambodian sand were being mined from Koh Kong each month by concessionaires including LYP, a haul estimated to be worth $248 million at the time.[38]

Environmentalists warned that untrammeled dredging threatened fish stocks and delicate mangrove ecosystems by churning up the seabed and spilling effluents into the water. Fishermen spoke of similar disruptions. Hauling his net out of the deep green waters of the Koh Pao River, 38-year-old Chun Doeun told me about the unusual behavior of the local crabs, which had recently been paddling up to the water's surface. "[This] is a strange habit for this kind of species. Crabs always dwell on the riverbed," he said, as a sand-filled barge puttered past, bound for a cargo ship glued to a blue horizon. Doeun had been fishing the area for 15 years, and said his catches had never been so low.

Little of the province has been spared. Farther down the coast, the government has carved out a huge chunk of Botum Sakor National Park and granted it to a Chinese company with plans to spend $3.8 billion on building a fantasy tourist resort. If things go according to plan, large swathes of unspoiled jungle will become a self-contained city featuring hotels, golf courses, a port, and a casino ("Angkor Wat on Sea"), linked by a 64-kilometer access highway. Forest and wildlife have already been destroyed, killed, or displaced, as have more than a thousand local residents.[39]

To the north, in remote corners of the thickly forested Cardamom Mountains, loggers operate far from the reach of the law. The rivers that course through the jungle valleys have been earmarked for hydropower dam developments which threaten to inundate the homes of hundreds of villagers and create opportunities for the "removal" of old-growth forest.[40] Back down in the plains, there is sugar. In September 2006, 250 families were thrown off their land in Sre Ambel district to make way for a sugar plantation owned by Ly Yong Phat. "The police destroyed the villagers' crops and houses with a bulldozer and brutally attacked the villagers who resisted the eviction," the Asian Human Rights Commission reported. Five people were reported injured; another two were shot.[41] Hundreds now toil in the sugar fields for small wages.

Contrary to the Cambodian government's claims, its economic land concession program has failed to benefit most people in rural areas. The real result has been a spate of land disputes which are seldom resolved fairly and have left tens of thousands of families homeless. Historically, Cambodia never had a serious problem with landlessness. Life was harsh, but there was almost always enough land to go around, and more could always be cleared. When Cambodia adopted a system of private property in 1989, land distribution was relatively egalitarian; but by 2007, after more than a decade of Hunsenomics, the richest 10 percent of the population owned 64 percent of the land and the top 1 percent an estimated 20–30 percent.[42] More than a fifth of the rural population is now landless, while another 45 percent of households own less than a hectare—an amount that barely allows farmers to meet subsistence needs.[43] Slowly, Cambodia's land crisis is turning its people from small landowners into a landless working class, laboring on plantations and garment factory floors.

The social effects are particularly acute in Ratanakkiri, home to a large population of ethnic minority peoples. The province—its name means "mountain of gems"—sits at the fulcrum of Indochina, where Virachey's dense Dragon's Tail tapers off into the upland wilds of the country's extreme northeast. For decades, war and revolution conspired to keep Ratanakkiri wild and isolated. In the 1960s, senior Khmer Rouge leaders plotted their revolution from bases deep in its jungle; later, US pilots banked over green jungles and dropped their payloads on hidden Viet Cong supply trails. Until recently, Ratanakkiri remained nearly untouched by the outside world. Only with the coming of peace and stability have new roads opened up the northeast, exposing this region of waterfalls, mountain spirits, and tribal peoples to the hurricane force of development.

When Pierre-Yves Clais first saw Ratanakkiri in 1992, at the start of his ten-month stint of military service in the French paratroopers, the province was still covered in thick jungle. Clais had ended up in Cambodia by chance. When he started his service, he hoped for a posting to Francophone West Africa, the backyard of the old colonial empire. Instead he found himself in the backwoods of Cambodia's northeast, wearing the light-blue helmet of the UNTAC military force. In support of the UN mission, he patrolled a wild land that had barely changed in hundreds of years. Leopard spots of Khmer Rouge resistance were still scattered here and there in the northeast, much of which remained inaccessible by road. To reach the isolated provincial capital, Banlung, it was safer—and more comfortable—to catch one of the Soviet-era Antonov 24 turboprops that skidded down every few days on a dusty landing strip in the center of town.

After being discharged in early 1993, Clais returned to Cambodia as a travel writer and tour guide, taking visitors on treks and dirt-bike explorations in every corner of the country. But he kept returning to Cambodia's Wild East, magnetized by the rugged life and the mystery of Ratanakkiri's minority peoples. "It reminded me of my army days, when I could wear the same military fatigues, be dirty, talk dirty," Clais recalled. Eventually he settled in Banlung, where he opened the Terres Rouges Lodge in 1998. "I was living all my childhood dreams," said Clais. "I'd always been a fan of the Apaches, and I saw the same sorts of people over there—wild tribes living in the forest, making these wonderful totems, that were totally forgotten."

But economic development wasn't far behind. In 2004, Cambodia and its neighbors created the Cambodia–Laos–Vietnam Development Triangle area, a scheme to develop the countries' remote border provinces and "modernize" the lives of the region's minority peoples. In the decade since, Ratanakkiri has been transformed. National Road 78, once an unpaved dirt road, was recently resurfaced with Chinese funds and is now an all-weather highway dissecting the province from east to west on its way to the Vietnamese border via Banlung. Huge swathes of Ratanakkiri's jungle, mostly secondary forests that ethnic minority peoples cultivate in a dispersed rotational system, have been converted into rubber, cassava, and cashew plantations. While patrolling along National Road 78 in 1992, Clais recalled having to dodge shots from Khmer Rouge hidden in the thick jungle. "We couldn't see the sky," he said. "Now the forest is kilometers away, if it exists at all."

The new roads have brought economic opportunity, and a wave of poor Khmer migrants from other parts of the country. Once a dusty frontier town, Banlung has grown into a bustling provincial capital with wide tarmacked roads, public parks, and a clutch of new government buildings. At night, the highway outside town is alive with the epileptic neon of karaoke bars and beer gardens. And then, in the blackness a few kilometers further out, begin the rubber plantations, the dark grids of *Hevea brasiliensis*, carpeting the country-side in every direction.

According to ADHOC, the government has granted ELCs to 27 companies in Ratanakkiri, covering more than 220,000 hectares. Almost half are located inside the Virachey National Park, which was opened up to ELC developments in early 2011, when Hun Sen granted two 70-year leases totaling 18,855 hectares to the tycoon Try Pheap.[44] In addition to his other business interests, Pheap has rapidly become the face of big-ticket enterprises in Ratanakkiri. To the south of Virachey, he runs a special economic zone and a casino on the Vietnamese border. In February 2013, he was granted the rights to all wood felled in ELCs across the entire province—an arrangement one observer said would only speed the degradation of Ratanakkiri's remaining forests.[45]

Fifty kilometers east of Banlung, in a small hut with a bamboo floor, 56-year-old Romas Thno shrugged his shoulders as he recalled the decade-long legal battle his people have waged to secure their land. Back in 2004, a businesswoman named Keat Kolney had arrived one day in this red-earthed village and informed its inhabitants that Hun Sen required 50 hectares of land to house disabled military veterans. After some discussion the villagers agreed, and Kolney organized a traditional, alcohol-enhanced ceremony to celebrate the deal. Once the villagers were drunk, they were presented with contracts to thumbprint. Instead of 50 hectares, however, the fuzzily viewed contract signed away 500. No army veterans ever arrived. Kolney's company cleared the land and began planting rubber trees. There was nothing the people of Kong Yu village could do. Keat Kolney was doubly connected: she was the sister of the finance minister Keat Chhon, and the wife of a senior official in the Ministry of Land Management. She was also seemingly protected by the provincial court in Banlung, which backed her claims against the people of Kong Yu, who have fought in vain to have the deal annulled.

Kong Yu's inhabitants belong to the Jarai ethnic group, an Austronesian people related to the Cham Muslims, to minority people in Vietnam, and, more distantly, to the Malay-speaking peoples of maritime Southeast Asia. At first glance, they have successfully absorbed the more visible aspects of modernization: motorbikes, Angry Birds baseball caps, artesian wells, laundry soap. But Romas Thno says the loss of their land has cut the community adrift. Having been deprived of their rotational farmlands and spirit forests, each family in Kong Yu now has just a hectare or two to cultivate—not nearly enough to support themselves. Many young people have been forced to take jobs on the rubber plantations. In Romas Thno's hut, a scraggly tortoiseshell cat limped across the floor as the somber 56-year-old quietly lit his pipe, puffing until the acrid smoke filled the dark room. "Now we have to do the same sort of farming as other Khmer people," he told me. "We've lost everything. Even our two ancestors' burial places were cleared to plant rubber trees."

When I visited Kong Yu in 2008, the rubber saplings were still small, and the village chief Romas Neath had angrily lamented the lack of action by the court. "We would speak one word, and [the judges] replied with ten," he said. "They have more power and rights than us." Four years on, Keat Kolney's rubber trees were nearing their gloomy maturity and the community seemed worn out by its struggle. Three different judges have now presided over the Kong Yu case, but still no verdict has been handed down. In a hut nearby, a group of men sat drinking in the middle of the day. Cows munched on the grass as women strung out lines of colored laundry. Romas Thno was resigned. "We just want to know who has won and who has lost," he said.

Back in Banlung, dusk was falling. Four-wheel drives covered in red dust roared through the city streets and children played on a white concrete monument commemorating the "liberation" of January 7. Sitting on the porch of his office, Pen Bonnar, then the provincial monitor for the human rights group ADHOC, explained how land disputes have erupted in all of Ratanakkiri's nine districts, mostly involving government-backed plantation firms. A serious man in a white short-sleeved shirt, Bonnar has worked in Ratanakkiri since 1999. In that time he has seen the toll that development has taken on its minority peoples. "Even though villagers' life wasn't developed in the past, they didn't have to worry about losing their land," he said, as the sun's last rays fell across the road outside.

Minority people are especially vulnerable to exploitation. Only a small number speak or read Khmer fluently. The Land Law contains generous provisions for indigenous peoples, including a recognition of community-based land rights, but, like the law as a whole, these have yet to be implemented. "A lot of businessmen have come to take over indigenous lands," Bonnar said, "and villagers are constantly worried, afraid that one day they'll lose theirs." A similar situation exists in Mondulkiri province to the south and Stung Treng to the west—two other provinces with sizeable ethnic minority populations.

Another threat in the northeast is hydropower. The Lower Sesan 2 dam, an $800 million project now under construction at the confluence of the Sesan and Srepok Rivers in Stung Treng, is set to displace around 5,000 mostly minority people. The Lower Sesan 2 project is just one of more than a dozen dams planned as part of a government policy to harness the power of the country's rivers and export electricity to Thailand and Vietnam. While hydropower could be a vital spur to development, environmentalists say the government's dam-building drive is ill-considered and threatens to damage Cambodia's teeming fisheries, which provide the country with 80 percent of its animal protein.

Much of the threat to Cambodia's fisheries comes from Mekong River dams upstream in Laos and China. But as Cambodia moves to develop its own hydropower capacity, the effects of distant dam projects could well be magnified closer to home. In the case of the Lower Sesan 2 project, donors have already called for a redesign after an environmental impact assessment found it would trigger changes in hydrology and water quality and cut off access to migratory fish for tens of thousands of people living along the river in Stung Treng and Ratanakkiri. Effects will also be felt downstream. By one estimate, the project will result in a 9 percent drop in fish stocks in the entire Mekong basin.[46] Despite the probable impacts, however, the government decided to press ahead with the Lower Sesan 2 project and several others, including some on the Mekong mainstream itself.

In an air-conditioned office in Banlung, the governor of Ratanakkiri arranged his three smartphones in a neat stack on the desk as he launched into an address on the subject of Hun Sen's national development policy. Pao Ham Phan wore tailored black pajamas with a gold pen peeking from the breast pocket. On one finger was a gold ring with a large green gemstone, and he wore thin-rimmed gold glasses which he adjusted now and then as he recited his catechism of progress. In recent years, he said, indigenous people have gone from living in traditional homes and practicing rotating cultivation to living on permanent farms like Khmers. Some now even own motorbikes and brick houses, and they no longer pray to the spirits when they get ill. New dams will bring electrification. New roads will bring further improvements. "When we have good roads everything develops faster," Ham Phan told me, as his boss smiled down from a framed poster on the wall and a dusty brass female *apsara* statue sat on a nearby shelf, frozen in mid-dance.

When asked about land disputes, Ham Phan blamed rights activists like Pen Bonnar for inciting opinion against the authorities. "He always makes problems," he said, unstacking his phones and building them into a new pile. "So far no company has taken over any villagers' land. If that was really the case, I'd have to find a resolution, but it's not like that. Ratanakkiri has changed from a cashew nut province into a rubber plantation province, and it will provide jobs for villagers."

Two decades after the great scramble for Cambodia began, an environment of desperation and alienation now grips some rural areas. Frustrated by the inability of authorities to resolve land disputes fairly, some people have begun taking matters into their own hands. In March 2010, violence erupted in Kampong Speu when police moved to enforce a Supreme Court eviction order and villagers fought back with stones and bamboo clubs. The following year at least 11 people were injured when a 300-strong force of police and military police arrived again to evict the residents. During the ensuing melee, a villager was shot and an officer beaten unconscious.[47] By the time Heng Chantha was killed in Broma village in May 2012, violent standoffs over land had become an almost monthly occurrence.

So far, such outbreaks of unrest have remained localized, but wider community activist networks have been established to oppose the great Cambodian land-grab. In 2000, villagers from Prey Lang forest formed the Prey Lang Community Network (PLCN), which shared information on forestry crimes and promoted cooperation between communities in the area. Today the network mobilizes campaigns against forest crimes, confronts illegal loggers, and destroys logging equipment found on forest patrols. In August 2011, PLCN activists made global headlines when they dressed up like characters from the hit film *Avatar* in order to draw attention to Prey Lang's plight. In Phnom Penh, the media-savvy protesters from Boeung Kak and Borei Keila began demonstrating with and on behalf of other communities affected by land-grabs. This dawning consciousness fostered and fed off an increasing sense that land-grabs and deforestation were systemic—that city dwellers and rural folk were all victims of the same political forces.

As a son of the soil, Hun Sen has always been aware of the dangers posed by rural discontent. In 2005, he warned government officials that land seizures could spark a "farmers' revolution"; two years later he declared a "war" on land-grabbing.[48] But as with illegal logging, the prime minister's pronouncements have had little effect. The government continued to issue ELCs on a massive scale. In 2011, it leased out 751,882 hectares—more than in any year since the ELC program began. Two-thirds of these concessions were in protected areas, since most of the country's agricultural land was already taken.[49]

As discontent mounted, Hun Sen was eventually forced to act. In May 2012, he announced a moratorium on the granting of new ELCs and a review of all existing concessions. He launched a military-style land titling drive led by a troupe of paid students—the "Heroic Samdech Techo Volunteer Youth"—drawn from pro-CPP youth organizations. Clad in army fatigues, the students fanned out across the country measuring out plots of land and issuing titles for local people. Hun Sen presented many of the deeds in person, choppering around the country with the usual ceremony. Sometimes he intervened personally to "save" people's land. After a violent land seizure in Sihanoukville in March 2013, Hun Sen reversed the decision of local authorities, dispatching the tycoon Mong Reththy to rebuild the homes of 29 families.[50]

While Hun Sen's white-knight titling program benefited many people—the government later claimed it had distributed 450,000 title deeds—it didn't do much to entrench land rights as a legal concept. As the "Heroic Samdech Techo Volunteer Youth" went about their work, the official government channels were bypassed and ignored. Land ownership would come—if it came—like everything else in Hun Sen's Cambodia: as a gift and an indulgence from above. Even though some people gained, the handouts failed to resolve the contradictions at the heart of Cambodia's politico-economic system. The youth land titling teams only operated in selected areas, and, like the earlier LMAP project, refused to demarcate disputed land—the holdings most in need of legal recognition.[51] The government also continued to award concessions in apparent violation of its own moratorium. From May 2012 until the end of that year, 33 new ELCs were reportedly granted.[52] Hun Sen claimed these were already in the pipeline, but with little reliable public information available there was no way to verify his claim. LICADHO said the loophole was "so big it swallows the ban itself."[53]

As initiatives have come from above, the government has moved to neutralize efforts by NGOs and community activists offering their own solutions to the land crisis. In Phnom Penh, riot police have been dispatched to quell anti-eviction protests. As we have seen, protesters from Boeung Kak lake were jailed, as was the independent broadcaster Mam Sonando, charged with inciting the Broma "uprising." In 2012, 232 people around the country were arrested in relation to land and housing issues. By the end of the year, 38 were still in prison and 50 were wanted by the authorities.[54] And still the land crisis kept claiming lives. In April 2012, the environmentalist Chut Wutty was shot dead. Six months later the battered body of Hang Serei Udom, a journalist who had written about the illegal timber trade in Ratanakkiri, was found stuffed into the trunk of his Toyota Camry on a cashew plantation.[55] No one has yet been brought to account for either killing.

The government's belated initiatives amounted to a recognition that the country's land crisis was now a threat to social stability, and conceivably its own hold on power. But they failed to restore equilibrium to the system. Land and resources remained the primitive currency of the CPP's shadow economy, providing business opportunities for the military, the police, the military police, and every layer of government above and between. While Cambodia's resources remained finite, the hunger of the patronage state continued to grow. More than ever, the needs of the rich and the needs of the poor pulled in opposite directions. Would they pull the country apart?

CHAPTER TEN

A Hundred Lotuses Blooming?

"Human Rights Are for Everyone." Overnight, the banners had appeared everywhere around town, shouting their message from walls and lampposts and above major roads. In their half-ignored ubiquity, they resembled the communist slogans of the 1980s, coaxing a reluctant Cambodian population to "build socialism." The message on the morning of December 10, 2012, however, was altogether different. It harked back to a wintry Paris day 64 years earlier, when the UN General Assembly voted to adopt the Universal Declaration of Human Rights.

Each year in Cambodia, when the government allows it, International Human Rights Day is marked by marches and celebrations. In 2012, drummers and dancers with colored masks led a march through Phnom Penh's peak-hour traffic under a banner that read, in English, "Congratulation of 64th anniversary of Human Rights Day." Participants in white T-shirts and blue *krama* scarves shouted slogans while activists spoke through bullhorns mounted on tuk-tuks. The march ended at Freedom Park, a paved "protest zone" in the center of town, where maybe a thousand students, garment workers, and NGO activists sat on plastic chairs beneath colorful marquees.

The day was blue-skied and sunny. Clusters of tethered balloons drifted over the crowd, trailing pennants emblazoned with the year's theme: "Business and Human Rights." Several foreign dignitaries were on hand to speak to the importance of the occasion. An official from the US embassy announced that "the promise of Cambodia's great people would only be realized when human rights are fully respected and all voices are heard." Among the voices heard that day were those of Nuth Sakhorn, one of the female garment workers shot by Chhouk Bundith in Bavet in February 2012, and an ethnic minority representative from Ratanakkiri, who spoke of his community's relentless retreat before the bulldozers.

The proceedings ended with more uplifting slogans. "Rights are the same for everyone!" a young man and woman shouted into a microphone. "We want an independent court system in our country!" "Cheer for Human Rights Day!" Each intervention aroused an enthusiastic response from the crowd. The optimistic mood lasted long after the plastic chairs had been stacked and loaded onto trucks. Tin Leang Eng, 22, a social work student from Phnom Penh University, took a break from her classes to attend with a handful of friends. "I think human rights are important, and I want all people to know the values of human rights," she told me as the crowd dispersed. The entire occasion might have made an uplifting item in a UN agency newsletter. It seemed like everything the "international community" had worked to create in Cambodia. It seemed like the country's democratic promise fulfilled.

But it, too, was a mirage of sorts. On the same morning, just a few blocks away, around a hundred protesters from Boeung Kak lake had attempted an impromptu Human Rights Day march to Prime Minister Hun Sen's office at the imposing Peace Palace. Tep Vanny was there, wearing a blue *krama* with a small Cambodian flag pinned in front. As the protesters moved forward, clutching lotus flowers and hand-drawn English signs for the benefit of the international press, they were met by a phalanx of riot police. The women in the group were pushed and jostled; they shouted as they pressed their hands against the hard plastic riot shields, each marked with the word "POLICE." Several fainted and had to be carried away.

Officially, the police had the law on their side. According to a Law on Peaceful Assembly passed in 2009, protests had to be approved in advance by the relevant authorities, and had to take place at specially designated "Freedom Parks." Even then, the right for NGOs and unions to march could be arbitrarily denied. Permission had previously been withdrawn for human rights forums, and "illegal" protests, by anti-eviction activists or anybody else, were frequently broken up by force.[1] All in all, it was a fitting end to Cambodia's most ostentatious—and incongruous—public holiday.

Four days before the two demonstrations, the CPP had marked International Human Rights Day by convening its inaugural "Human Rights Respect and Dignity Promotion" seminar. The keynote speaker at this misnamed event was Om Yentieng, a prime ministerial aide who headed two flimsy government institutions: the Cambodian Human Rights Commission and the Anti-Corruption Unit. Preaching to a choir of CPP officials, he described Cambodia as a "paradise" for NGOs and hailed the freedoms to be enjoyed under Hun Sen. "The government allows national and international newspapers as well as local and international organizations to be active," he said. All this took place "in accordance with democracy."[2]

What was wrong with Yentieng's statement? At first glance it could be hard to tell. Cambodian civil society was considerably freer than it is in most Asian nations. The country had fewer political prisoners than China, Vietnam, or Burma. It jailed fewer bloggers than Thailand or Vietnam, and prosecuted fewer journalists than Singapore. It had signed most of the UN's human rights conventions, and was the only country in Asia to celebrate International Human Rights Day as an official holiday. Yentieng's comments, spoken in commemoration of the founding of the international rights movement, seemed to contain both a claim and a challenge. Look around, he seemed to say. Is this not democracy?

Of all the positive legacies of the UNTAC mission, Cambodia's flourishing civil society sector has been perhaps the most substantial and lasting. When the UN pitched its blue tents in early 1992, hundreds of NGOs sprang up overnight and a rambunctious press rushed in to fill the vacuum of the preceding years. Suddenly there was great freedom and optimism. Millions in foreign aid flowed to local organizations, which became subcontractors of the international project to remake Cambodia and "save" it from a cruel past. Foreign advisors and consultants arrived by the planeload, and development projects of every sort were initiated. Cambodia's ramshackle socialist capital became an aid industry mecca, a steamy tropical outpost of what Alex de Waal has termed the "humanitarian international."[3]

Two decades on, little has changed. The sprawling UN mission and the main global development agencies remain comfortably ensconced in Phnom Penh. More than 2,600 NGOs are registered with the government, 80 percent of them local.[4] Civil society groups employ 43,000 people,[5] who are involved in every conceivable area of development, from good governance, land rights, environmental conservation, and gender equality, to healthcare, anti–human trafficking, and wildlife rescue. The mainline Cambodian human rights groups, including LICADHO and ADHOC, work tirelessly to monitor and document government abuses of every sort, and their findings are transmitted via a vigilant English-language press.

When UNTAC arrived many Cambodians still blanched at the word *angkar* ("organization"), which had terrifying connotations under the Khmer Rouge. But these benign *angkar* have since become a prominent part of people's lives, more trusted than corrupt state institutions like the police and the courts. Colorful NGO insignias hang on wooden village huts and on the headquarters of the big international development agencies; they are printed on T-shirts, banners, and the sides of hulking white four-wheel drives. Twenty years on, democracy, universal rights, and social justice are literally emblazoned on Cambodian civic life.

They also remain curiously superficial. Like the protesters at Freedom Park, Cambodian civil society flourishes within strictly defined limits. In certain times and places it operates freely, sometimes even providing services—say, in health and education—that the government patronage system fails to provide itself. But activists and journalists venturing into more sensitive areas quickly run afoul of the official consensus, which has subsumed nearly every independent Cambodian institution, from the media and the unions to the Boy Scouts, the Cambodian Red Cross, and the Buddhist monkhood. Twenty years after the UN jump-started civil society in Cambodia, it lives on under Hun Sen as a mirage for the benefit of well-intentioned foreigners and donor governments. While Cambodia remains freer than many other Asian countries, the outcome is a purposefully selective freedom—a system that Thun Saray, the head of ADHOC and a leading Cambodian activist, described with some resignation as "open, but closed." Indeed, few countries have seen such a wide gap between norms and realities.

Early in the morning on April 10, 2008, Lem Piseth was sitting up in bed watching television when his nine-year-old son ran into the house yelling. While sweeping out the yard of the family home in Battambang, Piseth's daughter Keokanitha had come across some strange metal objects. She called her brother, who immediately recognized them as bullets from a gun. Piseth, a reporter for Radio Free Asia (RFA), followed his children outside and there they were: half a dozen AK-47 rounds—gold, sleek, rocket-shaped—lying scattered in the dirt. He knew the discovery was no accident. For over a year, Piseth had been receiving threatening text messages and phone calls. All referred to reports he had filed for the US-funded RFA. The previous year, after a series of reports on illegal logging in Prey Lang forest, Piseth had received a call from a number he didn't recognize. When he replied a man's voice said:

"Is that you Lem Piseth?"

"Yes. Who are you?"

"You are insolent. Do you want to die?"

"Why are you insulting me like this?"

"Because of the story about the forest and know this, there will not be enough land to bury you in."[6]

After seeing the AK-47 bullets, Piseth rang one of his government sources, who told him powerful people were unhappy with his reporting. "I admit that I lost all courage as a strong reporter," he told me later. "The police and the government could not protect me from the threat, and they seemed not to care." Packing up his family, Piseth fled to Thailand and was later granted asylum in Norway.

On July 11 of the same year, just weeks out from the 2008 national election, Khim Sambo, an editor of the SRP-aligned *Moneakseka Khmer* newspaper, was gunned down along with his son in Phnom Penh. He too had written about corruption involving senior officials. Sambo's killer, like those responsible for the death of ten other Cambodian journalists since 1993, was never found; nor was there much of a search.

On the surface, Cambodia's media seems free enough. Prepublication censorship is rare. Colorful publications crowd the newsstands. The English-language *Phnom Penh Post* and *Cambodia Daily* publish hard-hitting reports on government corruption and rights abuses with little fear of reprisal. But most of the Khmer-language media is kept on a tight leash. In reality, an impartial press has never really existed in Cambodia. Even during the UNTAC spring, most of the publications that emerged were basically propaganda organs for political factions and prominent individuals within them.[7] Instead of pursuing the news with professionalism and balance, most papers shilled for their patrons, presenting a Punch-and-Judy narrative of Cambodian politics full of caricatures and personal insults. But at least there was a diversity of viewpoints, and a small but growing number of Cambodian journalists who did what they could to hold the powerful to account.

As appendages of political factions, media outlets were quickly drawn into the crossfire of the 1990s. Journalists were threatened, attacked, and shot dead in the street. Others were co-opted into progovernment publications. As Hun Sen's power grew and violence receded, the opposition Khmer-language press was brought to heel in the courts, where accusations of defamation or incitement were leveled by powerful people and then rubber-stamped by pliant judges. With no chance of winning, the threat of jail or insurmountable fines fostered self-censorship and, by 2010, had forced the closure or co-optation of most significant opposition outlets.

In March 2008, the SRP-aligned *Sralanh Khmer* inverted its editorial line when its publisher (also a SRP steering committee member) defected to the CPP and took the publication with him.[8] In June, Dam Sith, another high-ranking SRP figure who edited *Moneakseka Khmer*, was arrested on defamation and disinformation charges after quoting comments from Sam Rainsy accusing Foreign Minister Hor Namhong of crimes under the Khmer Rouge. Despite being released a week later on bail, the charges hung over Sith until mid-2009, when he wrote to the prime minister to express his "sincere apology" and beg for the charges to be dropped. In exchange, he promised to cease publication of the newspaper. The charges disappeared and the last edition rolled off the presses in mid-July. One observer described it to me as "the beginning of the end for press freedom in Cambodia."

A few weeks earlier Hang Chakra, the editor of *Khmer Machas Srok*, the other main SRP outlet, had been sentenced to a year's prison and fined 9 million riels (US$2,250) after being found guilty of disinformation for accusing Deputy Prime Minister Sok An and some of his cronies of corruption. The crackdown took place in tandem with legal attacks on opposition figures like Rainsy and Mu Sochua, who were prosecuted based on complaints by high-ranking "excellencies." The clamps were eventually released and *Moneakseka Khmer* was relaunched the following year. But a line had been drawn in the sand; everybody now knew just how far they could go.

Today, there's no need for overt censorship. To start with, the majority of the Khmer-language press is controlled by interests friendly to the CPP. The newspapers with the largest circulations—*Kampuchea Thmei, Koh Santepheap, Rasmei Kampuchea*—all toe the party line and the few small opposition papers that remain raise few alarms in Hun Sen's cabinet. The foreign press is similarly quarantined to an audience of NGO workers, expatriates, and English-speaking Cambodians living in the cities. The *Phnom Penh Post* and *Cambodia Daily* provide quality reporting and valuable training for young Khmer reporters, but they form their own part of the mirage—a highly visible advertisement of the government's "commitment" to press freedom. They are only given such freedom because they have little impact. One 2003 survey found that just 9 percent of respondents read a newspaper regularly—a function of both the low levels of literacy among the rural population and the lack of distribution outside Phnom Penh and the major towns.[9]

Most Cambodians receive their news and entertainment from television and radio, which are accordingly subject to tighter central control. The Ministry of Information has repeatedly refused opposition parties' requests for radio or television broadcast licenses. The official state television broadcaster, TVK, is run by the CPP and rarely offers the opposition airtime. (Ahead of the 2007 commune council elections, non-CPP candidates were forced to buy airtime on TVK with Australian aid money.)[10] Bayon TV is owned by Hun Sen's family and run by his daughter Hun Mana.[11] The remaining stations are overwhelmingly controlled by pliant business interests.

Political coverage, unsurprisingly, offers little more than a diet of government propaganda. "News" consists of footage of Hun Sen and other senior officials delivering speeches, slicing ribbons, and handing out gifts to the poor. "Analysis" consists of praise for Hun Sen's leadership or karaoke videos detailing Bun Rany's virtues as an advocate for the poor. There is no coverage of opposition politicians, unless it is to denigrate them. In the Apsara TV newsroom, a sign hangs from the wall, which reads, "Banned from broadcasting: Stories on human rights and land disputes."[12]

It is in radio that independent voices remain the strongest. The most outspoken station is Beehive Radio 105 FM, owned and managed by Mam Sonando, an iconoclastic former French disco owner and devout Buddhist. After three decades in Paris, Sonando returned to Cambodia in 1994 and obtained a radio license. Then, after a failed run in the 1998 election, Sonando dedicated himself to independent broadcasting full-time and was soon selling airtime to the US-funded RFA and Voice of America, which had been refused their own broadcast licenses. As an independent voice beamed into rural Cambodia, Sonando has come under frequent attack. In May 1997, assailants looted and ransacked the Beehive offices. Since then, Sonando has fled the country, had his radio license suspended, and has been jailed on three occasions—the last time following the Broma village "uprising" in 2012.

The Cambodian media, of course, have come a long way since UNTAC. Moeun Chhean Nariddh, who got his start as a reporter for the *Phnom Penh Post* in 1992 and now runs a media studies institute in Phnom Penh, says Cambodian reporters are now more professional than ever, pushing the boundaries when they can and occasionally slipping sensitive stories into the mainstream press. "Back [in the 1990s] journalists were fighting each other in their stories, but now there is solidarity," he told me. "Even the progovernment journalists and opposition journalists can sit at the same table and share stories." Cambodian readers have also become more sophisticated, more able to distinguish real stories from party propaganda.

Though there is an increasing appetite for serious news, journalists still tread a fine line in reporting on sensitive topics. According to one Khmer newspaper reporter, journalists writing sensitive stories are put on a "blacklist" at the Ministry of Interior. From there, the threats escalate. Some reporters receive "warnings" from Hun Sen's cabinet. Others receive calls from officials in the Council of Ministers—often ex-colleagues—who urge them, in the guise of friendly advice, to "do the right thing." Another tactic of choice is the threatening text message or anonymous call. In a 2007 survey of 150 journalists, 54 percent said they had been threatened with physical harm or legal action in the course of their work.[13] Occasionally the name of a recalcitrant journalist is broadcast on government-controlled television, where they are publicly labeled as "opposition," alienating them from friends and colleagues fearful of being tarred with the same brush.

Threats, as so often, come wrapped in inducements. In exchange for their acquiescence, reporters are often offered cash or jobs in the Press and Quick Reaction Unit, the ever-expanding public relations department attached to the Council of Ministers. A third of the respondents to the survey cited above said they knew a colleague who took bribes for not reporting stories, often to supplement paltry incomes or to ensure their family's safety.[14] One Khmer journalist who reported on a land dispute between villagers and a plantation firm owned by a leading tycoon recounted being summoned to his office after a string of critical articles. When he entered, the businessman was sullen and impatient. "He didn't say anything," the reporter told me. "Then he just said, 'what kind of car do you want?' "

For its own part, the Cambodian government has never admitted much of a distinction between the opposition press, opposition political parties, and independent civil society organizations. All are simply "opposition." This isn't as far-fetched as it might seem. Many Khmer-language opposition newspapers and local NGOs are openly anti-government. Kem Sokha, the vice-president of the Cambodia National Rescue Party (CNRP) and former head of the Cambodian Center for Human Rights, is just one civil society veteran with a long and undistinguished track record of bashing the Vietnamese and peddling anti-Hanoi conspiracy theories. Some notable exceptions aside, few Cambodian activists have put their necks out to denounce the use of racist anti-Vietnamese rhetoric by opposition politicians or defend the human rights of ethnic Vietnamese living in Cambodia. Many simply equate fighting oppression with fighting the CPP. As with Sam Rainsy, the language of democracy and universal rights is often used more to court international support than out of a commitment to principle.

Even for the more independent and professional NGOs, the undemocratic nature of the CPP's rule means that they often end up on the same side of the debate as opposition parties. Shared objectives are strengthened by personal and historical ties. Leading civil society figures come from the same generation of foreign-educated diaspora Cambodians who fought against the CPP in the 1980s and formed the leadership of opposition parties like Funcinpec, the BLDP, and the SRP. Politicians like Kem Sokha have even moved back and forth between the two camps.

As a result, Hun Sen and the CPP have always viewed civil society with suspicion. After the 1980s, when they were treated as pariahs by the democratic nations of the West, they saw UNTAC as merely a new and more sophisticated strategy for unseating them from power, a Trojan horse painted in pluralistic colors. The civil society groups that sprang from its flanks weren't the vanguard of a "new world order"; they were the fifth column for a hostile West. "Nongovernment" meant "antigovernment."

The attitude of Hun Sen and his opponents is consistent with a Cambodian political culture that has never tolerated much opposition. Sihanouk had little time for what we would today term "civil society." Lon Nol jailed critics and bumped off political dissidents with no concern for their rights. Pol Pot then elevated paranoia and terror into a self-consuming system of government. In a political culture where power is perceived as a reward for high stocks of merit rather than an outgrowth of a popular mandate, criticisms have often prompted violent reactions. To question a leader has traditionally been to question his merit, and hence his right to rule. Today, after two decades of electoral politics, the concept of a "loyal opposition" still doesn't exist in any meaningful way. No Cambodian leader has ever bowed gracefully to the will of the people as expressed through the ballot box, nor offered to work with the people who defeated him. If Hun Sen and his political opponents are united by anything, it's a Manichean perception of the other as illegitimate, disloyal and—most importantly—"un-Khmer."

Like its predecessors and opponents, Hun Sen's government has gone to great lengths to paint itself as the only true embodiment of "Khmerness." Everything on the other side of the equation—opposition parties, the press, foreign donors, NGOs, anyone advocating democratic principles—is pilloried as foreign and alien. Antigovernment demonstrations are "against" Khmer tradition, as are popular calls for social justice. Tep Vanny and the Boeung Kak lake protesters have been accused of lacking traditional values, of having suffered a "disappearance of national customs, traditions and Khmer culture."[15] Under Hun Sen, the very act of opposition is considered "un-Khmer." The only truly "Cambodian" attitude is to accept one's lot, thank the CPP for its charity, and provide an appreciative audience for Hun Sen during his rural excursions. In this "democracy with Khmer characteristics," Buddhism, a key facet of Khmer cultural identity, has naturally been of crucial importance.

On September 10, 2011, a Buddhist monk gathered up his scant belongings and strolled through the shady grounds of Wat Ounalom, the center of Cambodian Buddhism. After passing frangipani trees and a sacred gray stupa believed to contain an eyebrow hair of the Buddha, he walked through the tall carved gates facing the Tonlé Sap River, where the tranquility of the walled temple grounds gave way to the heat and noise of the city streets. The monk's name was Loun Sovath. He was 32 years old, with a broad jovial face framed by thin-rimmed glasses. He had been evicted on the personal order of Non Nget, the Supreme Patriarch of one of Cambodia's two main Buddhist sects. His transgression was to have taken part in public protests and to have offered blessings to people demonstrating against urban land evictions and other government abuses. According to the monastic authorities, these activities "contradicted" Buddhist principles.

Sovath had been courting conflict with the authorities since March 2009, when a land dispute erupted in his home village in the Chi Kraeng commune of Siem Reap. After police shot four protesting villagers, including his brother and nephew, the young monk took over the demonstrations. "The community broke," Sovath told me. "They were afraid, scared, quiet . . . We needed to stand up. We needed solidarity." Sovath's activism gained momentum. He traveled the country, speaking to communities fighting land-grabs and protecting forests. He became a fixture at protests across Cambodia, instantly recognizable by his flame-colored robes and beaming smile.

For as long as he can remember, Sovath had his heart set on entering the monkhood. He began studying the *dharma* at the age of 12. Four years later, he went to Oudong, the former Cambodian capital, where he studied under Sam Bunthoeun, a charismatic monk with a strong popular following. In sunbaked grounds at the foot of Oudong hill, Bunthoeun had established a flourishing Buddhist Meditation Center that focused on an imported strand of *vipassana* insight meditation. While at Oudong, Sovath came to see a disjuncture between the cardinal values of Buddhism and his country's self-destructive political dynamics. "When I was studying Buddhism, I learnt about the laws of Buddhism—justice, happiness, non-violence—and I compared it to the situation in Cambodia," he said, swiping a finger across his smartphone to check one of what seemed like a constant stream of messages from allies and well-wishers. "I saw many problems in Cambodian society."

When he was 19 years old, Sovath attended the "Democracy Square" protests that erupted after the 1998 election. What he saw left a deep impression. Monks chanted and waved Buddhist flags, leading demonstrations through the streets of Phnom Penh. *Wats* housing restive monks were barricaded by the police, while others were beaten by government thugs. During one protest, two monks were shot outside the US embassy and fire trucks were wheeled in to hose down the remaining protesters, who hid behind their orange parasols and chanted defiantly at their attackers. For the first time in decades, the monks were taking a stand.

As in Burma and Thailand, the Buddhist monkhood carries great moral authority in Cambodia. During the French period, monks and *achars* became involved in anticolonial agitation and some went on to play roles in the early communist movement. After the fall of Pol Pot, who tried to eradicate the country's Buddhist institutions, the re-emergence of the monkhood was tightly controlled. In September 1979, seven Khmer monks were ordained in Vietnam and became the core of a new religious hierarchy enmeshed with the networks of the Kampuchean People's Revolutionary Party. Monks sat on the party's Central Committee, and were given other political posts. By 1981, Tep Vong, the youngest of the seven, served as vice-president of the National

Assembly and Supreme Patriarch of a unified Buddhist order—an unprecedented melding of temporal and spiritual authority. Due to its close association with the Royal Palace, the Thommayut sect, the smaller of Cambodia's two Buddhist orders, was repressed in favor of the Mahanikay, which today controls around 90 percent of the country's pagodas. The traditional separation between the two orders wasn't re-established until Sihanouk's return to Cambodia in 1991.

As head of the Mahanikay order, Tep Vong has been unfailingly loyal to the CPP, overseeing a pliant monastic hierarchy that sanctifies government actions and discourages political agitation by the country's 60,000 monks. During the 1998 protests, Tep Vong reportedly called on Hun Sen's bodyguards and military police to flush out dissident monks holed up at Wat Ounalom.[16] In 2002, he banned monks from voting in elections, and instigated strict controls on their involvement in public protests. After human rights groups began using pagodas for public forums, he ordered them off-limits for political purposes.[17] All these actions were justified on the doctrinal grounds that monks should detach themselves from mundane life and adopt a neutral, compassionate stance. There was precedent for this—Cambodian monks had never voted prior to 1993—but the reintroduction of these rules had less to do with a concern for monks' spiritual attainment than with preventing them from mobilizing political opposition.

Like outspoken journalists, monks who believed they had a duty to stand up against worldly injustice were subject to harsh and sometimes violent treatment. At midday on February 6, 2003, Loun Sovath heard that his teacher Sam Bunthoeun had been shot by unidentified men outside Wat Lanka, a temple on Sihanouk Boulevard in Phnom Penh. Bunthoeun died in hospital two days later. The motive for the killing was never established. After a threadbare investigation the police concluded that it was the result of a "personal dispute."[18] But Bunthoeun had recently put himself in the government's crosshairs, speaking out strongly against Tep Vong's voting ban. Ian Harris, an expert on Cambodian Buddhism, writes that powerful government figures also saw Bunthoeun's popular *vipassana* meditation practice as a foreign, "un-Khmer" import.[19] After his death Bunthoeun's students bore his body to the Meditation Center in Oudong and had it embalmed. There it remains, displayed in a glass casket surrounded by bouquets of flowers and yellowing pictures of the departed monk.

Religious authorities have also come down hard on monks advocating on behalf of the Khmer Krom, the ethnic Khmer minority in southern Vietnam. In June 2007, Tep Vong ordered the arrest and defrocking of Tim Sakhorn, a monk-activist based in Takeo province, on the basis that he had violated Buddhist tenets by "harming Cambodian–Vietnamese solidarity" and using his religious status as a cover for distributing Khmer Krom propaganda.[20] On June 30, Sakhorn was forced into a car and driven to Vietnam, where he was tried and jailed for a year. Shortly after his release in mid-2008, he fled to Thailand, joining dozens of other Khmer Krom monks who had escaped crackdowns in Cambodia. Sakhorn was eventually granted asylum in Sweden.[21]

Needless to say, the stricture against monks' involvement in politics runs in just one direction. Far from remaining politically neutral, Tep Vong frequently praises the CPP, and has accused its opponents of "destroying the national identity."[22] A few entrepreneurial monks have even cuddled up to the powerful, offering tailor-made blessings and charms in exchange for donations to their *wats*, some of which have evolved into wealthy institutions complete with satellite populations of orphans, monk novices, and students from poor rural areas.[23] Wat Champuskaek, a pagoda on the Tonlé Bassac ten kilometers south of Phnom Penh, is the site of much conspicuous merit-making. Set in 12 hectares of pristine grounds, the temple offers a Disneyland version of Theravada Buddhism, all blue skies and swooping golden eaves. Gleaming new pagoda buildings tower amid hardwoods, mango orchards, and the funeral stupas of the departed rich.

Wat Champuskaek has a grisly past: under the Khmer Rouge it was used as an execution site, and its buildings were turned into granaries and storehouses for human excrement.[24] In a corner of the grounds a stupa filled with dusty skulls still stands as a reminder of the past, its paint peeling slowly in the shade. More recently, Wat Champuskaek has developed a reputation as a font of good fortune. Politicians, generals, and tycoons have offered the *wat* millions in charitable donations. A lavish reception hall, unveiled to a who's-who of VIPs in 2009, contains more than 5,000 Buddha statues donated by rich merit-seekers. There are Buddhas of every shape and size, fashioned from jade, bronze, glass, lacquered wood, and sandstone taken from ancient Angkorian quarries. They line the walls, crowd a raised altar, and stare down serenely from wall niches that light up at the flip of a switch. In the midst of this menagerie is a large grinning Buddha image covered with $200,000 worth of gold leaf.

Ta Ouk, a stooped 81-year-old who described himself as an assistant to the pagoda's chief monk, said the reason for the pagoda's success was simple. "After the rich people give presents, they always get success," he said, sitting on a soft carpet as birds fluttered about the ceiling, circling the chandeliers. Inscribed on the wall were the names of the VIPs who supported the hall's construction. Hun Sen's mother-in-law topped the list (she allegedly gave $470,000), followed by a cascade of names trailing zeroes and dollar signs down the wall. Elsewhere, I learnt that the refurbishment of the main pagoda building, completed in 1997, cost $590,000; a three-story dormitory for monks cost $492,524.[25]

The chief monk, Om Lim Heng, is a hard man to pin down. Since taking over the *wat* in the mid-1990s, Lim Heng has established a lucrative line in made-to-order blessings involving the sprinkling of holy water. A whiteboard in the reception hall testifies to the high demand for his holy services. In a single week of June 2013, he was scheduled to receive ceremonial candles from Chea Sim, pay a visit to the businesswoman Choeung Sopheap (of Pheapimex fame), bless a new garment factory, preside at an elite wedding, and attend the housewarming of the owner of an MSG factory. Another of his specialties is casting protective blessings on luxury cars.[26] Lim Heng is particularly close to Hun Sen, making regular house-calls over the river to Takhmao to perform private ceremonies at his Tiger's Lair. "If Hun Sen feels depressed, or uneasy inside, he has the monk give him a blessing. Then he feels better, relaxed," said Ngin Sophearak, a stocky tattooed soldier who has been driving Lim Heng to meetings with high-ranking people since 1999. In return, Lim Heng has had official honors lavished upon him: photos in the dining hall (price-tag, $300,000; completion date, 2000)[27] show Hun Sen bathing the monk with holy water and handing him royal decorations.

The Cambodian path to *nirvana*, it seems, now runs directly through the CPP. In 2006, Tep Vong was graced with the title of "Great Supreme Patriarch"— the first time in 150 years it had been awarded—and placed in overall charge of both Buddhist sects.[28] Soon afterward, Tep Vong revoked the voting ban on monks, but warned them against participating in any mass political movement critical of the government. It was their duty, he said, to show gratitude toward the ruling party and "live up to the January 7 *dharma*."[29] Around the same time the government appointed Hing Bun Heang, the commander of Hun Sen's personal bodyguard unit and a figure with no known expertise in Buddhist teachings, as head of a special "monk's congress" for resolving monastic disputes.[30]

At a time of rising popular discontent linked to land and natural resource issues, the government is particularly sensitive about any revival of religious activism. Not only does it push back against official definitions of what it means to be "Khmer" or "Buddhist"; it also raises the specter of a monk-led movement for social justice, articulated in a moral language familiar to ordinary people. In May 2012, Loun Sovath was seized by police during a protest and forced to sign an agreement promising to cease his political activities. He refused to give up his robes, but was cast out of the monkhood. No pagoda in the country would take him, and the only NGO willing to put him up was the human rights organization LICADHO.

Eventually, Sovath found more permanent lodgings at Wat Sammaki Reangsey, a shabby pagoda on Phnom Penh's outskirts that houses exiled Khmer Krom monks from southern Vietnam. Established in the mid-1990s by

Cambodians returning from overseas, Wat Sammaki Reangsey has never been recognized by the religious authorities; instead, its walls record the donations of Khmer communities from places like Paris, Long Beach, and Philadelphia. Here Sovath inhabits a small room with a thick security door, emerging to attend protests and make videos which he later posts to Facebook and YouTube. Despite the pressure from the authorities, Sovath says his religion and his activism remain inseparable. "The Buddhist monks stood up first, to fight for territory, to fight for justice, to fight for independence from the French," he said, as his phone rang again, flashing the name of another well-wisher. He apologized and picked up the call. Cambodia's "multimedia monk" is busy these days.

A year after Sam Bunthoeun was gunned down, another assassin pulled a trigger and inflicted a grievous wound on Cambodia's union movement. The circumstances were nearly identical. At 8:00 a.m. on January 22, 2004, Chea Vichea, the leader of one of Cambodia's oldest and most active labor unions, was buying a newspaper at the edge of Wat Lanka, just meters from where Bunthoeun was assassinated. While he was standing reading the day's headlines, a man dismounted from the back of a Honda motorcycle and pulled out a pistol. He fired three shots, hitting Vichea in the chest, head, and left arm. The man then fled with an accomplice.

There was little doubt as to the motive. Since taking over the Free Trade Union (FTU) in 1999, Vichea had become a prominent antigovernment critic and advocate for Cambodia's floating population of garment workers. Vichea had a magnetic presence. When he issued a call, workers turned out by the tens of thousands. In the few months leading up to his death, Vichea had been lying low after receiving a death threat linked to a high-ranking official. "I think they want to kill me," he told the filmmaker Bradley Cox shortly before his death, an interview which later appeared in Cox's moving 2011 film *Who Killed Chea Vichea?* "They know me very well, but I'm not afraid. If I afraid, [it's] like I die."

Vichea's killing was followed by an outpouring of grief. A crowd of 15,000 attended his funeral. Taken aback by the strength of the reactions, the authorities scrambled about for a culprit. Within a few days they had settled on two men with no clear link to the crime. They were Born Samnang, 23, and Sok Sam Oeun, 36. Phnom Penh's then police chief Heng Pov, now serving more than one hundred years in prison on a battery of charges including murder and extortion, declared that the men were guilty, based on a police sketch of dubious provenance, and paraded them before the press. Samnang wept before the cameras. While in custody, he had reportedly "confessed" and implicated Sam Oeun.

Even by Cambodian standards the investigation was a farce. Eyewitnesses said Samnang and Sam Oeun bore no resemblance to the men who carried out the shooting. Both men had alibis. Samnang soon retracted his confession, saying it had been coerced. The case was so flimsy that Heng Thirith, an investigating judge at Phnom Penh Municipal Court, threw it out for lack of evidence. Shortly after the ruling he was fired and reassigned to a remote part of the country, and the Appeal Court ordered the case to trial. On August 1, 2005, Samnang and Sam Oeun were found guilty of Vichea's killing and sentenced to 20 years jail. No one seriously believed their guilt. Vichea's brother even refused the $5,000 the two men were ordered to pay his family as compensation. "I would not want to accept any money, they were not the real killers," he said.[31]

Human rights groups clamored for the release of the two men. Amnesty International, with sublime understatement, announced that the case raised "serious concerns about the independence of the judiciary in Cambodia." A year later, Heng Pov, who had since fled Cambodia following a power struggle with the national police chief Hok Lundy, gave an interview to the French weekly *L'Express*, in which he admitted framing the two men on Hok Lundy's orders. "It did not take me long to understand that the two suspects, Born Samnang and Sok Sam Oeun, had nothing to do with the murder," he said. (Pov also accused Hun Sen and Hok Lundy of a raft of other crimes, including the March 1997 grenade attack and the unsolved 1999 shooting of the actress Piseth Pelika, supporting the unconfirmed allegation that she was murdered on the orders of Bun Rany.)[32]

Vichea's killing, followed by the murder of another FTU leader a few months later, cast a pall of fear over the labor movement. Since the mid-1990s, the unions had grown in tandem with Cambodia's garment sector, which had benefited from an arrangement that gave the country tariff-free access to the US market. Under the American scheme, Cambodia found a niche as an "ethical" destination for major clothing retailers—brands like Gap, Levi Strauss, and Abercrombie & Fitch—hoping to avoid the sweatshop stigmas of rock-bottom apparel producers like China and Bangladesh. Cambodia let inspectors from the International Labour Organization monitor its factories, and permitted collective action to improve working conditions—a freedom enshrined in a progressive Labor Law passed in 1997. "If we didn't respect the unions and the labor standards," Commerce Minister Cham Prasidh told the *New York Times* in 2005, "we would be killing the goose that lays the golden eggs."[33]

But the Cambodian government showed a limited tolerance for sustained industrial action. Police have been deployed to block May Day marches and strikes. Factories have fired workers who attempted to unionize or take collective action. In September 2010, an estimated 200,000 workers walked off the job, demanding a hike in the $61 monthly wage, an amount they said was far below what they needed to survive. It was the largest strike Cambodia's garment sector had ever seen, but came to an end after police were deployed, unionized workers were fired, and threats were made against labor leaders.[34] Cambodia's economy remains so heavily reliant on the garment sector that the government has acted decisively to stamp out any hint of instability in the sector.

Unions nonetheless represent an indigenous political force of increasing size and significance. Unlike Cambodian NGOs, many of which remain reliant on foreign funding, unions arose spontaneously in the 1990s to represent the interests of workers, who, despite the relatively decent conditions in Cambodian apparel factories, still lived close to the poverty line. Their collective bargaining efforts helped push garment workers' wages from $27 per month in 1996 to $45 in 2000.[35] From their inception, the labor unions were also closely aligned with the political opposition. Chea Vichea was a founding member of Sam Rainsy's Khmer Nation Party and garment workers appeared in large numbers at opposition rallies. By the time of his death, Vichea had helped politicize a large and growing slice of the working population. His appeal was all the more potent for being based on tangible demands, rather than abstract invocations of civil or political rights.

After Vichea's assassination, however, the union movement became cowed and divided. Dozens of progovernment and promanagement syndicates sprang up, swamping the handful of independent and opposition-aligned unions that remained. In a population of some 475,000 garment workers there are now an estimated 600 unions, most of them aligned to the government.[36] The emergence of these "official" syndicates has followed a familiar pattern. Like journalists, union leaders are paid or pressured to draw support away from independent and opposition-aligned groups. They can earn up to $10,000 per month by switching allegiances—an almost unimaginable amount for people who are often former garment workers themselves.[37]

Promanagement unions now take up a majority of the seats allotted to labor on the national committee that negotiates minimum-wage increases, considerably diluting the bargaining power of independent groups. This allows the government to keep wages competitive while preventing the unions from becoming the locus of a more broad-based political movement. Instead of letting independent, democratic unions flourish—the sort of groups that could engage in serious collective bargaining on behalf of workers—the government has tried to dilute the power of the labor movement by diffusing its membership among hundreds of groups.

Union leaders continue to work hard for better wages and working conditions, calling frequent strikes and walkouts. But even when they succeed the authorities try to take the credit. In March 2013, after months of negotiations, labor unions finally secured an increase in the monthly minimum wage from $61 to $80. (Nine months later, it was raised again to $100 amid fresh strikes.) Shortly afterwards, Hun Sen addressed a crowd of 4,000 garment workers belonging to a raft of pro-CPP unions. The prime minister claimed credit for securing the wage increase and urged workers to vote for the CPP at the upcoming election. "When Prime Minister Hun Sen asked, 'Who will vote for the CPP?' " one union leader told the *Cambodia Daily*, "all the people raised their hands and cheered for him."[38]

The Cambodian government's aim has never been to eliminate opposing voices entirely. Faced with the constant scrutiny of donors and human rights groups, its aim has been instead to create a mirage of freedom, keeping the country partway between outright freedom and outright repression. Maintaining the balance has naturally been a piecemeal process. At times it appears as if Cambodia is moving in the right direction. The government says the right things, loosens its restrictions on civil society, and passes nice-looking laws. Then, very often in election season, the situation deteriorates: lawsuits fly, protesters are hauled into court, and the cautious encouragement of donors and rights groups sours to "strong concerns." Eventually the government backs down and relaxes its controls. But since UNTAC, the ebbs and flows of the democratic tide have concealed a steady drift toward de facto one-party rule.

The mirage of apparent progress is everywhere. In 2006, after considerable lobbying, US officials convinced the Cambodian government to drop jail terms for the crime of defamation. In a diplomatic cable in May 2007, US officials hailed the move as an encouraging sign that reflected an increasingly free climate of expression, stating that the government was "allowing unprecedented criticism of its policies."[39] After the CPP's landslide win in the 2008 election, however, the boundaries of free expression rapidly converged. The mopping-up operations that followed the poll included legal attacks on journalists and government critics and the passage of new laws intended—if not designed outright—to curtail free expression.

The Law on Peaceful Assembly (2009) and the Law on Anti-Corruption (2010) would both be used to target opponents. A new Penal Code, which came into effect in December 2010, replacing an old UNTAC-era code, contained an expanded arsenal of charges that could be used to muzzle critics. Thanks partly to US efforts, the charge of defamation still didn't carry jail terms, but it *did* carry fines of up to 10 million riels ($2,500), which would transmute into jail-time for those lacking the money to pay. But forget defamation—critics could be charged with insult; offense against state authorities; intimidation of a public official; malicious denunciation; breach of professional secrecy; threats; threats to cause damage; taking advantage of a vulnerable person; and instigation. Then there was the one-size-fits-all, the masterpiece of legal fuzziness: "incitement." This charge included any speech that encouraged the commission of a felony, the disturbance of public security, or discrimination on the basis of ethnicity, nationality, race, or religion.[40] It carried jail terms of up to three years. And it could mean just about anything.

These laws have already been brought to bear on anti-eviction protesters and human rights defenders. Behind the mirage they remain, hanging over government critics. Most potentially restrictive in this respect is a proposed Law on Associations and Nongovernment Organizations. The legislation, still in draft form as of mid-2014, envisions complex registration requirements for every type of NGO and civil society group in Cambodia. The government has argued that it needs the new law to regulate Cambodia's unwieldy NGO sector, which runs the gamut from well-run professional organizations to bogus for-profit "orphanages". In 2008, Hun Sen announced that the NGOs were "out of control" and that civil society might be used as a cover for terrorism and other nefarious activities.[41] Critics countered that legal mechanisms already existed for weeding out fraudulent or criminal activities in the NGO sector and that the new law—like those mentioned above—would likely be applied selectively against outspoken organizations.

With much of Cambodian civil society now either cowed or "harmonized" with the official consensus, one sector of society may yet succeed in resisting the current trend: the internet. Cambodia is currently in the midst of a connectivity boom. In 2010, just 320,000 Cambodians had access to the internet; by the end of 2013, that number had climbed to 3.8 million—nearly a quarter of the population—according to the Ministry of Posts and Telecommunications,[42] driven by the proliferation of web-enabled smartphones and cheap 3G mobile data. Young Cambodians, especially those living in urban areas, have embraced social media networks like Facebook, which now counts 742,220 Cambodian users.[43]

While Cambodia's internet penetration rate still lags far behind countries like Thailand and Vietnam, the recent increases in internet usage have had disproportionate effects. By 2013, social media sites like Facebook and YouTube threatened the CPP's monopoly on news and information, helping publicize the activities of anti-eviction activists and other government critics. The monk Loun Sovath was active on social media, as were the Boeung Kak lake activists. Barred from accessing most of the state media and with limited resources to disseminate its message in rural areas, the Cambodia National Rescue Party has also developed a robust online presence. By early 2014, Sam Rainsy had accumulated 417,000 Facebook "likes," to Hun Sen's 185,000.

"If we look at TV and radio in Cambodia, they are affiliated to the ruling party. Luckily we have social media," said Ou Ritthy, who runs Politikoffee, a political discussion group that meets in coffee shops every two weeks and coordinates its meetings over Facebook. Ritthy, a 26-year-old from Pursat who works as a communications officer with Oxfam, is the picture of a new generation of connected Cambodians. During our interview, his smartphone beamed in updates from social media; his MacBook sat open next to a half-finished cappuccino. Over the past few years, Ritthy said, patterns of internet use have changed. "Before [young people] used them only for entertainment," he said of social media sites like Facebook. "Later, when we had big social events, like land-grabbing, social issues, violence, protests, people started talking about this. Gradually they changed from using [it] for entertainment to using it for social issues."

Though the Cambodian web remains relatively unshackled, the government has warned that "crimes" committed online will be subject to similar penalties to those committed elsewhere. One of the first cases tried under the new Penal Code was that of Seng Kunnakar, a logistics officer with the World Food Programme, who was arrested in December 2010, after printing out and sharing materials from KI-Media—an anti-government news blog based overseas. Kunnakar was arrested on a Friday; on Sunday, the municipal court convened and after a brief trial sentenced him to six months' jail. The charge: "incitement."

The following month, some Cambodian web users began noticing that the popular blogspot.com domain, which hosted KI-Media and other political blogs, was inaccessible. Other antigovernment sites, including that of Ung Bun Heang, the late Khmer-Australian political cartoonist whose creations poured invective on the CPP and the Vietnamese, also seemed to have dropped offline. In February, the foreign-language press published leaked emails from an official in the Ministry of Posts and Telecommunications ordering leading ISPs to block the domains. Minister So Khun denied any formal policy of censorship, but told the *Cambodia Daily* that ISPs had the right to block pages that insulted "government leaders" or otherwise offended Cambodian culture or morality.[44] Eventually some ISPs lifted the restrictions.

The government is currently readying a new "cyber law," expected to be passed in the latter half of 2014, a draft of which proposed outlawing any online communication that slandered government agencies or affected the country's "political cohesiveness." One official said the cyber bill would prevent "ill-willed people or bad mood people from spreading false information."[45] It later issued a stricture banning internet cafés within a 500-meter radius of schools—a decree that, if fully implemented (so far it hasn't been), would result in the closure of most of Phnom Penh's internet cafés. Then, early in 2013, a schoolteacher was summoned for questioning after he accused traffic police of corruption on Facebook. The Cambodian web remains small, but internet and social media use is only likely to spread further as Cambodia develops and technology becomes more affordable. Whether the CPP's time-honored system of control will be able to migrate to the diffuse world of the internet remains to be seen.

On September 25, 2013, Cambodia's Supreme Court released Born Samnang and Sok Sam Oeun, the men convicted of killing Chea Vichea. It had been nearly a decade since their arrest, around half of which the men had spent in prison, jailed for a crime they didn't commit. As the judge read out the ruling, applause broke out in the courtroom and the two men dropped to their knees. As they left the building, Sam Oeun raised his hands and shouted: "I would like the world to know that I, Sok Sam Oeun, have been freed and Cambodia does have justice . . . People across the world: believe that Cambodia has justice."[46]

The story of Sok Sam Oeun and Born Samnang had taken several cruel twists since their initial conviction. In early 2009, the pair were released on appeal and returned for a time to their old lives. Then, after four years of freedom, the court ordered them rearrested and there was more tearful bewilderment as the two men were taken back into custody. Their final release took place in a period of loosening after the 2013 election, in which the CNRP made large gains on the back of widespread discontent with the CPP's rule (see Epilogue). The two men had spent 2,073 days in prison, but there was no hint of compensation for their wrongful arrest and imprisonment. Samnang and Sam Oeun were free, but Vichea's killers remained at large. The case was officially "open," but no one expected justice.

In May 2013, the Free Trade Union held a small ceremony in a park close to Wat Lanka and unveiled a statue of Chea Vichea. It was slightly smaller than life-size, and depicted him in a familiar stance, speaking into a small microphone during a rally. For six years, Chea Mony, Vichea's brother and now head of the FTU, had sought government permission to erect the statue as a symbol of the bravery and compassion with which Vichea had fought to advance workers' rights. In early 2012, Hun Sen signed off on his proposal, and even ordered the city authorities to cover part of the statue's cost. (They eventually provided $5,000 out of $7,000.)

But there was one unpublicized condition. The FTU would have to cease its yearly marches calling for the killers of Chea Vichea to be brought to justice.[47] Instead of responding to rising popular discontent with concrete reforms, the government offered another empty concession. Instead of human rights, Cambodia had "International Human Rights Day." Instead of freedom of expression there was "Freedom Park." Now workers seeking justice for a murdered figurehead had been thrown another harmless symbol—a small statue that gazed over a busy intersection, its right arm draped with loops of jasmine, its hand raised as if in some sort of silent curse or benediction.

CHAPTER ELEVEN

An Improbable State

Sister Denise Coughlan called it the "House of Betrayal." From the outside, there wasn't much to see. It sat on a quiet street on the outskirts of Phnom Penh, crouching behind tangled foliage and a tall corrugated iron fence. Until a few years ago, this inconspicuous facade had concealed a sanctuary, a safe-house used by asylum seekers fleeing persecution in Iran, Afghanistan, North Korea, Burma, Vietnam, and parts of Africa. Drawn by Cambodia's porous borders, hundreds of desperate people had been put up there by refugee aid groups as their applications for political asylum filtered through the local office of the UN High Commissioner for Refugees (UNHCR). For many of them, the dwelling was a short stop on the way to a better life in the West.

All this changed in late 2009, when the compound briefly housed a group of 22 asylum seekers from China. They were Uighurs, members of a Turkic-speaking Muslim minority group from Xinjiang province in the country's west. They had fled a harsh official crackdown following protests in July that had devolved into one of the worst episodes of ethnic violence in China in decades. Police had detained hundreds of Uighurs for their alleged participation in the rioting. Several Uighurs were sentenced to death in guilty-until-proven-innocent trials. Others were reportedly "disappeared" by Chinese security forces.

After an arduous overland journey across China and down the coastal spine of Vietnam, the Uighurs had trickled over the Cambodian border in small groups throughout October and November. The group, which included a pregnant woman with two small children, was taken in by a number of refugee aid NGOs, including Coughlan's Jesuit Refugee Service (JRS), which gave them food and shelter. The UNHCR office issued letters stating that they were "Persons of Concern" under the agency's protection. They were told to wait while the government assessed their asylum claims.

The Uighur case might have remained an obscure footnote were it not for the American media coverage which publicized their presence in Cambodia.[1] When the story broke, the Chinese government immediately branded the Uighurs "criminals" and demanded their return. As one of the few Asian countries to have signed the 1951 UN Refugee Convention, Cambodia was legally obliged to conduct a fair assessment of the Uighurs' asylum claims and to prevent their "refoulement"—their return to any country where they were likely to face torture or mistreatment. Faced with a choice between Chinese demands and its obligations under the Refugee Convention, Ilshat Hassan of the World Uighur Congress expressed hope that the Cambodian government would do the right thing, and show the world it was "a responsible, accountable government" that abided by international law.[2]

Officials at UNHCR were equally optimistic. In mid-2008, the agency had signed an agreement with the government transferring asylum-seeker processing to a new Cambodian Refugee Office under the Ministry of Interior. In a press release marking the agreement, UNHCR hailed Cambodia as a potential "refugee model" for Southeast Asia.[3] All that was necessary for the final handover was the passage of a new refugee subdecree law, then in its final stages of drafting. After years of training and "capacity building," UNHCR was confident that the Cambodians understood their legal obligations—and would implement them accordingly.

The timing for the Uighurs could hardly have been worse. In mid-December, China's then-Vice President Xi Jinping was due to arrive in Cambodia for a high-profile state visit, carrying a fat portfolio of grants and loan agreements worth some $1.2 billion. The promise of this economic bonanza gave Beijing huge leverage over the Cambodian government. On December 19, the day before Xi's arrival, the Uighurs were taken to Phnom Penh International Airport at gunpoint and bundled aboard a charter flight to China. Human rights activists and Western diplomats voiced their outrage, but the calculation for the Cambodians was brutally simple: for each asylum seeker that it "refouled," the government received the equivalent of $60 million.*

Just a few days earlier, it looked like the government might resist China's pressure. Government spokesmen confirmed that immigration officials were working with UNHCR to process the Uighurs' asylum claims. On December 16, in response to concerns from Western embassies and refugee advocates, police rounded up the Uighurs from various locations and took them to a single location, supposedly for their protection. The following day they were installed at

---

* Of the original group of 22 Uighurs, two managed to slip away prior to the deportation.

the Phnom Penh refugee safe-house, as Interior Minister Sar Kheng assured US officials that the government was "on the road" to resolving their asylum claims.[4]

Then, suddenly, the Cambodian position shifted. On December 17, Prime Minister Hun Sen signed Cambodia's long-awaited refugee subdecree. The law, pushed through ahead of schedule, contained a last-minute addition—a clause giving the Interior Minister the power to deny, terminate, or remove the protection status granted by UNHCR and send asylum seekers home.

On December 18, a ministry spokesman declared that the Uighurs "were not real refugees" but rather "criminals escaping from China and involved with a terrorist organization."[5] Police armed with machine guns entered the safe-house compound, and forced the Uighurs to board a bus with curtains drawn over the windows. Those who asked where they were going were answered with kicks and blows. The group was driven to an Interior Ministry detention center where they were held in two small cells, some in handcuffs. Shortly before their departure, Sara Colm, a researcher for Human Rights Watch, had received a text message from one of the Uighurs, a young man named Yusup. "Please help us out," he wrote, "otherwise we are going to be killed."[6] A few hours later, Yusup and his compatriots were gone.

Most observers were stunned by the speed of the reversal. Denise Coughlan, the Australian nun who headed JRS and was closely involved in the Uighur case, was shocked at how quickly a house of refuge became a house of betrayal. "Like sheep going to the slaughter, the people went to the safe-house clearly believing they were going to be protected," she told me. "How they can call a pregnant mother with two children in her arms a terrorist is beyond my imagination."

The next morning, Xi Jinping and his entourage touched down in Siem Reap and drove into town along a sunny street lined with waving schoolchildren and strings of Chinese flags. Beijing's president-in-waiting posed for photos at Angkor Wat and then flew to Phnom Penh, where Cambodian soldiers in white uniforms saluted him outside the Sino-modernist building housing the Council of Ministers—a recent $30 million "gift" from Beijing. After inking their seven-figure deal, Xi and Hun Sen toasted the agreement with champagne. The two men clinked glasses, and the news cameras flashed their silver over a new apogee in Sino-Cambodian relations.

The deportation of the Uighurs was a vivid illustration of China's growing power in Cambodia, capping a decade in which it had risen to become perhaps the most important foreign influence over Hun Sen's government. Today, Chinese state banks act like a giant cash box for the Cambodian government, bankrolling the construction of bridges, hydropower dams, real estate projects, and tourist resorts. Chinese-built highways have opened up remote corners of the country. Beijing has given around $2.7 billion in loans and grants since 1992, most of them in the last decade.[7] Bilateral trade has also boomed. While Thailand and the United States remain Cambodia's top trade partners, China is well on the way to eclipsing both.

Chinese influence has also taken softer forms. In recent years dozens of Chinese-language schools have opened their doors in Phnom Penh; with more than 15,000 students, the Duanhua School is the largest in the world outside mainland China. Chinese tour groups flood in increasing numbers to the temples of Angkor, while businessmen from Hong Kong and southern China have established lucrative connections with members of Cambodia's Chinese-speaking Sino-Khmer elite.

Things have come a long way in two decades. In late 1991, when Chinese diplomats accompanied Prince Sihanouk on his return to Cambodia from Beijing, history still cast a long shadow. Throughout the 1980s, while China continued to back the Khmer Rouge, the PRK had openly discriminated against Cambodia's ethnic Chinese community and Hun Sen had described China as "the root of everything that was evil" in the country.[8] After Tiananmen Square and the end of the Cold War, however, Chinese leaders jettisoned Pol Pot and returned to the foreign policy goals of imperial times: unifying the realm by securing peace and stability on China's southern periphery and forestalling Taiwan's moves toward formal independence. Hun Sen's rise in the 1990s suddenly made him an attractive partner. Not only did he welcome Chinese aid and investment; he also shared Beijing's skepticism about Western calls for democratic reform.

Hun Sen's July 1997 putsch against Prince Ranariddh, and the chilly Western reaction that followed, paved the way for the expansion of diplomatic ties. Claiming that Funcinpec had received covert support from Taiwan, Hun Sen shut down the Taiwanese trade office in Phnom Penh, rebuffing a government that was then one of Cambodia's largest investors. Beijing was pleased by the gesture. A few months later, China delivered 116 military cargo trucks and 70 jeeps valued at $2.8 million, offsetting the freeze in military aid imposed by the US and Western governments after Ranariddh's ouster.[9]

In November 2000, Chinese President Jiang Zemin paid a landmark visit to Cambodia—the first by a Chinese leader since 1963. He was greeted by the usual rent-a-crowd of cheering schoolchildren and fluttering red pennants, a scene of confected celebration that one analyst compared to "a festive papal visit to a devoutly Catholic nation."[10] In the florid ceremonies that marked the visit, neither Jiang nor Hun Sen made any public mention of the two countries' strained history. A handful of protesters who turned out and hoisted banners protesting China's support for Pol Pot were quickly bundled out of sight by police.[11] The Khmer Rouge period was forgotten, a bloody historical slate hosed clean with promises of cash and political support. Hun Sen told Jiang that Cambodia's relations with China were "a precious gift," and "of long-term and strategic significance for our country."[12]

Chinese cash started flowing into Cambodia. Official delegations shuttled between Beijing and Phnom Penh, brokering loans, releasing sunny communiqués, and spouting paeans to Sino-Cambodian amity. China wrote off millions in Cambodian debt dating back to the 1960s. Prime Minister Wen Jiabao visited in April 2006, bringing economic aid totaling $600 million. Two years later, Cambodia hosted lavish celebrations marking the fiftieth anniversary of diplomatic relations with Beijing. In a cable to Washington, US Ambassador Carol Rodley described the extent of the official events, which included an endless banquet cycle and a list of official visitors "so long that the Chinese embassy's political and economic officers have complained . . . that they never get any rest."[13]

By the time the Uighur asylum seekers trickled into Cambodia from Vietnam, the "China model" of authoritarian capitalism loomed as a direct challenge to the democratic system imported by the UN and sustained for years by foreign money. Whenever donor countries put pressure on Hun Sen to improve governance and enact reforms, China stepped in to relieve the pressure with loans and investments. Beijing's sales pitch was simple. It hewed to a doctrine of mutual noninterference. It made no demands on how Hun Sen ran the country. "China respects the political decisions of Cambodia," Hun Sen said in September 2009, cutting the ribbon on a $128 million Chinese-funded bridge over the Tonlé Sap. "They build bridges and roads and there are no complicated conditions."

Chinese support has also allowed Hun Sen to offset the traditionally strong influence of Vietnam and Thailand. This is particularly the case with Hanoi. Since the early 1990s, Cambodia and its old patron have remained fast friends, united by proximity and the historical ties between the two countries' ruling parties. Military relations are enmeshed; Metfone, one of Cambodia's largest telecoms operators, is run by the Vietnamese military-owned enterprise Viettel. Cross-border trade has boomed since the signing of the supplemental border treaty in October 2005. While Vietnamese influence remains a combustive issue in Cambodian politics, the Phnom Penh–Hanoi axis is no longer the special, quasi-colonial relationship it once was. The new power calculus was on display at the ASEAN Foreign Ministers' Meeting held in Phnom Penh in July 2012. When the meeting discussed territorial disputes in the South China Sea,

Cambodia sided with Beijing, leaving its old ally—and other ASEAN claimant states like the Philippines—out in the cold. Hun Sen is "very shrewd," one senior Vietnamese diplomat confided to US officials in 2006. He listened to Vietnamese leaders only when it was "convenient and profitable for him to do so."[14]

Hun Sen has been happy to toe the Chinese line in other ways. He has given Chinese firms open access to Cambodian land and resources. He has voiced frequent support for the "One China" policy. As it has frequently done for Vietnam, Cambodia has also deported political activists and other "undesirables" wanted by the Chinese government. In August 2002, Cambodia barred the Dalai Lama from attending a Buddhism conference, shortly before it deported two Falun Gong activists to China, disregarding their pending asylum claims.[15] When the Uighurs arrived in Cambodia, tired and desperate after their long journey from western China, it wasn't hard to predict that politics would trump law, that the government would put its obligation to China above its obligation under the Refugee Convention. The only surprising thing was UNHCR's failure to see the warning signs.

China's rising influence loomed over the regular aid summit that was convened in Phnom Penh in June 2010, six months after the deportation of the Uighurs. The venue was the Palais du Gouvernement, a musty gray Art-Deco edifice built to house the French colonial administration in the 1930s. Set along the Tonlé Sap riverside in tropical gardens filled with topiary hedges and outspread Traveler's Palms, the building had played some interesting walk-on roles in Cambodia's modern history. In the late 1970s, it was where Pol Pot received "fraternal" foreign guests. Later, it housed the UNTAC mission. On this particular morning, diplomats and aid officials filed through iron doors into an air-conditioned hall with a dark green board announcing the "3rd Cambodia Development Cooperation Forum." For the next two days it would be the backdrop to a surreal sort of theater.

At the top of the bill was a keynote speech by Prime Minister Hun Sen. The topic: his government's commitment to "deep reform." Hun Sen's audience, facing each other around a long horseshoe of tables draped with gold fabric, was drawn from the foreign governments and international financial institutions that had bankrolled Cambodia's development since the early 1990s. They put on headphones and listened as Hun Sen ran through a list of his government's achievements. After 20 years of donor talk-shops, he had learnt the language well. He spoke of "ownership" and "multifaceted development." "Sustainability" and "efficiency" both received a dutiful airing. The government's goal was an "operation-oriented administration with high productivity, responsibility, and capacity." Hun Sen hailed the government's "significant progress" in education and its "remarkable progress" in healthcare. "The Royal Government will continue legal and judicial reform," he announced circularly, "by implementing the Strategy for Legal and Judicial Reform."

It was all quite meaningless. The meetings of the Cambodia Development Cooperation Forum (CDCF) had taken place in various guises, and had undergone several name changes, since the first donor meeting was held in Tokyo in 1992. In that time, Cambodia had received around $12 billion in foreign aid,[16] while showing a more or less complete lack of progress on the various reform "benchmarks" formulated by its Western "partners". Donor conditionalities had done little to alter Cambodia's destructive political dynamic. Land-grabs, forestry crimes, and high-level corruption—the oxygen of the CPP's patronage state—remained endemic. Despite years of assistance, social services like healthcare and education still relied heavily on foreign aid, and even then remained in a dire state. Very little aid money seemed to reach the people whom it was theoretically intended to help.

With China backstopping Hun Sen's domestic agenda, diplomats and donor agency representatives seemed more resigned than ever. The Cambodian government had made it clear that it intended to pursue "hard" infrastructure development over the sorts of "soft" development—human rights, democratic reform, good governance—that would undermine its hold on power. A few months earlier, the US had announced the cancellation of a shipment of 100 military trucks, a punishment of sorts for the deportation of the Uighurs. The Chinese then stepped in with a shipment that was nearly twice the size.

With their influence on the wane, Western governments faced a choice. They could walk away from the field and leave it to China, or they could remain, pursuing their own strategic agendas, and hope for the best. Most opted for engagement. And so as Hun Sen droned on, spouting buzzwords and promises, his audience did what they had done at every previous meeting: they pretended to believe him. The next day—June 3, 2010—donor representatives laid out their aid "indications" for the coming 18 months. They added up to $1.1 billion. This meandering vaudeville had culminated in a grand finale: the largest aid pledge in Cambodia's history.

Despite all the promises, the third CDCF meeting turned out to be the last. Not long afterwards the Cambodian government cancelled the event scheduled for 2012 and postponed it indefinitely. They didn't give a reason, but the obvious assumption was that due to Chinese backing, and the possibility of a windfall from oil and gas revenues, Hun Sen was no longer willing to endure the theater of donor criticism. As the projector machines were switched off and the doors clanked shut in the Palais du Gouvernement, an era came to an end—the last era in which Western donors could claim any significant say in Cambodia's future. In NGO-speak, Hun Sen had finally taken full "owner-ship" of his country's development.

Where did things go wrong?

The opening of Cambodia to international aid 20 years earlier had taken place in an atmosphere of great optimism. The arrival of the UN coincided with the dawning of what many people hoped would be a new post–Cold War interna-tional order, in which the challenges of peace, justice, democratic develop-ment, and poverty alleviation would all diminish under the sustained efforts of a so-called "international community" working in tandem with empowered local NGOs. The general assumption was that Cambodia had been wiped developmentally clean by the Khmer Rouge, and was thus an ideal test for new theories of peace building and democratic development. Guilt about the Western role in Cambodia's past intersected with hope about its future. Cambodia became an international project, a new "White Man's Burden," a blank slate awaiting its inscription with universal rights and democratic values.

Infusing this new civilizing mission was an overweening confidence that economic and political development had reached its zenith after the Cold War—that the world was drifting inevitably, à la Francis Fukuyama, toward the adoption of free markets and Western-style democracy. This was matched by the rise of global discourses plotting out the path to the promised land, which any country could tread if it adopted the recommended formulas. The World Bank and the International Monetary Fund brought their free market templates, which would trim back the state and improve Cambodia's global "competitiveness." Others prioritized the building of democratic institutions and the crafting of progressive laws. "Development" in this sense was simply a matter of assembling the right set of instructions and then shoveling money toward their implementation.

This approach took little heed of local contexts and conditions. The agenda was set by drop-in development missionaries with little or no knowledge of Cambodia and its history. From this perspective, of course, Cambodia and its history were mostly beside the point. The most important political and social questions had all been settled. The country's main problem wasn't its political culture, with its mesh of patrimonial relationships and the amassing of power by self-focused elites, but rather its lack of capacity to implement known solu-tions. If the world was trending inevitably in the direction of democracy, universal rights, and all things good and true, all Cambodia needed was a little developmental nudge. All it needed was to have its capacity "built."

But Cambodia in 1992 was hardly a blank slate. The CPP had spent the previous decade rebuilding a shattered nation and sinking deep political roots, and it resented the arrival of the UN, with its long tail of foreign consultants and Panglossian NGO "action plans." For Hun Sen and his colleagues, history was still very much a work in progress. All the talk of democracy they saw as a moral cover for the interests of foreign powers that had openly or clandestinely supported the Khmer Rouge throughout the 1980s. The CPP desperately needed aid money to counter the drop-off in Soviet rubles, but resisted any reform that would undermine its own power.

All the while, donors, parachuted into the optimistic maelstrom of the early 1990s, proceeded as if Cambodia had returned to a developmental Year Zero. "People assumed nothing happened in Cambodia during the '80s," recalled Darryl Bullen, an Australian development consultant who first visited Cambodia in the middle of that decade. Foreign donors took the view that Cambodia was "a clean sheet, that there'd been an election, and that therefore that all the public servants that'd previously been in positions of power were just going to roll over and have their tummies tickled."

The coup de force of July 1997 demonstrated just how far theory diverged from reality. When the dust settled, and the flawed 1998 election had restored Hun Sen's legitimacy, the donors reassessed. They announced that aid disbursements would now be tied to a set of reform benchmarks, known as "Joint Monitoring Indicators." Various bodies and mechanisms were contrived to monitor the targets. There were the 18 Technical Working Groups (TWGs), which fed plans and reform recommendations in various sectors into the Government-Donor Coordination Committee, another aid talk-shop which met periodically in Phnom Penh. Crowning this edifice of red tape was the Consultative Group (CG) meeting, held roughly every 18 months and chaired by the World Bank. Renamed the CDCF in 2007, these meetings were the highest-level forum for donors to assess the Cambodian government's "performance"—the use of the word revealed more than it intended—on this dizzying array of reform indicators.

Even after the jolt of July 1997, many donor and UN officials still took it for granted that the world had reached a final consensus about how development should proceed. As UN resident coordinator Dominique McAdams put it in 2003, "The role of the development partners is certainly not to make the choice for [Cambodia]. The role of the development partners is to empower the country so the country can make the right choice."[17] McAdams's statement made clear that the idea of "country-owned" development, like the idea of a final international "consensus" around liberal democracy and free markets, was a pleasant fiction. From this perspective, it didn't really matter what Cambodian leaders wanted, a fact Hun Sen recognized, if only for self-serving reasons, when he denounced the "neocolonial" demands of the

West. The fundamental fact, however, is that he needed the aid—and donors needed a pretext for giving it.

The result was mirage politics in its purest form: a convergence of interests between a government willing to offer symbolic gestures of reform, and a donor "community" willing to accept them. Laws were easy enough to pass and elections were easy enough to stage. Statistics could be massaged to give an impression of progress. For Hun Sen, putting on the right "performance" was all too easy.

A great deal of effort went into maintaining the illusion of reform. Cambodian officials assembled turgid progress reports and attended TWG meetings, which, according to one former government consultant, quickly devolved into a "smokescreen" for inaction. The TWG on land, perhaps the most important, was chaired by an official from the Ministry of Land Management, which had nothing to do with the granting of economic land concessions to big business—one of the main issues the TWG sought to address. For all their plans and recommendations, the TWGs were "technical" bodies that did little to address the issue of political incentives. "Nobody believed in them," the consultant told me. "After a while nobody high-ranking attended those meetings."

Soon enough the CG/CDCF summits had devolved into a ritual of scripted hypocrisy. From the donors there were diplomatic complaints about benchmarks missed and pledges unfulfilled. "It was like being beaten with a feather cushion," said Bullen. From the government there were speeches stuffed with promises. From both sides there were calls for more "coordination," more "capacity building", more consultants to write more reports that would end up collecting dust on a shelf in an NGO office somewhere. And there was always more aid, averaging around half a billion dollars per year. Looming over everything was the legacy of the Khmer Rouge, which gave both sides a handy pretext ("weak capacity") for the slow pace of reform. For the watchdog group Global Witness, the whole process amounted to a "mass exercise in intellectual dishonesty."[18]

Diplomats and other officials based in Phnom Penh were far from ignorant of these problems. Privately, they often expressed frustration at the lack of meaningful reform, but had no real power to alter the dynamic of engagement. Far from being an "international community" united in vision and purpose—perhaps the crowning cliché of the post-Cold War consensus—donor countries resembled a pack of absent parents trying to impose discipline on a misbehaving child. Aid was highly fragmented among the big multilateral lenders—the World Bank, the IMF, and the Asian Development Bank (ADB)—the big international NGOs, and national governments. Decisions about aid were made not in Phnom Penh, but in far-off capitals, each pursuing its own institutional and foreign policy agenda. The result on the ground was developmental chaos. By 2007, Cambodia had 35 different "development partners" supporting more than 700 projects over a wide range of sectors. These were in turn monitored by around 1,000 "project implementation units," steering committees, and working groups set up by NGOs and development agencies.[19]

Efforts to coordinate this tangle of disbursements have proven as fruitless as more specific reforms. The Council for the Development of Cambodia (CDC), a body set up in 1994 to help coordinate development efforts, quickly went the way of most Cambodian government institutions. One foreign consultant who assisted in setting up the body said that instead of helping harmonize aid disbursals, CDC officials "opted for plain brown paper bags full of cash" siphoned off from development loans. The lack of coordination allowed Hun Sen to do to donors what he did to his political opponents: play them off against one another, while slowly redefining the terms of engagement.

Whatever the views of their representatives in Phnom Penh, foreign governments were mostly happy with Cambodia's progress. To the extent that Cambodia registered at all in foreign capitals, it was as a troubled nation finally at peace and on the path toward economic development. Early on, key donors like France, Japan, and Australia came to accept the stabilizing power of the CPP. They saw that Cambodia, for the first time in generations, was no longer exporting instability to the region. Fifteen years after the UN peacekeeping operation, Cambodians were wearing the blue helmets themselves: starting in 2006, Cambodian soldiers and demining teams took part in several UN operations in Sudan, Chad, and Lebanon. In the meantime, Cambodia had emerged as a player on the regional and global stage. Hun Sen proudly chaired ASEAN for the first time in 2002; two years later Cambodia joined the World Trade Organization.

There was also money to be made. Australian and Japanese mining firms jostled for mineral exploration rights to large swathes of eastern Cambodia, while global oil corporations—including the US giant Chevron and its French counterpart Total—made plays for access to Cambodia's offshore oil reserves. The possibility of investment opportunities gave foreign governments a new and lucrative reason to work with Hun Sen.

Even the US, long one of Hun Sen's strongest critics, learned to stop worrying and love (or at least tolerate) the strongman. In the aftermath of July 1997, when Congress froze direct aid, the US State Department had paid little attention to Cambodia. Policy was controlled informally by a small group of human rights activists, democracy evangelists, and Congressmen united by their strong animus against Hun Sen. At the center of this nest of "Cambodia hawks" was Dana Rohrabacher, the California Republican who in 1998 had described Hun Sen as a "new Pol Pot" and called for his indictment on genocide charges. Another was his fellow Republican Mitch McConnell, the Senate majority whip and chairman of its Foreign Operations Subcommittee. In June 2003, McConnell introduced the Cambodia Democracy and Accountability Bill, which promised the country an additional $21.5 million in development assistance provided that "new leadership in Cambodia has been elected in free and fair elections, and that Prime Minister Hun Sen is no longer in power."

The bill didn't pass, but its clear double-standard—that the only legitimate election was one that selected the candidate preferred by the US—grated on many officials in Phnom Penh. One of them was the new US ambassador, Charles Ray. After the "hanging chads" and the 2000 election fiasco in Florida, McConnell's attitude struck Ray as hubristic. "It took us more than 200 years to get close to democracy," he told me. "To expect a country that's never had it to do it overnight, that's a bit—that's a reach."

Ray's background and outlook were military. He grew up on a farm near Center, a speck on the map of eastern Texas, close to the Louisiana border. His childhood ambition echoed the old US Army pitch—to "see the world." He signed up, served two tours in Vietnam, and was decorated twice, before joining the State Department. When Ray arrived in Phnom Penh in late 2002, becoming the first African-American ambassador to Cambodia, his first impression was that it resembled Bangkok in the 1960s, except that the traffic was lighter and "there wasn't quite as much street hustling." The legacy of Vietnam also continued to color attitudes towards Cambodia back in Washington. Under the influence of McConnell and Rohrabacher, Hun Sen remained a pariah, and ambassadors who tried to argue for engagement were cast as apologists.

A particularly influential member of this circle was Paul Grove, McConnell's chief aide and a staff director on the Senate Foreign Operations Subcommittee. Grove harbored a strong antipathy towards Hun Sen. In the mid-1990s, he had worked in Cambodia with the International Republican Institute, which offered close support to Sam Rainsy's party. During the March 1997 grenade attack, Grove's friend and successor at IRI, Ron Abney, was injured by a piece of shrapnel—an event that triggered the FBI's aborted investigation into the attack (see Chapter 4). Like Abney, Grove was close to Rainsy and was outraged by Hun Sen's ruthless consolidation of power. The only acceptable option for the US, he and McConnell argued in a series of newspaper op-eds in 2002 and 2003, was "regime change." Hun Sen was another Saddam Hussein: another dictator impeding the global spread of democracy. Like Hussein, he had to go.

Ray had little time for the ideological noises coming out of Congress. For all of Hun Sen's authoritarian excesses, Congress's stance had resulted in few positive changes in Cambodia. For better or worse, Ray opted to deal with Cambodia's realities as he found them. After the terror attacks of 9/11, Cambodia assumed a new importance in Washington. In 2003, US authorities learned that the Indonesian terrorist Hambali, responsible for the 2002 bombing in Bali, had spent time hiding out in Phnom Penh. Since the US had no real relationship with the Cambodian military, which was responsible for border control, Ray set about re-establishing ties with Hun Sen and getting Washington on board. For his own part, Hun Sen quickly adapted to the rhetoric of the Bush administration. He pledged Cambodia's support in the global War on Terror and raided mosques thought to be harboring radical Islamists. In June 2003, Cambodia happily signed a so-called "Article 98 agreement," promising not to hand US citizens to the International Criminal Court in the Hague.[20]

Ray felt that he could do business with Hun Sen. The two men conversed in Vietnamese and shared an occasional game of golf. Grudgingly, Congress came around. In Washington, one Congressman told Ray to make it clear that even if Hun Sen could help fight Islamic extremism, he wanted the Cambodian leader to know he had few friends on Capitol Hill. On his return to Phnom Penh, Ray met with Hun Sen and delivered the Congressman's message. "He looked at me, he sort of laughed, and he said, 'I can live with that.' " The moratorium on military assistance was lifted in 2005.

Relations have been improving ever since. In 2007, under Ray's successor Joseph Mussomeli, the US resumed direct foreign assistance to the Cambodian government. The Peace Corps arrived and there were visits of US Navy vessels for the first time in three decades. This partnership continued following the Obama administration's much publicized "pivot" toward Asia, aimed at counter-balancing the rise of China. In 2008, Hun Sen gave his 35-year-old son, Hun Manet—a graduate of the US Military Academy at West Point—command of a National Counterterrorism Special Force, established with US assistance. The following year the two countries exchanged defense attachés and subsequently initiated Angkor Sentinel, an annual joint military exercise. The US remained one of Cambodia's main trade partners, taking the lion's share of its garment exports. By 2013, the United States had earmarked $70 million in annual aid for Cambodia. Most went to NGOs, but the sum also included around $6 million in aid to the Cambodian military.

Washington had finally learnt to live with Hun Sen.

But American policy toward Cambodia remained contradictory. While the State Department and the Pentagon worked to build closer ties, hawks like Rohrabacher kept up their Congressional chorus, denouncing Hun Sen and calling for cuts in aid. These inconsistencies were on display in November 2012, when President Obama arrived in Phnom Penh to attend the East Asia Summit—the first ever visit to Cambodia by a sitting US president. Hun Sen, determined to milk the occasion for maximum legitimacy, smiled for the cameras as he shook the President's hand. But Obama was standoffish. During a closed-door meeting he berated Hun Sen for human rights violations and the arrest of anti-eviction activists. Just hours earlier in Burma, he had congratulated President Thein Sein and offered him a "hand of friendship" as his country embarked on historic political reforms. Now, to mollify Congress, he was lecturing Hun Sen about human rights. The Cambodians were enraged at being compared to Burma, the Southeast Asian pariah state par excellence. Adding insult to injury, Obama also declined to pay a visit to Sihanouk's sarcophagus, then lying in state at the Royal Palace, following his death the month before.

But the greatest indictment of Obama's trip, perhaps, was that it did little to improve things in Cambodia. The world had changed since the early 1990s. The US was no longer the "indispensable nation", as Madeleine Albright had once put it. With Chinese backing, countries like Cambodia could now push back against US and Western demands for human rights and democratic reform. Strategic realignments in the region meant that America now needed Hun Sen more than Hun Sen needed America—a reality that was symbolized by the sight that met Obama's motorcade when it arrived at the Peace Palace for the summit meetings. Here the Cambodians had pointedly hung two large banners that read "Long Live the People's Republic of China."

The decision was ultimately pragmatic. Western governments accepted Hun Sen because they realized they couldn't get anything done without him, either for Cambodia or for themselves. But working with Hun Sen meant accepting his terms of engagement. It meant jettisoning the democratic project of the early 1990s in favor of a narrative of development quarantined from politics and untethered from the structures of power that were the root cause of so many of Cambodia's problems. This is where history had ended up: not with democracy and universal rights, but with "partnership"—and paralysis.

There must have been moments during the Third Cambodia Development Cooperation Forum—somewhere between Hun Sen's keynote performance and the aid pledges that closed the event—when diplomats and donor representatives looked up from their tables of Joint Monitoring Indicators and asked themselves: what had 20 years and billions in aid achieved in Cambodia?

In theory, foreign aid should be a temporary measure, tapering off as a country becomes more able to fund development for itself. If mapped on a graph, the ideal trajectory would resemble a flat "X", in which the first line, representing foreign aid and international NGO activities, declines, while a second, representing the capability of government and local NGOs, moves upward. The goal of international NGOs and donor agencies, then, is essentially their own obsolescence: the shifting of the graph to the point where government and local organizations have assumed most of the burden and internationals play no more than a supporting role. "Your job is to basically put yourself out of work," said Brian Lund, the head of Oxfam America, who has worked in Cambodia for more than 10 years.

Since the early 1990s, when the two lines of the potential "X" were at their widest, aid has helped rebuild Cambodia's physical infrastructure and contributed in some part to its economic resurgence. International agencies have provided vital humanitarian aid during flash floods and periods of drought. In the health sector, malaria and HIV/AIDS infection rates have been reduced to manageable levels thanks to external funding for drugs, training, and education campaigns. (Some credit should perhaps also be given to rampant deforestation, which has reduced the breeding areas of malaria-bearing mosquitos.) The reports and websites of NGOs paint a picture of onward progress, with inspiring PR copy framing slideshows of smiling Cambodian schoolchildren and rice farmers. On the whole, however, it's hard to pinpoint many successes that would survive an overnight cut in aid, anything that is truly—to use another buzzword worn almost meaningless from overuse—"sustainable."

Today, the two arms of the development graph remain far apart. Cambodia is still highly dependent on outside assistance for social services like health, education, and rural development, where donor-funded NGOs continue to fill gaps in the public sector. From 2002 until 2010, Cambodia derived around half of its budget from aid, but the tax revenues that would ideally replace foreign assistance have flat-lined: as a percentage of GDP, tax revenues crept from 8.2 percent of GDP in 2002 to just 10 percent in 2011—a low figure by global standards.[21] The government has focused instead on the informal "tax" of patronage—the cash that the rich and powerful pour, usually on request, into VIP charity projects and CPP re-election campaigns.

"Cambodian people have never paid direct tax," said Ok Serei Sopheak, a development consultant who has worked for the World Bank and other major institutions. Foreign investors are given generous tax holidays, and none of the taxes that are collected, such as VAT and import duties, have the psychological impact of a tax on income. "As long as you don't pay tax on revenue, you don't have that concept of the civil servant owing you something," Sopheak said. In his research on the impacts of aid in Cambodia, the Khmer-American political scientist Sophal Ear has reached a similar conclusion, arguing that by reducing the government's need to fund itself through taxes, aid has lessened domestic pressure for accountability, and therefore undermined democracy and the rule of law.[22]

The extent of the dependence is also evident in the fact that around a third of foreign aid to Cambodia goes toward "technical assistance"—the hiring of highly paid foreign development consultants to write reports and project assessments. According to one experienced "technical assistant," foreign consultants can earn up to $1,000 per day on short-term contracts—amounts justified by their command of the esoteric language of the World Bank and other development bureaucracies. In 2002, according to ActionAid, donors paid 700 international consultants an estimated $50–70 million, an amount roughly equivalent to the wage bills for 160,000 Cambodian civil servants.[23] Technical assistance has since fallen gradually, from as much as half of all aid money in 2004,[24] but the continuing dependence on this foreign "consultariat" ensures that large amounts of aid simply flow back out of the country.

Today, Cambodia is stuck in a dependence spiral, in which a stubborn lack of government "capacity" is matched by continuing aid disbursals. What started out as an investment in Cambodia's future in the early 1990s has evolved into an entrenched development complex that has eroded democracy, undermined the livelihoods of the poor, and given powerful elites a free hand to keep plundering the nation's resources for their own gain.

As key international donors made their political accommodations with the Cambodian government, their development priorities also started to shift. Facing a tightening of overseas aid budgets and fatigued at the slow pace of reform, they started quietly pulling money out of the areas that have seen the least progress. Most withdrew from forestry, land, and the judiciary. In 2010, a donor-funded salary supplements scheme for civil servants, which had tried and failed to reform the state bureaucracy (a reservoir of CPP patronage), was canceled. The next year, the United Kingdom stopped its bilateral aid program and closed its local development office. Denmark has done the same, as has Canada, after its development agency CIDA was merged with the Department of Foreign Affairs and International Trade in 2013.

Those donors that remained—France, Australia, Germany, the US, and Japan are among the largest—started pressing for more concrete results, both in their own projects and in those they were willing to support. Forceful advocacy and democracy promotion, once reflected in the implicit pro-opposition bias of groups like the IRI and the USAID-funded Cambodian Center for Human Rights (CCHR), were on the way out. "Core funding," the broad financial backing of Cambodian NGOs, gave way to smaller, more targeted disbursals. One foreign rights advocate said international backers are now "more interested in short-term results, in accepting the status quo ... They've put most of their eggs in the government's basket."

Though the largest Cambodian human rights NGOs remain outspoken, vocal advocacy is becoming taboo for donors. Ou Virak, the US-educated president of CCHR, told me:

> Hun Sen is telling the donors, if you want to engage and work with me on reforms, don't bring up human rights, don't bring up democracy, don't bring up any of these things. The donors keep coming up with strategies to use the government, to change the government from within ... The CPP is much smarter than that. But you don't need to be smart to play the donors, because the donors don't really care about the outcome. Perception is more important than the result, more important than anything else.

Seeking the greatest "outcomes" at the smallest cost, donors have shifted their focus to social sectors like health and education, especially those linked to the UN's Millennium Development Goals (MDGs), global development targets set for 2015. Needs in these areas have the advantage of being both genuinely pressing—many Cambodian people still need food and medicine—and seemingly quarantined from politics. They are also easy to quantify, giving donors tangible outputs—schoolchildren enrolled, health centers opened—that can be easily summarized in year-end reports. As one long-time Cambodian development expert put it, "those donors subscribing to the MDG goals want to justify their presence. They need positive indicators. And because of lack of government services for the people, it's easy to step in."

Service provision and MDG targets may be expedient for donors, but the focus on statistical measures can be misleading—especially with government agencies fudging the stats. "Monitoring indicators are about counting," said Caroline McCausland, the head of ActionAid in Cambodia. "They're not about quality, and they're not about change. So you can say Cambodia's made huge steps forward, it's got 90 percent enrollment in schools. Brilliant. But where's the quality? There's no improvement on that level. In many ways it's gone backwards." And there's another effect: while donors keep filling gaps, the government can keep ignoring its most basic responsibilities, diverting its resources into the patronage state. All this perpetuates Cambodia's dependence on the foreign aid dollar.

The accommodation between donors and government has exacerbated the tendency to view political problems—which is to say, most problems—as "technical" issues. As the Australian political scientist Michael Wesley has observed, the "narrow focus" on technocratic tasks is handy for Western

donors eager to avoid resonances of neocolonialism.[25] In Cambodia, this
has been a prescription for failure. Land and forestry reforms based on
"technical support" to corrupt ministries have failed to address the political
incentive to steal land and cut down trees, and therefore failed to solve the
problem. Helping Cambodia create a constitution and laws enshrining human
rights did nothing to guarantee their implementation. One might also mention
UNHCR's support to the Cambodian Refugee Office, which proceeded
in apparent ignorance at what would happen when politics and law came, as
they inevitably would, into conflict.

This way of thinking is so pervasive that an analysis published by the
Brookings Institution in 2008 could offer a detailed anatomy of aid effectiveness in Cambodia and barely mention the realities of politics or patronage. It
summed up its argument:

> To enhance aid effectiveness, some key challenges desperately need to be
> addressed. These include the use of program-based approaches (PBAs), the
> strengthening of [Technical Working Groups], promoting the role of civil
> society organizations, improving government systems, particularly public
> financial management, and finally improving the database on aid delivery
> and management.[26]

All these things mattered on some level. But without directly addressing the
political obstacles that stand in the way of these prescriptions, they are reduced
to tautology—an assertion that aid effectiveness could be improved by
improving the effectiveness of aid.

Most diagnoses of Cambodia's development complex overlook the reality
that highly skilled and dedicated Cambodian officials—and there are many—
remain constrained by the political logic of the system. Brian Lund of Oxfam
recalled meeting Cambodian agricultural extension officers who have "ten
times the training" he received back in Australia, but no way to apply it. If the
adherence to templates and models began as idealistic, rooted in the post–
Cold War narrative of constant forward progress, it ended as pragmatic, a way
of keeping the development complex humming down the path of least political
resistance.

All of which brings us to the United Nations, whose 24 entrenched agencies
in Phnom Penh form a sort of Ground Zero for the Cambodian development
complex. Two decades after UNTAC, the UN mission is still cemented to its
headquarters in Phnom Penh by a strong institutional inertia and a pervasive
fear of losing its access. This is not in itself exceptional. Everywhere it operates,
the UN is forced to work closely with host governments, which has led to a

global tendency for UN personnel to tread carefully on sensitive issues. In Cambodia, however, escalating government pressure has forced the global organization into a particularly ineffective position.

In March 2010, the Ministry of Foreign Affairs wrote to Douglas Broderick, the UN's Resident Coordinator, threatening to revoke his diplomatic status and expel him from the country. Broderick had issued a statement mildly criticizing the passage of the government's new Anti-Corruption Law. According to one ex-UN employee, the incident made a strong impression at headquarters. "Nobody else wants to get a letter like that, whether or not that letter had any substance," the former staffer said. In the UN, risk aversion has now been elevated into a philosophy of management. One international NGO director summarized the prevailing thought process as, "Get through your posting without ruffling any feathers, get a few ticks, move on to the next posting."

A notable exception is the Office of the High Commissioner for Human Rights (OHCHR), the one UN agency with a mandate to speak out about sensitive issues. OHCHR, established in 1993 to carry on the work of UNTAC's Human Rights Component, has always had a fraught relationship with the Cambodian government. Since the mid-1990s, the government has made repeated attempts to close the office down, and the UN's special rapporteurs for human rights, independent experts who work closely with OHCHR, have come in for the full "Hun Sen treatment." In 2001, Hun Sen referred to the Austrian lawyer Peter Leuprecht as "stupid." His Kenyan successor, Yash Ghai, would be described variously as "deranged," "lazy," and a "short-term tourist."[27]

While OHCHR remains in Phnom Penh, the office has slowly been muzzled by the reluctance of other UN agencies to support it in times of trouble. In July 2010, a few months after the government threatened Broderick with expulsion, the long-serving head of OHCHR in Cambodia, Christophe Peschoux, faced a similar problem. Peschoux made some comments to a local newspaper that criticized the government's deportation of two Thai nationals suspected of bombing a political party office in Bangkok. As with Broderick, the government took immediate action, requesting his removal. When OHCHR in Geneva refused, he was declared persona non grata and government officials refused to meet with him. Shortly afterward, unable to work, he left for a new posting in Geneva. During the entire affair, the other UN agencies in Phnom Penh did nothing to publicly protest his treatment. "They didn't back him at all," said one foreign aid worker.

Peschoux understood how Cambodia worked as well as just about any foreigner. He had studied it for more than 25 years. As head of OHCHR, he worked patiently with the government on a range of human rights issues. In areas where government officials were cooperative, like prison reform, he had seen gradual progress. As Peschoux told an interviewer shortly before his departure, he made a point of using public advocacy sparingly, reserving it only for cases where dialogue failed to produce results.[28] But as soon as he crossed that line, the government withdrew its cooperation. "It's an impossible situation," said the former UN worker. "It's a Catch-22. The UN can't achieve most of its aims without working with the government—that's what it does, that's what its job is—but that does mean that some compromises have to be made."

For OHCHR, compromise has meant a reduction in public advocacy. For the UN system as a whole, it has resulted in projects and initiatives that are so bleached of anything sensitive and vetted at so many levels that they attain a sort of sublime blandness. To mark the centenary of International Women's Day in March 2011, for example, the UN mission in Phnom Penh announced that it was "collaborating with youth organizations to ask Cambodian youth to send text messages from their mobile phones promoting gender equality and the rights of women and girls." Whether this quixotic scheme would have any effect was open to question for a host of reasons. But it ticked the right boxes. Gender. Technology. Youth. The consultants got paid and the UN got some more ballast for its annual reports.

The other large multilateral institutions are marked by similar tendencies. Like UN agency heads, the country directors of the World Bank, the IMF, and the ADB sit on a global career conveyor that prizes good relations with host governments. Despite recent talk of stricter accountability—a belated response to years of theft and corruption scandals—global financial bureaucracies still have three main imperatives: lend, lend, and lend some more. The World Bank froze its funding to Cambodia in 2011 over the Boeung Kak lake eviction, but, by late 2013, it had initiated two new projects using auxiliary "trust funds" provided by other donors.[29] Ou Virak of CCHR, whom the World Bank approached for support for its plans to restart loans, said disengagement was simply "not an option." As he said, "Their aim is to be here 10 years or 15 years."

Where the UN has crossed the road to reach the middle, the World Bank and ADB continue to apply their neoliberal economic models in apparent disregard for Cambodia's political and social context. The outcome, as in many other developing countries, has been ambiguous. Free market templates have stoked economic growth, yielding an impressive annual crop of GDP growth figures, but they have also produced a typhoon capitalism that has empowered a predatory elite, opened up a massive gap between rich and poor, and undercut one of their supposedly central priorities: poverty reduction.

The accommodations that are made at the top invariably trickle downward, to the international and local NGOs that rely on donor funding. Like the Cambodian government, these groups have been forced to adapt the agendas and language of outside patrons. Increasing amounts of time are now spent writing funding proposals and progress reports servicing long lists of donor requirements. These can range from the ideological—like the onerous restrictions the US government places on the offering of abortion services by American-funded health NGOs—to simply what is considered important in global development circles at any given time. There is plenty of money to combat HIV/AIDS, for instance, but much less for fighting diabetes. Climate change has emerged as a sexy field, despite the fact that landlessness, debt, and the transformation of the rural agricultural economy will swallow most Cambodian farmers long before global warming does.

As donor countries have shifted in recent years toward short-termism and instant results, NGOs have moved in the same direction. Faced with government pressure, shorter-term disbursals of funds, and donor pressures to "engage," many Cambodian NGOs have retreated into a tame conference culture characterized by the liberal use of PowerPoint bromides and euphemistic development jargon. At these workshops, held every day at a dozen hotel conference halls in Phnom Penh, deeply political questions about good governance and human rights—even seemingly less political issues like health and education—are expressed in the deadening language of "hurdles" and "cross-cutting issues."

A whole generation of Cambodian NGO workers has been trained in the use of this clotted cant. This language finds its supreme manifestation in the hundreds of grant proposals and reports that are churned out each year by the development complex. (If Pol Pot were alive today, it's not hard to imagine him talking about "mainstreaming" the party line.) But NGO language, a sort of development Newspeak, also has more pernicious effects. Wittingly or not, the use of such soft language chimes with the official agenda, which is to keep development safely quarantined from politics.

As with the UN, this inertia is reinforced by NGO bureaucracies that are self-focused and protective of operational turf. It is true that some NGOs have closed their Cambodia offices and moved on, fulfilling the goal of obsolescence. In 2009, for instance, Médecins sans Frontières Belgium pulled out of Cambodia after determining that its emergency mandate no longer applied. At the time, its outgoing country director, Philippe Berneau, told me that MSF thought Cambodia now had the "capacity" to deal with major health problems on its own (though he wondered about its willingness). In early

2011, the Lutheran World Federation nationalized its operations in Cambodia under the name "Life with Dignity."

But these groups remain a small minority. While most NGOs pay lip service to the idea of putting themselves out of business, they treat their mandates as basically permanent. Instead of pursuing self-obsolescence, they accept aid dependency—and their roles in propping up hollowed-out public services—as a fact of life. "I'm still on a career path," said the head of one major international NGO, describing the situation faced by many of his colleagues. "Instead of thinking about how I'm going to continue to reduce my presence, my footprint, most of the time I'm thinking of how I'm going to keep my staff . . . I don't want to preside over the demise of my organization." Of the international NGOs in Cambodia, "probably half" have no defined exit plan, the director said.

In large part this reflects Cambodia's peculiar place in the global development industry. The country is no longer the prestigious posting it was in the early 1990s. In career terms, it is now relatively low on the global totempole—a place without the urgency of a Syria or South Sudan. At the same time it is a surprisingly comfortable place to live and work. The Phnom Penh expat life is a sybaritic blur of cheap entertainment, running the gamut from panini bars and yoga classes to hip cafés, "social enterprise" setups, and cocktail happy hours. Rent and domestic help are inexpensive, internet connections are fast, and just about every sort of indulgence is imported from abroad. "They don't call it the 'Play Penh' for nothing," said Weh Yeoh, a Sydney native and Cambodia-based co-founder of whydev.org, a website that scrutinizes the ethics and business of aid.

Each year, hundreds of prospective foreign aid workers rotate through the country, taking jobs as program managers, legal consultants, volunteers, and interns with a wide spectrum of NGOs and nonprofits. Living in an extraterritorial settlement sustained by aid money, few expatriates "really engage with Cambodian culture," Yeoh said. "They don't learn the language—90 percent of them don't learn the language. They're basically living this lifestyle that they lived back in Australia or America or wherever, except that they have more money relative to how much things cost." The heads of large development agencies and NGOs can often earn six-figure salaries—tax-free in the case of the UN—which include health plans, school allowances, and other perks. A spell in Cambodia is generally a comfortable step on the way to somewhere else, and everybody wants to leave with a gold star on their CV.

Those who stay longer soon learn that achieving lasting results in the Cambodian development complex is extremely tough, in large part for these very reasons. "I've had people say to me, 'this is the most difficult country I have ever worked in,' " said McCausland of ActionAid, who has lived in Cambodia since 1995. "There are very few places where you can go and meet with the government, who will just blatantly say yes, yes, yes to everything and do absolutely nothing, take [your] $3 million, produce absolutely nothing, and then get another $3 million." Veteran aid workers, often people of the highest integrity, find themselves in much the same position as well-intentioned government officials: constrained by a system that they have little power to change. For the rest, life is good enough in Phnom Penh that it's easy to let things slide, to accept a broken system, to drift through a posting—forgetting all the while that the Cambodian mirage is thickest not at the horizon, but at the center.

After 20 years of meandering development, a growing number of NGOs are beginning to question the current model of development and to push back against the shift toward short-term results and statistical bean-counting, especially among those groups—such as Oxfam, ActionAid, and some of the church-based charities—with independent sources of funding. Some international NGOs have wound up their operations, or established plans for handing them over to Cambodian nationals. The recent growth of community activism around land and natural resources has also offered an alternative role for NGOs, which is to support local developments rather than simply substituting for them. This is the role played courageously by Cambodia's largest human rights groups, which still receive strong backing from abroad. Most NGOs, however, don't enjoy the luxury of independence. They remain beholden to the donor cycle, reliant on outside money and therefore unable to challenge a flawed paradigm.

Until foreign governments reassess their approach to development— an unlikely event, give the economic and strategic agendas at play—the destructive pattern of aid in Cambodia shows few signs of abating. Every three or four years a new crop of NGO directors and UN agency staff arrives in Cambodia full of optimism. New development projects are introduced. Old, failed ones are resurrected. When things don't work out, many grow frustrated and leave, having decided they are powerless to affect change. In some ways, they are right. Twenty years after it arose during the UNTAC mission, the Cambodian development complex has attained its own uncontrollable inertia. Like a runaway four-wheel drive with a bottomless tank, it plunges onward, inscribing a wide and endless circle.

The result is more than an aid economy; it is an aid society, marked by relationships of dependence at every level, between donors, government officials, NGOs, and ordinary people. In the villages, far from the foreign capitals where donors tally up their indicators and publish their annual reports, this pattern is nothing new. For centuries, Cambodian farmers and rural folk have depended on those more powerful than they are, whether they are government chiefs or NGO workers offering handouts and training sessions. From the perspective of the village, the distinctions are cosmetic. One treats the people as a subject of charity, the other as a subject of "capacity building." Both see the rural population as a malleable entity, traumatized by the Khmer Rouge and subsequent years of conflict, and so in desperate need of guidance from the outside.

Since the poor are rarely asked for their opinion about development, they are often the first to suffer its unintended consequences. Far from "empowering" local people, the development complex and its templates of betterment have merely reinforced an age-old pattern, in which well-dressed outsiders drive into a village, briefly break the surface of rural life with gifts and promises, and then vanish back to where they came from. If people there are lucky, the ripples subside quickly.

CHAPTER TWELVE

UNTAC Redux

The man in the hammock swung gently back and forth, one leg dangling free. On a nearby chair lay a pouch of tobacco and a splayed volume of Buddhist sutras. Above, a straw roof provided protection from the hot afternoon, which was silent except for a faint strain of music coming from a transistor radio somewhere nearby. Slowly, the old man stirred and sat up. He was in his early seventies, with thinning ash-gray hair and a creased brow. As he shook himself awake, a young man brought him a pair of dark green trousers. He dressed and settled back down in his hammock, taking a pinch of tobacco and rolling it into a stubby facsimile of a cigarette. Then he began to talk.

Ta Sanh Cheung village was a peaceful place. The fields all around blazed emerald green, with wooden stilt-houses sitting in groves of banana trees. At a dusty village junction was a large illustration of a man prying apart an old rocket—a warning against dismantling the unexploded remnants of war that still littered this pocket of western Cambodia. Now and then a child passed unsteadily on a bicycle. In front of small shacks stood racks of old Coca-Cola bottles filled with gasoline, dyed yellow, red, candy-green.

To all appearances, the old man napping away the afternoon grew rice or maize, like most families in Ta Sanh Cheung. But Meas Muth was no ordinary peasant. When the Khmer Rouge movement capitulated in the late 1990s, he was one of the last commanders to give up the fight. When I met him in 2011, Muth's name had just appeared on documents leaked from the UN-backed tribunal set up in 2006 to try surviving leaders of the Khmer Rouge. Prosecutors described him as a harsh leader who had a hand in killings and purges, and recommended he be put on trial for crimes against humanity.

Muth's home stood in a quiet corner of the village, a lavish residence by local standards, topped with satellite dishes and blue ceramic tiles. After his defection in December 1998, Muth was made a two-star general in the

Cambodian army. To the local farmers, many of them grizzled former Khmer Rouge fighters, he became a sort of revered Buddhist patriarch, constructing a new pagoda—a wooden structure with blue shutters and painted *naga* statues— and showering local residents with advice about matters both agricultural and spiritual. Like most former Khmer Rouge, Muth disavowed any responsibility for what took place during the 1970s. He was just a servant of his nation, he told me, "a lower officer with a job to protect Cambodian independence and neutrality." He blamed the United States for its B-52 bombing raids, and Prince Sihanouk, for calling the Cambodian people to rise up against the Lon Nol regime. "If the court does not sentence those from the beginning and only starts to sentence at the end and in the middle, how can it be fair?" he said, speaking almost inaudibly. "I didn't create the war. I was a victim that was forced to join in."

Historians tell a different story. They describe how Muth rose in the early 1970s through the military ranks in Democratic Kampuchea's Southwest Zone, then under the control of his father-in-law Ta Mok, nicknamed "the Butcher," the architect of many of Pol Pot's purges. When the regime came to power, Muth was appointed head of the navy—a prominent position within the DK military apparatus, with responsibility for Cambodia's coasts and the port-town of Kampong Som (since renamed Sihanoukville). Along with Sou Met, the head of the air force, he allegedly played a direct role in purging military cadres and sending them to the fearsome S-21 security prison in Phnom Penh, where they were subsequently tortured and killed.

In 2001, the academics Steve Heder and Brian Tittemore published an influential paper which laid out "compelling evidence" of the pair's involvement in killings and purges. According to the paper, Muth and Met attended regular meetings of the General Staff of the Revolutionary Army of Kampuchea, indicating their "close involvement and knowledge of the Party's arrest, interrogation and execution policies."[1] When the Khmer Rouge tribunal was established, Muth seemed like an ideal target for prosecution. But despite all the evidence against him—and the extensive paper trail wending its way from his leafy rural sanctuary into a dark thicket of killings and disappearances—he will probably never see the inside of a courtroom.

In February 2012, Cambodia's war crimes court—the Extraordinary Chambers in the Courts of Cambodia (ECCC)—celebrated its first big victory. A panel of Supreme Court judges upheld a 2010 conviction against Kaing Guek Eav, also known as Comrade Duch—the gaunt figure who ran S-21 prison. The judges handed him the maximum possible sentence: life in prison. It was the first time a Khmer Rouge figure had been sentenced, beyond all appeal, for his role in the human experiment that called itself "Democratic Kampuchea."

Four more defendants were also on trial in Case 002, the court's second, more complex proceeding. There was Nuon Chea, the steely dogmatist who served as "Brother Number Two" to Pol Pot, and Khieu Samphan, DK's head of state. The last two were a married couple: Ieng Sary, the former foreign minister, and his wife, Ieng Thirith, its minister of social affairs. All four had surrendered in the late 1990s in exchange for amnesties; then, in 2007, they were wrenched from quiet retirements and locked up to await trial at the ECCC, a "mixed" court which paired UN and Cambodian judges. As the Duch case came to a close, the message coming out of the court was one of account-ability and justice long delayed.

Behind the scenes, however, the tribunal was unraveling. In March 2012, the international co-investigating judge, a Swiss named Laurent Kasper-Ansermet, resigned his post after months of standoffs with the Cambodian government. At the center of the dispute was the question of whether the tribunal should pursue two further investigations, known as Case 003 and Case 004, which the government vehemently opposed. Meas Muth was named in the third case along with Sou Met (who died in mid-2013); the fourth was focused on three more mid-ranking DK cadres, all still leading quiet lives in the countryside.

After his resignation, Kasper-Ansermet released a scathing report describing the "serious irregularities, dysfunctions, and violations of proper due process of law" that he witnessed at the ECCC. He claimed that Cambodian staff, including his counterpart, the national co-investigating judge, You Bunleng, had stymied his investigations into Cases 003 and 004 by with-holding the official seal of the investigating judges' office and refusing him access to court translators and drivers.[2] These five prospective defendants allegedly had a hand in hundreds of thousands of deaths, many more than were killed at S-21 on Duch's watch. Without government cooperation, however, there was no chance of the cases ever reaching trial.

At the crux of the dispute sat widely divergent conceptions of justice: of why the Cambodian tribunal was set up and what it aimed to achieve. The international courts that had been established after the Cold War to try the perpetrators of atrocities committed in places like Rwanda and the former Yugoslavia all blended justice and politics in sometimes uncomfortable meas-ures. But the Cambodia tribunal stood apart as a product of pure political expediency. Its fraught and tangled history represented in concentrated mini-ature the fraught and tangled relationship between Cambodia and the "inter-national community." Cambodia's war crimes tribunal began in politics. In all likelihood that's also where it would end.

There's no doubt Cambodia is in need of some sort of a reckoning. If there's one unifying theme to the country's relationship with its ghastly past, it is the profound lack of resolution. After overthrowing the Khmer Rouge in 1979, the ruling CPP promoted rituals of remembering, but also of forgetting. There was much talk of liberation, of "January 7," but most perpetrators were amnestied or left alone and allowed to return to civilian life, often alongside their former victims. For political reasons the history of DK wasn't properly taught in schools until 2007, and younger generations of Cambodians still have little sense of the scope of the tragedy that befell their country.

In 1979, most Khmer Rouge survivors picked up the pieces and moved on as best they could. Some found consolation in traditional religion; others simply chose silence. "They've tried to find ways to cope with this thing, without any help, with empty hands," said Youk Chhang, a Khmer Rouge survivor and director of the Documentation Center of Cambodia (DC-Cam), a US-funded institute that documents DK-era crimes. "They deal with the skulls, with the graves, with missing family members, all kinds of things. They're on their own. And they've become exhausted."

From the very moment of Cambodia's liberation from the Khmer Rouge on January 7, 1979, the new People's Republic of Kampuchea based its legitimacy on the fact that it had freed Cambodia from the "genocidal clique" of Pol Pot and Ieng Sary. One of the new regime's first acts was to set up a People's Revolutionary Tribunal which tried the two leaders and condemned them to death in absentia. The five-day trial took place at Vann Molyvann's Chaktomuk Theater. Memories and emotions were raw. "They tried to select good victims who could speak out clearly with detail," recalled Thun Saray, one of those who collected evidence for the tribunal. "Everybody, after they listened, they cried, everyone cried."

But the world's first genocide trial was designed to serve entirely political ends. Its length and verdicts were set in advance, and the lawyer assigned to defend Pol Pot and Ieng Sary denounced them as "criminally insane monsters" who deserved the death penalty. Throughout the 1980s, responsibility for Khmer Rouge crimes was ascribed solely to these two individuals, who were vilified as "fascists" so as to distance them from orthodox communism and its adherents. To underscore the point, Vietnamese museum experts transformed S-21 prison into a grisly "museum of genocide," still popular with tourists today, featuring an infamous map of Cambodia fashioned from human skulls and bones. (The map was dismantled in 2002.) In schools, children were fed a politically filtered catechism of horror, with the "Pol Pot–Ieng Sary clique" and its Chinese patrons in starring roles. "Living prisoners first had to dig their own graves and then they were buried," recounted one high school primer from 1988. "Some prisoners had their gallbladders removed by the Khmer Rouge cadre, and then the gallbladders were sent to Beijing . . ."[3]

While the new regime unleashed a barrage of propaganda reminding Cambodians how they suffered under Pol Pot, its administration and top leadership were filled with former members of the regime. As a political and practical necessity, accountability for past crimes took a back seat to the challenges of restoring the economy and fighting the civil war. To encourage defections from the resistance armies fighting the Vietnamese occupation, the PRK offered amnesties to former Khmer Rouge, promising to overlook their past actions. As noted in Chapter 2, the policy allowed the new government to draw a line under the past and absolve its own leadership, while keeping the door open for future defections.

Starting in 1984, the PRK staged annual "Days of Anger" when victims delivered speeches condemning the "genocidal clique" and actors re-enacted the liberation of January 7. These still take place every year at Choeung Ek, the partially exhumed killing field on the outskirts of Phnom Penh where thousands of S-21 victims were executed and thrown into pits. Taken together, S-21, the "killing fields", and the Days of Anger became the stage for a selective telling of history, one that featured a handful of genocidal masterminds, millions of innocent victims, and a patriotic vanguard that delivered them from the nightmare.

If this didn't look much like real justice and accountability, at least it was something. Throughout the 1980s, the UN, the US and other Western governments showed nearly no interest in putting the Khmer Rouge on trial. Even after the Paris Peace Agreements were signed in 1991, political support for trials was elusive. The Western governments that framed the treaty were more concerned with detaching themselves from the Cambodian conflict than in dredging up the past, and so the agreements made no reference to accountability. Under Chinese pressure, all references to genocide or specific atrocities were whited out of the final treaty.

This question of justice was left to a small number of Western scholars and activists centered around the Campaign to Oppose the Return of the Khmer Rouge (CORKR), established in the late 1980s in Washington. Under the leadership of its executive director, Craig Etcheson, CORKR worked tirelessly to gather evidence and rally support for prosecutions. In the end it was the actions of the Khmer Rouge themselves that opened the door to trials. Pol Pot's return to civil war in the 1990s put him beyond political rehabilitation. In July 1994, the Cambodian government officially outlawed the Khmer Rouge, and, after years of patient lobbying by CORKR and other activists, the idea of a trial started to gain traction in foreign capitals. In April of that year, the US Congress passed the Cambodia Genocide Justice Act, which made support for a Khmer Rouge tribunal official US policy and provided funding for the establishment of the Cambodian Genocide Program at Yale University, as well as a local field office, DC-Cam, which set about gathering evidence of DK-era crimes.

A couple of years later, as DK forces began defecting to the government in droves, the UN finally got engaged. The first feelers were put out by Thomas Hammarberg, who arrived in Cambodia as the Secretary-General's special representative for human rights in mid-1996. In his encounters with ordinary people, Hammarberg recalled hearing strong support for trials. After the establishment of the Yugoslavia and Rwanda tribunals in 1993 and 1994, he thought it obscene that piles of skulls still lay in the open in Cambodia while known killers tended their gardens. With the Khmer Rouge on the verge of collapse, it seemed like a perfect time to press the case for justice.

On June 21, 1997, just two weeks before Hun Sen's violent overthrow of Prince Ranariddh, Hammarberg convinced both leaders to sign a letter to the new UN Secretary-General, Kofi Annan, formally requesting UN assistance for a tribunal. Shrewdly playing on the fierce rivalry between the two politicians, then competing for the allegiance of the remaining Khmer Rouge fighters, Hammarberg first approached the Funcinpec leader. Then he presented Hun Sen with Ranariddh's signature and challenged him to add his own. Having agitated for years for the trial of leading Khmer Rouge figures, Hun Sen could hardly afford to be outflanked by a political rival. He too signed. And so the seed of the ECCC was planted firmly in Cambodia's domestic political tangle.

In New York, the gears of the UN's bureaucracy creaked slowly into motion. Annan dispatched a Group of Experts to study the feasibility of a trial. Their report, released in early 1999, foreshadowed the problems and divisions to come. The experts concluded that trials against surviving Khmer Rouge leaders were workable, but should only take place in The Hague or in another outside country. The Cambodian courts were simply too corrupt, and only a fully international court could guard against government meddling. "The more insulated the tribunal can be from domestic politics," the report concluded, "the better."[4]

For Hun Sen this was out of the question. If trials were to take place, they would be in his courts and on his terms. One reason was that he wanted control over the scope of any potential prosecutions. Under the government's amnesty policy, thousands of Khmer Rouge soldiers and mid-level cadres had already been reintegrated into Cambodian society, with little regard for their past actions. The question of who should be tried was sensitive for many in the CPP. Chea Sim, the elderly CPP president, had served as party secretary of Sector 20, in DK's Eastern Zone, which was ravaged by purges in 1977–8. Heng Samrin had been commander of the zone's Fourth Division, suspected of massacring Vietnamese civilians during cross-border incursions in 1977. Did these leaders have a hand in Khmer Rouge atrocities?

The same question hung over key members of Hun Sen's cabinet. The finance minister, Keat Chhon, had worked in the DK Foreign Ministry under Ieng Sary and didn't defect until 1984, settling in France and going on to a career in the UN before returning to Cambodia in 1992 and becoming an economic advisor to Hun Sen. Then there was Hor Namhong, Hun Sen's long-serving foreign minister. As a young diplomat, Namhong had rallied to Prince Sihanouk's government-in-exile in 1970, representing it in Paris and Havana. After the Khmer Rouge took power in April 1975, he joined an exodus of intellectuals and diplomats called back home to serve the revolution. Upon arrival, he was immediately sent to Boeung Trabek, a prison in Phnom Penh where hundreds of intellectuals were sent for re-education and many subsequently perished. Namhong was spared and reportedly helped run the camp as the "chief" of its detainees.[5] A biographical file kept at the Stasi archives in Berlin describes Namhong as an ordinary prisoner who served as a camp "director" (*Leiter*) and enjoyed privileges not accorded other inmates, such as presenting the camp to Ieng Sary during inspections. Namhong has consistently denied any hand in atrocities, and has filed defamation suits against journalists and other individuals—including King Sihanouk and Sam Rainsy—who have alleged otherwise. Whether or not he and others were guilty of anything, the CPP opposed any court that might air the question in public.

From the start, Hun Sen took an instrumental view of justice, supporting trials when it was politically expedient and then cooling off once the Khmer Rouge were on the verge of collapse. When Khieu Samphan and Nuon Chea defected to the government in December 1998, dealing the movement its final death-blow, Hun Sen extended his "warmest welcome" to the pair and promised privately not to hand them over to an international court. The two ageing *genocidaires* rang in the New Year in the seaside resort town of Sihanoukville, visited Angkor Wat, and then returned to civilian life as free men, to a chorus of outrage from victims and rights advocates. Years earlier, Hun Sen had excoriated the pair as two Khmer Rouge "ringleaders" who should be put in the dock. Now he argued that intemperate moves toward trials could threaten the country's fragile peace. It was time to "dig a hole and bury the past."[6]

As the debate raged between Hun Sen and his critics, the government made two important arrests. The first was of Ta Mok, captured by the Cambodian military in March 1999. At around the same time, the Irish photographer Nic Dunlop stumbled unexpectedly across a skinny, buck-toothed man living in the backwoods of Samlaut. Two decades after the regime's fall, Comrade Duch, the former chief of S-21, was alive and well. He had converted to Christianity and taken a job in the district education office. Soon after Dunlop and the American journalist Nate Thayer published their landmark interview with Duch, he too was arrested. Duch appeared resigned to his fate. Whether he would be tried, he told Dunlop, was now "up to Hun Sen and Jesus."[7]

Still smarting from the Group of Experts report, Hun Sen announced that the two prisoners would be tried domestically. The UN renewed its calls for an international trial. During a visit to Phnom Penh in April 1999, US Senator John Kerry helped break the deadlock by floating the novel idea of a "mixed" tribunal, one that would include both domestic and international personnel. Kerry's proposal got the negotiations back on track. But translating the "mixed" tribunal formula into something that was acceptable to both sides would take years of agonizing negotiations, without ever resolving the underlying disagreement. The only trial the UN wanted was one Hun Sen couldn't control; the only trial Hun Sen wanted was one he could.

The Cambodia tribunal negotiations coincided with the high noon of international criminal justice. The ad hoc tribunals for Rwanda and the former Yugoslavia had produced a momentum that led directly to the Rome Statute and the creation, in 2002, of the International Criminal Court (ICC) in The Hague. To their many boosters, these international tribunals embodied the promise of the Nuremberg war crimes trials of the 1940s, a legacy frozen by the superpower calculations of the Cold War. Kofi Annan hailed the establishment of the ICC as "a gift of hope to future generations, and a giant step forward in the march towards universal human rights and the rule of law."[8] In the brave new post–Cold War order, tyrants and mass murderers would no longer be able to bank on impunity. State sovereignty would no longer be absolute.

Unfortunately, the new world had turned out a lot like the old one. The early 1990s were years of massacre and genocide—Rwanda, Somalia, Bosnia—in which foreign governments seemed as reluctant as ever to intervene and put an end to the killing. What the West could offer, however, were trials after the fact. The international criminal courts were totems of universal values, but also represented the failure of those values to be applied while genocide and mass killings were actually in progress. Within a few years the great shining idea of the post–Cold War age—an end to genocide and crimes against humanity—had been downgraded and farmed out to these new organs of international justice.

In Cambodia, too, the idea of a tribunal was loaded with deferred hopes. Hun Sen's brutal seizure of power in July 1997 had seemingly sounded the death-knell for the democratic system implanted by the UNTAC peace-keeping mission. Frustrated with their inability to prevent Cambodia's slide back into authoritarianism, many activists and observers turned their focus to the past. "No peace without justice," was the rallying cry. Without addressing the crimes of the past, they said, it would be impossible to tackle the problems of the present.[9]

The idea of a Khmer Rouge tribunal soon became a blank screen for the projection of every sort of individual and institutional agenda. A court could bring reconciliation, "healing," a reckoning with Cambodia's dark past. It could help end the country's "culture of impunity" and advance international criminal jurisprudence. For the CPP, it was a chance to bolster its own liberation myth. For the CPP's opponents, it was a chance to pick it apart. That many of these aims were overambitious and contradictory didn't prevent the tribunal from being seen implicitly as a rerun of the UNTAC mission—another transformational foreign intervention that would reset Cambodian politics and put the country once again on a democratic path.

In August 1999, the UN and the Cambodian government began negotiations over the shape of the Khmer Rouge tribunal. At the first morning session, the two sides took their seats along opposite sides of a polished wooden table at the Council of Ministers. On one side sat Deputy Prime Minister Sok An, head of the government's new high-level tribunal task force. On the other sat Ralph Zacklin, the UN's Assistant Secretary-General for Legal Affairs. Zacklin, a brusque British lawyer, had worked for more than two decades to advance the idea of a norms-based international order. He had had a hand in the establishment of the Yugoslavia and Rwanda tribunals, and would later play a role in setting up the Special Court for Sierra Leone. In Cambodia, he faced a government with a very different view of justice, and how it should be pursued.

There were two main disagreements between the UN and the Cambodians. The first was the balance of power within a "mixed" tribunal. Whose laws would prevail and which side would have a majority of judges? The second related to the court's jurisdiction. Both sides agreed that only leading Khmer Rouge figures would be indicted—a tribunal aiming to try thousands of low-level perpetrators was clearly impractical—and there were too many skeletons in too many closets to extend the court's temporal jurisdiction beyond 1975-9. But this was where the agreement ended. As in 1979, the Cambodian government wanted to try a hand-picked clique of DK leaders. The UN favored a more open-ended legal process.

These differences were underpinned by fundamentally divergent percep-
tions of justice. Like the development experts who jetted into Cambodia
during the UNTAC years, Zacklin and his legal team were dedicated profes-
sionals with little experience of Cambodia and how it operated. From a legal
standpoint, of course, it didn't much matter. The law, after all, was the law:
neutral, universal, categorical. The UN's prime concern was whether the
tribunal would uphold international standards of due process.

The Cambodians, on the other hand, saw justice in essentially political
terms. They pointed out that when the Khmer Rouge were still a threat, it was
their own policy of force and diplomacy that had brought them to heel, not the
proclamations and "mandates" of the UN. Hun Sen and other Cambodia officials questioned whether the UN even had the moral authority to lecture it
about justice, given the fact that Pol Pot's men sat in the UN General Assembly
until 1991, and they bristled at the arrogance of the UN's lawyers, who seemed
to look upon them with enlightened disdain. Straight away it was clear the two
sides were "on completely opposite paths," recalled Zacklin, who retired from
the UN in 2005. "The Cambodian side did not truly want to have a tribunal at
all. For political reasons they had decided to go ahead with the calls for a
tribunal while at the same time ensuring that whatever form it took it would
not escape their control."[10] The talks shuddered to a halt.

Once again, the Americans helped break the deadlock. Since the passage of
the Cambodia Genocide Justice Act in 1994, the Clinton administration had
become perhaps the most energetic international proponent of a trial for the
Khmer Rouge. In 1997, it had even drawn up plans to arrest Pol Pot and spirit
him off for trial in a third country, a scheme which was foiled by his death the
following year. The commitment stemmed partly from guilt about past
American actions in Cambodia, but also figured as a way for the US to reclaim
the moral high ground and bolster its supposedly redemptive role in international affairs. To get the talks back on track, Washington turned to its
Ambassador-at-Large for War Crimes Issues, David Scheffer, who raised the
idea of establishing a "special chambers" within the Cambodian court system,
filled with local and foreign jurists. Under Scheffer's plan, judicial decisions
would be determined by a so-called "supermajority"; Cambodian judges
would form a majority, but would require the vote of at least one international
judge for any important decision.

Zacklin and his boss, Hans Corell, the UN's Swedish chief legal counsel,
were hesitant to accept the supermajority formula. But it was an easier sell for
the Cambodians. For Hun Sen, it offered the possibility of allowing him
control over the tribunal while also benefiting from international involvement.
As a further lure, US officials also made it clear that increased aid was in the

offing if Hun Sen accepted the deal, and pressed the UN to adopt a more "flex-ible" approach to the negotiations—that is, to dilute its demands. The bar inched downwards. In January 2001, Cambodia unilaterally passed a draft law for the establishment of the ECCC, containing many of the terms to which the UN had previously objected.

In early 2002, Annan abruptly pulled out of the negotiations. A few weeks earlier, Corell had signed an agreement setting up the Special Court for Sierra Leone (SCSL), which featured a similar "mixed" model to the proposed Cambodian court. Unlike the Cambodians, the authorities in Freetown had willingly agreed to a majority of international judges and other UN demands. Compared to the ease of setting up the SCSL, Cambodia suddenly seemed like too much trouble. "My feeling in negotiating with Sierra Leone is that they wanted a truly independent court," Corell told me. What Cambodia wanted was something else entirely, "a creature that would not fulfill international standards for criminal justice, and still bear the emblem of the UN."

Organizations like Human Rights Watch supported the UN's move, along with many Cambodian NGOs. Others took the opposite view. One of the few dissenters in Cambodian civil society was Youk Chhang of DC-Cam, who said the world shouldn't abandon its efforts to bring the Khmer Rouge to justice. Scheffer agreed, writing that the insistence on "near-perfect justice" risked "losing the good for the sake of the unattainable."[11] As the debate raged, inter-national pressure mounted on the UN. Like the Americans, Cambodia's other donor countries all had their own political reasons for wanting the court to succeed. In November 2002, France and Japan sponsored a General Assembly resolution "authorizing" Annan to return to the negotiations. Corell was effec-tively ordered back to Cambodia to resume talks. "Basically my hands were tied," he said. Without the backing of UN member states, he had no choice but to make a deal. In March 2003, the UN and the Cambodian government finally reached an agreement for the establishment of the ECCC.

Human rights groups were unimpressed. Mike Jendrzejczyk of Human Rights Watch said that it represented "the lowest standards yet for a tribunal with UN participation."[12] In a candid report to the General Assembly, Annan expressed his worry about the lack of guarantees for due process and warned that if the Cambodian government deviated from its obligations, the UN would withdraw from the court. On June 6, 2003, the ECCC Framework Agreement was officially signed at the Chaktomuk Theater, where the 1979 trial had taken place a quarter-century before. Corell smiled as he shook Sok An's hand, but he still had deep misgivings about the agreement. For better or worse, the Khmer Rouge tribunal was finally a reality.

Six years of tortuous negotiations gave birth to a tribunal that was "hybrid" in the worst sense. The ECCC Agreement created a court with two parallel "sides"—one international, one Cambodian—supported by separate budgets and administrations. There were two prosecutors and two investigating judges and a specially constituted Pre-Trial Chamber to resolve any disputes that might arise between them. As an extension of the political compromises that marked the negotiations, distrust and delay were built into the ECCC's very structure. The verdict of David Tolbert, a former deputy prosecutor at the Yugoslavia tribunal, was damning: "It would be hard to design a much worse system even if you wanted to."[13]

Problems became apparent even before the court opened its doors in mid-2006. In May of that year, the government announced the names of the 17 local judges who would serve in the ECCC. Some were competent individuals, but the CVs of others made for deflating reading. On the list was Ney Thol, the president of the military court, who had presided over the political show-trial of SRP lawmaker Cheam Channy in 2005. There was also a candidate who had previously admitted to taking bribes, and another with no actual experience as a judge.[14] In theory, the appointments were made by the Supreme Council of the Magistracy—the body intended to oversee the Cambodian judiciary—but it later emerged that Hun Sen had had the final say.[15]

It was naive, perhaps, to expect anything else. Cambodia had never known a truly independent judiciary. Historically, the law had been whatever those in power decided it was, a reality still reflected in the fact that the Khmer word usually used for "prisoner," neak thos, literally means "guilty person."[16] Behind the mirage of legislation adopted to impress foreign donors, musty provincial courthouses amounted to a money-making scheme. To pass the oral exam at the Cambodian Bar Association was said to cost $30,000. Entry to the Royal School of Judges and Prosecutors cost twice that amount.[17] Qualifications were generally irrelevant. Even judges with experience and integrity rose and fell by the dictates of patronage. At the ECCC, the international judges and their Cambodian colleagues operated in very different worlds.

When Tolbert arrived in Cambodia on a UN trouble-shooting mission in April 2008, he was shocked. A laconic North Carolinian, Tolbert had just wound up a five-year stint at the Yugoslavia tribunal. To Cambodia he brought long experience with the nuts and bolts of international criminal law. As the UN's first special expert to the ECCC, his job was simple: get the tribunal into a shape to allow it to begin holding trials. After the arrests of the four Case 002 suspects in early 2007, however, things had ground to a halt. Tolbert found a court that was administratively in a state of "near-disaster." "They didn't have the judicial infrastructure in place," he told me. "They didn't have the court management systems in place, they didn't have much of anything in place."

Then there was the issue of corruption. In February 2007, the Open Society Justice Initiative (OSJI), a court monitoring group funded by the Soros Foundation, had aired allegations that Cambodian staff at the ECCC were paying a portion of their salaries to their boss, the Cambodian administrator Sean Visoth. It called for an immediate investigation. The government's first reaction was to lash out at OSJI, threatening to expel it from Cambodia; the UN's was to wait for the issue to go away. But in mid-2008, after further reports of corruption, the UN was eventually forced to act. The UNDP, then providing backing to the Cambodian side of the ECCC, froze its funds until the issue was addressed.

In late 2008, a deal of sorts was reached. Visoth was cashiered and sent on indefinite "medical leave," and the court agreed to set up a new anticorruption mechanism. Another round of negotiations ensued to hash out the details. Hoping to avoid further delays, key donor countries again pushed the UN to compromise. The final formula consisted of a single anticorruption counsellor, appointed by the Cambodians. The lucky candidate was Uth Chhorn, the head of the National Audit Authority, a mirage-body which in seven years of operations had yet to make any of its reports public.[18] It wasn't a good sign. The new anticorruption body was "a face-saving, essentially empty mechanism," said Heather Ryan, then head of OSJI's Cambodia office. But it achieved its main purpose, giving donors just enough confidence to keep the ECCC moving toward its first case.

On March 31, 2009, a 67-year-old Cambodian man rose and prepared to address a packed auditorium on a military base 15 kilometers outside Phnom Penh. He wore a short-sleeved white shirt and baggy gray trousers fastened high on his skinny frame with a leather belt. The old man adjusted his reading glasses. Clutching a pile of papers tightly with his right hand, he began to read aloud: "I would like to express my regret and my deepest sorrow . . ." The man's name was Kaing Guek Eav, but most people in the audience knew him as Duch. As head of S-21 prison, he had presided over the death of at least 12,272 people, who were interrogated, forced to sign what were almost all false confessions, and, in all but a handful of cases, executed.

Thirty years on, Duch faced a panel of judges. The zealous light in his eyes was replaced by a rheumy gaze. Behind a screen of glass hundreds of people, including a number of survivors of S-21, watched and listened. "I know that the crimes I committed against the lives of those people, including women and children, are intolerably and unforgivably serious crimes," Duch said. "My plea is that you leave the door open for me to seek forgiveness." Duch's contrition was not unexpected—his lawyers hoped it would ensure a mitigation of the sentence he faced on charges of homicide, torture, crimes against humanity, and war crimes—but it was nonetheless a powerful moment. When else since the fall of the Khmer Rouge had a leading figure admitted his guilt, acknowledged the suffering of his victims, and pleaded for forgiveness?

Over the following months, Duch's trial laid bare the machinery of death over which he had presided with fanatical attention to detail. Some of the most powerful testimony was given by Vann Nath, an artist who managed to survive S-21 after Duch put him to work making paintings and sculptures of Brother Number One. He told of being shackled by the feet along with dozens of prisoners in one of the converted school buildings at S-21, where inmates were kicked and beaten by guards for the smallest infractions. There were frequent disappearances. Screams from the interrogation rooms pierced the afternoon heat.

After the prison was turned into a museum and its archives opened to the public, Nath looked up his S-21 file and found a chilling annotation, written in Duch's hand. It said, *keep for use temporarily*. For this white-haired man, who carried the traumas of his experiences to his grave in 2011, testifying at the ECCC was vital for educating young people about a grisly past that many of them could still hardly believe. "I never imagined that I would be able to sit in this courtroom today," he said during his testimony in 2009. "This is my privilege. This is my honour. I do not want anything more than that. What I want is something that is intangible, that is justice for those that already died."[19]

During the Duch trial, public interest in the ECCC soared. By the trial's end, some 3 million Cambodians had tuned in to the televised trial coverage. Around 31,000 people traveled to the court to witness the proceedings in person.[20] The long negotiations between the Cambodian government and the UN now suddenly seemed worthwhile. But the successes were marred by long delays. Duch freely admitted his guilt and there was a paper trail linking him directly to S-21, but because of the convoluted structure of the court, hearings dragged on for eight months. The trial "meandered here and there and everywhere," said Ieng Sary's defense lawyer Michael Karnavas. "It should have been a two-month presentation [of evidence] . . . You could have had a judgment in one month, and then that would have been the end of it."

It wasn't until July 2010 that Duch was convicted and sentenced to 35 years prison—a term reduced to just 19 to reflect the defendant's cooperation with the court and a period of illegal detention that followed his arrest in 1999. The verdict was historic, but the apparent leniency of the sentence bewildered many victims. Here was a man who as a prisoner of the ECCC enjoyed better standards of nutrition and healthcare than most Cambodians. Here was a man who admitted being responsible for thousands of deaths, yet received a lighter sentence than some petty criminals. "I am not satisfied!" S-21 survivor Chum Mey cried outside the courtroom after the verdict was handed down. "We are victims two times, once in the Khmer Rouge time and now once again."[21]

Defense and prosecution both appealed the verdict. In February 2012, the Supreme Court Chamber made its final ruling, increasing Duch's sentence to life. Victims applauded the harsher sentence, but the judgment dropped any recognition of Duch's eight-year illegal detention, which rights activists saw as a breach of the defendant's rights. Nothing better illustrated the difficulty the tribunal had in reconciling international legal standards with Cambodian realities. In their initial verdict, ECCC judges hewed to international standards, but left many victims deflated. On appeal, victims got what they wanted, but only after legal standards were watered down somewhat. "International standards" of justice had collided with very different local understandings.

Aside from the delays, Duch's trial proceeded with relatively little friction, in large part because it offered a compelling narrative of contrition and redemption which moved along politically predictable lines. Like the CPP's official version of history, it treated S-21 as the pivot of the Khmer Rouge nightmare, overlooking the tens of thousands who had perished at forgotten rural prisons like Wat O Trakuon, described in the opening chapter of this book. For better or worse, Duch and his prison had become emblematic of Democratic Kampuchea.

If Case 001 was relatively straightforward, Case 002 loomed as a legal and political labyrinth. Its mammoth indictment ran to 772 pages, and included charges of forced evacuations, forced marriage, torture, executions, enslavement, and genocide against ethnic Vietnamese and Cham Muslim populations. Its four defendants—Nuon Chea, Khieu Samphan, Ieng Sary, and Ieng Thirith—denied every charge. Instead of admitting their clients' guilt and pleading for mitigation, as Duch's lawyers did, the Case 002 defense teams made it clear that they planned to put the ECCC itself on trial, aggressively highlighting instances of corruption and political interference.

Political roadblocks had already gone up during the investigative phase, when the first international co-investigating judge, Marcel Lemonde, summonsed six Cambodian officials for questioning in 2009. They included Chea Sim, Heng Samrin, Keat Chhon, and Hor Namhong—the four senior government officials believed to have the closest links to the Khmer Rouge. The summonses were all ignored, and Lemonde's Cambodian counterpart, You Bunleng, refused to put his name to the documents.

All this was a prelude to the ECCC's most explosive dispute: whether to pursue indictments beyond the five defendants already in custody. The final ECCC Agreement had defined its jurisdiction as being over "senior leaders" of DK and "those most responsible" for atrocities and other serious crimes. It was a vague formulation and both sides had differing interpretations. As before, UN staff saw the final number of defendants as a question to be determined by the evidence, while Hun Sen decided that the trial would end after Case 002. Moving further, he said repeatedly, risked plunging the country back into "civil war."

A return to war was never likely, of course. Most Khmer Rouge fighters had long put down their weapons and returned to rural life. But Hun Sen's rhetoric signaled his continuing discomfort at the prospect of a court process that could roam freely. None of the Case 003 and Case 004 suspects was indispensable; after all, Hun Sen had turned over the Case 002 suspects, backtracking on earlier assurances that they would never face trial. But some of the new suspects held roughly equivalent ranks to sitting members of government. If the tribunal moved its focus downward, what was to stop it from moving sideways?

The first disagreements over the new cases had arisen in late 2008, when Robert Petit, then international co-prosecutor, submitted six additional names to the court for investigation. Petit's Cambodian counterpart Chea Leang, a niece of Deputy Prime Minister Sok An, objected, in language that closely mirrored Hun Sen's views on the matter. The dispute between the two prosecutors was forwarded to the Pre-Trial Chamber, which split along national lines—the foreign judges in favor of the new cases, the Cambodians against.

According to the court's rules, the lack of a supermajority decision in the Pre-Trial Chamber meant the new cases could proceed. In September 2009, Cases 003 and 004 were forwarded to the co-investigating judges. Named in the submissions were five suspects, including Meas Muth, and an impressive array of evidence that they orchestrated vast purges of the DK apparatus. For a moment it looked as if the system was working: despite opposition from the Cambodian judges, the case had moved forward. But the disagreement over the new cases had merely been kicked down the hall. As the investigation opened, Hun Sen made his opposition clear and again warned of civil war. "I will not let anyone, either Cambodian or foreigner, ruin this peace," he said.[22]

Following the prime minister's lead, Cambodian judges found excuses to slow progress on the new cases. You Bunleng refused to take part in the Case 003 investigations, and Judge Lemonde proceeded alone. There were few complaints to be heard from the UN and the ECCC's foreign donors. They were more concerned about pushing forward with Case 001 and Case 002, the tribunal's headlining events. Besides, Case 003 was technically moving forward:

investigations had started, and US officials hailed this as "another sign of progress" and one that "vindicated" the inclusion of the supermajority provision.[23] For the time being, the problem could be ignored.

In November 2010, however, Lemonde resigned his post and the cases passed to a new German co-investigating judge, Siegfried Blunk. From the beginning, Blunk showed little inclination to pursue them. After four months, he and Bunleng announced the closure of the Case 003 investigation. Many tribunal observers saw it as a bewildering move. Neither of the two prospective defendants had been interviewed, and few field investigations had been carried out. When the international co-prosecutor, Andrew Cayley, requested further investigations, Blunk and Bunleng refused. Later, the Pre-Trial Chamber backed their decision, cleaving again along national–international lines.

What motivated Blunk to close the case? One court insider described him as "lazy and crazy—and that made for a pretty lethal combination." In a rare interview, the judge maintained his decision was based on precedents from the Sierra Leone tribunal.[24] Casting an eye over the evidence against Meas Muth and Sou Met, however, it was not hard to draw a line between the skimpy investigation and the government's well-known opposition to the case. Blunk's staff certainly seemed to see it this way. Most of his foreign investigative staff quit in disgust. On his way out the door, consultant Steve Heder penned a resignation letter criticizing the closure of the investigation and "the toxic atmosphere of what is now a professionally dysfunctional office."[25]

Four months later, Blunk resigned, denying to the last that he had played any role in burying Case 003. He left just a few weeks before the two international judges on the Pre-Trial Chamber accused him of altering and backdating documents in the Case 003 file—an act an OSJI court monitor described as "*prima facie* evidence of serious misconduct."[26] Still, the UN showed little desire to ask questions about Blunk. As the Case 003 controversy unfolded, the UN had stuck safely to the realm of words, beaming out periodic statements of "concern" and making rather meaningless calls for the Cambodians to refrain from interfering in the court's work. When the UN's legal counsel Patricia O'Brien flew to Phnom Penh after Blunk's resignation, she all but ruled out a formal investigation. If the probe uncovered anything, she reportedly told one NGO leader, the defense teams would have a "field day" and it could "undermine Case 002."[27]

It seemed to boil down to a simple trade-off. Cases 003 and 004 would be jettisoned in order to save the all-important second trial. The only other option for the UN was to threaten withdrawal from the court, as Kofi Annan had suggested a decade earlier. But to walk away from the ECCC with just one conviction would be both an admission of failure and a colossal waste of money. The choice was between compromise and failure, between a mirage of justice and no justice at all. "All of this was foreseeable," Ralph Zacklin told me in an email. "It is the direct result of the type of agreement concluded, and in my view was inevitable once the decision was made to compromise."

It was the sort of send-off his own regime would never have permitted: an elaborate Buddhist ceremony that ended with prayers, reminiscences, and the crackle of fireworks in an inky night sky. On March 14, 2013, Ieng Sary was rushed from his holding cell at the ECCC to the Khmer-Soviet Friendship Hospital in Phnom Penh, where he died of cardiac arrest. He was 87. For a week afterward, hundreds of white-clad mourners turned out in Malai, his old stronghold along the Thai border, to pay their respects to a man they remembered as a comrade and patriot. To just about everyone else, Sary enjoys the dubious distinction of being the only person in history to be charged with genocide twice: first in 1979 and again, three decades later, by the ECCC.

On the day of his funeral, monks chanted as farmers and former guerrilla fighters arrived at Sary's villa to pay their respects. His gold-colored casket sat next to mountains of flowers. When evening fell, the casket was moved into a two-story crematorium strung with blinking colored lights. During a ten-minute eulogy, Sary's daughter Hun Vanny made just one reference to his involvement with the Khmer Rouge, a period when "he sacrificed his life by leaving his wife and family, moving from place to place." Paying a final farewell was Sary's frail widow and fellow ECCC defendant Ieng Thirith, who was led to the base of the crematorium for a moment before being bundled into a van and driven away. The previous September, the ECCC had ruled that she was unfit to stand trial due to dementia, and she was released into a vegetative, house-bound retirement. After Thirith's departure, the fuse of the crematorium was lit by Y Chhean, the governor of Pailin province, a former bodyguard of Pol Pot and subordinate of Sary who had defected with him in 1996. Fireworks flowered overhead as the casket caught fire. Gongs clattered and clanged. Smoke from the crematorium was piped into the night sky like tractor exhaust as a haunting moan burst from the loudspeakers—a crude imitation of an elephant's roar, intended to ward off evil spirits.

Back in Phnom Penh, the ECCC pressed on with Case 002. With one of its defendants now dead and another ruled unfit to stand trial, the frailty of the remaining two now became a pressing concern. Nuon Chea and Khieu Samphan were both in their eighties, and in precarious health. In order to quicken the proceedings, judges had sliced up the massive Case 002 indictment into a series of "mini-trials," the first of which (Case 002/01) focused on the forced evacuation of Phnom Penh in April 1975 and the subsequent execution of former Lon Nol officials. The goal was to secure judgments before the accused died, whether "for stealing a loaf of bread," one ECCC lawyer said, "or for the crime of genocide."

On the whole, the ECCC's lawyers and judges persevered with diligence and professionalism. With controversy raging outside the courtroom, it was easy to overlook the compelling testimony that was being offered inside. Over 18 months of evidence hearings, the Khmer Rouge evacuation of Phnom Penh was recalled in dramatic detail. Witnesses and civil parties spoke of the frenzy and panic that gripped the city as the war-swollen population was set on a forced march out of the city, and then dispersed to work camps across the country.

In December 2012, Denise Affonço, author of the harrowing memoir *To The End of Hell*, gave a dramatic account of her ordeal under the Khmer Rouge. Despite having a job at the French embassy, the half-French, half-Vietnamese Affonço remained in Phnom Penh after April 17. Her husband, Seng, a devoted communist, was convinced the Khmer Rouge had benign intentions and even celebrated the end of the war by giving young soldiers cans of Chinese beer. Soon after the evacuation of the city, he was executed. Affonço ended up in a remote part of Battambang, where she was put to work on what was known as the "Widows' Dyke." Taking the stand, she described DK as a desert: "We were in a rice exporting country, or at least previously. We had no rice to eat. A country full of fruit trees; for four years, I never saw a single orange. We no longer had any medicines. We had no hygienic products, either; no candles, no electricity, no water. We lived like people out of the caves."[28]

Later, victims registered as civil parties to the case confronted Nuon Chea and Khieu Samphan with harrowing stories of loss and suffering. One was Chan Sopheap, who lost 13 brothers and sisters to overwork and starvation on DK work communes. "I have always wondered why the three years, eight months, and 20 days [of Khmer Rouge rule] was so cruel," she told the court. "Why did they do all of this atrocity? I have endured tremendous suffering."[29]

In October 2013, the court heard closing statements in Case 002/01. Throughout the entire trial, the defendants had maintained their innocence. Khieu Samphan had watched on impassively; Nuon Chea had observed most of the proceedings from behind sunglasses, or by video link from his cell. The two men offered their condolences to victims, but denied any personal responsibility. The evacuation of Phnom Penh, they said, had been carried out to spare people from US bombing attacks and minimize the difficulties faced in the city. On October 31, 2013, the last day of the trial, the two old men appeared in court to make their final statements. Reading from a prepared address, Nuon Chea called for his release and deflected responsibility in a familiar direction. "Vietnam had agents infiltrated in party ranks and the army in order to destroy [the] Revolution, kill Cambodian people, and annexed [sic] Cambodian territory, which had been a long-term ambition of Vietnam," he said.[30] It was a virtual echo of the justifications Pol Pot gave in his interview with Nate Thayer in 1997.

Ten days earlier, prosecutors had wrapped up their case, calling for the two defendants to be sentenced to life in prison. "There are few graver threats to humanity than those posed by those so blinded by ideology, beliefs, or religion that they are willing to do anything, to employ any means, however destructive or unlawful, to achieve their goals," Deputy Co-Prosecutor William Smith told the chamber. Nuon Chea was "a bitter man who sees foreign imperialists, the CIA, KGB, and Vietnamese spies lurking around every corner." Khieu Samphan, meanwhile, had presented himself implausibly as "the only man in all of Cambodia who knew nothing, saw nothing, and heard nothing."[31]

As the trial came to an end, with a judgment expected in August 2014, a glaring question remained: what next? When the ECCC was set up, the UN had initially promised donors that trials would take around three years. In reality, securing three convictions had taken eight years and cost around $200 million. By 2012, donors had grown fatigued and increasingly reluctant to provide the voluntary tranches of funding that kept the court afloat. The Cambodian government, too, was slow in ponying up money for the national side of the court, leaving Cambodian staff working without pay for months at a time. When the Case 002 indictment was severed into smaller sections, few people at the court had given any thought to what might come next.

In late 2013, with judgments now in sight, OSJI urged the UN, donor countries, and the Cambodian government to make up their minds. They could either give the ECCC their full backing to see out the second phase of Case 002, or admit the practical and political difficulties and wind things up. Characteristically, they did neither. They continued dispensing droplets of funding that left the court limping forward. Prosecutors busied themselves with preparations for Case 002/02, the staff working on short-term contracts, and initial hearings began in July 2014. But serious questions remained as to whether there would be enough money to see it through. As one ECCC judge told me, "there's so little trust as to where all this is going to end."

More vexed was the issue of Cases 003 and 004. After Siegfried Blunk's departure, the Cambodians had again held up proceedings by blocking the approval of the reserve international co-investigating judge, Laurent Kasper-Ansermet, who had arrived in late 2011 and thrown himself into his work. Kasper-Ansermet was keen on social media. Via Twitter, he had denounced Blunk's closure of Case 003 and promised to reopen the investigations. The Supreme Council of the Magistracy seized on his tweets as a pretext—probably a legitimate one—to block his appointment. After his rejection and subsequent resignation, the 003 and 004 investigations received a new lease on life under a new co-investigating judge, Mark Harmon. But it all seemed futile. Barring a change of heart by Hun Sen, the cases stood little chance of proceeding to trial. Again, the donors dithered. They provided funds to keep Harmon's investigations on-going, which allowed them to say the process was working, at least on their side. But all it did was kick the can of confrontation a little further down the road.

This was no small issue. The controversy over Cases 003 and 004 cut to a dilemma at the heart of international justice. While the international criminal courts were all political creations, serving the interests of the powerful players that established them, it was unclear just where the threshold lay. How far could legal standards be politically compromised before the proceedings lost all value? The ECCC had always been tightly circumscribed by politics, its jurisdiction restricted to a narrow historical window and a small number of defendants. At the same time the UN claimed a moral and political authority ("the legacy of Nuremberg") on the basis that it represented universal legal norms. The problem with legal norms, however, was that they were categorical and absolute. To compromise them a fraction was, by definition, to compromise them in their entirety.[32]

It was a contradiction that Cases 003 and 004 cast into stark relief. The UN and the donors might be morally or politically justified in sacrificing the two cases in order to save Case 002, but legally speaking, such a compromise could well call into question the legitimacy of the entire enterprise. The outcome, one court insider said, would then be "something very close to what the 1979 trials were, just maybe dressed up a bit better." If that was the case, it begged the question: why need the UN and the "international community" be involved at all? If verdicts were what mattered—and if it was accepted that legal corners could be trimmed in the process—couldn't Hun Sen do it all more quickly and cheaply on his own?

The truth is that the court's main backers—Australia, Japan, France, and the US—wanted it both ways. They wanted credit for bringing justice to Cambodia, but not if it carried a burdensome political cost. They spoke loftily of the ECCC's example to the Cambodian legal system, but then pressured the UN to make compromises that reinforced a pattern of political meddling in the courts. In short, they took a series of messy political accommodations and concealed them behind a mirage of justice. That many foreign officials were genuinely motivated by a desire to see justice done did little to alter the fact that supporting the ECCC was a useful way for Western governments to bolster their moral credentials while supporting an undemocratic status quo. As the journalist Philip Short put it in his biography of Pol Pot, "trying the surviving Khmer Rouge leaders for past crimes offers an alibi for doing nothing about present ones."[33]

Whatever happened, Hun Sen stood to profit. If the ECCC succeeded, he could take credit for himself. If it failed, he could blame the UN for yet again abandoning the Cambodian people. Since the court's inception, Hun Sen, the UN, and the major donors had all pursued primarily political aims. The only difference was that the Cambodians had never pretended otherwise. This always put Hun Sen at an advantage; unlike the UN and the donor countries, he was free from the burden of dressing up political calculations in the language of moral uplift.

Only two people survived the massacres of the Cham Muslims in Sambor Meas village. Him Man and his wife Him Jas live in a dim corrugated iron shack with a roof slanting down to a hatch overlooking the fast-moving waters of the Mekong River. Four decades ago, in 1977, when Khmer Rouge soldiers rounded up the Chams and marched them to the killing field at Wat O Trakuon, the couple escaped by jumping into a stream and hiding out beneath a thick carpet of water hyacinth. Man, still sprightly at 60 years of age, has since become something of a folk hero in Sambor Meas. Everybody in the village knows *Kamphlaok*, as he is nicknamed, after the Khmer word for "water hyacinth." They all eagerly pointed out the winding dirt path that led to his home.

Man has told the story of his daring escape many times. As he ran through the familiar narrative, he grew animated, shouting, jumping up, drawing imaginary lines on the wood-plank floor to indicate the location of pivotal rivers and trees. Neighbors crowded around, adding their own details and embellishments. When asked about the ECCC, Man and his neighbors grew quiet. For a moment there was no sound but the crackle of a nearby cooking fire. Man then said he was happy to see senior leaders on trial. Everybody was. But like many other people in the village, he wanted something the ECCC, with its international standards, would never be able to provide. "To satisfy us, they should be killed," he said, to nods of agreement from those around him. "These people owe us their blood."

What will be the ultimate legacy of the ECCC in places like Sambor Meas? Nobody really knows. To be sure, there have been many positives to the tribunal's work. One of the greatest was the massive historical archive created by the trials, a gift to a future generation of historians and researchers. Another was the education of young people about the DK period. In 2007, DC-Cam published a history textbook that is now widely used in Cambodian schools, something that is hard to imagine without the momentum generated by the ECCC. People have finally grown comfortable with openly discussing the crimes of the Khmer Rouge. For DC-Cam's Youk Chhang, there was power in simply seeing once-untouchable figures like Ieng Sary on trial.

But in a broader sense, the ECCC has struggled to live up to massively inflated expectations. Long before the first trial had started, the court bore the crushing burden of dashed democratic hopes. It became a sort of UNTAC Redux, a legalistic salve for the woes of democratic demoralization. It soon formed an entire wing of the Cambodian development complex, employing dozens of mostly foreign lawyers, judges, experts, and commentators. The more people analyzed and debated the court and its supposed benefits, the more expectations were forced to the outer limits of the possible.

There was a notable absence from most of these discussions. While everybody ventriloquized the victims of the Khmer Rouge, the vast majority remained silent, with little say as to the sort of justice they wanted to see, if any at all. Surveys conducted in December 2010 found that while there was strong support and awareness of the trials at the ECCC, they weren't a high priority. A full 98 percent of those polled said the economy, jobs, and poverty reduction were more important than justice; 83 percent said the government should address people's daily problems rather than crimes committed more than three decades earlier.[34]

As far as international legal advocates were concerned, however, the question was already settled. Though they cared deeply about how the court might benefit victims, they assumed, axiomatically, that international legal norms dovetailed with the needs and desires of ordinary people. That Cambodia was a poor, rural Buddhist society with no historical experience of independent courts or impartial justice—to say nothing of the atomizing effect of conflict and mass killing—was largely irrelevant. If anything, it only increased the urgency of the task. Like the development industry, the international justice project had a global, universal scope. "As much as anyone," the British political scientist Stephen Hopgood has written, "the beneficiaries of international trials are international advocates. Victims are collateral damage, the raw material for building the machinery of interventionary power necessary to do good in a world of sovereigns."[35]

It was perhaps inevitable that the Khmer Rouge tribunal would fail to reconcile the irreconcilable, to map the visionary abstractions of international law onto the messy realities of contemporary Cambodia. And so the legacy of Nuremberg, implanted on the banks of the Mekong, produced another mirage—perhaps the most disorienting mirage of all.

The Fading Mirage

On July 28, 2013, the people of Cambodia went to the polls and signaled an unambiguous desire for change. The CPP, hubristic and over-confident, reeled as its share of National Assembly seats was slashed from 90 to just 68—its worst electoral showing since 1998. The remaining 55 seats were won by the resurgent Cambodia National Rescue Party (CNRP), which had deftly capitalized on the smoldering discontent with CPP rule.

The CNRP's return might have been even more impressive were it not for the widespread "irregularities" that were suspected to have distorted the electoral process. One NGO audit conducted before the election claimed that 9 percent of voter names were missing from the national roster. A further one in ten belonged to "ghost voters" who were either deceased, or had never existed to begin with. On election day, thousands of opposition voters arrived at polling stations only to find that someone else had already cast a vote in their name. In Phnom Penh, tensions over voter lists erupted into a small riot in which a mob burned two police trucks while chanting slogans against the government and its supposed Vietnamese backers.

By nightfall, an uneasy calm prevailed in Phnom Penh. Police were deployed throughout the city and the roads were closed around Hun Sen's mansion near the Independence Monument. Sensing political turmoil, people rushed to withdraw cash from ATMs and to fill jerry cans with petrol. How would Hun Sen react to the election results? Officially, his party had lost 22 seats. If this was what the CPP-dominated National Election Committee was willing to admit, many Cambodians asked, then what was the real number?

It was in many ways the perfect political storm. When the CNRP was formed in mid-2012, it was unclear how prepared it would be to fight an effective national election campaign. Sam Rainsy, the president of the new party, remained in exile abroad, flitting between foreign capitals in a bid to get

Cambodia's, and his own, travails back on the international agenda. There were also concerns about Rainsy's relationship with the CNRP's vice-president Kem Sokha, the popular former head of the Human Rights Party (HRP). Past merger plans had foundered on the issue of which leader should enjoy prominence in the new party, and some questioned whether the two men could work constructively together.

All of these apprehensions were swept aside in the weeks leading up to the election, as huge crowds turned out for CNRP rallies. The opposition wave gathered momentum when Hun Sen, in a bid to assuage international opinion, secured a royal pardon for Rainsy, allowing him to return to Cambodia for the final week of the campaign. It was a major miscalculation. When Rainsy landed in Phnom Penh on the humid morning of July 19, after nearly four years in exile, he received a hero's welcome. Tens of thousands of people streamed out to the airport, and the roads were so crowded that it took five hours for Rainsy's motorcade to reach the center of town. As the triumphal procession inched forward, throngs of party supporters streamed past on motorbikes and trooped along the roadside in the heat, snapping photos with iPads and holding up homemade signs featuring the CNRP's rising sun emblem. The crowds chanted "Change! Change! Change!" as people squeezed onto balconies to see Rainsy's slow, triumphant march back into Cambodian politics.

When Rainsy and Sokha reached Freedom Park in the center of town, they strode out onto a stage overlooking a crowd of tens of thousands, a mottled sea of blue and yellow spread out under gathering storm clouds. Party anthems blared from stacks of amplifiers and supporters danced joyfully. After four years on the political margins, Rainsy had surged back to center stage. In an electric half-hour speech, the first of the frenzied week of campaigning to come, he promised increased wages, the cancellation of economic land concessions, and an end to Vietnamese encroachments. "Today," he told the crowd, "we are writing a new page of Cambodian history."

The 2013 election was the youngest Cambodia had ever seen. Around 3.5 million of the country's 9.5 million registered voters were under 30 years of age, and 1.5 million of them had voted for the first time. Shifting demographics meant that the CPP's old political formula—liberation from the Khmer Rouge plus stability plus basic economic development—was gradually losing its potency. A large majority of the Cambodian population now had no memory of the Khmer Rouge, and were no longer willing to accept Pol Pot's nightmare as a benchmark.

First-time voters, born since the UNTAC mission of 1992–3, were growing up in a very different country from the one their parents and grandparents had known. Hun Sen's long reign had transformed Cambodian society. Land-grabs and indebtedness had disrupted the traditional rural economy and swept tens of thousands from the land. As rural folk moved to the cities, they escaped the smothering influence of CPP village chiefs and commune authorities, joining a burgeoning working class of garment and construction workers. The CNRP's election campaign cleverly targeted this new urban population with promises of better wages and pensions for elderly relatives, which they relayed back to their villages during the Khmer New Year holiday.

Voters also had greater access to information than ever before. The proliferation of mobile internet access and social media networks like Facebook had loosened the CPP's control of the political narrative and given the opposition a direct channel of communication with the electorate. The second-order effects were if anything even more profound. As ordinary people became more connected, they acquired a sense of political consciousness and common grievance that had previously been pre-empted by Hun Sen's Jovian personality cult and the CPP's near-monopoly control on the Khmer-language media. Voters I spoke to during the campaign evinced a growing sense that local issues—landgrabs, deforestation, corrupt local officials—were systemic in nature. Fewer people at demonstrations carried portraits of Hun Sen, calling for his lordly intercession in local disputes. More people criticized the government openly.

For the previous three decades, Hun Sen had pursued development in a highly selective manner. Like Prince Norodom Sihanouk, he succeeded in bringing Cambodia into the modern world, but did so via the old methods: hierarchy, patronage, and the dictates of absolute power. For a long time, it seemed to work. In 1979, the CPP had inherited a scarred and traumatized nation, in which Hun Sen and his colleagues were able to draw on a vast reservoir of fear and craving for security. But Hun Sen's status quo relied on the assumption that as Cambodia modernized its people would remain the same—essentially passive and "Khmer," haunted and immune to the modern world. By 2013, the contradiction seemed to be stretching his political consensus to breaking point.

Hun Sen clearly sensed that things were changing, but he responded in the only way he knew how: with more threats and more handouts. In 2012, the government launched a land-titling drive to neutralize concern over land seizures and tenure security. In the first half of 2013, Hun Sen presided over the inauguration of 22 Buddhist pagodas, many located in key "swing districts" where the party had leaked support at the previous year's commune elections. Addressing audiences of rural folk, he warned that the benefits of CPP rule—its infrastructure projects and patronage of religious institutions—would come to an end if it lost the election. Again and again, he warned of "internal war" if the opposition came to power.

The CPP also made tin-eared attempts to woo younger voters. This consisted in the main of paying students—the going rate was 20,000 riels (about $5) per day—to drive through the streets of major towns waving flags and blaring progovernment dance music. The sons of party grandees—Hun Sen's youngest son, Hun Many, his son-in-law Dy Vichea, and Sok Sokan, the son of Deputy Prime Minister Sok An—were run as candidates in a bid to boost the party's youth "appeal." Before the election, the CPP released a slick campaign video featuring karaoke star Nop Panharith, who crooned homilies to Hun Sen's leadership as Angkor Wat loomed inevitably and CPP youth activists formed a giant number "4"—the party's position on the ballot—on the roof of the Canadia Tower. None of this addressed the real concerns of young people: jobs, education, and the heavy burden of everyday corruption. Hun Sen, a leader who once said his political philosophy was to "know reality" seemed more out of touch with it than ever.

In his younger years, Hun Sen had been different. He was ruthlessly practical, and unafraid to solicit advice before acting upon political reality. But as the years went by, power had worked its corrupting influence. Hun Sen had grown rich, entangled in the web of powerful interests that sustained his rule. By identifying his own interests with those of the nation as a whole, he had also, like many a Cambodian leader before him, courted hubris. His confidence inflated by an endless procession of political victories—over the opposition, over factional foes, over the "international community"—Hun Sen stumbled into the dictators' trap. He started believing his own propaganda.

The 2013 election, as on many occasions in the past, was followed by political deadlock. Rainsy and Sokha claimed electoral fraud had robbed them of victory, and called for a UN-backed investigation. To drive home their demands, they boycotted the first session of the new National Assembly in September and initiated a campaign of colorful public demonstrations at Freedom Park. Hun Sen refused the opposition's demands, and the NEC duly formalized the CPP's 68–55 election victory.

As the stalemate dragged on, the CNRP's election complaints coalesced into a broader social movement. Garment workers took to the streets, demanding a hike in the monthly minimum wage to $160. Key labor unions joined the CNRP protests, and marched in honor of the tenth anniversary of Chea Vichea's killing. Teachers threatened to strike, garbage collectors walked off the job, and Buddhist monks defied their superiors to attend protests. In late 2013, tens of thousands of people marched through Phnom Penh calling openly for Hun Sen's resignation. It was the greatest challenge to his rule in 15 years. In early January 2014, garment worker protests on the outskirts of the city degenerated into violence when police fired live ammunition at demonstrators, killing five people. The government responded by banning public gatherings. Freedom Park, now unexpectedly living up to its name as a symbol of political resistance, was sealed off with steel barriers and loops of razor wire.

Stung by the voters' verdict, Hun Sen promised sweeping reforms. In September 2013, he gave a six-hour speech in which he told officials to "scrub your body" and "heal our disease."[1] The party borrowed from the most popular elements of the CNRP's platform and announced wage hikes for teachers, garment workers, and civil servants. Hun Sen's student land-titling teams returned to the field. Judges released from prison the two men framed for the Chea Vichea killing, and Yorm Bopha, the anti-eviction activist from Boeung Kak lake. Concurrently, the government announced a cabinet reshuffle. Many-armed Sok An saw his clutch of chairmanships slashed. Commerce Minister Cham Prasidh was cashiered and kicked upstairs to a new Ministry of Industry and Handicrafts. Taking Prasidh's place was Sun Chanthol, a former General Electric executive who had returned to Cambodia in the 1990s. The Ministry of Education was given to Hang Chuon Naron, widely regarded as one of the CPP's most capable technocrats, who immediately announced reforms and promised to tackle schoolyard corruption. The government pledged to clean up the court system.

The promise of reform sounded neat in theory. In practice, it did little to slow the destructive inertia of the CPP's system of obligation and reward. In the countryside, the land-grabs and deforestation continued unabated. In mid-2014, the *Cambodia Daily* reported that the Lower Sesan 2 dam project in Stung Treng province was being used as a giant laundry for illegally felled timber, a scheme that it linked to Kith Meng, the chairman of the Royal Group, and another firm owned by Sok Vanna, a brother of Sokimex chairman Sok Kong.[2] In mid-2016, I reported for *Forbes Asia* on the extensive logging operations run by the businessman Try Pheap. Having risen high in the CPP firmament since the 2013 election, Pheap's timber concern continued the hollowing out of the Boeung Per Wildlife Sanctuary in northern Cambodia.[3]

While the CNRP was boycotting parliament, CPP lawmakers approved a series of judicial reforms that formalized the executive's control over the courts. The new laws, the product of years of "partnership" with foreign donors, were passed just as the courts were prosecuting a series of spurious cases against demonstrators arrested during the post-election protests. The comically flawed proceedings all ended the same way, with guilty verdicts for the accused, who were then freed under suspended sentences. Stung by a sharp loss of public trust, Hun Sen and the CPP were doubling down on the old strategies: dispensing patronage and gifts, while arresting critics, dishing out court summonses, and in general sustaining an atmosphere of fear and foreboding.

If it was unclear whether tweaks to the Cambodian political system would allow Hun Sen to retain his hold on power, it also remained to be seen whether the opposition offered a credible alternative. The CNRP was good at organizing street protests, but there was no indication the party had the resources to run the country, nor any concrete plan to pay for the massive wage hikes and pensions it promised voters. There remained a Jekyll-and-Hyde quality to the party and its president. To a foreign audience, Sam Rainsy still presented himself as a democratic freedom fighter, fluent in the pieties of the humanitarian international. On his 2013 campaign tour, however, Rainsy's speeches were filled with the same sorts of nationalistic rhetoric as in the 1990s. "We have been eating sour Vietnamese soup for 30 years," he told a cheering crowd in Svay Rieng on July 25. "It's time for that to stop." Later, in a speech near Prey Lang forest, Rainsy declared that "the *yuon* are taking the Khmer land to kill the Khmer people."[4]

Rainsy's bipolar politics were reflected within the CNRP itself. Figures like Mu Sochua, who rose to prominence during her Kafkaesque legal spat with Hun Sen in 2009, represented what might be termed the "Berkeley wing" of the party: liberal, progressive, and antiracist. But many others in the CNRP still clung to the anti-Vietnamese resistance dogmas of the 1980s, viewing Hun Sen's government as illegitimate by definition due to its past connection with Hanoi. In June 2014, during a speech at Wat Sammaki Reangsey, Kem Sokha went so far as to blame Vietnam for the bridge stampede at Diamond Island during the 2010 Water Festival, which had killed 353 people and injured many hundreds more. "They created the scene to kill Khmers at Koh Pich," he said.[5]

In this way, Sam Rainsy and Kem Sokha held a mirror to the uncompromising attitude of the CPP. Like successions of Cambodian regimes, both parties saw themselves as the exclusive embodiment of the national interest, standing against the forces of disunity and foreign infiltration. Hun Sen's opponents, too, knew the importance of appearances. Since UNTAC, liberal rhetoric had been a ready shortcut to international sympathy. Whatever their degree of personal conviction, CNRP politicians had learned to speak the language of their foreign patrons. Liberal overtures thus coexisted and intermingled with the familiar tropes of Cambodian politics: the appeals to outside powers, the inverse fear of outside domination.

On August 5, 2014, the CNRP's 55 elected lawmakers were finally sworn in to the National Assembly, bringing an end to the deadlock that had paralyzed Cambodian politics for nearly a year. As the CNRP parliamentarians entered the Assembly building, clad in orange pantaloons and white tunics, Phnom Penh reverted to its usual rhythm. Freedom Park, barricaded and guarded since protests at the beginning of the year, was reopened and restored to the public. An uneasy political peace pertained.

A few weeks earlier, the two parties had agreed to a truce aimed at ending the political stalemate. The agreement was born not of amity but of confrontation. On July 15, during an opposition protest to "free Freedom Park," CNRP supporters had set upon a squad of thuggish district security guards, beating several of them bloody. In the aftermath, seven CNRP politicians were arrested, pasted with exaggerated charges, and locked up at Prey Sar prison. In characteristic Cambodian style, tension yielded to negotiation, which quickly dissolved the deadlock.

Under the terms of the truce, the CNRP promised to join parliament and end its campaign of confrontation. In exchange, the CPP pledged to rewrite electoral laws, add CNRP appointees to the NEC, and grant the opposition party a license for its own television station. Hun Sen and Rainsy also proclaimed a "culture of dialogue," promising to end the vicious insults which had flown between them since the 2013 election. The pact was sealed in late July, when the two leaders dined together with their families at a Phnom Penh hotel, snapping a selfie that quickly went viral on Facebook. At the first full session of the National Assembly, Rainsy hailed a new beginning for Cambodian politics. "To guarantee the implementation of this agreement, both parties must carry it out with optimism, honesty, and belief in each other, even though we will be met with obstacles and difficulties," he said in an address to the parliament. Hun Sen described the occasion in slightly less sunny terms as "the start of a long process together."

The "culture of dialogue" came under immediate strain. Despite all the talk of reconciliation, steadfast commitment was lacking on both sides. The CPP and CNRP never strayed from their common view of politics as a game of winner-takes-all, in which neither was willing to give any but the most temporary, grudging concessions. Tensions increased when nationalist elements in the CNRP, taking advantage of the more relaxed political atmosphere, launched a public campaign against alleged Vietnamese encroachments in eastern Cambodia. In mid-2015, scattered groups of activists began trooping down to rural Svay Rieng and Kratie, Cambodian flags rippling, to "inspect" the placement of border markers, on one occasion coming to blows with Vietnamese villagers and security personnel.

Vietnam, as always, was a red-line issue for Hun Sen. Instead of responding to opposition claims in the spirit of dialogue, he pivoted back to the political offensive. In July 2015, a judge convicted and jailed 11 CNRP members for "insurrection," in connection with the melee that had taken place at Freedom Park the year before. The same month, CPP lawmakers voted to approve the controversial Law on Associations and Nongovernment Organizations, imposing a suite of tight regulations on Cambodia's large NGO sector. On August 15,

Hong Sok Hour, a long-serving opposition senator, was arrested and charged with treason after he posted a fake section of a 1979 border treaty on Facebook, implicitly accusing the CPP government of ceding territory to Vietnam.

The tensions escalated sharply. After Sok Hour's arrest, Hun Sen gave a string of barnstorming speeches in which he described Rainsy as the leader of "a gang of thieves destroying the stability of this country," and likened the CNRP's post-election protests to a "color revolution" aiming to overthrow his government. On October 26, two CNRP parliamentarians, Kong Sophea and Nhay Chamroeun, were dragged from their cars and beaten in the street by progovernment thugs after a National Assembly session. CPP lawmakers then voted to remove Kem Sokha from his post as the Assembly's vice-president, a position he had been granted under the terms of the July 2014 truce.

The final break came after Rainsy began comparing himself to Burma's Aung San Suu Kyi, who led her National League for Democracy to a lopsided victory in the country's election on November 8. In the aftermath, Rainsy posted on Facebook old photos of himself with the Burmese Nobel laureate. He juxtaposed images of the 1988 protests in Burma, put down with ruthless force by the country's military, with photographs of recent CNRP rallies. He predicted, "The wind of freedom that is blowing throughout the world will also reach Cambodia in the very near future."

As ever, Hun Sen had had his own ideas about history's direction. Later that month, when Rainsy flew to South Korea for meetings with Cambodian expatriates there, the courts activated a dormant defamation conviction against the CNRP leader and ordered his arrest, effectively stranding him overseas. In response, Rainsy took to Facebook, branding Hun Sen a "dictator" and comparing himself once again to Aung San Suu Kyi. More charges and jail terms would be filed against Rainsy in due course as the "culture of dialogue" collapsed into a period of renewed animosity.

By this point, much of Cambodia's bitter political combat was playing out online. In surveys conducted in 2016, the Asia Foundation and the Phnom Penh-based Open Institute found that some 48 percent of Cambodians now owned a smartphone, more than twice the number as in 2013. The same year, the internet became the most important source of news and information for Cambodians, eclipsing television and radio for the first time.[6] In exile abroad, Facebook became Rainsy's main line of communication with the Cambodian public, which he used to goad Hun Sen from afar. Hun Sen, too, had embraced the internet, belatedly but with considerable zeal. The prime minister's aides had maintained a Facebook page in his name since before 2013, but Hun Sen only acknowledged ownership in September 2015, after it notched its millionth "like."

From that point on, the Cambodian leader was a born-again digital convert, rarely seen without a smartphone in hand. His public addresses now incorporated a new ritual, in which he would descend from the podium and pose for selfies with his audience. Hun Sen's Facebook page was used to promote CPP achievements and to sand down the rough edges of the Cambodian leader's belligerent public image. Between footage of bridge-openings and livestreamed speeches, the page featured old family photos of Hun Sen with Bun Rany and their children. Other posts offered a glimpse into Hun Sen's private life, everything from his exercise regimen and medical checkups to selfies snapped at ASEAN Summit meetings. As Ou Ritthy of Politikoffee described it to me, "He is trying to show the public that he's a good leader, a good father, a good husband."

With Rainsy out of the immediate picture, the Cambodian government now turned its repressive attentions toward his deputy. As the head of the Cambodian Center for Human Rights and, later, the Human Rights Party, Kem Sokha had traveled the country from end to end, holding small public seminars and patiently accruing a political profile. From this base, the 2013 election had shot him to national prominence. As the new de facto leader of the Cambodian opposition, he represented a more formidable challenge for Hun Sen than his old rival Rainsy. First of all, Sokha was much closer to Hun Sen in political style. Over the years, he had elaborated a close intimacy with rural audiences: he was fluent in their grassroots idiom and attuned to their workaday concerns. Secondly, Sokha also showed little inclination to leave the country during times of tension. During the crackdown of 2005–6, he had spent time in prison and shown a nuggety resilience in the face of political attacks. While Rainsy beat a tactical retreat to Paris, Sokha struck trenches on Cambodian soil.

In the early months of 2016, Sokha was targeted by a complicated "sex scandal" involving a 25-year-old hairdresser, leaked recordings of phone conversations, and confected allegations of witness tampering. Accused of "procuring prostitution," Sokha holed up in the CNRP party headquarters, where he would remain for six months. By this point, five other people, including four staffers from the local human rights group ADHOC, had also been arrested in connection with the scandal.

By this point, increasing numbers of CNRP supporters were facing criminal charges connected to their activities online. In March, a court sentenced a 25-year-old student to 18 months' prison after he issued a Facebook call for a "color revolution" to overthrow the government. In April, it was the turn of Um Sam An, a CNRP parliamentarian, after he made Facebook posts accusing the CPP of using Vietnamese-drawn maps in its border demarcation efforts. The CPP showed no more toleration for online speech than it did for dissenting journalists or human rights defenders. For a brief shining moment, the growth of the internet had outpaced the government's repressive capacity. Now the aperture of free expression was being closed over.

As the crackdown reached its peak in late June of 2016, I phoned Dr. Kem Ley, a well-known activist and popular political commentator, and asked for his forecast of where Cambodia was headed. He was pessimistic. With the CPP locked in a struggle to maintain its "political life" in the face of rising opposition, Kem Ley saw little chance of Cambodia experiencing anything like Aung San Suu Kyi's resounding election triumph the previous November. "No," he said over the crackly line, "this will not be like Burma." A couple of weeks later, at just after half past eight in the morning of July 10, Kem Ley was shot and killed while drinking his morning coffee at a Caltex service station in downtown Phnom Penh. The bullets were fired from close range by an unemployed former soldier who was picked up in the street by police shortly afterward. When asked for his name, the sinewy 43-year-old offered a chilling sobriquet: "Chuob Samlap"—literally, "Meet Kill."

Kem Ley's assassination shocked and appalled the nation. Over the past few years, the medical doctor and researcher, who had worked with a range of local and international NGOs since the late 1990s, had become an increasingly conspicuous presence in Cambodian politics. In 2014, after growing disillusioned with the CNRP and its leaders, he had established Khmer for Khmer, a grassroots advocacy network, and had become widely known for his outspoken commentaries on Khmer-language radio. He had recently registered a new political party—the Grassroots Democracy Party—and had plans to run in the commune elections scheduled for June 2017. By the time of his murder, Kem Ley occupied a perilous niche: popular enough to pose a threat to entrenched interests, yet lacking the protective armor of a substantial international profile.

Kem Ley's killing was striking for being unexpected, yet to many Cambodians, so chillingly familiar. It recalled, in many of its specifics, the violence of the 1990s and early 2000s: high morning, a busy public place, the shots expertly and lethally placed. On July 24, hundreds of thousands of Cambodians accompanied Kem Ley's body on its final, 70-kilometer journey to his home village in Takeo. It was the greatest display of public mourning since Sihanouk's passing in 2012.

Shortly after Kem Ley's killing, I left Cambodia after more than eight years of living and working in the country. It was a melancholy juncture, as the incipient expectations of 2013 were ground under the relentless turn of the political wheel. In the weeks leading up to his assassination, Kem Ley had posted on his Facebook page a series of "fables": short prose tales that anatomized Cambodia's psychology of obedience to the powerful. One such fable, dated July 2, just a few days before his death, told the story of a man named Uncle Sao, who works in the garden of his boss, Uncle Sok:

> One day, the sun is shining very strongly and Uncle Sao starts watering the flowers, leading his boss to come and praise him, and to be very happy that his gardener knows how to water the flowers so well. Only a moment later, it starts raining very heavily, so the gardener decides to stop watering the garden. The boss comes back to look again and, not seeing the gardener watering the flowers this time, shouts out: "Why haven't you continued to water the flowers?" The servant says, "It's raining, boss! No need to water them now." The boss scolds him: "If you're afraid of getting wet, why not bring an umbrella to cover you as you water the garden?" Uncle Sao, afraid of his boss's power, continues watering the garden, even though it's raining so heavily. In a society that concentrates power on individuals without the ability to think deeply when it comes to administration, even when the orders are wrong and endowed with danger, it does not matter. The people in the system must follow, whether the rain pours or not.

In the early hours of September 4, 2017, the final edition of Cambodia's oldest English-language daily rolled off the presses. The *Cambodia Daily* was a respected pillar of the country's small independent media. True to its slogan— "All the News Without Fear or Favor"—the newspaper had accrued a reputation for meticulous reporting and hard-hitting exposés, which belied its unassuming letter-sized format. A month earlier, the Cambodian government had sent the paper's publishers a $6.3 million tax bill, ordering them to pay up or "pack up." They had no choice but to fold.

The front page of the newspaper's last edition featured a grainy cellphone photo of Kem Sokha, now the CNRP's president, being taken into custody by police. Flanked by a portly officer in khaki uniform and baseball cap, Sokha wore a crumpled, untucked shirt, his face frozen into a rictus of surprise. Accompanying the photo was a parting shot in the form of an oversized headline: "Descent Into Outright Dictatorship."[7]

Three months before Sokha's arrest, Cambodia had held its fourth round of commune elections. The political climate was chilled to freezing. Ahead of the June 4 polls, Hun Sen had issued a warning to any wavering voters. In a speech that the *Cambodia Daily* described as a "mammoth three-hour rant," he accused the CNRP of plotting a "color revolution" and said the armed forces stood ready to see off any challenge. Raising up the specter of the chaos then engulfing Middle Eastern nations like Libya, Syria, and Iraq, he announced that he was willing to "eliminate 100 or 200 people" in order to preserve the CPP's hold on power.[8]

Despite Hun Sen's threats, the CNRP once again made considerable gains. In 2012, the Sam Rainsy Party and HRP had won a combined total of 30.7 percent of the vote, yielding the two parties just 40 commune chief positions out of 1,633. Five years later, the CNRP's proportion of the vote leapt to 43.8 percent. Consolidated now under a single party, this translated to 489 of the country's 1,646 commune chiefs. The result was less dramatic than in 2013, but posed just as serious a threat to the CPP's hold on power. For the first time, the CNRP had gained a significant political presence at the grassroots. Unlike the party's 55 lawmakers, safely quarantined in Phnom Penh, the CNRP's new commune chiefs threatened to begin boring directly into the CPP's rural bedrock. They immediately got to work organizing local members in advance of the national elections due in July 2018.

The CPP responded to the commune election results with a redoubling of the pressure. Shortly after midnight on September 3, Kem Sokha was arrested at his home in Phnom Penh and held at the maximum security Trapaing Phlong prison in eastern Cambodia, close to the Vietnamese border. He was subsequently charged with treason for conspiring with foreign governments to launch a "color revolution" aimed at sweeping the CPP from power. In November, a Phnom Penh court used the charge as a pretext to order the dissolution of the CNRP itself. Across the country, CNRP signs were torn down, and the rising sun on the front of the party's headquarters on National Road 2 was effaced with white paint. The CNRP's 55 National Assembly seats were assumed by the CPP; some of its commune council seats were distributed to a number of smaller allied parties. Most of the CNRP's senior leadership fled the country.

In this climate, the national election of July 2018, eagerly anticipated by Cambodia watchers since the tumultuous events five years earlier, took place in a strange vacuum of suspended expectations. With its only real challenger forced out of the race, the CPP ran virtually unopposed, and few were surprised when the NEC declared that it had won every seat in the National Assembly. As Western governments criticized Hun Sen's brazen consolidation of power, government spokesmen pointed to the 20-odd small parties, including a new-look Funcinpec under Prince Norodom Ranariddh, as proof that Cambodia remained a viable multiparty democracy. It convinced nobody.

The crackdown left Cambodia's leader in a more dominant position than ever. In June 2015, Hun Sen's long-time rival Chea Sim, the president of the CPP and the Senate, had died at the age of 82. In the wake of his elaborate state funeral, the CPP anointed Hun Sen as the new president of the party. To the extent that there was a meaningful distinction between party and state, Hun Sen was now the unchallenged leader of both, even if rival ambitions continued to bubble away beneath the CPP's shell of unity.

As he climbed to a new zenith of power, Hun Sen began sizing up his place in Cambodian history. In February 2016, work began on a memorial on Phnom Penh's Chruoy Changvar peninsula, dedicated to Hun Sen's political legacy, particularly his "win-win" policy, which was credited with engineering the collapse of the Khmer Rouge and bringing an end to Cambodia's long civil war. The Win-Win Monument, as it was officially termed, was inaugurated on December 29, 2018, the twentieth anniversary of the conflict's end. Located on eight hectares of land donated by the tycoon Ly Yong Phat, the monument featured a 33-meter-tall pinnacle of concrete, skirted by reflective pools and roughly landscaped gardens. Beneath, a subterranean gallery housed a collection of artifacts, and running clockwise around the monument's base were 400 meters of carved limestone bas-reliefs illustrating the official CPP version of Cambodia's recent history.

Early one evening in September 2019, I drove out to visit Hun Sen's shrine to himself. Like many public parks, the Win-Win Monument attracted a sparse crowd of locals who exercised and let their children dash across the wide paved expanse. Along the entryway, women sold illuminated plastic whirligigs and cold drinks from orange tubs filled with ice. From its field of stone paving, the monument speared a cloud-spangled sky.

For an hour, I carefully followed the bas-reliefs clockwise around the base of the monument. Here, graven in limestone, like the otherworldly bas-reliefs of Angkor Wat, was Hun Sen's *telos*: the story of how an unlikely leader unified his people and ushered them toward peace and prosperity. In fairytale tableaux, the carvings depicted Hun Sen's defection from the Khmer Rouge in 1977, his perilous flight to Vietnam, and his role in the overthrow of the Pol Pot regime. They showed the rebirth of Cambodian culture and Buddhist ritual under the CPP's beneficent hand. Carvings illustrated Sihanouk's return to Cambodia in 1991, the arrival of the UNTAC peacekeepers, and the reintegration of former Khmer Rouge fighters into Cambodian society.

The final quadrant of bas-reliefs was dedicated to the fruits of Hun Sen's reign. There was the prime minister in dictator shades, with military officers in tow; further on, he greeted soldiers as they embarked on a UN peacekeeping mission, against a backdrop of Cambodian flags. Hun Sen was even shown taking cellphone selfies with his supporters, smiling, benevolent, beloved. The circumambulatory narrative concluded with a carving of Hun Sen in military uniform, extending an arm of greeting.

Capped by the CPP's sweep of National Assembly seats, the political crackdown of 2017–18 far exceeded the repressive cycles of the past. Indeed, in many ways, it represented Hun Sen's final repudiation of the international settlement that had created Cambodia's democratic system in 1991. For the first time, the Cambodian government had gone beyond the usual targets—opposition members, union leaders, and land rights activists—to attack prominent institutions, like the *Cambodia Daily*, which had been established during the UNTAC mission of 1992–3. Another casualty was my old newspaper the *Phnom Penh Post*, sold under government pressure in May 2018 to a consortium of Malaysian investors with links to the CPP. The National Democratic Institute, an American-funded democracy promotion group, was told to pack up and leave. The US-funded Radio Free Asia also closed its local bureau. It had taken 30 years, but Hun Sen was freeing himself of a foreign intervention that he had never accepted or viewed as legitimate. Cambodia's democratic mirage was finally beginning to fade.

That Hun Sen was able to take such drastic actions to reset Cambodian politics spoke to the robust support he now enjoyed from China. By the time I left Cambodia in 2016, Beijing had risen to become the country's number one trading partner and leading source of foreign direct investment; it was also the top source of tourists to the country. Under the Belt and Road Initiative (BRI), the headline foreign policy initiative of China's supreme leader Xi Jinping, China had poured hundreds of millions of dollars into Cambodia to build dams, highways, power plants, and special economic zones. In Phnom Penh, Chinese high-rise apartments were reorienting the city's skyline. Chinese-built bridges swept over the nation's rivers. Officials engaged in a blur of bilateral visits, capped by the arrival in October 2016 of Xi himself. China's president described Cambodia warmly as an "iron-clad friend."[9]

Returning to Cambodia in 2018 to research a new book on China's rising influence in Southeast Asia, I was astonished by the growth of the mainland Chinese investment presence in Phnom Penh. Previously concentrated in the old Chinatown along Monivong Boulevard, Chinese restaurants, businesses, and expatriates were now visible just about everywhere. A more radical transformation was underway in Sihanoukville on the coast, which had metamorphosed from a shabby tourist backwater into a sordid gambling mecca sustained by the Chinese tourist dollar. On a visit in September of that year, high-rise hotels and apartment buildings pressed up into the evening sky. City streets crumbled under the weight of cranes and cement trucks, while rainwater gathered in the ruts. The focus of Sihanoukville's development were its dozens of Chinese-run casinos: bantam venues that glowed like illuminated amber in the nighttime murk. Inside, the baccarat tables were ringed by gamblers—mostly jumpy young Chinese men in T-shirts—who smoked and glowered over the baize. On the coral arc of O'Chheuteal Beach, the beer-swilling Western backpackers had been almost entirely replaced by Chinese nationals: an apt metaphor for Cambodia's eastward shift.

As a foreign patron, China offered Hun Sen just about everything he wanted. Instead of lecturing him about how he ran his country, the Chinese spoke of national sovereignty and "non-interference": the right of every country to choose its own political path. After Kem Sokha's arrest, a Chinese Foreign Ministry spokesperson responded by saying that Beijing supported "the Cambodian government's effort to uphold national security and stability."[10] When Western nations suspended support for the 2018 election, China donated laptops, computers, and voting booths to the NEC. More importantly, Chinese leaders offered Hun Sen the one thing he had never received from the West: legitimacy. As he put it in February 2018, during the groundbreaking for a $57 million Chinese-funded bridge close to his native village in Kampong Cham, "The Chinese leaders respect me highly and treat me as an equal."[11]

Fortified by Chinese backing, the Cambodian government was increasingly numb to Western opinion. As its political crackdown accelerated in 2017, the government met European and American criticisms with irate assertions of sovereignty. That April, the Cambodian Foreign Ministry issued an 11-page "white paper" defending its record and slamming Western governments for colluding with NGOs and media outlets that had "twisted historical facts and events in an attempt to portray a negative image of Cambodia."[12]

In response to criticisms from the US, Hun Sen revived all of his old resentments. He savaged Washington for its carpet bombing of Cambodia in the 1960s and 1970s and its support of the Khmer Rouge throughout the 1980s. In early 2017, Cambodia suspended its participation in Angkor Sentinel, a military exercise it had held with the US Army since 2010, just a month after holding its first joint exercise with China's People's Liberation Army, and kicked out a US naval engineering battalion that was in Cambodia building schools and maternity wards. By implication, the government accused the US of colluding with Kem Sokha and the CNRP to launch a "color revolution" to topple his government from power.

It wasn't long before Hun Sen's embrace of China was attracting keen attention in Washington. Under the administration of President Donald Trump, who had entered office in January 2017, the Obama administration's cautious "rebalance" to Asia had given way to a strident and increasingly confrontational stance toward China. This soon crystalized into a broad bipartisan consensus that viewed Beijing as a hostile power seeking to overturn the US-backed global security order. Politicians and pundits sketched the lines of a grand ideological struggle, even a new Cold War, pitting authoritarian China against the democracies of the West. Viewed through this binary lens, the Cambodian government's authoritarian turn, and its cheerful embrace of Chinese largesse, put it squarely on the wrong side of the line.

American concerns focused on a Chinese tourism development in Koh Kong province, across the bay from Sihanoukville (see Chapter 9). Here a Tianjin-based company known as the Union Development Group (UDG) had been granted a colossal 36,000-hectare concession fronting the Gulf of Thailand. UDG's planned resort development included an airport and deep-water seaport, which analysts believed could be used by the Chinese navy and air force. In July 2019, even as the Cambodian government was denying that it intended to permit a Chinese military presence on its soil, the *Wall Street Journal* reported that the two countries had signed a secret agreement granting China exclusive access rights to the Ream Naval Base near Sihanoukville for a period of 30 years. After the publication of the article, the US State Department expressed concern that a Chinese military presence would threaten the coherence of ASEAN and "disturb peace and stability in Southeast Asia."[13]

Throughout 2019 and into early 2020, Western governments increased their pressure on Phnom Penh. The European Union announced a partial suspension of Cambodia's tariff-free access to the European market, the destination of more than a third of Cambodia's exports, threatening to damage industries that employ hundreds of thousands of workers. Hun Sen critics in the US Congress tabled several bills calling for the imposition of economic sanctions and travel bans on senior Cambodian officials. One of them, the Cambodia Accountability and Return on Investment Act of 2019, demanded that Cambodia release Kem Sokha (he had since been transferred to house arrest) and dismiss the charges against him. It also urged the Cambodian government to "protect its sovereignty from interference" by China. At the same time, the US Treasury Department imposed sanctions on several of Hun Sen's close associates, including the logging baron Try Pheap, Hing Bun Hieng, the head of Hun Sen's bodyguard unit, and General Kun Kim, among his closest satraps in the military.

Western concerns were fanned by the CNRP's exiled leaders. Sam Rainsy cycled through the capitals of the West, depicting Hun Sen as a Chinese puppet and calling for harsh sanctions. Previously, Rainsy had paid little attention to China's creeping inroads in Cambodia. In 2014, he had even declared that the CNRP supported China's maritime claims in the South China Sea, on the logic that anyone opposing Vietnam must be Cambodia's friend. As he told his supporters, "The islands belong to China."[14] Ever alert to the preoccupations of would-be Western allies, Rainsy tuned his lobbying efforts to the new anti-China mood now prevailing in many Western capitals. He warned of China's "invasion" of Cambodia and the perils of the nation becoming snared "by massive, opaque debts to China, which it cannot repay."[15]

Still, Hun Sen showed no sign of yielding. He responded to the pressure by telling Western countries to "stop treating Cambodia as a toy" and announced he was "done taking orders" from foreigners.[16] In a speech at the United Nations in Geneva in July 2019, he described the 2018 election as "free, fair and just," and called Cambodia a "land of freedom."[17] He praised Japan, which pragmatically continued to offer ample infrastructure funding in competition with China's BRI projects. The predictable result of Western pressure was to increase further Hun Sen's reliance on Chinese support. In 2018, China's Ambassador Xiong Bo compared the Sino-Cambodian friendship to a fine red wine: "The longer it is," he said, "the better taste it has."

In truth, the Western powers bore a share of the responsibility for Cambodia's turn toward China. When the Paris Peace Agreements were signed in 1991, Cambodia's fate had converged with a global narrative of progress, and an expectation, widespread in the West, that history had reached its preordained democratic end. Cambodia appeared to fit the template perfectly. Its suffering during the 1960s and 1970s dramatized the human cost of Cold War realpolitik. Then, with the coming of the UN in 1992, the land of the "killing fields" came to embody a narrative of suffering and redemption through the good offices of Western aid workers and a well-intentioned "international community."

Even as it dissipated elsewhere, this liberal promise persisted in Cambodia, preserved as if in amber. Viewing Cambodia as small and strategically unimportant, many Western powers felt that it was a place where they could press a human rights agenda without incurring much of a strategic cost. Yet Cambodia's "special" status rankled the CPP and its leadership, for whom the Paris Agreements had always posed an implicit threat. To Hun Sen and his colleagues, the 1991 settlement was built on a bedrock of Western hypocrisy, and driven forward by a double standard that demanded more of Cambodia that most neighboring countries. For a government that rejected liberal democratic norms, it was unsurprising that Western attempts at democracy promotion, especially when pursued so selectively, would be perceived as a project of regime change. The fact that opposition figures like Sam Rainsy fastened to democracy promotion efforts to advance their own political aims only underscored the CPP's sense of paranoia and siege.

Hun Sen's embrace of China was in some ways the logical outcome of the political contradictions contained in the Paris Agreements, a pact that set the stage for a spectacular, albeit slow-motion, collision between two incommensurable worldviews. In avowing to transform Cambodia into a liberal democracy (even if their actions rarely matched their words), Western governments seemed not to grasp the ideological and revolutionary scope of their ambition, nor the existential threat it posed to the CPP and other entrenched interests. They also failed to take account of how much the world had changed since 1991. From Brexit to the rise of Trump to the renaissance of China, global power shifts were quickly closing the parenthesis on a post-Cold War era in which there had been a broad international consensus around globalization, neoliberal capitalism, and democratic government. Dreams of liberal order were giving way to a new era of multipolarity and superpower competition: a world of hardening borders and resurgent national sovereignty. Although it was easy to overlook, Cambodia's trajectory reflected this broader global turn. If the nation embodied the liberal hopes of the post-Cold War era, it also reflected the disillusion that set in as the world, starting out for Francis Fukuyama's democratic promised land, found itself confronting a liberal mirage.

For all its messianic overtones, the international political settlement of the early 1990s was merely the latest in a long line of frustrated outside interventions in Cambodia's affairs. Since the decline of the Angkorian empire, a weak Cambodian state had been the subject of repeated foreign schemes, including the nation-building efforts of the Vietnamese imperial court, the *mission civilisatrice* of the French, and Hanoi's socialist project in the 1980s. Powerless to resist these incursions, Cambodian rulers became skilled in appealing to external powers and channeling outside energy into domestic struggles. Sihanouk and Hun Sen, the most successful modern Cambodian leaders, were masters in this art of political dissimulation and harnessing. They turned a mirror outward, so that foreigners arriving in an exotic land very often saw their own political interests and ideological presuppositions reflected back at them. Much the same was true of opposition leaders like Sam Rainsy and Kem Sokha.

It could be hard to see through the scattershot refractions. As the French sociologist Serge Thion wrote in 1993, "Khmer reality lies shrouded by many veils."[18] The Thais, the Vietnamese, the French, the Americans, the Chinese, the Vietnamese (again), and the "international community": all left their mark on Cambodia, although none succeeded in imposing its own norms or fundamentally altering the mindset of Cambodia's leaders. From long experience, Cambodians knew that foreign influences were evanescent. As outsiders came, so too would they eventually depart. Like water finding its lowest point, Cambodian ways had a manner of persisting through cycles of social and political change.

This is not to deny that the international presence had brought benefits to the Cambodian people. For one thing, Western scrutiny imposed limits on Hun Sen. It ensured that as bad as things got, the country always had fewer political prisoners than Burma or Vietnam or Laos, and, for a time, presented a freer face to the world than many other Southeast Asian nations. The desire for foreign legitimacy led Hun Sen to allow Sam Rainsy's return before the 2013 election; during the post-election protests, outside scrutiny meant the CPP had to tread carefully in suppressing popular calls for change. The government did use violent means to break the deadlock, but things could well have been a lot worse. In many ways, a mirage of democracy was better than no democracy at all. But this unsteady status quo was dependent on a balance of external power that was always destined to change as wealth and power shifted gradually to the east.

The removal of these limits did little to alter the fundamental challenges facing Hun Sen. In January 2020, the Cambodian leader marked his thirty-fifth year in power, with perhaps a decade more to come. He was now 67 years of age, and beginning to contemplate how best to ensure that his legacy, such as it was, survived beyond his own rule. The obstacles facing Hun Sen were legion. Internationally, the Cambodian leader's suspicion and resentment had led him into a paralyzing overreliance on China, and into the crosshairs of an increasingly belligerent US security establishment. As Sino-American tensions grew, Cambodia and its people risked once again being squeezed in a contest between dueling superpowers.

Domestically, the CPP's essential challenge remained the same: keeping pace with the rapid evolutions of Cambodian society. Freed from the friction of formal opposition, the ruling party still faced the genuine popular discontent that had fueled the CNRP's popularity in the first instance. The dissolution of the CNRP in 2017 did nothing to resolve the contradiction at the heart of the Cambodian political system: that true reform would undermine the very economic interests that sustained it.

With the CPP in near-total control of the political landscape, it was just as likely that threats to Hun Sen's authority would emerge from within. Behind a unified front, the CPP had always been riven by rivalries over power and its spoils. While Hun Sen had imposed his will over the party, the eventual handover of power to a successor—widely believed to be his eldest son, Hun Manet—loomed as a point at which internal tensions could break into the open. A stable succession plan was necessary to secure Hun Sen's legacy, but it remained to be seen whether Manet was skillful enough to keep the CPP's webs of interlinked but competing interests in a state of satisfied and stable acquiescence. Raised in a context of privilege and comfort, it was by no means clear that Manet enjoyed the confidence of the CPP's veteran leaders and moneymen, nor the mixture of cunning and ruthlessness that had kept his father at the slippery apex of Cambodian politics for more than four decades. The career of Prince Norodom Ranariddh offers ample evidence that political acumen is rarely heritable.

With Beijing's backing, Hun Sen has more freedom to address these challenges in his own fashion. Paradoxically, he also finds himself more constrained. Cambodia's elections have never been free or fair, but they were usually competitive enough to offer the CPP leadership a gauge of popular opinion. Lacking any meaningful political opposition, the party now faced an informational vacuum, in which it could easily ignore or underestimate the extent of popular disaffection. Absent the guardrails of Western scrutiny, there was a growing risk of Hun Sen misreading public sentiment, or leaning more heavily on raw coercion to preserve his hold on power. An aging leader's obsession with maintaining stability at all costs portended further rounds of instability to come.

Cambodia's political trajectory since the end of the Cold War offers some sobering lessons. The first is that political changes imposed on nations from the outside are rarely sustainable over the long run. While the world managed to fashion a democratic system for Cambodia, there was no inherent magic in these institutions to magnetize the people that filled them. The political philosopher John Dunn has described democracy as "a self-indigenizing category": one that takes on the coloration of the social conditions and political economy of the nation in which it is embedded.[19] In general, the politically exalted tends downward into the deep water of local customs and relations of power. The corollary is that true political change, if it comes to Cambodia, will come not from above—from a shape-shifting "international community"— but from below, from the Cambodian people themselves.

In October 2013, three months after that year's disputed national election, I paid a visit to Bavet to interview Bun Chenda, the young woman who was shot by Chhouk Bundith outside the Kaoway Sportswear Factory in February 2012. In the 18 months since the incident, Chenda had married and moved out of her parents' home. She still worked at the factory with her 24-year-old husband, and sent regular payments back to her parents in the village of Prek Pdav. "If I can save money I'd like to open a grocery shop," she said, as we sat at a small café on the highway, where semi-trailers thundered past, border-bound.

Like most Cambodians, Chenda probably intuited that the country's democratic system was a mirage. But after years of winning the people's support with peace and rudimentary development, Hun Sen's government was now facing real political pressures from ordinary folk like her: from garment workers, monks, evicted farmers, opposition politicians, and human rights defenders. Before the 2013 election, Chenda had supported Hun Sen, like most people in her village; after the shooting, she cast a vote for Sam Rainsy and Kem Sokha. "I hope when the CNRP wins more support, they will quickly find justice for us," she said.

Her comments suggested that despite the tortuous turns of Cambodia's elite politics, the nation had crossed a threshold of sorts. No longer was

Cambodia its own island, as it had been for much of history, inward-looking and cut off from the world. Slowly, expectations were rising and a young population was beginning to demand more from its vain and self-obsessed political class. It all pointed the way to a better future: probably not a fully democratic one, but at least one that was marginally more accountable and responsive to the needs of ordinary people. There was some reason to hope that in the future beyond Hun Sen, destructive political patterns might give way to something fairer and more just. After so many years of hardship and uncertainty, the Cambodian people would deserve nothing less.

Notes

Preface to the Paperback Edition

1. John Marston, "Cambodia: Transnational Pressures and Local Agendas," *Southeast Asian Affairs 2002* (Singapore: Institute of Southeast Asian Studies, 2002), 95.

Introduction: A Mirage on the Mekong

1. May Titthara and David Boyle, "Court Avoids Warrant for Governor of Bavet," *Phnom Penh Post*, March 6, 2012.
2. Thomas Beller, "An Unflinching Look," *Cambodia Daily*, August 20, 2003.
3. Michael Hayes, "Ten Years After," *Phnom Penh Post*, July 19–August 1, 2002.
4. Denise Hruby and Hul Reaksmey, "Hunger Reduced, Malnourishment Next Issue," *Cambodia Daily*, October 17, 2013.
5. Joel Brinkley, *Cambodia's Curse: The Modern History of a Troubled Land* (New York: Public Affairs, 2011), 353.

1 Against the Ages

1. David P. Chandler, *The Tragedy of Cambodian History: Politics, War, and Revolution since 1945* (Chiang Mai: Silkworm, 1994), 6.
2. David P. Chandler, *A History of Cambodia* (Boulder: Westview, 2008), 105.
3. Philip Short, *Pol Pot: Anatomy of a Nightmare* (New York: Holt, 2004), 25.
4. Chandler, *A History of Cambodia*, 121.
5. Cited in Milton Osborne, *Phnom Penh: A Cultural and Literary History* (Oxford: Signal, 2008), 85.
6. By 1921, Vietnamese migrants made up 7 percent of Cambodia's population. See Nayan Chanda, *Brother Enemy: The War after the War* (New York: Macmillan, 1986), 56.
7. David P. Chandler, "Normative Poems (Chbap) and Pre-colonial Cambodian Society," *Journal of Southeast Asian Studies* 15, no. 2 (Sept. 1984): 271–79, at 279.
8. Chandler, *A History of Cambodia*, 195.
9. Chandler, *The Tragedy of Cambodian History*, 168.
10. John Pilger, *Heroes* (Cambridge: South End Press, 2002), 386.
11. David P. Chandler, *Brother Number One: A Political Biography of Pol Pot* (Boulder: Westview, 1999), 64.
12. Taylor Owen and Ben Kiernan, "Roots of U.S. Troubles in Afghanistan: Civilian Bombing Casualties and the Cambodian Precedent," *The Asia-Pacific Journal*, June 28, 2010.
13. William Shawcross, *Sideshow: Kissinger, Nixon, and the Destruction of Cambodia* (New York: Simon & Schuster, 1979).
14. Elizabeth Becker, "Who Are the Khmer Rouge?" *Washington Post*, March 10, 1974.

15. Samantha Power, *A Problem from Hell: America and the Age of Genocide* (New York: HarperCollins, 2003), 100.
16. Lewis M. Simons, "Khmer Rouge: Victors' Incongruities Begin with Sihanouk," *Washington Post*, April 18, 1975.
17. Becker, "Who Are the Khmer Rouge?"
18. Elizabeth Becker, *When the War Was Over: Cambodia and the Khmer Rouge Revolution* (New York: Public Affairs, 1998), 141.
19. "Living History Interview with Ambassador Kenneth Quinn," *Transnational Law and Contemporary Problems* 17, no. 1 (Oct. 2007): 165–85, at 174.
20. Kenneth M. Quinn, "The Khmer Krahom Program to Create a Communist Society in Southern Cambodia," airgram from US Consulate General Can Tho, February 20, 1974, 19–20.
21. "Living History Interview with Ambassador Kenneth Quinn," 176.
22. Johnny Brannon, "Oahu Became Home for Ex-Cambodian Leader's Exile," *Honolulu Advertiser*, October 22, 2007.
23. François Ponchaud, *Cambodia: Year Zero* (New York: Holt, Rinehart & Winston, 1978), 5.
24. Kassie Neou's story, here and in subsequent chapters, is based on an interview conducted on August 29, 2012.
25. Saing Soenthrith, "A Journalist's Account of the Khmer Rouge," *Cambodia Daily*, May 17, 2004.
26. Short, *Pol Pot*, 275.
27. Chanda, *Brother Enemy*, 44.
28. For a detailed account of Chinese aid to DK, see Andrew Mertha, *Brothers in Arms: Chinese Aid to the Khmer Rouge, 1975–1979* (Ithaca: Cornell University Press, 2014).
29. For one survivor's account of S-21, see Vann Nath, *A Cambodian Prison Portrait: One Year in the Khmer Rouge's S-21* (Bangkok: White Lotus, 1998).
30. Jamie F. Metzl, *Western Responses to Human Rights Abuses in Cambodia, 1975–80* (New York: St. Martin's Press, 1996), 51 and 91.
31. The Ieng Sary interview appeared in the magazine's international edition. See James Pringle, " 'We Do Not Copy,' " *Newsweek*, September 8, 1975.
32. Author interview with Charles Twining, December 21, 2012.
33. This and following sections are based on an interview with Gunnar Bergström, conducted on August 30, 2012. Recollections of Bergström's trip, including a series of color photos, were later published in *Living Hell: Democratic Kampuchea, August 1978* (Phnom Penh: Documentation Center of Cambodia, 2008).
34. David Kline, *Kampuchea: A Photo Record of the First American Visit since April 1975* (Chicago: Liberator Press, 1979), 3.
35. Noam Chomsky and Edward S. Herman, "Distortions at Fourth Hand," *The Nation*, June 6, 1977.
36. Becker, *When the War Was Over*, 316.
37. Foreign Broadcast Information Service, *Daily Report, Asia & Pacific*, August 27, 1978.
38. Rithy Panh, *The Elimination*, trans. John Cullen (London: The Clerkenwell Press, 2013), 1.
39. Ben Kiernan, *The Pol Pot Regime: Race, Power, and Genocide in Cambodia under the Khmer Rouge, 1975–79* (New Haven: Yale University Press, 1996), 357.
40. David P. Chandler, *Voices from S-21: Terror and History in Pol Pot's Secret Prison* (Berkeley: University of California Press, 1999), 73.
41. Kiernan, *The Pol Pot Regime*, 387.
42. Evan Gottesman, *Cambodia after the Khmer Rouge: Inside the Politics of Nation-Building* (New Haven: Yale University Press, 2003), 8.
43. Short, *Pol Pot*, 397.
44. Foreign Broadcast Information Service, *Daily Report, Asia & Pacific*, January 5, 1979.

2 The Second Revolution

1. Elizabeth Becker, *When the War Was Over: Cambodia and the Khmer Rouge Revolution* (New York: Public Affairs, 1998), 399.

2. Harish C. Mehta and Julie B. Mehta, *Strongman: The Extraordinary Life of Hun Sen* (Singapore: Marshall Cavendish, 2013), 124.

3. Author interview with Ouk Bunchhoeun, October 2, 2012.

4. When he joined the communists in 1970, Hun Sen gave his birthdate as April 4, 1951 in a bid to conceal his young age from recruiters.

5. Interviews by Ben Kiernan, October 21, 1980, Cambodian Genocide Program, Yale University.

6. Ben Kiernan, *The Pol Pot Regime: Race, Power, and Genocide in Cambodia under the Khmer Rouge, 1975–79* (New Haven: Yale University Press, 1996), 266 and 370.

7. Translated material from the Central Stasi Archives Berlin, provided by Bernd Schaefer, Woodrow Wilson International Center, Washington, DC. Hun Sen told his biographers that the Vietnamese gave him the slightly different name "Mai Phuc," meaning "happiness forever," so as not to "attract attention, or give rise to suspicions." See Mehta and Mehta, *Strongman*, 115.

8. Ibid.

9. Michael Leifer, "Kampuchea in 1979: From Dry Season to Dry Season," *Asian Survey* 20, no. 1 (Jan. 1980): 33–41, at 39.

10. Kathleen Gough, "Interviews in Kampuchea," *Bulletin of Concerned Asian Scholars* 14, no. 4 (Oct.–Dec. 1982): 55–65, at 56.

11. Hoang Nguyen, *The Vietnam-Kampuchea Conflict* (Hanoi: Foreign Languages Publishing House, 1979), 43. See also Evan Gottesman, *Cambodia after the Khmer Rouge: Inside the Politics of Nation-Building* (New Haven: Yale University Press, 2003), 8.

12. Nayan Chanda, *Brother Enemy: The War after the War* (New York: Macmillan, 1986), 347.

13. Tom Fawthrop and Helen Jarvis, *Getting Away with Genocide: Elusive Justice and the Khmer Rouge Tribunal* (London: Pluto Press, 2004), 56.

14. Becker, *When the War Was Over*, 435.

15. Samantha Power, *A Problem from Hell: America and the Age of Genocide* (New York: HarperCollins, 2003), 150.

16. Fawthrop and Jarvis, *Getting Away with Genocide*, 39.

17. Author interview with Jacques Bekaert, March 13, 2009.

18. For a detailed account of the formation of the KPNLF, see Justin Corfield, *A History of the Cambodian Non-Communist Resistance 1975–1983* (Clayton, Victoria: Centre of Southeast Asian Studies, Monash University, 1991).

19. John Burgess, "Khmer Rouge, Fighting to Regain Power, Admit 'Mistakes,' " *Washington Post*, August 10, 1980.

20. Serge Thion, *Watching Cambodia: Ten Paths to Enter the Cambodian Tangle* (Bangkok: White Lotus, 1993), 125.

21. John Pilger, *Heroes* (Cambridge: South End Press, 2002), 449.

22. Author interview with Prince Sisowath Sirirath, July 27, 2012.

23. Kelvin Rowley, "Second Life, Second Death: The Khmer Rouge after 1978," in Susan E. Cook, ed., *Genocide in Cambodia and Rwanda: New Perspectives* (New Haven: Yale Center for International and Area Studies, 2004), 202. For the KPNLF and ANS figures, see Timothy Carney, "Kampuchea in 1982: Political and Military Escalation," *Asian Survey* 23, no. 1 (Jan. 1983): 73–83, at 78.

24. Markus Karbaum, "The Paper Trail," *Southeast Asia Globe*, April 2013.

25. Gottesman, *Cambodia after the Khmer Rouge*, 208–9. See also Colin Campbell, "Defectors Detail Hanoi Rule in Running Cambodia," *New York Times*, October 8, 1982.

26. For instance, see Jacques Bekaert, *Cambodian Diary: Tales of a Divided Nation, 1983–1986* (Bangkok: White Lotus, 1997), 22.

27. For Rogachev's meeting with Hun Sen, see Becker, *When the War Was Over*, 440–3.

28. Author interview with Bill Herod, July 27, 2012.

29. See Mehta and Mehta, *Strongman*, 107.

30. Michael Vickery, "Phnom Penh Decays behind a Bustling Cheerful Façade," *Canberra Times*, October 22, 1981.

31. "Julie Andrews to Seek Aid for Orphans," *New Straits Times*, September 11, 1982.

32. Brian Eads, "Hatred of the Khmer Rouge Helps Unite Cambodians," *Observer*, May 29, 1983.

33. Material from the Central Stasi Archives Berlin (GDR, State Security, HA II, April 26, 1983), provided by Bernd Schaefer, Woodrow Wilson International Center, Washington, DC.

34. Author interview with Ouk Bunchhoeun, October 2, 2012.

35. Gottesman, *Cambodia after the Khmer Rouge*, 102–3.

36. Until 1993, Cambodia's only criminal code was Decree-Law 2, passed by the PRK in June 1980, which interpreted all forms of offense under the rubric of "counterrevolutionary" dissent. See ibid., 241.

37. Ibid., 53–4, 60 and 75.

38. Ibid., 131.

39. Shortly after the Congress, Hanoi veterans Chea Soth and Bou Thang were removed as ministers of planning and defense in favor of Chea Chanto, a former National Bank of Cambodia employee who now serves as the bank's governor, and Koy Buntha, another young technocrat. For the make-up of the KPRP Central Committee as of late 1985, see Michael Vickery, *Kampuchea: Politics, Economics and Society* (London: Frances Pinter, 1986), 80–1. By the 2000s three notable Hanoi veterans—Bou Thang, Say Phouthang, and Chea Soth—still retained leading positions on the Central Committee of the Cambodian People's Party, the successor to the KPRP. At the national level, however, they wielded little power.

40. Regarding the border agreements, see Gottesman, *Cambodia after the Khmer Rouge*, 209–11. See also Ramses Amer, "Border Conflicts between Cambodia and Vietnam," *IBRU Boundary and Security Bulletin* (Summer 1997): 80–8, at 81–2.

41. These details are taken from the author's interview with Pen Sovan, January 27, 2014. On previous occasions, Sovan has accused Hun Sen himself of responsibility for Chan Si's death. See "Sam Rainsy Uses Pen Sovann to Attack Hun Sen's Background," *Cambodia Daily*, May 1, 1998. Regarding allegations of Hun Sen's involvement in Chan Si's death, see Slocomb, *The People's Republic of Kampuchea*, 143–4; Gottesman, *Cambodia after the Khmer Rouge*, 134.

42. Author interview with Khieu Kanharith, March 13, 2013.

43. Gottesman, *Cambodia after the Khmer Rouge*, 208.

44. Email correspondence with Jacques Bekaert, December 2012.

45. Author interview with Khieu Kanharith, March 13, 2013.

46. Gottesman, *Cambodia after the Khmer Rouge*, 333.

47. Ibid., 331–2.

48. Ibid., 329.

49. Michael Vickery, "The Cambodian People's Party: Where Has It Come From, Where Is It Going?" in *Southeast Asian Affairs 1994* (Singapore: Institute of Southeast Asian Studies, 1994), 110.

50. Nayan Chanda, "Cambodia in 1986: Beginning to Tire," *Asian Survey* 27, no. 1 (Jan. 1987): 115–24, at 118.

51. Margaret Slocomb, "The K5 Gamble: National Defense and Nation Building under the People's Republic of Kampuchea," *Journal of Southeast Asian Studies* 32, no. 2 (2001): 195–210, at 202–3.

52. Author interview with Timothy Carney, July 21, 2012.

53. Benny Widyono, *Dancing in Shadows: Sihanouk, the Khmer Rouge, and the United Nations in Cambodia* (Lanham: Rowman & Littlefield, 2008), xxii.

54. Chanda, "Cambodia in 1986," 122.

55. Author interview with Pung Chhiv Kek, August 8, 2012.

56. Thion, *Watching Cambodia*, xxiii.

57. Nayan Chanda, "Cambodia in 1987: Sihanouk on Centre Stage," *Asian Survey* 28, no. 1 (Jan. 1988): 105–15, at 114–15.

58. Thion, *Watching Cambodia*, 198.

59. Slocomb, *The People's Republic of Kampuchea*, 271, n38.
60. Michael Vickery dates this independence from the KPRP's Fifth Party Congress in 1985, which saw an influx of a large number of technocrats and young officials who identified neither with Vietnam, nor with communism. See Vickery, "The Cambodian People's Party," 107–8.

3 The Wages of Peace

1. Elaine Ganley, "Cambodian Peace Treaty Signed in Effort to End 13-Year Civil War," Associated Press, October 23, 1991.
2. Francis Fukuyama, "The End of History?" *National Interest*, Summer 1989.
3. Alan Riding, "4 Parties in Cambodian War Sign U.N.-Backed Peace Pact," *New York Times*, October 24, 1991.
4. Julio A. Jeldres, "Cambodia's Relations with France since the Paris Agreements of 1991," in Pou Sothirak, Geoff Wade, and Mark Hong, eds, *Cambodia: Progress and Challenges since 1991* (Singapore: Institute of Southeast Asian Studies, 2012), 137.
5. Tiziano Terzani, "An Indecent Peace," *Far Eastern Economic Review*, June 25, 1992.
6. David P. Chandler, *Brother Number One: A Political Biography of Pol Pot* (Boulder: Westview, 1999), 174.
7. Mike Yeong, "Cambodia 1991: Lasting Peace or Decent Interval?" in *Southeast Asian Affairs 1992* (Singapore: Institute of Southeast Asian Studies, 1992), 106.
8. Benny Widyono, *Dancing in Shadows: Sihanouk, the Khmer Rouge, and the United Nations in Cambodia* (Lanham: Rowman & Littlefield, 2008), 87.
9. Keith B. Richburg, "Hun Sen Making an Impact," *Washington Post*, June 22, 1989; Steven Erlanger, "In Phnom Penh, Vietnam's 'Puppet' Is Finding His Voice," *New York Times*, August 27, 1989.
10. Dominic Faulder, "Grand Manipulator," *Asiaweek*, September 27, 1996. See also "Hun Sen Gets Hospital Treatment in Tokyo," Reuters, April 24, 1991.
11. Richburg, "Hun Sen Making an Impact."
12. Thach Saren, ". . . Does Anybody Care?" *Washington Post*, October 30, 1989; Thach Saren, "Don't Excuse Hun Sen and Heng Samrin," *Washington Post*, November 29, 1989.
13. "Cambodia's Hun Sen Is Himself Khmer Rouge," *New York Times*, December 7, 1989.
14. Harish C. Mehta and Julie B. Mehta, *Strongman: The Extraordinary Life of Hun Sen* (Singapore: Marshall Cavendish, 2013), 70.
15. Interviews by Ben Kiernan, October 21, 1980, Cambodian Genocide Program, Yale University. See also Ben Kiernan, *The Pol Pot Regime: Race, Power, and Genocide in Cambodia under the Khmer Rouge, 1975–79* (New Haven: Yale University Press, 1996), 254. Serge Thion claims similarly that Hun Sen became a communist messenger in March 1967. See Serge Thion, *Watching Cambodia: Ten Paths to Enter the Cambodian Tangle* (Bangkok: White Lotus, 1993), xxiii.
16. Translated material from the Central Stasi Archives Berlin provided by Bernd Schaefer, Woodrow Wilson International Center in Washington, DC, December 2012. The dates in the Stasi biography are presumably based on what Hun Sen told the Vietnamese after his defection in 1977. According to the file, Hun Sen left school and began work at a factory of some kind in Kampong Cham in 1967, where he faced persecution due to "activities against Sihanouk." After fleeing to Memot he again "joined the struggle of the peasants" and moved north up the Mekong to Kratie, where he worked as a water seller until the fall of Sihanouk in March 1970.
17. Mehta and Mehta, *Strongman*, 93. See also Chou Meng, "A Talk with Prime Minister Hun Sen," *Cultural Survival Quarterly* 14, no. 3 (Fall 1990).
18. Mehta and Mehta, *Strongman*, 95–6. See also Barry Wain, "A Complex Pragmatist, Hun Sen Remains Enigma with Elusive Beliefs," *Wall Street Journal*, July 6, 1999.
19. In late 1998, after a resolution in the US House of Representatives condemned Hun Sen as "one of the leaders of the Cambodian genocide," historians Steve Heder and Craig

Etcheson, two leading authorities on the Khmer Rouge, wrote to Congress to say that the accusation had "no basis in fact or law." See Jeff Smith, "Rohrabacher Rebuked for Attack on Hun Sen," *Cambodia Daily*, September 30, 1998. Regarding House Resolution 553 see Tom Fawthrop, " 'Irresponsible' and 'Baseless' Anti-Hun Sen Campaign Hits US Congress," *Phnom Penh Post*, October 2–15, 1998.

20. Evan Gottesman, *Cambodia after the Khmer Rouge: Inside the Politics of Nation-Building* (New Haven: Yale University Press, 2003), 279.

21. Raoul M. Jennar, *Cambodian Chronicles*, vol. 1: *Bungling a Peace Plan, 1989–1991* (Bangkok: White Lotus, 1998), 34.

22. Amnesty International, *State of Cambodia: Arrest and Detention of Government Officials* (September 1990).

23. Charles P. Wallace, "A Humble Populist Hero Emerges in Cambodia," *Los Angeles Times*, September 18, 1990.

24. Richburg, "Hun Sen Making an Impact."

25. Valerie Strauss, "Washington Sees a New Hun Sen," *Washington Post*, March 27, 1992.

26. Jeremy J. Stone, *Every Man Should Try: The Adventures of a Public Interest Activist* (New York: Public Affairs, 1999), 287.

27. Ibid., 288.

28. Barbara Crossette, "Cambodia Chief, a Communist Survivor, Is Welcomed in U.S.," *New York Times*, March 25, 1992.

29. Strauss, "Washington Sees a New Hun Sen."

30. *Financial Times*, Special Survey, November 22, 1982. Cited in Nigel Harris, *The End of the Third World: Newly Industrialising Countries and the Decline of Ideology* (Harmondsworth: Penguin, 1987), 61.

31. Cited in an interview with Hun Sen published in the *Cambodia Daily* on January 1–4, 2002. At http://cnv.org.kh/en/?p=185 (accessed Mar. 2014).

32. "The Prince of Political Tides," *Newsweek*, November 24, 1991.

33. David W. Roberts, *Political Transition in Cambodia 1991–99: Power, Elitism, and Democracy* (New York: Palgrave, 2001), 63. For a good account of the events of November 17, see Thion, *Watching Cambodia*, 188–92.

34. Author interview with Charles Twining, December 21, 2012.

35. Yeong, "Cambodia 1991," 117.

36. Margaret Slocomb, *The People's Republic of Kampuchea, 1979–1989: The Revolution after Pol Pot* (Chiang Mai: Silkworm, 2003), 268.

37. Gottesman, *Cambodia after the Khmer Rouge*, 318–19.

38. Grant Curtis, *Cambodia Reborn? The Transition to Democracy and Development* (Washington, DC: Brookings Institution Press, 1998), 71.

39. Stan Sesser, *The Lands of Charm and Cruelty* (New York: Knopf, 1993), 128.

40. David E. Sanger, "Corrupt Officials in Cambodia Put the Country Up for Sale," *New York Times*, December 27, 1991.

41. Among the victims was Tea Bun Long, a 59-year-old SOC official who was abducted from outside his home and killed on January 22. Prior to his killing, Bun Long had reportedly spoken out about corruption in the CPP's ranks. See Amnesty International, *State of Cambodia: Human Rights Developments: 1 October 1991 to 31 January 1992* (March 1992).

42. Caroline Hughes, *Dependent Communities: Aid and Politics in Cambodia and East Timor* (Ithaca, NY: Cornell Southeast Asia Program, 2009), 92.

43. Henry Kamm, *Cambodia: Report from a Stricken Land* (New York: Arcade, 1998), 212.

44. Ibid., 221.

45. The riel was worth 380 to the US dollar in December 1991; within a year it was trading at 2,400 to the dollar. See Gary Klintworth, "Cambodia 1992: Hopes Fading," in *Southeast Asian Affairs 1993* (Singapore: Institute of Southeast Asian Studies, 1993), 121.

46. Bridget Byrne, Rachel Marcus, and Tanya Powers-Stevens, *Gender, Conflict and Development* (Brighton: Institute of Development Studies, 1995), 12.

47. "Profile: Bureaucrat at Large in the Balkans," *Independent*, April 30, 1994.

48. Yasushi Akashi, "An Assessment of the United Nations Transitional Authority in Cambodia (UNTAC)," in Pou Sothirak, Geoff Wade, and Mark Hong, eds, *Cambodia: Progress and Challenges since 1991* (Singapore: Institute of Southeast Asian Studies, 2012), 157–8.

49. Cited in MacAlister Brown and Joseph J. Zasloff, *Cambodia Confounds the Peacemakers, 1979–1998* (Ithaca: Cornell University Press, 1998), 141–3. See also Nate Thayer, "Shakeup in KR Hierarchy" *Phnom Penh Post*, January 28–February 10, 1994.

50. Klintworth, "Cambodia 1992," 120.

51. Ibid., 119.

52. For a detailed description of the incident, see Widyono, *Dancing in Shadows*, 77.

53. Nayan Chanda, " 'Isolate Khmer Rouge,' " *Far Eastern Economic Review*, July 30, 1992.

54. William Shawcross, *Deliver Us from Evil: Peacekeepers and Warlords in a World of Endless Conflict* (London: Bloomsbury, 2001), 58.

55. Widyono, *Dancing in Shadows*, 63.

56. Ibid., 78.

57. Foreign Broadcast Information Service, *Daily Report, East Asia*, April 6, 1993.

58. Kevin Barrington, "KR Open Bloody Anti-Poll Campaign," *Phnom Penh Post*, May 7–20, 1993.

59. Judy Ledgerwood, "Patterns of CPP Repression and Violence during the UNTAC Period," in Steve Heder and Judy Ledgerwood, eds, *Propaganda, Politics and Violence in Cambodia: Democratic Transition under United Nations Peace-Keeping* (Armonk: M. E. Sharpe, 1996), 118.

60. Ibid., 122.

61. Kate Frieson, "The Politics of Getting the Vote in Cambodia," in Heder and Ledgerwood, eds, *Propaganda, Politics and Violence in Cambodia*, 195.

62. Ibid., 196. See also Human Rights Watch, *"Tell Them That I Want to Kill Them": Two Decades of Impunity in Hun Sen's Cambodia* (New York, November 2012), 13–22.

63. Author interview with Benny Widyono, July 2008.

64. Michael Hayes, "Ranariddh Kicks off Campaign," *Phnom Penh Post*, April 23–May 6, 1993. See also Ker Munthit, "Ranariddh Grounded," *Phnom Penh Post*, May 7–20, 1993.

65. Nayan Chanda, "Blood Brothers," *Far Eastern Economic Review*, December 3, 1992.

66. Jay Jordens, "Persecution of Cambodia's Ethnic Vietnamese Communities during and since the UNTAC Period," in Heder and Ledgerwood, eds, *Propaganda, Politics and Violence in Cambodia*, 138.

67. Kevin Barrington, "Massacre Condemned But . . ." *Phnom Penh Post*, March 26–April 8, 1993.

68. "Hun Sen 'Reluctant to Intervene' for Vietnamese," *Bangkok Post*, April 5, 1993.

69. Jordens, "Persecution of Cambodia's Ethnic Vietnamese Communities," 139.

70. Caroline Hughes, *UNTAC in Cambodia: The Impact on Human Rights* (Singapore: Institute of Southeast Asian Studies, 1996), 69.

71. David Rieff, *A Bed for the Night: Humanitarianism in Crisis* (London: Vintage, 2002), 156.

72. Widyono, *Dancing in Shadows*, 120.

73. "Voters Mob Polling Stations," *Phnom Penh Post*, June 6–17, 1993.

74. Ker Munthit, "Akashi: Election 'Free and Fair,' " *Phnom Penh Post*, June 6–17, 1993.

75. This is the view of Michael Vickery, who points to a meeting between Sihanouk and his son Chakrapong on June 9, the day before the "secession" was announced. See Michael Vickery, *Cambodia: A Political Survey* (Phnom Penh: Funan, 2007), 92.

76. The Paris Agreements stated that a new government not be formed until after the drafting and promulgation of a constitution by the newly elected constituent assembly.

77. Nate Thayer, "Sihanouk Back at the Helm," *Phnom Penh Post*, June 18–July 1, 1993.

78. Author interview with Timothy Carney, July 21, 2012.

79. Chris Burslem, "UNHCR Ultimatum on Thefts," *Phnom Penh Post*, September 24–October 7, 1993.

80. Widyono, *Dancing in Shadows*, 130.
81. Mark Dodd, "King Warns Graft May Empower KR," *Phnom Penh Post*, May 20–June 6, 1994.
82. See, for instance, Henry Porter, "Days of Shame," *Guardian*, November 17, 1999.
83. Shawcross, *Deliver Us from Evil*, 98.

4 A False Dawn

1. "Developments in Cambodia: Hearing before the Subcommittee on Asia and Pacific Affairs of the Committee on Foreign Affairs, House of Representatives," October 27, 1993. At http://www.archive.org/stream/developmentsinca00unit/developmentsin-ca00unit_djvu.txt (accessed Mar. 2014).
2. "Aust Diplomat's Cambodia Analysis," *Phnom Penh Post*, November 4–17, 1994.
3. Henry Kamm, *Cambodia: Report from a Stricken Land* (New York: Arcade, 1998), 233.
4. Nayan Chanda and Nate Thayer, "Things Fall Apart," *Far Eastern Economic Review*, May 19, 1994.
5. "Aust Diplomat's Cambodia Analysis."
6. Human Rights Watch, *"Tell Them That I Want to Kill Them": Two Decades of Impunity in Hun Sen's Cambodia* (New York, November 2012), 27. See also Nate Thayer, "Army's Dossier of Shame," *Phnom Penh Post*, August 12–25, 1994.
7. MacAlister Brown and Joseph J. Zasloff, *Cambodia Confounds the Peacemakers, 1979–1998* (Ithaca: Cornell University Press, 1998), 258.
8. Norodom Sihanouk, *Shadows over Angkor: Memoirs of His Majesty King Norodom Sihanouk of Cambodia*, trans. Julio A. Jeldres (Phnom Penh: Monument Books, 2005), 61.
9. Norodom Sihanouk, "Forging Cambodian Nationhood," *Far Eastern Economic Review*, January 13, 1994.
10. Nate Thayer, "King Talks of Taking Power," *Phnom Penh Post*, June 17–30, 1994. See also Nate Thayer, "Last Act: Sihanouk's Plan to Retake the Reins of Power," *Far Eastern Economic Review*, June 23, 1994.
11. "Premier Hun Sen Replies to the King," *Phnom Penh Post*, July 1–14, 1994.
12. John Ogden, "King Washes His Hands of Politics," *Phnom Penh Post*, July 1–14, 1994.
13. Nate Thayer, "Standing Up to Father," *Far Eastern Economic Review*, June 30, 1994.
14. Harish C. Mehta, "Cambodia: A Year of Consolidation," in *Southeast Asian Affairs 1996* (Singapore: Institute of Southeast Asian Studies, 1996), 118.
15. Barton Biggs, "Slain Editor Pressured by Gov't, Letters Show," *Cambodia Daily*, September 9–11, 1994.
16. "Cambodia: Sam the Whipper," *Time*, July 21, 1958.
17. Regarding Sary's disappearance, see David P. Chandler, *The Tragedy of Cambodian History: Politics, War, and Revolution since 1945* (Chiang Mai: Silkworm, 1994), 99–101. Rainsy believes his father was shot in the southern Lao province of Pakse in late 1962 or early 1963, on the orders of Son Ngoc Thanh. His account is given in Sam Rainsy, *We Didn't Start the Fire: My Struggle for Democracy in Cambodia* (Chiang Mai: Silkworm, 2013), 11–22.
18. Rainsy, *We Didn't Start the Fire*, 27–8.
19. Benny Widyono, *Dancing in Shadows: Sihanouk, the Khmer Rouge, and the United Nations in Cambodia* (Lanham: Rowman & Littlefield, 2008), 204.
20. Cited in Brown and Zasloff, *Cambodia Confounds the Peacemakers*, 226.
21. Jason Barber and Christine Chaumeau, "Teng Boonma: The Man with the Money," *Phnom Penh Post*, May 17–30, 1996.
22. Ker Munthit, "Boon Ma Fires Off Complaint to RAC," *Phnom Penh Post*, April 18–May 1, 1997.
23. For a detailed profile of Teng Bunma, including the allegations of drug trafficking, see Nate Thayer, "Medellin on the Mekong," *Far Eastern Economic Review*, November 23, 1995.
24. "Statement by Parliamentary Vice-Minister for Foreign Affairs Koji Kakizawa at the Ministerial Conference on Rehabilitation and Reconstruction of Cambodia, Tokyo,

June 22, 1992." At http://www.mofa.go.jp/policy/other/bluebook/1992/1992-appendix-2. htm (accessed Mar. 2014).

25. Joel Brinkley, *Cambodia's Curse: The Modern History of a Troubled Land* (New York: Public Affairs, 2011), 89.

26. Author interview with Charles Twining, December 21, 2012.

27. "PM's 'Vital Issues' Report: Full Text," *Phnom Penh Post*, August 25–September 7, 1995.

28. For details of the attack on *Sereipheap Thmei*, see Jason Barber and Ker Munthit, "The Hun Sen Town of Kraingyov," *Phnom Penh Post*, November 3–16, 1995. Hun Sen's reaction to the incident is cited in Amnesty International, *Cambodia: Diminishing Respect for Human Rights* (London, May 28, 1996), 46–47.

29. "Drawing the Lines of 'Acceptable' Democracy," *Phnom Penh Post*, November 3–16, 1995.

30. Human Rights Watch, *"Tell Them That I Want to Kill Them"*, 32.

31. Author interview with Son Soubert, July 3, 2012.

32. Brown and Zasloff, *Cambodia Confounds the Peacemakers*, 243.

33. Amnesty International, *Kingdom of Cambodia: Killing of Thun Bun Ly* (May 20, 1996).

34. Foreign Broadcast Information Service, *Daily Report, East Asia*, December 4, 1995.

35. Elisabeth Pisani, "Hun Sen Wants Political Strings Cut from Donor Aid Packages," *Asia Times*, March 4, 1996.

36. Steve Heder, "Political Theatre in the 2003 Cambodian Elections," in Julia C. Strauss and Donal Cruise O'Brien, eds, *Staging Politics: Power and Performance in Asia and Africa* (London: I. B. Tauris, 2007), 161.

37. Ker Munthit, "Ranariddh Defends His Actions," *Phnom Penh Post*, December 1–14, 1995.

38. "Further Evidence of Hun Sen's Mental State," diplomatic cable from US Embassy Phnom Penh (95PHNOMPENH3751), November 14, 1995.

39. For details on the Tiger's Lair compound, see Michael Hayes, "All Eyes on PMs' Bodyguard Units," *Phnom Penh Post*, May 2–15, 1997. The salary of Hun Sen's bodyguards is cited in Widyono, *Dancing in Shadows*, 217.

40. Hayes, "All Eyes on PMs' Bodyguard Units."

41. Of the 24 CPP members in the new government, 11 were widely considered Hun Sen allies, with just two belonging squarely in the Chea Sim group. Ten more were without known affiliations, but due to their "relative youth or intellectual background" could be presumed to be closer to Hun Sen than Chea Sim. See Michael Vickery, *Cambodia: A Political Survey* (Phnom Penh: Funan, 2007), 121–2.

42. Brad Adams, "Marking the Anniversary of the Cambodian Coup Attempt," *Cambodia Daily*, July 2, 2014.

43. Khatharya Um, "Cambodia in 1994: The Year of Transition," *Asian Survey* 35, no. 1 (Jan. 1995): 76–83, at 77.

44. See "Further Evidence of Hun Sen's Mental State," diplomatic cable from US Embassy Phnom Penh (95PHNOMPENH3751), November 14, 1995.

45. Adams, "Marking the Anniversary of the Cambodian Coup Attempt." For a contemporary account of the coup attempt and its aftermath, see "How the Plot Unfolded," *Phnom Penh Post*, July 15–28, 1994. For more on the factional nature of the event, see Nate Thayer, " 'Coup' Plot Thickens," *Phnom Penh Post*, July 15–28, 1994. In a 2002 interview with the *Cambodia Daily*, Hun Sen put the plot down to "a person in the CPP." Interview available at http://cnv.org.kh/en/?p=185 (accessed Mar. 2014).

46. Widyono, *Dancing in Shadows*, 213–14.

47. Jason Barber and Ker Munthit, "CPP Draws Line in the Sand" *Phnom Penh Post*, April 5–18, 1996.

48. "Hun Sen: 'Live and Die with the People,' " *Phnom Penh Post*, May 3–16, 1997.

49. Ibid.

50. Widyono, *Dancing in Shadows*, 231.

51. Foreign Broadcast Information Service, *Daily Report, East Asia*, August 7, 1996.

52. A good account of Hun Sen's visit to Pailin is given in Widyono, *Dancing in Shadows*, 233–6.

53. Ker Munthit, "Smiles All Round as One-Time Foes Join Hands in NUF," *Phnom Penh Post*, March 7–20, 1997.

54. " 'This Time We Will Fight,' " *Asiaweek*, March 23, 1997.

55. Jason Barber and Christine Chaumeau, "Slaughter on Sunday—March 30, 1997," *Phnom Penh Post*, April 4–17, 1997.

56. Ibid.

57. See, for instance, Amnesty International, "Kingdom of Cambodia: Grenade Attack on a Peaceful Demonstration," press release, March 31, 1997. For a full account of the attack and its aftermath, see Rich Garella and Eric Pape, "A Tragedy of No Importance," *Mother Jones*, April 2005. A longer version of the article is available online at http://www.cambodiagrenade.info/ (accessed Mar. 2014).

58. Ibid. See note at http://www.cambodiagrenade.info/main/note0700e.html (accessed Mar. 2014).

59. Douglas Gillison, "FBI Found Partner Lacking in 1997 Investigation," *Cambodia Daily*, December 10, 2009.

60. Douglas Gillison, "Documents Chart Thwarting of '97 Investigation," *Cambodia Daily*, December 9, 2009.

61. Ibid.

62. "FBI's Report on Rainsy Rally Bombing," *Phnom Penh Post*, October 15–28, 1999.

63. Douglas Gillison, "FBI Weakened Grenade Report to Congress," *Cambodia Daily*, January 11, 2011.

64. Douglas Gillison, "'97 Attack Case Shelved after 8 Long Years," *Cambodia Daily*, January 10, 2011.

65. Nick Lenaghan and Claudia Rizzi, "Weapons Seizure Ignites Party Sniping," *Phnom Penh Post*, May 30–June 12, 1997.

66. "Son Sen and Yun Yat: Living by the Sword," *Phnom Penh Post*, June 27–July 10, 1997.

67. For a detailed description of Pol Pot's trial, see Nate Thayer, "Brother Number Zero," *Far Eastern Economic Review*, August 7, 1997; Nate Thayer, "Brother Enemy No. 1," *Phnom Penh Post*, August 15–28, 1997.

68. Thayer, "Brother Number Zero."

69. Author interview with Gordon Longmuir, August 27, 2012.

70. Brad Adams, "Brigade 911 Had Brutal History before Garment Factory Strike," *Cambodia Daily*, January 9, 2014.

71. United Nations Centre for Human Rights, *Evidence of Summary Executions, Torture and Missing Persons since July 2–7, 1997* (August 21, 1997), 2. See also Jason Barber and Claudia Rizzi, "Funcinpec Military Chiefs Hunted Down," *Phnom Penh Post*, July 12–24, 1997.

72. United Nations Centre for Human Rights, *Evidence of Summary Executions*, 24.

73. Ministry of Foreign Affairs and International Cooperation, "White Paper: Background on the July 1997 Crisis," July 9, 1997.

74. Seth Mydans, "Hun Sen Says He's Enjoying Being Cambodia's Sole Ruler," *New York Times*, July 11, 1997.

75. Jason Barber, "Democracy from the Barrel of a Gun," *Phnom Penh Post*, July 12–24, 1997.

76. Keith B. Richburg and R. Jeffrey Smith, "Cambodia: U.N. Success Story Fouled," *Washington Post*, July 13, 1997.

77. Seth Mydans, "Cambodia: Quandary for Diplomats," *New York Times*, July 12, 1997.

78. The phrase is taken from William Branigin and R. Jeffrey Smith, "Saddam Hun Sen? Fear and Loathing after the Coup in Cambodia," *Washington Post*, July 20, 1997.

79. Elizabeth Moorthy, "Ambassador under Fire from DC . . ." *Phnom Penh Post*, August 29–September 11, 1997.

80. "Hun Sen Is Becoming Cambodia's New Pol Pot," statement by Dana Rohrabacher in the US House of Representatives, Friday, September 11, 1998.

81. Tina Rosenberg, "Hun Sen Stages an Election," *New York Times*, August 30, 1998.

82. Associated Press, August 11, 1997. Cited in Brown and Zasloff, *Cambodia Confounds the Peacemakers*, 265.

83. Brinkley, *Cambodia's Curse*, 140.

84. Cited in Seth Mydans, "Cambodia's Coup Leader Puts on a Democratic Face," *New York Times*, July 14, 1997.

85. Philip Gourevitch, "Pol Pot's Children," *The New Yorker*, August 10, 1998.

86. The 11-member NEC was theoretically neutral. In practice, however, the CPP came to dominate the election committees at the provincial level. See "Provincial Commissions Show Huge Party Bias," *Phnom Penh Post*, April 10–23, 1998. For more on the history of the NEC, see "Cambodia: Systematic Problems Undermine Elections," statement from Human Rights Watch, July 26, 2013.

87. Human Rights Watch, *Cambodia: Fair Elections Not Possible* (New York, June 1998).

88. The elderly Son Sann retired from active politics in January 1997 and died in Paris in December 2000, at the age of 89.

89. Solarz's comment was widely disseminated in the media, though some claim he was quoted out of context. See Ron Abney, "Groupie-Like Gushing," *Phnom Penh Post*, August 29–September 11, 2003; Stephen Solarz, "Cambodia: A Reasonably Fair Election," *Washington Post*, September 4, 1998.

90. Bou Saroeun and James Eckardt, "CPP Demos: The Empire Strikes Back," *Phnom Penh Post*, September 18–October 1, 1998.

91. Harish C. Mehta and Julie B. Mehta, *Strongman: The Extraordinary Life of Hun Sen* (Singapore: Marshall Cavendish, 2013), 318–19.

92. In 1999 two SRP members were arrested for the crime and then released for lack of evidence. See Saing Soenthrith, "Activists Accused in Rocket Attack Released from Prison," *Cambodia Daily*, March 7, 2000. In 2008 Hun Sen again accused the SRP of involvement in the attack. See Yun Samean, "PM Orders Probe into SRP Plot Charges," *Cambodia Daily*, June 16, 2008.

93. Michael Hayes, "Another Chapter Opens as Hun Sen Gives Prince Ranariddh the Deal," *Phnom Penh Post*, November 27–December 10, 1998.

94. Nate Thayer, "Day of Reckoning," *Far Eastern Economic Review*, October 30, 1997.

95. Seth Mydans, "At Cremation of Pol Pot, No Tears Shed," *New York Times*, April 19, 1998.

96. Ta Mok's comments are cited in David P. Chandler, *Brother Number One: A Political Biography of Pol Pot* (Boulder: Westview, 1999), 186.

5 Potemkin Democracy

1. Statistics are taken from United Nations Development Programme, *Human Development Report 2000* (New York: UNDP, 2000).

2. Samreth Sopha and Eric Pape, "Budget '98: 43% for Army and Police," *Phnom Penh Post*, December 5–18, 1997.

3. Michael Hayes, "Another Chapter Opens as Hun Sen Gives Prince Ranariddh the Deal," *Phnom Penh Post*, November 27–December 10, 1998.

4. Human Rights Watch, *Landmine Monitor Report 2000* (New York, August 2000), 387. For landmine casualty figures for 1998 and 1999, see ibid., 26.

5. Stuart Hughes, "Cambodia's Landmine Victims," *BBC News*, November 11, 2003.

6. Regarding the *L'Express* allegations, see "Extracts From Piseth Pelika's Diary," *Phnom Penh Post*, October 15–28, 1999; Annette Marcher, "Bun Rany Fails to Act on Pelika Diary," *Phnom Penh Post*, October 27–November 9, 2000.

7. Jeff Smith and Kay Kimsong, "Acid-Laced Vengeance," *Cambodia Daily*, February 5–6, 2000.

8. Men Kimseng, "Official Blames Wife in 1999 Acid Attack," Voice of America, August 24, 2009.

9. Michael Vickery, *Cambodia: 1975–1982* (Chiang Mai: Silkworm, 1999), 7. See also Alex Hinton, *Why Did They Kill?: Cambodia in the Shadow of Genocide* (Berkeley: University of California Press, 2005).

10. Lee Kuan Yew, *From Third World to First: the Singapore Story: 1965–2000* (New York: HarperCollins, 2000), 328. Slocomb's comments are cited in Richard Wood, "Cambodia's Rulers 'Like Gods in Valhalla,'" *Phnom Penh Post*, July 16–29, 2004.

11. Lee, *From Third World to First*, 328.

12. "Opening Speech to the Cambodia Consultative Group Meeting, Tokyo, Japan, 25–26 February 1999," *Cambodia New Vision*, February 1999.

13. For overviews of the CMAC corruption scandal, see Joe Cochrane, "Clearing a Minefield of Graft," *South China Morning Post*, May 23, 1999; Dominic Faulder, "An International Minefield," *Asiaweek*, September 17, 1999.

14. Phelim Kyne, "Sam Sotha Bounces Back from Disgrace," *Phnom Penh Post*, September 17–30, 1999.

15. Patrick Falby, "Fraud Found in Demobilization Process," *Phnom Penh Post*, October 25–November 7, 2002.

16. Yun Samean, "Gov't Parries World Bank's Graft Charge," *Cambodia Daily*, January 17, 2005.

17. Brian Calvert and Seth Meixner, "Donors Offer a Healthy $635 Million in Aid," *Cambodia Daily*, June 22, 2002.

18. Details on the statue and its symbolism are given in Caroline Hughes, *The Political Economy of Cambodia's Transition, 1991–2001* (New York: RoutledgeCurzon, 2003), 182.

19. Human Rights Watch, *"Tell Them That I Want to Kill Them": Two Decades of Impunity in Hun Sen's Cambodia* (New York, November 2012), 40.

20. Ibid., 43.

21. Steve Heder, "Cambodia in 2010: Hun Sen's Further Consolidation," *Asian Survey* 51, no. 1 (Jan.–Feb. 2011): 208–14, at 208–9.

22. Sorpong Peou, "Hun Sen's Pre-emptive Coup: Causes and Consequences," in *Southeast Asian Affairs 1998* (Singapore: Institute of Southeast Asian Studies, 1998), 98–9.

23. "Inside Funcinpec: Cracks Apparent," *Phnom Penh Post*, April 30–May 13, 1999.

24. Andrew Wells-Dang, "Republican Group Meddles in Cambodia," *Asia Times Online*, April 16, 2004. One party leader would later admit that IRI "are outspoken in their support for SRP." See Derek Cheng, " 'Tenuous Democracy' Blamed for IRI Pullout," *Phnom Penh Post*, February 25–March 10, 2005.

25. Tom Fawthrop, "The Axis of the Republican Right," *Irrawaddy*, August 2003.

26. Stew Magnuson and Kay Kimsong, "On Campaign Trail, Sam Rainsy Pledges to Oust Vietnamese," *Cambodia Daily*, July 21, 1998.

27. Cited in David W. Roberts, *Political Transition in Cambodia 1991–99: Power, Elitism, and Democracy* (New York: Palgrave, 2001), 194.

28. James Eckardt and Chea Sotheacheath, "Diary of a Demonstration," *Phnom Penh Post*, September 4–17, 1998.

29. Kay Kimsong and Debra Boyce, "Angry Mobs Kill at Least 4 Vietnamese," *Cambodia Daily*, September 5, 1998.

30. The food poisoning story was reported by *Samleng Samapheap* (September 3–4, 1998) and *Neak Prayuth* (September 4–5). See Caroline Hughes, "Transforming Oppositions in Cambodia," *Global Society* 15, no. 3 (2001): 295–318, at 311, n45. For the "plot" against Sihanouk's aircraft, see "Diplomats Aghast at Paper's Yarn," *Phnom Penh Post*, September 1–14, 2000.

31. Human Rights Watch, *Cambodia's Commune Elections: Setting the Stage for the 2003 National Elections* (New York, April 2002).

32. Seth Mydans, "Cambodian Leader Rules As If from the Throne," *New York Times*, March 19, 2002.

33. Karen Emmons, "Chess Player, Philosopher, a Leader of the Country: A Sunday Spent with Hun Sen," *Phnom Penh Post*, December 1–14, 1995.

34. Eric C. Bjornlund, *Beyond Free and Fair: Monitoring Elections and Building Democracy* (Washington, DC: Woodrow Wilson Center Press, 2004), 190.

35. Sam Rainsy, "A Call for International Standards in Cambodia," address to National Press Club, Washington, DC, April 10, 2002.

36. Mydans, "Cambodian Leader Rules As If from the Throne."

37. Vong Sokheng, "Funcinpec Plans Pre-Election Shuffle," *Phnom Penh Post*, May 11–24, 2001.

38. Steve Heder, "Hun Sen's Consolidation: Death or Beginning of Reform?" in *Southeast Asian Affairs 2005* (Singapore: Institute of Southeast Asian Studies, 2005), 117–18.

39. "Murder of a Man with No Enemies," *Phnom Penh Post*, February 28–March 13, 2003. See also Human Rights Watch, *"Tell Them That I Want to Kill Them"*, 50–2.

40. "The Run-up to Cambodia's 2003 National Assembly Election," Human Rights Watch briefing paper, June 2003.

41. Saing Soenthrith and Porter Barron, "2 Men Given 20 Years for Om Radsady Killing," *Cambodia Daily*, October 28, 2004.

42. David Shaftel, "Observer Groups: 31 People Killed in Pre-Election Period," *Cambodia Daily*, July 26, 2003.

43. See Luke Reynolds and Yun Samean, "Ranariddh, Hun Sen Sign Coalition Deal," *Cambodia Daily*, July 1, 2004; "Ministry Names 146 Undersecretaries of State," *Cambodia Daily*, July 21, 2004.

44. "Prince Gets Helicopter," *Cambodia Daily*, July 1, 2004; Yun Samean, "Gov't Returns Plane Once Owned by Ranariddh," *Cambodia Daily*, July 12, 2004.

45. Wency Leung, "Back to Square One," *Cambodia Daily*, July 24–25, 2004.

46. Saing Soenthrith and Yun Samean, "Chea Sim Leaves, Creating Political Crisis," *Cambodia Daily*, July 14, 2004; Luke Hunt and Michael Hayes, "New Government Formed after Chea Sim Leaves the Country," *Phnom Penh Post*, July 16–29, 2004.

47. "King: Future Kings Will Only Be Puppets," *Cambodia Daily*, July 19, 2004.

48. Luke Reynolds, "Flex of Muscle May Signal Split within CPP," *Cambodia Daily*, July 14, 2004.

49. Yun Samean, "Deadlock Is Over: Govt Is Formed," *Cambodia Daily*, July 16, 2004.

50. Liam Cochrane, "Sihamoni Crowned New King," *Phnom Penh Post*, November 4–18, 2004.

51. Editorial in *Pracheachon*, May 24, 1992. Cited in K. Viviane Frings, "The Cambodian People's Party and Sihanouk," *Journal of Contemporary Asia* 25, no. 3 (1995): 356–65, at 359–60.

52. The city also has roads named after Nehru, Tito, Kim Il-sung, and Georgi Dimitrov, the first communist leader of Bulgaria.

53. Julio A. Jeldres, "King Sihanouk and the Future of Cambodia," *Australia and World Affairs*, no. 32 (Autumn 1997): 17–25, at 24.

54. "King Warns of Keen Balance between Success and Failure," *Phnom Penh Post*, May 31–June 13, 1996.

55. Seth Mydans, "The Royal Alter Ego Wields a Poison Pen in Cambodia," *New York Times*, June 29, 2003.

56. Patrick Falby, "Money Can't Buy You a King's Respect, but It's a Sure Path to Royal Honors," *Phnom Penh Post*, April 11–24, 2003.

57. Mydans, "The Royal Alter Ego Wields a Poison Pen in Cambodia."

58. Yun Samean, "PM Criticizes New Idea for King Selection," *Cambodia Daily*, August 19, 2002.

59. Mydans, "Cambodian Leader Rules As If from the Throne."

60. Milton Osborne, "Cambodia: Hun Sen Firmly in Control," in *Southeast Asian Affairs 2003* (Singapore: Institute of Southeast Asian Studies, 2003), 87.

61. According to Sihanouk's biographer Julio Jeldres, French Ambassador Gildas Le Lidec helped convince Hun Sen not to abolish the monarchy in 1997, saying it would be vital for ensuring peace and stability. See Julio A. Jeldres, "Cambodia's Relations with France since the Paris Agreements of 1991," in Pou Sothirak, Geoff Wade, and Mark Hong, eds, *Cambodia: Progress and Challenges since 1991* (Singapore: Institute of Southeast Asian Studies, 2012), 145.

62. "Cambodia's Man Who Won't Be King—Ranariddh's Snit Fit," diplomatic cable from US Embassy Phnom Penh (04PHNOMPENH1701), October 29, 2004.

63. The account of the crackdown on the SRP is based on that given in Heder, "Hun Sen's Consolidation," 121–2.

64. "Military Court Tries Cambodia MP," *BBC News*, August 8, 2005.

65. Vong Sokheng and Charles McDermid, "Rainsy Thunders against 'Fascist' State," *Phnom Penh Post*, December 31, 2005–January 12, 2006.
66. Samantha Melamed and Pin Sisovann, "Cambodian Arrests in International Media Spotlight," *Cambodia Daily*, January 17, 2006.
67. Author's email correspondence with Joseph Mussomeli, February 24, 2013. See also Seth Mydans, "In Cambodia, a Harsh Crackdown," *New York Times*, January 8, 2006.
68. Joel Brinkley, *Cambodia's Curse: The Modern History of a Troubled Land* (New York: Public Affairs, 2011), 149.
69. Charles McDermid, "Brave New Political World Unfolds," *Phnom Penh Post*, February 24–March 9, 2006.
70. Sophal Ear, *Aid Dependence in Cambodia: How Foreign Assistance Undermines Democracy* (New York: Columbia University Press, 2013), 131.

6 The Peasant King

1. The new appointees to the Politburo were Chea Chanto, Cheam Yeap, Chhay Than, Ek Sam Ol, Khuon Sudary, Ouk Rabun, Pen Panha, and Som Kimsuor. See "CPP Adds Eight to Top Echelon," *Phnom Penh Post*, February 11–24, 2005. For the expansion of the Central Committee, see Vong Sokheng, "Governing Parties Cement their Reign," *Phnom Penh Post*, December 2–15, 2005.
2. Cited in Craig Guthrie, "Towards Hun Sen's Cambodia," *Asia Times Online*, July 23, 2008.
3. Luke Reynolds, "CPP Uses Council of Ministers to Wield Power," *Cambodia Daily*, March 5, 2004.
4. Vong Sokheng and Charles McDermid, " 'Prepare Your Coffin,' PM Tells Royalists," *Phnom Penh Post*, September 21–October 5, 2006.
5. Vong Sokheng and Charles McDermid, "Troubled Funcinpec on the Ropes," *Phnom Penh Post*, March 24–April 6, 2006.
6. Cat Barton and Vong Sokheng, "Ranariddh Quits Politics," *Phnom Penh Post*, October 3, 2008.
7. Lor Chandara and Richard Sine, "Hun Sen Credits Cambodians for 1991 Peace," *Cambodia Daily*, October 23, 2001.
8. "Samdech Techo Hun Sen: On the Issue of Responsibility As a Leader and Compassion As a Human Being with a Golden Heart," Council of Ministers Press and Quick Reaction Unit, October 8, 2012.
9. These are the latest statistics available from Hun Sen's cabinet. See http://cnv.org.kh/en/?page_id=125 (accessed Mar. 2014).
10. "A School in Mali Named after PM Hun Sen," Agence Kampuchea Presse, March 21, 2013.
11. The rules for gaining *oknha* status are laid down in a 1993 subdecree. See Kheang Un, "Patronage Politics and Hybrid Democracy: Political Change in Cambodia, 1993–2003," *Asian Perspective* 29, no. 2 (2005): 203–30, at 225.
12. Regarding the historical role of the *oknha*, see David P. Chandler, *A History of Cambodia* (Boulder: Westview, 2008), 130–6.
13. Chea Sotheacheath, "From Strongman to Songman: Hun Sen Pens the Blues," *Phnom Penh Post*, January 30–February 12, 1998; Seth Mydans, "When He Writes a Song, Cambodia Better Listen," *New York Times*, July 15, 1998. For more on Hun Sen's musical "career," see "Hun Sen Shares His Music in Effort to Preserve Tradition," *Cambodia Daily*, January 10, 2000.
14. Julia Wallace, "Cambodian Strongman and Karaoke King," *New York Times*, January 18, 2013.
15. Adhémard Leclère, *Histoire du Cambodge* (Paris: Paul Geuthner, 1914), 238–78; translated and cited by Astrid Norén-Nilsson, "Performance as (Re)Incarnation: The Sdech Kân Narrative," *Journal of Southeast Asian Studies* (Feb. 2013): 4–23, at 11–12.
16. Harish C. Mehta and Julie B. Mehta, *Strongman: The Extraordinary Life of Hun Sen* (Singapore: Marshall Cavendish, 2013), 64.

17. "Selected Comments at the Visit to the Former Palace of Sanlob Prey Nokor in the District of Ponnhea Krek, Kampong Cham Province," *Cambodia New Vision*, February 26, 2006.

18. Ros Chantraboth, *Preah Sdech Kân* (Phnom Penh: Bânnakear Angkor, 2007); translated and cited in Norén-Nilsson, "Performance as (Re)Incarnation," 19.

19. See, for instance, "Selected Comments at the Inauguration of the Bayon TV and Radio Station," *Cambodia New Vision*, March 11, 2007.

20. According to Norén-Nilsson, the first statue of Sdech Kan was created in 2006. Others have since appeared across the country, including a mounted statue of Kan in Kampong Cham commissioned by a tycoon, Oknha Sim Vanna, on Hun Sen's orders. Sculptors have also been commissioned to create two statues of General Ta Di, one of Kan's military commanders, in the guise of Hing Bun Heang, the chief of Hun Sen's bodyguard unit. See Norén-Nilsson, "Performance as (Re)Incarnation," 21.

21. Ibid., 13.

22. See Leang Delux, "History: Hun Sen Finances a Book about Sdech Korn," *Cambodge Soir*, March 29, 2007. The book was authored by Ros Chantraboth of the Royal Academy of Cambodia (RAC), an institution that might be described as the "academic arm" of the CPP, under the control of Sok An and the Council of Ministers. For information on the reissue of the *sloeung* coin, see http://www.nbc.org.kh/english/nbc_gallery/more_info.php?id=4 (accessed Mar. 2014).

23. One such event took place on February 25, 2010, performed by "the artists of the Department of Guards of Samdech Techo Hun Sen." See http://www.sangsalapak.org.kh/2010/02/23/festival.html (accessed Mar. 2014).

24. The Peace Palace was inaugurated in October 2010. Its name in Khmer, *vimean santepheap*, translates literally as "Peace Monument."

25. Sam Rith, "PM Defends Divisive Celebration," *Phnom Penh Post*, January 7, 2009.

26. For a perceptive discussion of Cambodian political culture, see Trude Jacobsen and Martin Stuart-Fox, "Power and Political Culture in Cambodia," Working Paper Series No. 200, Asia Research Institute, National University of Singapore, May 2013.

27. Sebastian Strangio and Vong Sokheng, "Poll Start Sees Vote Buy Claims," *Phnom Penh Post*, May 1, 2009.

28. Kate Bartlett, "King Father Communicated through His Website until the Very End," *Cambodia Daily*, October 16, 2012.

29. Neou Vannarin, "Heng Samrin Defends Rights Record," *Cambodia Daily*, January 8, 2013.

30. Neou Vannarin, "Hun Sen Cites 'Miracle' for His Role in Royal Cremation," *Cambodia Daily*, February 15, 2013; Meas Sokchea, " 'Miracle' Cremation: PM Hun Sen," *Phnom Penh Post*, February 15, 2013.

31. Denis Gray, "Cambodia's 'Puppet King' Slowly Becomes a Prisoner in his Own Palace," Associated Press, May 30, 2011.

32. Denise Heywood, "The Artiste, the Ambassador, the Prince," *Phnom Penh Post*, April 21–May 4, 1995.

33. James Pringle, "The Death of Cambodia's Nimble Prince," *Asia Sentinel*, October 15, 2012.

34. Heywood, "The Artiste, the Ambassador, the Prince."

35. "Gov't Is Cool to Idea of King's Forum," *Cambodia Daily*, November 25, 2004.

36. Colin Meyn, "The Moral Authority of the Monarch," *Cambodia Daily*, October 31, 2012.

37. Author interview with Julio A. Jeldres, February 2, 2013.

38. Colin Meyn and Mech Dara, "Late King Sihanouk's Cremation Site Will Cost $5 Million," *Cambodia Daily*, December 17, 2012; Kaing Menghun and Colin Meyn, "Palace Minister Concerned over Cremation Site Financing," *Cambodia Daily*, January 16, 2013.

39. Hul Reaksmey and Alex Willemyns, "Grand Plans for $80-Billion Capital City Fit for a Techo," *Cambodia Daily*, August 9, 2013.

7 Hunsenomics and Its Discontents

1. George Styllis, "Tourism Not Affected by Deadlock," *Cambodia Daily*, January 30, 2014.
2. Vong Sokheng and Anette Marcher, "Sokimex and Government Revisit Angkor Deal," *Phnom Penh Post*, August 18–31, 2000.
3. Cheang Sokha, "Eurasie Travel to Challenge Angkor Wat Ticket Deal," *Phnom Penh Post*, May 20–June 2, 2005.
4. Kay Kimsong and Erik Wasson, "Gov't Extends Sokimex Ticket Deal at Angkor," *Cambodia Daily*, August 18, 2005.
5. Hor Kimsay, "Angkor Wat Revenue at $51 Million for Last Year," *Phnom Penh Post*, July 17, 2013.
6. "Cambodia's Top Ten Tycoons," diplomatic cable from US Embassy Phnom Penh (07PHNOMPENH1034), August 9, 2007.
7. Evan Gottesman, *Cambodia after the Khmer Rouge: Inside the Politics of Nation-Building* (New Haven: Yale University Press, 2003), 316.
8. Elisabeth Pisani, "Caltex Rises to Cambodia Petrol Challenge," *Asia Times*, May 29, 1996.
9. See http://www.sokimex.com.kh/sokimex_group/index.php?page=company-profile (accessed Mar. 2014).
10. Stephen O'Connell and Yin Soeum, "All That Glitters Seems to Be . . . Sokimex," *Phnom Penh Post*, April 28–May 11, 2000.
11. Sokimex was also granted the right to develop the old T3 prison in Phnom Penh, which has been earmarked for the development of a 15-story hotel and commercial complex. Details of the "prison swap" arrangements can be found in LICADHO, *Human Rights and Cambodia's Prisons: Prison Conditions 2002 and 2003* (Phnom Penh, October 2004), 7–8.
12. "It's a Family Affair," *Phnom Penh Post*, February 23–March 8, 2007.
13. Author interview with foreign auditor, March 2013.
14. See, for instance, Denise Hruby, "Neutrality of Red Cross in Question after Bun Rany's Speech," *Cambodia Daily*, November 2–3, 2013.
15. Neou Vannarin, "CPP's Elite Showers Red Cross with Millions," *Cambodia Daily*, May 9, 2013.
16. Neou Vannarin, "Hun Sen Says CPP Largess Will End If Election Is Lost," *Cambodia Daily*, March 6, 2013.
17. Phorn Bopha, "Hun Sen Encourages Cambodians to Emulate Chinese-Style Wealth," *Cambodia Daily*, December 30, 2012.
18. Stephane Guimbert, *Cambodia 1998–2008: An Episode of Rapid Growth* (Washington, DC: World Bank, April 2010), 7.
19. World Bank, *Where Have All the Poor Gone? Poverty Assessment 2013* (Washington, DC, November 2013), xiii.
20. According to the World Bank, "lower middle-income countries" are those with per capita annual income between $1,025 and $4,035.
21. Daniel de Carteret, "Garment Exports Rose 20 Percent Last Year," *Phnom Penh Post*, February 4, 2014.
22. Gottesman, *Cambodia after the Khmer Rouge*, 318.
23. Caroline Hughes, *Dependent Communities: Aid and Politics in Cambodia and East Timor* (Ithaca: Cornell Southeast Asia Program, 2009), 165.
24. Sophal Ear, *Aid Dependence in Cambodia: How Foreign Assistance Undermines Democracy* (New York: Columbia University Press, 2013), 136–7.
25. While Cambodia's Gini coefficient fell from 0.374 in 2007 to 0.282 in 2011, indicating lessening income inequality, the gap between the rich and the poor has increased in absolute terms. See World Bank, *Where Have All the Poor Gone?*, xvi.
26. Ibid.
27. Binxin Yu and Xinshen Diao, "Cambodia's Agricultural Strategy: Future Development Options for the Rice Sector," Policy Discussion Paper, Cambodia Development Research Institute, Phnom Penh. March 2011, 1.
28. Ibid.

29. For annual rice production figures for 1994–2008, see table at ibid., 26. For rice production and export figures for 2013, see Hul Reaksmey, "Rice Exports Rise by More Than 170,000 Tons," *Cambodia Daily*, January 3, 2014.

30. May Kunmakara, "Million-Tonne Goal Still a Challenge," *Phnom Penh Post*, September 28, 2012.

31. Yu and Diao, "Cambodia's Agricultural Strategy," 1.

32. Ibid., 11. The UN Food and Agriculture Organization estimated that in 2006, just 9 percent of the country's total cultivated area were irrigated. FAO statistics are available at   http://www.fao.org/nr/water/aquastat/countries_regions/cambodia/tables.pdf (accessed Mar. 2014).

33. One 2005 report found that medical issues were a greater cause of land sales even than crop failure. See Yagura Kenjiro, "Why Illness Causes More Serious Economic Damage Than Crop Failure in Rural Cambodia," *Development and Change* 36, no. 4 (July 2005): 759–83.

34. Ear, *Aid Dependence in Cambodia*, 34. For the 2010 figure, see United Nations Development Programme, *Cambodia Human Development Report 2013* (Phnom Penh, 2013), 158.

35. Marwaan Macan-Markar, "In Cambodia, Women Fear Death at Childbirth," *Inter Press Service*, April 1, 2011.

36. Statistics are from WHO's Global Health Observatory, at http://apps.who.int/gho/data/node.main.1?lang=en (accessed Mar. 2014).

37. Chhay Channyda, "PM Urges Better Medical Care," *Phnom Penh Post*, March 29, 2013.

38. Mech Dara and Kate Bartlett, "Desperate for a Cure, Thousands Flock to Child Healer," *Cambodia Daily*, October 30, 2013.

39. International Organization for Migration, *Counter Trafficking and Assistance to Vulnerable Migrants: Annual Report of Activities 2011* (Geneva: IOM, 2012), 17.

40. Sen David, "Illegal Migration Ticking Up," *Phnom Penh Post*, March 27, 2013.

41. "Wat Phnom Junior Highschool Renamed," *Cambodia Daily*, June 9, 2003.

42. Kuch Naren and Zsombor Peter, "Spending on Defense and Security Up 17% in 2014," *Cambodia Daily*, November 8, 2013.

43. Laignee Barron and Mom Kunthear, "School Buildings 'Failing Test,'" *Phnom Penh Post*, October 17, 2013.

44. See *Cambodia Labour Force and Child Labour Survey 2012* (Phnom Penh: National Institute of Statistics and International Labour Organization, November 2013), 27.

45. Ben Woods and Chin Chan, "Education Minister Rails against Lack of Funding," *Cambodia Daily*, January 31, 2013.

46. UNDP statistics are available at http://www.kh.undp.org/content/cambodia/en/home/countryinfo/ (accessed Jun. 2014).

47. Mong Reththy's biography is available at http://www.mongreththy.com/index.php?page=social_activities (accessed Apr. 2014).

48. "Cambodia's Top Ten Tycoons," diplomatic cable from US Embassy Phnom Penh.

49. Global Witness, *Cambodia's Family Trees: Illegal Logging and the Stripping of Public Assets by Cambodia's Elite* (London, June 2007), 85.

50. Ibid., 84.

51. Philip Heijmans and Simon Marks, "Small Signs Show Investors Slowly Diversifying in Cambodia," *Cambodia Daily*, August 11–12, 2012.

52. Interview with foreign banker, Phnom Penh, March 2013.

53. Global Witness, *Country for Sale: How Cambodia's Elite Has Captured the Country's Extractive Industries* (London, February 2009), 56–7.

54. Thet Sambath and Chun Sophal, "Anti-Graft Legislation in Sight: Govt," *Phnom Penh Post*, September 19, 2008.

55. Sebastian Strangio, "Crunch Time in Corruption Fight," *Phnom Penh Post*, April 2, 2010.

56. Regarding the allegations against Om Yentieng, see Global Witness, *Country for Sale*, 27 and 29.

57. "Cambodian PM Declares Assets in Anti-Graft Push," Agence France-Presse, April 1, 2011.

8 "A City With No Smoke and No Sound"

1. Helen Grant Ross and Darryl Collins, *Building Cambodia: 'New Khmer Architecture'*, *1953–1970* (Bangkok: Key, 2006), 28–9.
2. Borei Keila's use during the civil war was detailed during recent testimony at the Khmer Rouge tribunal. See " 'There Were So Many Wounded': Civil Party Recalls the Fall of Phnom Penh," *Cambodia Tribunal Monitor*, November 14, 2012. For its use under the Khmer Rouge, see "Civil Party Details Political Education in Phnom Penh," *Cambodia Tribunal Monitor*, August 27, 2012.
3. "For Justice and State of Law (Public Disorder at Borey Keila)," Phnom Penh Municipality statement, January 6, 2012.
4. Sahmakum Teang Tnaut, *A Tale of Two Cities: Review of the Development Paradigm in Phnom Penh* (Phnom Penh, August 2012), 15–16.
5. "Resettling Phnom Penh—54 and Counting?" Sahmakum Teang Tnaut Factsheet, January 2013, 1.
6. John Pilger, *Heroes* (Cambridge: South End Press, 2002), 390.
7. Harish C. Mehta and Julie B. Mehta, *Strongman: The Extraordinary Life of Hun Sen* (Singapore: Marshall Cavendish, 2013), 142.
8. Seth Mydans, "Stampede in Cambodia Leaves Hundreds Dead," *New York Times*, November 22, 2010.
9. "Cambodia Plans Asia's Tallest Building," Associated Press, September 2, 2010.
10. Simon Lewis and Phorn Bopha, "Phnom Penh's Wealthy Seek a Quieter Life," *Cambodia Daily*, April 16, 2013.
11. Ibid.
12. Sam Rith and Liam Cochrane, "Koh Pich: Island in a Stream of Greed," *Phnom Penh Post*, June 3–16, 2005.
13. "Selected Impromptu Comments during the Groundbreaking Ceremony to Launch the Construction of the Stoeng Meanjei Overpass," *Cambodia New Vision*, November 26, 2011.
14. Global Witness has calculated that Pheapimex holds 1,333,931 hectares in logging and economic land concessions. See Global Witness, *Cambodia's Family Trees: Illegal Logging and the Stripping of Public Assets by Cambodia's Elite* (London, June 2007), 77.
15. "Aide-memoire on Development Process of Boeung Kak Area," statement from Phnom Penh Municipality, June 19, 2012. At http://www.phnompenh.gov.kh/news-aide-memoire-on-development-process-of-boeung-kak-area-3024.html (accessed Mar. 2014).
16. "Cambodia: Release Mother Imprisoned for Housing Rights Activism," statement from Amnesty International, June 3, 2013. At http://www.amnesty.org/en/news/cambodia-release-mother-imprisoned-housing-rights-activism-2013-06-03 (accessed Mar. 2014).
17. "World Bank Board of Executive Directors Considers Inspection Panel Report on Cambodia Land Management and Administration Project," World Bank press release, March 8, 2011. At http://web.worldbank.org/WBSITE/EXTERNAL/COUNTRIES/EASTASIAPACIFICEXT/CAMBODIAEXTN/0,,contentMDK:22851984~menuPK:293861~pagePK:2865066~piPK:2865079~theSitePK:293856,00.html (accessed Mar. 2014).
18. James O'Toole and Khouth Sophak Chakrya, "World Bank Blunder," *Phnom Penh Post*, March 10, 2011.
19. Milton Osborne, *Phnom Penh: A Cultural and Literary History* (Oxford: Signal, 2008), 132.
20. Cited in Robert Turnbull, "View from Phnom Penh," *Architectural Review* 215, no. 1287 (May 1, 2004).
21. For a moving account of the building's demolition, see Moeun Chhean Nariddh, "A Bassac Theater Tale," *Phnom Penh Post*, January 11–23, 2008. On the building's background, see Ross and Collins, *Building Cambodia*, 26–7.
22. Helen Grant Ross, "Comment: Sports Complex under Threat," *Phnom Penh Post*, September 13–26, 2002. Regarding the history of the complex, see Ross and Collins, *Building Cambodia*, 210–29.
23. Willem Paling, "Planning a Future for Phnom Penh: Mega Projects, Aid Dependence and Disjointed Governance," *Urban Studies* 49, no. 13 (Oct. 2012): 2889–912, at 2898.

24. Robbie Corey-Boulet and May Titthara, "What's Age Got to Do with It?" *Phnom Penh Post*, February 4, 2009. Regarding the Renakse conflict, see Robbie Corey-Boulet and May Titthara, "Landmark Hotel in the Firing Line," *Phnom Penh Post*, February 10, 2009.

25. James O'Toole and Cheang Sokha, "Property Swaps Linked to Pheapimex," *Phnom Penh Post*, March 26, 2010.

26. Phann Ana, "Ministry Swaps Complex Next to Royal Palace," *Cambodia Daily*, August 22, 2005.

27. "Report of the Special Rapporteur on Adequate Housing as a Component of the Right to an Adequate Standard of Living, Miloon Kothari," UN Commission on Human Rights, Economic and Social Council, E/CN.4/2006/41/Add.3, March 21, 2006, 9.

28. Sam Rith, "Downtown Siem Reap Police Station Latest to Be Traded Away," *Phnom Penh Post*, September 9–21, 2005.

29. Lee Berthiaume and Prak Chan Thul, "UN Envoy Says Public Evictions Punishing Poor," *Cambodia Daily*, August 24, 2005.

30. Neou Vannarin and Julia Wallace, "Almost Entire Siem Reap Provincial Government Property Swapped and Primed to Move," *Cambodia Daily*, March 18, 2010; Phorn Bopha, "After Land Swap, Siem Reap Government Moves Again," *Cambodia Daily*, September 6, 2013.

31. Brendan Brady and Neth Pheaktra, "City, Developer Demolish Dey Krahorm Homes," *Phnom Penh Post*, January 24, 2009.

32. Aun Pheap and Joshua Wilwohl, "Phnom Penh Parking Problem Worsens Traffic," *Cambodia Daily*, December 5, 2012.

33. William E. Todd, "Keeping Cambodians Safe on the Roads," *Cambodia Herald*, April 7, 2013.

34. "Cops Cover Powerful SUV Killer's Identity," *Phnom Penh Post*, August 8, 2008; Chrann Chamroeun, "Hun Sen's Relative Admits to Hit-and-Run," *Phnom Penh Post*, August 14, 2008.

35. Kevin Doyle, "Court Intrigue," *Time*, January 19, 2004.

36. Nick McKenzie and Richard Baker, "Drugs: Our Man in Cambodia," *The Age*, March 26, 2012; Phorn Bopha and Simon Lewis, "Hun To Hits Back at Allegations of Drug Smuggling," *Cambodia Daily*, March 28, 2012.

37. "Cambodian Leader's Nephew Arrested on Murder Charges," Associated Press, November 26, 2003; Doyle, "Court Intrigue."

38. "Hun Sen's Nephew Convicted of Unintentional Murder," Associated Press, March 11, 2004.

39. "Cambodia: Getting Away with Murder," statement from Amnesty International, December 22, 2004. At http://www.amnesty.org/es/node/8781 (accessed Mar. 2014).

40. "Cambodian PM's Nephew Cleared," *BBC News*, December 21, 2004.

41. See, for instance, Vong Sokheng and Brendan Brady, "Hun Sen Orders Crackdown on Children of the Rich and Powerful," *Phnom Penh Post*, November 16–29, 2007.

42. Khy Sovuthy, "Koh Kong Shooting Suspect Not Investigated," *Cambodia Daily*, August 28, 2012.

43. Mom Kunthear and Sebastian Strangio, "Fresh Street Sweeps Mar Summit Opening," *Phnom Penh Post*, May 29, 2009.

44. May Titthara and Khouth Sophak Chakrya, "More Protests Nipped in Bud," *Phnom Penh Post*, November 20, 2012; Aun Pheap and Joshua Wilwohl, "Mass Eviction Looms Ahead of East Asia Summit," *Cambodia Daily*, October 4, 2012.

45. Khouth Sophak Chakrya, Mom Kunthear, and Shane Worrell, "Clean Sweep for ASEAN," *Phnom Penh Post*, November 9, 2012.

46. "Illegal Arrests & Social Affairs Centers: Time for Govt Action, Not More Denials," statement from LICADHO, November 9, 2008. At http://www.licadho-cambodia.org/press/files/193LICADHOPRActionNotDenials08.pdf (accessed Mar. 2014).

47. Human Rights Watch, *"Skin on the Cable": The Illegal Arrest, Arbitrary Detention and Torture of People Who Use Drugs in Cambodia* (New York, January 2010), 4.

48. Ibid., 58.

49. Human Rights Watch, *Off the Streets: Arbitrary Detention and Other Abuses against Sex Workers in Cambodia* (New York, July 2010), 37.

9 The Scramble for Cambodia

1. This figure is from the human rights group ADHOC. See Paul Vrieze and Kuch Naren, "Carving up Cambodia," *Cambodia Daily*, March 10–11, 2012.
2. May Titthara, "Protesters Injured As Guards Fire," *Phnom Penh Post*, January 19, 2013.
3. "LICADHO Calls for Investigation into Deadly Kratie Shooting," statement from LICADHO, May 17, 2012. At http://www.licadho-cambodia.org/pressrelease. php?perm=277 (accessed Mar. 2014).
4. Zsombor Peter and Aun Pheap, "In 'Rebel' Village, Fond Memories of a Slain Girl," *Cambodia Daily*, May 16, 2013.
5. Global Witness, *Cambodia's Family Trees: Illegal Logging and the Stripping of Public Assets by Cambodia's Elite* (London, June 2007), 29–47.
6. Kuch Naren and Paul Vrieze, "Government Drafts a Plan to Protect Prey Long," *Cambodia Daily*, February 3, 2012.
7. ADHOC, *A Turning Point? Land, Housing and Natural Resources in Cambodia in 2012* (Phnom Penh, February 2013), 41. See also Vrieze and Naren, "Carving Up Cambodia."
8. Cited in May Titthara and Daniel Sherrell, "Protected Forest 'Is Finished,' " *Phnom Penh Post*, August 11, 2011.
9. Historical forest cover statistics are taken from Philippe Le Billon, "Logging in Muddy Waters: The Politics of Forest Exploitation in Cambodia," *Critical Asian Studies* 34, no. 4 (2002): 563–86, at 565, n9.
10. Angela Gennino and Sara Colm, "Forests Threatened by Logging Free-for-All," *Phnom Penh Post*, July 24–August 6, 1992.
11. Global Witness, *Country for Sale: How Cambodia's Elite Has Captured the Country's Extractive Industries* (London, February 2009), 13.
12. Michele-Ann Okolotowicz, "Mareth Tells of Illegal Logging 'Catastrophe,' " *Phnom Penh Post*, July 29–August 11, 1994.
13. Le Billon, "Logging in Muddy Waters," 570.
14. Global Witness, *Cambodia's Family Trees*, 12.
15. Hurley Scroggins, "World Bank Paints Bleak Logging Picture," *Phnom Penh Post*, March 27–April 9, 1998.
16. Sorpong Peou, "Cambodia: A New Glimpse of Hope?" in *Southeast Asian Affairs 1997* (Singapore: Institute of Southeast Asian Studies, 1997), 92.
17. Matthew Grainger, "IMF Freezes Funding," *Phnom Penh Post*, May 31–June 13, 1996; Global Witness, *Cambodia's Family Trees*, 18.
18. Global Witness, *Cambodia's Family Trees*, 29.
19. Ibid., 61.
20. Michael Richardson, "Illegal Logging Topples Cambodia's Forests," *New York Times*, June 21, 2002.
21. "Cambodia Ditches Logging Watchdog," *BBC News*, January 29, 2003.
22. Yun Samean and Douglas Gillison, "Global Witness Decries Report Ban; Probe Ordered," *Cambodia Daily*, June 5, 2007.
23. Cheang Sokha and Chhay Channyda, "Hun Sen Fires Forestry Director," *Phnom Penh Post*, April 7, 2010.
24. Official figures were published by the UN Food and Agriculture Organization as part of its Forest Resources Assessment for 2010. At http://www.fao.org/forestry/fra/fra2010/ en/ (accessed Mar. 2014). Environmentalists claim the government's forest cover statistics are vastly exaggerated. According to satellite maps published in late 2013 by Open Development Cambodia, total forest cover stood at 46.3%. The maps also showed that dense forest had fallen from 34.5% in 2000 to just 10.8% in 2013. Maps and data available at http://www.opendevelopmentcambodia.net/briefings/forest-cover/ (accessed Mar. 2014).

25. Douglas Gillison, "World Bank Seeking Answers over Dragon's Tail," *Cambodia Daily*, August 17, 2007.

26. World Bank, "Biodiversity and Protected Areas Management Project, Annual Project Progress Report 2004," 11.

27. Jeremy Hance, "Exploring Asia's Lost World," interview with Greg McCann, mongabay. com, May 3, 2012. At http://news.mongabay.com/2012/0503-hance_mccann_interview. html (accessed Mar. 2014).

28. Matthew Smith, "Patronage and Corruption in Cambodian Forestry," Master's thesis, University of Oslo, June 2007, 60.

29. Prak Chan Thul, "R'kiri Ex-Governor Gets 17 Years for Illegal Logging," *Cambodia Daily*, November 24, 2006.

30. Smith, "Patronage and Corruption in Cambodian Forestry," 68–70. Regarding Bou Thang's background, see Ben Kiernan, *The Pol Pot Regime: Race, Power, and Genocide in Cambodia under the Khmer Rouge, 1975–79* (New Haven: Yale University Press, 1996), 83; Timothy Carney, "Heng Samrin's Armed Forces and the Military Balance in Cambodia." *International Journal of Politics* 16, no. 3 (Fall 1986): 150–85, at 157.

31. World Bank, "The Biodiversity and Protected Areas Management Project: Implementation Completion and Results Report," October 15, 2008, 11–12.

32. Regarding the allocation of mineral exploration rights, see Global Witness, *Country for Sale*, 15–34.

33. Ibid., 49.

34. George McLeod, "Cambodia Finds Oil and Changing Fortunes," *Bangkok Post*, December 17, 2006.

35. Simon Lewis, "BHP Billiton Faces Bribery Charges after Abandoned Project," *Cambodia Daily*, August 19, 2013.

36. Vrieze and Naren, "Carving Up Cambodia."

37. "Cambodia's Top Ten Tycoons," diplomatic cable from US Embassy Phnom Penh (07PHNOMPENH1034), August 9, 2007.

38. Regarding Cambodia's sand industry, see Global Witness, *Shifting Sand: How Singapore's Demand for Cambodian Sand Threatens Ecosystems and Undermines Good Governance* (London, 2010), 17.

39. Andrew R. C. Marshall and Prak Chan Thul, "China Gambles on Cambodia's Shrinking Forests," Reuters, March 7, 2012.

40. May Titthara, David Boyle, and Danson Cheong, "Last Days of a Valley Damned," *Phnom Penh Post*, February 8, 2013.

41. "Cambodia: Two Villagers Shot and Several Injured during the Illegal Forced Eviction in Koh Kong," statement from Asian Human Rights Commission, September 28, 2006. At http://www.humanrights.asia/news/urgent-appeals/UA-321-2006 (accessed Mar. 2014).

42. Caroline Hughes, "Cambodia in 2007: Development and Dispossession," *Asian Survey* 48, no. 1 (Jan.–Feb. 2008): 69–74, at 71.

43. United Nations Development Programme, *Cambodia Human Development Report 2011* (Phnom Penh, 2011), 39.

44. ADHOC, *A Turning Point?*, 41; Van Roeun and Douglas Gillison, "Virachey National Park Now Open to Rubber, Agribusiness," *Cambodia Daily*, March 8, 2011.

45. Kuch Naren, "Firm Given Rights to All ELC Timber in Ratanakkiri," *Cambodia Daily*, May 8, 2013.

46. Sam Rith and Sebastian Strangio, "Sesan II Dam Report Cites Impact Fears," *Phnom Penh Post*, August 19, 2009. See also Dene-Hern Chen and Kuch Naren, "International Donors Call for Redesign of Sesan 2 Hydro Dam," *Cambodia Daily*, July 4, 2013.

47. May Titthara, "Land Disputes Flare in Kampong Speu," *Phnom Penh Post*, March 19, 2010; May Titthara, "Violent Scenes in a Rice Paddy," *Phnom Penh Post*, June 10, 2011.

48. Vong Sokheng, "Stop Land Theft, Warns Hun Sen," *Phnom Penh Post*, December 16–29, 2005; Sue-Lyn Moyle and Aun Pheap, "Prime Minister Talks Tough on Land-Grabbing Issues," *Phnom Penh Post*, April 6–19, 2007.

49. ADHOC, *Report of Land and Housing Rights 2011* (Phnom Penh, March 2012), 1.

50. Kaing Menghun, "Hun Sen Has Last Word on Preah Sihanouk Eviction," *Cambodia Daily*, March 21, 2013.
51. Phorn Bopha, "Hun Sen Says Students Will Not Measure Disputed Land," *Cambodia Daily*, August 2, 2012.
52. ADHOC, *A Turning Point?*, 34.
53. Vong Sokheng, "PM Defends Economic Land Concession Signings," *Phnom Penh Post*, June 27, 2012.
54. ADHOC, *A Turning Point?*, 3.
55. Chhay Channyda, "Stringer Who Reported on Logging Found Dead," *Phnom Penh Post*, September 12, 2012.

10 A Hundred Lotuses Blooming?

1. LICADHO, *The Delusion of Progress: Cambodia's Legislative Assault on Freedom of Expression* (Phnom Penh, October 2011), 27-8.
2. Aun Pheap, "CPP Marks Human Rights Day Early, Lauds Its Achievements," *Cambodia Daily*, December 6, 2012.
3. Alex de Waal, "An Emancipatory Imperium? Power and Principle in the Humanitarian International," in Didier Fassin and Mariella Pandolfi, eds, *Contemporary States of Emergency: The Politics of Military and Humanitarian Interventions* (New York: Zone Books, 2010).
4. "Information on Civil Society in Cambodia," diplomatic cable from US Embassy Phnom Penh (08PHNOMPENH922), November 14, 2008.
5. David Kaner, "CSOs Look for New Ways to Access Funding," *Cambodia Daily*, June 26, 2013.
6. "Death Threat Made against Radio Free Asia Journalist," statement from Reporters without Borders, June 19, 2007. At http://en.rsf.org/cambodia-death-threat-made-against-radio-19-06-2007,22609.html (accessed Mar. 2014).
7. By 1995 Cambodia had an estimated 90 newspapers. See LICADHO, *Reading between the Lines: How Politics, Money and Fear Control Cambodia's Media* (Phnom Penh, May 2008), 6.
8. Ibid., 41; Yun Samean, "*Sralanh Khmer* Newspaper Publisher Confirms Defection to CPP," *Cambodia Daily*, March 28, 2008.
9. LICADHO, *Reading between the Lines*, 8-9.
10. "Bucking a Disturbing Trend in Southeast Asia: Press Freedom in Cambodia," diplomatic cable from US Embassy Phnom Penh (07PHNOMPENH682), May 17, 2007.
11. LICADHO, *Reading between the Lines*, 29.
12. Author interview with Moeun Chhean Nariddh, July 10, 2013.
13. LICADHO, *Reading between the Lines*, 56.
14. Ibid., 21.
15. "Aide-Memoire on Development Process of Boeung Kak Area," statement from Phnom Penh Municipality, June 19, 2012. At http://www.phnompenh.gov.kh/news-aide-memoire-on-development-process-of-boeung-kak-area-3024.html (accessed Mar. 2014).
16. Ian Harris, *Cambodian Buddhism: History and Practice* (Chiang Mai: Silkworm, 2006), 219.
17. "PM's Bodyguard Leads Monks in Path Towards Harmonious Support for CPP," diplomatic cable from US Embassy Phnom Penh (06PHNOMPENH2172), December 11, 2006.
18. Human Rights Watch, *"Tell Them That I Want to Kill Them": Two Decades of Impunity in Hun Sen's Cambodia* (New York, November 2012), 51.
19. Ian Harris, "Buddhism in Cambodia since 1993," in Pou Sothirak, Geoff Wade, and Mark Hong, eds, *Cambodia: Progress and Challenges since 1991* (Singapore: Institute of Southeast Asian Studies, 2012), 330.
20. Human Rights Watch, *On the Margins: Rights Abuses of Ethnic Khmer in Vietnam's Mekong Delta* (New York, January 2009), 67. See also Yun Samean, "Tep Vong Orders Khmer Krom Monk Defrocked," *Cambodia Daily*, July 2, 2007.

21. Cheang Sokha and Sebastian Strangio, "Sweden Takes in Sakhorn," *Phnom Penh Post*, July 6, 2009.

22. Sam Rith and Charles McDermid, "Great Supreme Patriarch," *Phnom Penh Post*, December 15–28, 2006.

23. Harris, *Cambodian Buddhism*, 222.

24. Howard J. De Nike, John Quigley, and Kenneth J. Robinson, eds, *Genocide in Cambodia: Documents from the Trial of Pol Pot and Ieng Sary* (Philadelphia: University of Pennsylvania Press, 2000), 281.

25. The first figure is from an inscription outside the pagoda hall. The second is taken from "Selected Comments at the Inauguration of the Great Residential Hall of Buddhist Monks in the Pagoda of Champuh Kaek," *Cambodia New Vision*, August 28, 2007.

26. Harris, *Cambodian Buddhism*, 221–2; Anette Marcher and Bou Saroeun, " 'Oh, Give Me the Simple Life,' " *Phnom Penh Post*, March 17–30, 2000.

27. Marcher and Saroeun, " 'Oh, Give Me the Simple Life.' "

28. After Tep Vong's elevation, his deputy, Non Nget, took over as head of the Mahanikay order. See Lor Chandara, "Buddhist Head Becomes Great Supreme Patriarch," *Cambodia Daily*, May 25, 2006.

29. Lor Chandara and John Maloy, "Top Buddhist Warns against 'People Power,' " *Cambodia Daily*, November 30, 2006.

30. Kuch Naren and John Maloy, "Hing Bun Heang Appointed to Monk Assembly," *Cambodia Daily*, October 26, 2006.

31. " 'Nothing to Do with the Murder,' " statement from Amnesty International, May 1, 2008.

32. "Les Basses Oeuvres de Hun Sen," *L'Express*, August 17, 2006.

33. Elizabeth Becker, "Cambodia's Garment Makers Hold Off a Vast Chinese Challenge," *New York Times*, May 12, 2005.

34. "Violence after Strike Leaders Barred in Kandal," *Cambodia Daily*, September 20, 2010; Mom Kunthear, "Workers Fired for Illegal Strike," *Phnom Penh Post*, September 27, 2010.

35. Caroline Hughes, *Dependent Communities: Aid and Politics in Cambodia and East Timor* (Ithaca: Cornell Southeast Asia Program, 2009), 131.

36. Colin Meyn and Kaing Menghun, "In Garment Sector, a Labor Movement Divided," *Cambodia Daily*, December 16, 2012.

37. Author interview with Dave Welsh, the American Center for International Labor Solidarity, April 5, 2013.

38. Neou Vannarin, "Hun Sen Seeks Garment Factory Worker Vote," *Cambodia Daily*, April 30, 2013.

39. "Bucking a Disturbing Trend in Southeast Asia: Press Freedom in Cambodia," diplomatic cable from US Embassy Phnom Penh (07PHNOMPENH682), May 17, 2007.

40. LICADHO, *The Delusion of Progress*, 11–15.

41. Andrew Nette, "New Cambodia Laws May Curb NGO Activity," *Inter Press Service*, December 15, 2008.

42. Ben Sokhean, "Mobile Users Top 20 Million, Internet Usage Still Rising," *Cambodia Daily*, March 27, 2014.

43. Facebook user statistics are from Internet World Stats, at http://www.internetworldstats.com (accessed Mar. 2014).

44. "E-mails Point to Collusion in Gov't Censorship," *Cambodia Daily*, February 18, 2011.

45. Bridget Di Certo and Kim Yuthana, "The 'Ill-Willed' Spark Cyber Law: Officials," *Phnom Penh Post*, May 24, 2012.

46. May Titthara and Abby Seiff, "Scapegoat 'Killers' Acquitted," *Phnom Penh Post*, September 26, 2013.

47. Author interview with civil society leader, May 2013.

11 An Improbable State

1. John Pomfret, "Uighur Protesters Land in Cambodia," *Washington Post*, December 3, 2009.

2. Sebastian Strangio, "Uighurs 'Criminals': Beijing," *Phnom Penh Post*, December 16, 2009.

3. "Cambodia on Track to Become Refugee Model for Southeast Asia," UNHCR, October 20, 2008. At http://www.unhcr.org/48fc78034.html (accessed Mar. 2014).

4. "Ambassador Discusses Uighurs and Drug Rehabilitation with Deputy Prime Minister Sar Kheng," diplomatic cable from US Embassy Phnom Penh (09PHNOMPENH926), December 17, 2009.

5. "Corrected Copy – Deportation Scenario for 20 Uighur Asylum-Seekers," diplomatic cable from US Embassy Phnom Penh (09PHNOMPENH954), December 21, 2009.

6. Sara Colm, "Analysis: Inside Perspective on Uighurs," *Phnom Penh Post*, December 20, 2010.

7. Chun Han Wong, "Cambodia's Hun Sen Slams U.S. Threats over Aid," *Wall Street Journal*, August 3, 2013.

8. Bertil Lintner, "The Day of Reckoning in Cambodia?" *Far Eastern Economic Review*, March 2009.

9. Julio A. Jeldres, "China-Cambodia: More Than Just Friends?" *Asia Times Online*, September 16, 2003.

10. Joshua Kurlantzick, "China's Charm Offensive in Southeast Asia," *Current History*, September 2006.

11. Saing Soenthrith, "Not All Were Happy to See the President," *Cambodia Daily*, November 14, 2000.

12. "Jiang Makes 4-point Proposal to Boost China-Cambodian Ties," *People's Daily*, November 14, 2000.

13. "Cambodia's Year of China," diplomatic cable from US Embassy Phnom Penh (08PHNOMPENH1027), December 25, 2008.

14. "A/S Hill Discusses Burma, Cambodia, Laos, China with Senior Vietnamese Diplomats," diplomatic cable from US Embassy Hanoi (06HANOI244), February 6, 2006.

15. Lor Chandara, "Officials: Dalai Lama Can't Attend Buddhism Conference," *Cambodia Daily*, August 7, 2002; Saing Soenthrith and Kevin Doyle, "2 Falun Gong Practitioners Deported Despite UN Protection," *Cambodia Daily*, August 14, 2002.

16. *Cambodia Development Effectiveness Report 2011* (Phnom Penh: Cambodian Rehabilitation and Development Board), 14.

17. Kevin Doyle, "10 Years Later," *Cambodia Daily*, June 14–15, 2003.

18. Sebastian Strangio and Nguon Sovan, "$1.1 Billion Pledged in Donor Aid," *Phnom Penh Post*, June 4, 2010.

19. Ek Chanboreth and Sok Hach, "Aid Effectiveness in Cambodia," Wolfensohn Center for Development Working Paper 7, Brookings Institution, Washington, DC, December 2008, 20–3.

20. Michael Vickery, *Cambodia: A Political Survey* (Phnom Penh: Funan, 2007), 180.

21. Statistics from World DataBank, at http://databank.worldbank.org/ (accessed Mar. 2014).

22. Sophal Ear, *Aid Dependence in Cambodia: How Foreign Assistance Undermines Democracy* (New York: Columbia University Press, 2013), 57.

23. ActionAid International, *Real Aid: An Agenda for Making Aid Work* (Johannesburg, June 2005), 22.

24. Daniel Ten Kate, "Donor Aid Consumed in Mountain of Reports," *Cambodia Daily*, August 19, 2004.

25. Michael Wesley, "The State of the Art on the Art of State Building," *Global Governance* 14, no. 3 (July–Sept. 2008): 369–85, at 375.

26. Chanboreth and Hach, "Aid Effectiveness in Cambodia," 40.

27. "Cambodia Snipes at Former UN Human Rights Envoy," Deutsche Presse-Agentur, September 22, 2008.

28. Thomas Miller, " 'Sometimes We Have to Speak Out, We Cannot Remain Silent': Peschoux," *Phnom Penh Post*, March 25, 2011.

29. Zsombor Peter, "World Bank Says Freeze on Lending Remains," *Cambodia Daily*, November 6, 2013.

12 UNTAC Redux

1. Steve Heder and Brian D. Tittemore, *Seven Candidates for Prosecution: Accountability for the Crimes of the Khmer Rouge* (Washington, DC: War Crimes Research Office, American University, 2001), 100.

2. Julia Wallace, "Judge Details 'Dysfunction' at Tribunal," *Cambodia Daily*, March 22, 2012.

3. PRK Lecture Book, level 5, part 1, 1988 (Documentation Center of Cambodia Archive D24335), 189–90.

4. "Report of the Group of Experts for Cambodia Established Pursuant to General Assembly Resolution 52/135," United Nations, February 18, 1999, 68.

5. For a detailed exploration of these issues, see Kelly McEvers and Thet Sambath, "Clouded History: Government Leaders and the Khmer Rouge," *Cambodia Daily*, July 1–2, 2000.

6. Seth Mydans, "Cambodian Leader Resists Punishing Top Khmer Rouge," *New York Times*, December 29, 1998.

7. Nic Dunlop, "KR Torture Chief Admits to Mass Murder," *Phnom Penh Post*, April 30–May 13, 1999.

8. David Bosco, *Rough Justice: The International Criminal Court in a World of Power Politics* (Oxford: Oxford University Press, 2014), 3.

9. For instances of this view, see Craig Etcheson, "Nightmare of a History: Philip Short's Pol Pot," *Phnom Penh Post*, December 17–30, 2004; Nayan Chanda, "The Man Who Made Cambodia Hell," *Washington Post*, February 27, 2005.

10. Author's email correspondence with Ralph Zacklin, September 10, 2013.

11. David Scheffer, "Justice for Cambodia," *New York Times*, December 21, 2002.

12. "UN: Khmer Rouge Tribunal Flawed," statement from Human Rights Watch, April 30, 2003.

13. Author interview with David Tolbert, September 12, 2013.

14. Regarding the ECCC judges, see LICADHO, *Human Rights in Cambodia: The Charade of Justice* (Phnom Penh, December 2007), 25.

15. Douglas Gillison, "Officials Mum on KR Tribunal Judicial Appointments Memo," *Cambodia Daily*, June 20–21, 2009.

16. David P. Chandler, "Will There Be a Trial for the Khmer Rouge?" *Ethics and International Affairs* 14, no. 1 (Mar. 2000): 67–82, at 81.

17. Author interview with Michael Karnavas, March 26, 2013.

18. Sophal Ear, "Cambodian 'Justice,' " *Wall Street Journal*, September 1, 2009.

19. Official transcript of ECCC Case 001, Trial Day 35, ECCC, June 26, 2009. For more on Nath's story, see Vann Nath, *A Cambodian Prison Portrait: One Year in the Khmer Rouge's S-21* (Bangkok: White Lotus, 1998).

20. Kheang Un and Judy Ledgerwood, "Is the Trial of 'Duch' a Catalyst for Change in Cambodia's Courts?" *Asia-Pacific Issues*, no. 95 (June 2010): 1–12, at 4–5. Case 001 attendance figures are available at http://www.eccc.gov.kh/en/case/topic/1 (accessed Mar. 2014).

21. Seth Mydans, "Anger in Cambodia over Khmer Rouge Sentence," *New York Times*, July 26, 2010.

22. Neou Vannarin and Douglas Gillison, "Hun Sen Again Warns ECCC of Civil War," *Cambodia Daily*, September 8, 2009.

23. "Khmer Rouge Tribunal: Five More for Prosecution," diplomatic cable from US Embassy Phnom Penh (09PHNOMPENH648), September 1, 2009.

24. Stéphanie Giry, "Necessary Scapegoats? The Making of the Khmer Rouge Tribunal," *New York Review* blog, July 23, 2012.

25. Douglas Gillison, "UN Legal Team Walk Out on Stymied KR Cases," *Cambodia Daily*, June 13, 2011.

26. Mary Kozlovski, "Judges Decry KRT Missteps," *Phnom Penh Post*, October 26, 2011.

27. Julia Wallace, "Nuon Chea Takes Meddling Charge to Court," *Cambodia Daily*, October 24, 2011.

28. Official transcript of ECCC Case 002, Trial Day 139, ECCC, December 12, 2012.
29. Official transcript of ECCC Case 002, Trial Day 185, ECCC, May 29, 2013.
30. Official transcript of ECCC Case 002, Trial Day 224, ECCC, October 31, 2013.
31. Official transcript of ECCC Case 002, Trial Day 218, ECCC, October 21, 2013.
32. David Rieff, *A Bed for the Night: Humanitarianism in Crisis* (London: Vintage, 2002), 286.
33. Philip Short, *Pol Pot: Anatomy of a Nightmare* (New York: Holt, 2004), 447.
34. *After the First Trial: A Population-Based Survey on Knowledge and Perception of Justice and the Extraordinary Chambers in the Courts of Cambodia*, Human Rights Center, University of California, Berkeley, School of Law, June 2011, 19.
35. Stephen Hopgood, *The Endtimes of Human Rights* (Ithaca: Cornell University Press, 2013), 126.

Epilogue: The Fading Mirage

1. Khy Sovuthy, "Hun Sen Moves Ahead With 'Reform' Plan, Minus Opposition," *Cambodia Daily*, January 30, 2014.
2. Matt Blomberg and Phann Ana, "Sesan II Reservoir a Laundry for Illegal Timber," *Cambodia Daily*, June 6, 2014.
3. Sebastian Strangio, "Crony in the Forest," *Forbes Asia*, August 2016.
4. "Cambodia: An Interview with Opposition Leader Sam Rainsy," *The Diplomat*, January 10, 2014.
5. Mech Dara, "CNRP Verbally Attacks CPP at Kampuchea Krom Ceremony," *Cambodia Daily*, June 5, 2014.
6. Kimchhoy Phong, Lihol Srou, and Javier Solá, "Mobile Phones and Internet Use in Cambodia 2016" (Phnom Penh: The Asia Foundation, 2016), 9, 24.
7. Matthew Tostevin and Prak Chan Thul, "Cambodian Paper Shuts with 'Dictatorship' Parting Shot," *Reuters*, September 4, 2017.
8. Kuch Naren, "Hun Sen Goes on Tirade Against Opponents," *Cambodia Daily*, May 26, 2017.
9. Khy Sovuthy, Ben Paviour, and Khuon Narim, "China's President Xi Arrives Bearing Gifts," *Cambodia Daily*, October 14, 2016.
10. Available at https://www.fmprc.gov.cn/mfa_eng/xwfw_665399/s2510_665401/t1489891.shtml.
11. Hannah Beech, "Embracing China, Facebook and Himself, Cambodia's Ruler Digs In," *New York Times*, March 17, 2018.
12. Available at https://pressocm.gov.kh/en/archives/12845.
13. Jeremy Page, Gordon Lubold, and Rob Taylor, "Deal for Naval Outpost in Cambodia Furthers China's Quest for Military Network," *Wall Street Journal*, July 21, 2019.
14. Kuch Naren, "Rainsy Says CNRP Backs China, Not Vietnam, in Sea Dispute," *Cambodia Daily*, January 11–12, 2014.
15. Sam Rainsy, "China's Cambodian Invasion," *Project Syndicate*, August 2, 2019.
16. "If You Have Jobs, Don't Listen to Propaganda: PM Hun Sen Tells Workers," *Fresh News*, February 20, 2019; "Cambodia's PM Hun Sen Unveils 'Strategy' to Offset Loss of EU Trade Scheme," *Radio Free Asia*, March 29, 2019.
17. Clare Baldwin and Andrew R.C. Marshall, "Khmer Riche," *Reuters*, October 16, 2019.
18. Serge Thion, *Watching Cambodia: Ten Paths to Enter the Cambodian Tangle* (Bangkok: White Lotus, 1993), xi–xii.
19. John Dunn, *Breaking Democracy's Spell* (New Haven: Yale University Press, 2014), 93–4.

Further Reading

For a general introduction to Cambodia and its history, interested readers would do well to start with David P. Chandler, *A History of Cambodia* (Boulder, 2008), or John Tully, *A Short History of Cambodia: From Empire to Survival* (Sydney, 2006), both of which offer good overviews of the country's story from premodern times to the present. Another valuable volume is Chandler's *Facing the Cambodian Past: Selected Essays, 1971–1994* (Chiang Mai, 1998), which contains articles on topics ranging from the Angkorian period to the regime of Democratic Kampuchea. The Chinese envoy Zhou Daguan's thirteenth-century chronicle of his visit to Angkor offers one of the only descriptive accounts of life as it might have been lived under the Angkorian God-Kings. The best translation is that by Peter Harris, published as *A Record of Cambodia: The Land and Its People* (Chiang Mai, 2007).

On the French protectorate (1863–1953), two detailed studies recommend themselves: Penny Edwards, *Cambodge: The Cultivation of a Nation, 1860–1945* (Honolulu, 2007), and John Tully, *France on the Mekong: A History of the Protectorate in Cambodia, 1863–1953* (Lanham, 2002). For post-independence Cambodia, Chandler's *The Tragedy of Cambodian History: Politics, War, and Revolution since 1945* (Chiang Mai, 1994) is a detailed and highly readable study of the backdrop to Pol Pot's revolution. Ben Kiernan's *How Pol Pot Came to Power: Colonialism, Nationalism and Communism in Cambodia, 1930–1975* (New Haven, 2004) is a similarly accomplished academic study of the roots of the Cambodian communist movement, from Saloth Sar to Son Ngoc Thanh. Milton Osborne's *Sihanouk: Prince of Light, Prince of Darkness* (Chiang Mai, 1994) offers a critical take on the "golden age" of the 1950s and 1960s.

There are ample accounts of the years of Democratic Kampuchea. Kiernan's *The Pol Pot Regime: Race, Power, and Genocide in Cambodia under the Khmer Rouge, 1975–79* (New Haven and London, 1996) is an intricately detailed study, based on lengthy interviews conducted shortly after the fall of the regime. For a vivid journalistic treatment of Democratic Kampuchea, see Elizabeth Becker, *When the War Was Over: Cambodia and the Khmer Rouge Revolution* (New York, 1998), which includes Becker's memorable account of her visit to Cambodia and meeting with Pol Pot in late 1978. On Pol Pot's life, see Chandler, *Brother Number One: A Political Biography of Pol Pot* (Boulder, 1999). This can be read profitably alongside Philip Short's *Pol Pot: Anatomy of a Nightmare* (New York, 2004), which benefited from the opening of former Khmer Rouge zones in the late 1990s, and draws on extensive interviews with former members of the regime.

For a view of Democratic Kampuchea from the one-eyed perspective of a radical Western sympathizer, see *Kampuchea: A Photo Record of the First American Visit since April 1975* (Chicago, 1979), the record of a group of US fellow-travelers who visited DK in April 1978. Contrasting recollections from Gunnar Bergström's visit to Cambodia, including a series of rare color photos, are included in *Living Hell: Democratic Kampuchea, August 1978* (Phnom Penh, 2008).

In addition to studies by journalists and historians, dozens of Cambodian survivors have written of their experiences under the Khmer Rouge. Among the best are U Sam Oeur, *Crossing Three Wildernesses: A Memoir* (Minneapolis, 2005); Rithy Panh, *The Elimination*, translated by John Cullen (New York, 2012), which formed the basis for his Oscar-nominated 2013 film *The Missing Picture*; and Haing S. Ngor with Roger Warner, *A Cambodian Odyssey* (London, 1987), which tells the story of Haing S. Ngor, who survived the Khmer Rouge and then went on to depict the story of Dith Pran as an actor in Roland Joffé's 1984 film *The Killing Fields*.

Another fascinating memoir is *To the End of Hell: One Woman's Struggle to Survive Cambodia's Khmer Rouge* (London, 2007), written by Denise Affonço, a half-French, half-Vietnamese woman who gave testimony at both the People's Revolutionary Tribunal in 1979 and at the ECCC (Extraordinary Chambers in the Courts of Cambodia) in 2012. Laurence Picq's *Beyond the Horizon: Five Years with the Khmer Rouge* (New York, 1989) tells the rare story of an idealistic French woman who spent the Khmer Rouge years working in Ieng Sary's Foreign Ministry.

For an examination of S-21 prison, see Vann Nath, *A Cambodian Prison Portrait: One Year in the Khmer Rouge's S-21* (Bangkok, 1998). David Chandler's *Voices from S-21: Terror and History in Pol Pot's Secret Prison* (Berkeley, 1999) is an exhaustive study of S-21 which draws on the prison's archives. For more on Comrade Duch, the gaunt former schoolteacher who ran the facility, see Nic Dunlop's *The Lost Executioner: A Story of the Khmer Rouge* (London,

2005), which details the author's intriguing discovery of Duch in the Cambodian countryside in 1999.

There are fewer studies of Cambodia after the collapse of the Pol Pot regime in 1979. The most detailed is Evan Gottesman's *After the Khmer Rouge: Inside the Politics of Nation Building* (New Haven, 2003), which draws on the PRK's voluminous archives to produce a nuanced account of an impoverished country's internal dynamics during the 1980s. See also Michael Vickery, *Kampuchea: Politics, Economics and Society* (London, 1986), and Margaret Slocomb, *The People's Republic of Kampuchea, 1979-1989: The Revolution after Pol Pot* (Chiang Mai, 2003), a more sympathetic treatment of the period also based on archival sources.

Another good source on the 1980s is Jacques Bekaert's *Cambodian Diary: Tales of a Divided Nation, 1983-1986* (Bangkok, 1997) and *Cambodian Diary: A Long Road to Peace, 1987-1993* (Bangkok, 1998). These two volumes collect the weekly columns published by the author in the *Bangkok Post*, and include a good deal of anecdote and analysis, both from the border and from Phnom Penh. Serge Thion's *Watching Cambodia: Ten Paths to Enter the Cambodian Tangle* (Bangkok, 1993) is likewise a worthwhile collection of essays on Cambodian politics, including Thion's account of a journey to a Khmer Rouge "liberated zone" in 1972 and a scathing description of Cambodia's collision with the new world hopes of the UNTAC years.

For a detailed treatment of the geopolitical backdrop of the 1980s, see Nayan Chanda, *Brother Enemy: The War after the War* (New York, 1986); and William Shawcross, *The Quality of Mercy: Cambodia, Holocaust and the Modern Conscience* (New York, 1984), which focuses on the international relief effort of the early 1980s. Another detailed volume is Grant Evans and Kelvin Rowley, *Red Brotherhood at War: Vietnam, Cambodia and Laos since 1975* (New York, 1990). Eva Mysliwiec's *Punishing the Poor: The International Isolation of Kampuchea* (Oxford, 1988) attacks the international indifference to Cambodia's suffering under the moral contortions of Cold War realpolitik.

For the UNTAC and post-UNTAC years, see MacAlister Brown and Joseph J. Zasloff, *Cambodia Confounds the Peacemakers, 1979-1998* (Ithaca, 1998); and David W. Roberts, *Political Transition in Cambodia 1991-99: Power, Elitism, and Democracy* (New York, 2001). William Shawcross has a perceptive account of the UNTAC years in his *Deliver Us from Evil: Peacekeepers and Warlords in a World of Endless Conflict* (London, 2001), which draws comparisons with the other UN peacekeeping missions of the 1990s.

In *Dancing in Shadows: Sihanouk, the Khmer Rouge, and the United Nations in Cambodia* (Lanham, 2008), former UN official Benny Widyono offers a colorful insider account of Cambodian politics throughout the 1990s. Another illuminating volume on the UNTAC years is Steve Heder and Judy Ledgerwood, eds, *Propaganda, Politics and Violence in Cambodia: Democratic Transition under United Nations Peace-Keeping* (Armonk, 1996), a series of essays on the country's sudden encounter with the "international community." For discussions of Cambodian culture in the post–Khmer Rouge years, see May M. Ebihara, Carol A. Mortland, and Judy Ledgerwood, eds, *Cambodian Culture since 1975: Homeland and Exile* (Ithaca, 1994).

There are surprisingly few book-length treatments of Cambodian politics since the late 1990s. Among the most recent and perceptive up to this time are Caroline Hughes, *The Political Economy of Cambodia's Transition, 1991–2001* (New York, 2003) and Sorpong Peou, *Intervention and Change in Cambodia: Towards Democracy?* (Singapore, 2000). Pou Sothirak, Geoff Wade, and Mark Hong, eds, *Cambodia: Progress and Challenges since 1991* (Singapore: 2012), published to coincide with the twentieth anniversary of UNTAC, is a useful collection of essays on a wide range of subjects relating to contemporary Cambodia. Michael Vickery has also assembled dozens of previously published essays and articles in a collection titled *Kicking the Vietnam Syndrome in Cambodia* (2010), covering the years 1975–2010, available online at http://michaelvickery.org/vickery2010kicking.pdf.

The only full-length biography of Hun Sen in English is Harish C. Mehta and Julie B. Mehta's *Strongman: The Extraordinary Life of Hun Sen* (Singapore, 2013), a hagiographic of the Cambodian leader's life and career. For a contrasting, but equally biased, account of the country's recent history, see Sam Rainsy's memoir, *We Didn't Start the Fire: My Struggle for Democracy in Cambodia* (Chiang Mai, 2013), which mixes an interesting account of Rainsy's early life in Cambodia and France with a selective account of his later political career.

For the past decade's economic development and its impacts on Cambodia, see Caroline Hughes and Kheang Un, eds, *Cambodia's Economic Transformation* (Copenhagen, 2011). On Buddhism and contemporary Cambodian religion, see Ian Harris, *Cambodian Buddhism: History and Practice* (Chiang Mai, 2006), and Alexandra Kent and David P. Chandler, eds, *People of Virtue: Reconfiguring Religion, Power and Moral Order in Cambodia Today* (Copenhagen, 2008), an illuminating collection of essays on Buddhism and folk religion.

The development of Phnom Penh since precolonial times is described in Milton Osborne's lively *Phnom Penh: A Cultural and Literary History* (Oxford, 2008), drawing on the author's early encounters with the city as an Australian diplomat in the 1950s. *Building Cambodia: 'New Khmer Architecture', 1953–1970* (Bangkok, 2006), by Helen Grant Ross and Darryl Collins, offers a visual chronicle of the modern Khmer architecture movement of the 1960s and 1970s, including detailed discussions of Vann Molyvann and his work.

On foreign aid and Cambodia's "development complex," see Caroline Hughes's meticulous study, *Dependent Communities: Aid and Politics in Cambodia and East Timor* (Ithaca, 2009); and Sophal Ear, *Aid Dependence in Cambodia: How Foreign Assistance Undermines Democracy* (New York, 2013). The crisis in Cambodian education is covered in great detail in David M. Ayres, *Anatomy of a Crisis: Education, Development, and the State in Cambodia, 1953–1998* (Chiang Mai, 2003).

For the history of Cambodia's relationship with the US, the most comprehensive treatment is given by Kenton Clymer in his *Troubled Relations: The United States and Cambodia since 1870* (DeKalb, 2007). For the disastrous American involvement in Cambodia during the Sihanouk and Lon Nol years, including the fierce carpet-bombing campaign of the late 1960s and early 1970s, see William Shawcross, *Sideshow: Kissinger, Nixon, and the Destruction of Cambodia* (New York, 1979).

For an account of Cambodia's relationship with China running from the 1950s to the present, see Sophie Richardson, *China, Cambodia, and the Five Principles of Peaceful Coexistence* (New York, 2009). Andrew Mertha's *Brothers in Arms: Chinese Aid to the Khmer Rouge, 1975–1979* (Ithaca, 2014) is a recent study that casts much needed light on Beijing's support of Pol Pot.

Good background on the issue of Khmer Rouge accountability and the progress of the Extraordinary Chambers in the Courts of Cambodia can be found in Steve Heder and Brian D. Tittemore, *Seven Candidates for Prosecution: Accountability for the Crimes of the Khmer Rouge* (Washington, DC, 2001); Tom Fawthrop and Helen Jarvis, *Getting Away with Genocide: Elusive Justice and the Khmer Rouge Tribunal* (London, 2004); and Peter Maguire, *Facing Death in Cambodia* (New York, 2005), which mixes the author's personal travelogue with an examination of the collision between accountability and superpower prerogatives. The most detailed and up-to-date account of the tribunal's creation and legal evolution is *Hybrid Justice: The Extraordinary Chambers in the Courts of Cambodia* (Ann Arbor, 2014), by John D. Ciorciari and Anne Heindel.

Illustration Acknowledgments

All those not listed are author's own.

1 Documentation Center of Cambodia; 2 Documentation Center of Cambodia; 3 Agence Kampuchea Presse; 4 Agence Kampuchea Presse; 5 Agence Kampuchea Presse; 6 Agence Kampuchea Presse; 7 Agence Kampuchea Presse; 8 Timothy Carney; 9 Private Collection of Ambassador Julio Jeldres; 10 Agence Kampuchea Presse; 11 Chip Hires/Gamma-Rapho via Getty Images; 12 Agence Kampuchea Presse; 13 Peter Charlesworth/LightRocket via Getty Images; 14 AP Photo/Ou Neakiry; 15 Michael Hayes; 16 Prasit Sangrungueng/AFP/Getty Images; 17 Michael Hayes; 18 Tang Chhin Sothy/AFP/Getty Images; 19 Agence Kampuchea Presse; 20 Robert Carmichael; 21 Heng Chivoan/Phnom Penh Post; 22 Pha Lina/Phnom Penh Post; 25 Will Baxter; 27 Will Baxter; 29 Scott Howes; 30 ECCC/Mark Peters; 33 Ben Woods.

Acknowledgments

This book, like all long-term research projects, was a significant undertaking, and would not have been possible without the support of a wide group of people. Among the many scholars, comrades, and colleagues who offered assistance and otherwise helped shape my views on contemporary Cambodia, I'd like to thank Rupert Abbott, Kate Bartlett, Will Baxter, Elizabeth Becker, David Boyle, Brendan Brady, Robert Carmichael, Youk Chhang, Clair Duffy, Julio A. Jeldres, Michael Karnavas, Scott Leiper, Brian Lund, Truong Mealy, Chhim Savuth, Abby Seiff, Carl Thayer, Prince Sisowath Thomico, Ou Virak, Julia Wallace, and Hayley Welgus. I am also grateful to Michael Hayes, Cat Barton, and Seth Meixner, my editors at the *Phnom Penh Post*, for setting me on the right path during my first years in Cambodia.

I owe a special debt of gratitude to the historian David Chandler, who was supportive of the project from the very start, and read over numerous drafts of the typescript, making useful suggestions and significant improvements to the text. Mary Kozlovski generously read over the initial drafts, zeroing in on errors both factual and interpretative, and offering other valuable advice. William Blakeley, Robert Carmichael, Anne Heindel, Don Jameson, and Peter Maguire also donated their time in reading over all or part of the typescript.

Throughout two and a half years of research and writing, I was assisted in translation and reporting by Thor Sina, Sany Sinary, May Titthara, and Neou Vannarin. A special thanks goes to the unflappable Pheng Sokhenin, who endured numerous sojourns through the Cambodian countryside and always went out of his way to help me in my work. Phorn Bopha at the *Cambodia Daily* and Sam Rith at the *Phnom Penh Post* provided valuable contacts. I cannot begin to thank all my interviewees, in city and country, who were very generous with their time in sharing recollections. Each contributed in some measure to the final product.

I am also grateful to Youk Chhang, Nhean Socheat, and Khamboly Dy at the Documentation Center of Cambodia, for their assistance in tracking down documents and photos in their archives. A similar thanks is due to Khieu Kanharith, Hun Yukthun, Nuon Maly and all the staff at Agence Kampuchea Presse, who allowed me access to their fascinating photo archive and kindly tolerated my requests for scans and negatives. At the *Phnom Penh Post*, Alan Parkhouse and Scott Howes allowed me access to the newspaper's photographs, while Gunnar Bergström, Timothy Carney, Michael Hayes, Julio A. Jeldres, and Son Soubert all donated images from their personal collections. Bernd Schaefer of the Woodrow Wilson International Center in Washington, DC, kindly shared documents held at the Central Stasi Archive in Berlin.

At Yale University Press, I owe a special thanks to Phoebe Clapham, for conceiving of this project back in 2012 and providing judicious suggestions on my initial drafts, and to Heather McCallum, Candida Brazil, and Tami Halliday for guiding the project expertly to its conclusion. Ann Bone was a superb copy editor, helping rescue me from the inevitable pitfalls of mixed metaphors, misplaced commas, and botched citations.

Finally, I'd like to thank my parents and family back in Melbourne who have offered support, encouragement, love, and a comfortable base of operations during my spells back in Australia. This book wouldn't have been possible without you.

Index

Printed and bound by CPI Group (UK) Ltd, Croydon, CR0 4YY

26/03/2025

14648056-0001